THE SAS DRIVER'S SURVIVAL HANDBOOK

How to stay safe and be confident
on and off the road

John 'Lofty' Wiseman

By the same author

THE SAS SURVIVAL HANDBOOK
THE SAS URBAN SURVIVAL HANDBOOK
THE SAS SURVIVAL FLICKBOOK
THE COLLINS GEM SAS SURVIVAL GUIDE

HarperCollins*Publishers*
77-85 Fulham Palace Road,
Hammersmith, London W6 8JB

Published by HarperCollinsPublishers 1997
9 8 7 6 5 4 3 2 1

A catalogue record for this book
is available from the British Library

ISBN 0 00 255831 9

Set in Berling and Neue Helvetica

Printed in Great Britain by
Scotprint Ltd, Musselburgh, Scotland

The SAS is famous for its daring exploits, on land, sea, and in the air. Raiding Pebble Island, storming the Iranian Embassy, and forays into enemy territory in the Gulf War, are just a few of their success stories. Getting into action quickly is paramount, and most people are familiar with their parachuting capability. What is not generally known is that the Regiment also uses many types of land vehicle to strike swiftly anywhere in the world, often under the worse conditions imaginable.

As well as driving in Arctic wastes, and negotiating the searing heat of the desert, the Regiment uses special driving skills for immediate response to any terrorist threat. This book is based on these skills, learnt over the course of many years spent perfecting these techniques in training and operations.

contents

1

ESSENTIALS 7

2

SAFE DRIVING 21

3

VEHICLE SECURITY 43

4

BAD-WEATHER DRIVING 55

foreword

Almost every family owns a car. In fact, it is not uncommon to find several vehicles per household, which means that every year more cars are introduced on to our congested roads, adding to the dangers and frustrations of motoring. The sheer volume of traffic results in gridlock and long delays. Drivers become impatient, and sometimes reckless, as they try to beat the jam and get to their destination on time. The result is that accidents that need never happen claim lives on a daily basis.

Motoring must be safe, and with a little forethought and common sense it can be. You don't need to be an expert mechanic to maintain your car in prime condition, and anyone who has passed the driving test has the capability to master the advanced skills required for defensive driving. The aim of this book is to teach safe, easy-to-learn techniques and instil the confidence you need to be able to drive anywhere safely.

If you need an incentive to learn, think about the thousands of people who are killed or maimed in road traffic accidents every year. The majority of victims will claim that their accident was someone else's fault. They may even be right – but that's no consolation when lives have been lost or ruined.

You have it in your power to prevent yourself becoming a victim. In the chapters that follow, I will take you through the dangers that face the modern motorist and teach you the safest strategies for dealing with them. Between us we will make the roads a safer place and bring the enjoyment back into motoring.

John 'Lofty' Wiseman
Hereford 1997

I dedicate this book to

MARILYN

WHO IS THE DRIVING FORCE BEHIND ME

Some people look on cars as toys for grown-ups. But driving is not just about freedom and thrills. It brings with it obligations, responsibilities and risks that cannot be ignored. So give serious thought both to how you drive and what you drive.

essentials

RULES AND REGULATIONS

FIT TO DRIVE Disabled drivers

SELECTING A CAR Size • Economy • Performance
• New or secondhand? • Where to buy • Inspecting a used car
• Test drive • Documentation checks

LEGAL PAPERWORK Registration documents • Road tax • Insurance

SURVIVAL KITS

rules and regulations

To a learner driver, trying to get to grips with the rules and regulations which apply to modern-day motorists, the list of prohibitions can seem endless. Having passed the test, many drivers set about disregarding whichever rules they think they can get away with. They forget all they ever learned about stopping distances and follow close behind the vehicle in front. They don't bother signalling their intentions to other drivers. They think far more about getting from A to B in the fastest possible time than they do about the dangers involved.

In other words, they acquire bad driving habits, but a combination of luck and skill at the controls allows them to get away with a near-miss where a new driver would crash head-on. Ironically, the more near-misses they have, the more they congratulate themselves – mistaking high-speed manoeuvres and fast reflexes for skilful driving.

In reality, skilful driving is all about recognizing hazards and making decisions in good time so as to avoid near-misses. It's about understanding the purpose of all those rules and regulations and road signs, and obeying them not because there's an examiner or a police officer breathing down your neck, but because it's the only safe way to drive. It's also about recognizing that, no matter how long it's been since you passed your test, there's always room for improvement.

This is a book for drivers who have passed their test and satisfied the authorities that they are competent to handle a car on the public highways, but who want to satisfy themselves that they can safely deal with any situation they might encounter. Later chapters will give detailed instructions on advanced and defensive driving skills, correcting skids, dealing with road rage, etc. But first let's tackle the basics: you and your car.

Fit to Drive

You have a legal obligation to make sure that you are medically fit to drive. Any health conditions likely to affect your driving must be reported to the authorities, and you should never drive under the influence of alcohol or drugs which may impair your ability (see Safe Driving).

Most countries, including Britain, require elderly drivers to renew their licences annually and declare themselves fit to drive. Often there are no medical tests, so it is up to the driver to be honest when filling in the forms. For your own safety and that of your passengers and other road users, seek confirmation from your doctor and optician that you are capable of driving safely.

Pregnant women, or mothers who have recently given birth, should also seek medical advice. Most can safely drive, but it's as well to be sure. Remember that you must wear a seat belt (adjust it so that the lap strap goes under the bump).

Vulnerable drivers will benefit greatly from membership of a motoring organization. In the event of a breakdown, you will be able to count on someone coming to your rescue. And if you notify the operator that you are pregnant or elderly or a woman alone, you should be given priority.

DISABLED DRIVERS

For someone who has mobility problems, a car can mean the difference between independence and being housebound. There are various government-sponsored schemes offering information and advice about buying specially adapted vehicles, tax concessions, and special parking permits or badges which allow the disabled to park in restricted areas. There are also associations catering for disabled motorists which give advice and campaign for better treatment and provisions.

There should be no problem getting insurance cover, but make sure you declare in full the nature of your disability and any special adaptations made to your car, otherwise the policy could be invalidated.

essentials

Able-bodied drivers can help by giving assistance when they see a broken-down car with a 'help – disabled' sign. Someone who is confined to a wheelchair cannot make their way to an emergency telephone, so be a good Samaritan and do what you can to help.

Selecting a Car

With such a huge variety of makes and models on offer, choosing the right car can be a daunting task. Before you start touring dealers' showrooms, your first priority must be to work out how much you can afford to spend. Running costs and maintenance will need to be taken into consideration when calculating your budget, because insurance, road tax, maintenance and replacement parts can add up to a substantial amount. If you are considering taking out a loan, make sure the monthly repayments are well within your means; aim too high and your car could end up being repossessed.

Having done your sums and fixed your price limit, don't let any salesman talk you into spending more than you can afford. Ask about hidden charges for delivery or number plates. You will be in a stronger negotiating position if you do a little research: check out motoring magazines for details of what optional extras – sunroofs, air-conditioning, cruise control, CD players, airbags, metallic paint, alloy wheels – are available, and a guide to current prices for new and used cars.

Think realistically about what it is you need from a car in terms of size, economy and performance. You might dream of sitting behind the wheel of a high-performance sports car, but if you have a large family a two-seater convertible is going to be too small, uneconomical, and therefore out of the question.

SIZE

How large a car you need will depend on the size – and age – of your family, and whether the car is required for business use involving long journeys or the transportation of heavy loads. For long motorway journeys, a large car will be much

LOANS

If you need to borrow money to buy a car, shop around for the most advantageous interest rates. The key figures to look out for are the APR (Annual-equivalent Percentage Rate) and the total amount payable (you may need to deduct the agreed cost of the car to find out how much the loan is costing you). Interest charges can mount up, so unless you find a dealer offering '0% finance' it's best to pay cash if you can afford to.

The four main finance schemes are:

'loan': a bank or finance company lend you the money, which you then pay back, with interest, over a fixed period. The car is yours, unless you fail to meet the payments.

'personal contract purchase' (pcp): many car manufacturers now offer these schemes, which look attractive because the monthly repayments are low. The unattractive part is the large final payment which must be made either in cash or by handing over the car. Keep an eye

on the credit charges, which can be high, and also mileage restrictions imposed by the dealer (you could find yourself limited to as little as 6000 miles per year).

'hire purchase': there are unlikely to be mileage restrictions in a hire purchase scheme, but the car remains the legal property of the lender until you make the final payment.

'personal leasing': this is basically a long-term rental agreement. You don't have to raise a deposit, but the car will never be yours and there could be mileage restrictions.

Whichever scheme you opt for, check the terms carefully. It's better to take the paperwork home with you overnight to read it through thoroughly before signing – if you allow yourself to be pressured into signing then and there, in the showroom, you may find you've committed yourself to something which is not in your best interest.

more comfortable – and for caravan-towing a powerful engine is a must.

If you have a large family or use the car to transport groups of children on the school run, a 'people carrier' or MPV (multi-purpose vehicle) may be the best option. These can seat seven adults in comfort, and some have room for the luggage, too. Estate cars can accommodate an average-sized family with room in the back for large loads or a couple of dogs. Hatchbacks are convenient for a small family, and usually the rear seats fold down to give extra space for luggage or shopping.

Because children can't be trusted not to tamper with door catches when travelling, they are safest in the back of a two-door car, or a four-door model fitted with childproof locks. Elderly passengers, on the other hand, will have difficulty manoeuvring themselves into the back seat of a two-door saloon or hatchback.

Will the car fit into your garage? It's a great boon if you can lock your car away securely when not in use, and it would be a waste to have to park on the street while your garage stands empty. If you don't have a garage, think twice before you buy a soft-top convertible. Thieves, vandals and even the neighbour's cat can slash their way through the cover in no time if you leave it on the street.

ECONOMY

Running costs vary depending on the size and specifications of the vehicle. Spares are more expensive on foreign and luxury cars. High-performance cars and large vehicles cost more to insure and give fewer miles to the gallon. Fuel consumption is substantially reduced with a small car, but the service intervals may be shorter than for large cars.

This is why it pays to study consumer or motoring magazines which publish comparative charts listing new and used cars by price, and showing details such as insurance group, top speed, fuel efficiency (miles/kilometres per gallon/litre in urban traffic and in top gear at speed), service intervals, and even the cost of a routine service. Manufacturers are now building cars that can go for up to 20,000 miles (32,000 km) between services, which works out a good deal cheaper to run than a new car whose warranty demands that you take it back to the garage every 6,000 miles (10,000 km).

PETROL VS. DIESEL

Cars with diesel engines cost more to buy, but offer better fuel economy, are more reliable, more tolerant of damp weather, and have a longer life span (diesels can be expected to cover as much as 200,000 miles/322,000 km, whereas a petrol-engined car would do well to make it to 150,000 miles/241,000 km). On the downside, diesels are noisy, the fuel smells, the engine labours when climbing hills, service intervals may be twice as frequent as for petrol-engined cars, and if they do go wrong they can be very expensive to repair.

Environmentally, unleaded petrol is a friendlier fuel than diesel. Catalytic converters reduce emissions of nitrogen oxides and particulates into the atmosphere, so even though they have to be replaced every few years, the cost is justified by improved air quality.

Whichever fuel you use, be careful not to breathe in the fumes as these contain cancer-causing agents.

PERFORMANCE

The higher the engine capacity the more powerful the car – and the more fuel it will consume. It will also cost more to insure. A small engine will do fine if you live in town and use your car mostly for short journeys, but opt for power if you regularly undertake long journeys and carry heavy loads, or use your car to tow a trailer or caravan.

For country roads, and in areas where winters are severe, it may be worth investing in a four-wheel drive vehicle. Anti-locking brakes, traction control, and power-assisted steering are other options you might consider to enhance the performance of your vehicle – at a price, of course. And the more you spend, the more it makes sense to invest in state-of-the-art security systems, such as immobilizers and alarms, to protect your car.

NEW OR SECONDHAND?

If you're on a tight budget, a new car will probably be way beyond your means. Those who can afford the outlay get a vehicle in mint condition which comes with a manufacturer's warranty covering you against mechanical failure, corrosion, and other defects for the first few years of the car's life. And because car design has improved over the years, your vehicle should be more fuel efficient, more reliable, and safer than an old secondhand car.

A few high-performance cars are in such demand that not only do they hold their value, they can be sold on at a profit. But this is the exception to the rule. Most cars depreciate in value from the moment you take delivery. In three years' time you will be lucky to get 50 per cent of what you paid, no matter how well you care for your car. Before buying a new car, find out how well that particular make and model holds its value (motoring magazines and price guides include this information in their comparative tables). Make sure you don't pay over the odds, ring around the dealers for the best deal you can get, and don't be afraid to haggle.

A nearly new car offers many advantages over brand new models and older used models. The car should be in excellent condition. Any defects will have had a chance to show themselves – and the first owner will have gone through the hassle of getting them sorted out under the manufacturer's warranty, saving you the trouble. There may even be a year or two still remaining on the guarantee. It's possible to pick up low-mileage models in good-as-new condition at knock-down prices.

If you're on a shoestring budget, you may have no alternative but to buy an old banger. Reliability matters more than style at this end of the market. Chances are that things will go wrong and parts will need replacing, so go for a make and model that is fairly common and check out the price of spares and repairs before you buy. Look for a vehicle with the minimum number of previous owners, and a mileage that matches the age of the car.

WHERE TO BUY

Buying secondhand is not without risk, but by buying wisely you can save a substantial amount. The cheapest way to buy secondhand is to scan used car advertisements placed by private sellers. Don't believe everything you read – car advertisements are full of misleading statements. 'One careful owner' may contain an element of truth – but you need to read between the lines and ask yourself how many lunatics have had the car since the careful owner parted with it. Beware the many pitfalls of buying privately: your legal rights are limited and there will be no warranty to fall back

on if things go wrong, so you need to carry out a thorough inspection (or have an expert carry out a professional examination), and to satisfy yourself that the seller is the lawful owner of the car and not a car thief. Don't let the seller bring the car to your house – you need to know their home address in case something goes wrong with the car and you have to seek compensation. Make sure, too, that you are not dealing with a car trader passing himself off as a private seller to dodge his legal obligations.

Auctions are cheaper still, but not an option for the faint-hearted. There's no opportunity to take the car for a test drive, very little legal comeback if the car has a serious mechanical fault, and even if there is a 'warranty' it expires one hour after the sale. You're buying on appearances, and having fallen for a car which looks the part, a novice can easily get carried away by the bidding and spend more than they intended. Visit an auction or two to get a feel for how the system works before you buy.

The safest route to buying a car is to visit a reputable dealer, preferably a member of a trade federation, as this way you will have the benefit of added legal safeguards should the car prove unsatisfactory. By shopping around, you should be able to find a showroom offering a choice of competitively priced secondhand cars with warranties and full service histories. They will have no objection to your taking the car for a long test drive or having it examined by an expert, and if you wish, you can trade in your old car (although it will fetch about 10 per cent more, on average, if you sell privately).

When buying a new car, you can save money by phoning dealers and asking what discounts they are prepared to offer – some will slash the list price by as much as 15 per cent. Because dealers have to meet manufacturer's monthly sales targets, wait until the end of the month when they are at their most vulnerable and desperate to sell. Don't give up if the first dealer you telephone refuses to budge – keep trying and you'll soon find one who will drop the price. Of course, if the car is so popular that dealers have problems meeting the demand, there will be no discount – but they might be prepared to offer an extended warranty or free insurance instead.

Having established which dealers offer the best prices, visit one or two showrooms and see whether you can negotiate further 'sweeteners' such as advantageous finance terms or a good part-exchange deal for your old car. The manufacturer's warranty will probably commit you to returning to that dealer for servicing and maintenance, so if you're not happy with the treatment you receive when you visit the showroom, don't buy.

INSPECTING A USED CAR

Always arrange to inspect a car in daylight hours. If it's dark or raining, you will not be able to get an accurate impression of the condition of the bodywork. Take along a knowledgeable friend, to help you with the inspection and to act as your witness should the need arise. Don't rush things, be methodical in your checks, and no matter how much you like the car, give yourself time to think it over before committing yourself to buy. Never let yourself be pressurized into buying.

If you are going to carry out a full inspection yourself, take along a small magnet, torch, mirror, and something to kneel or lie down on. You will need to crawl under the car to check the underbody, so dress appropriately. Alternatively, you can pay for a professional inspection (wherever secondhand cars are advertised, you will see advertisements for expert inspections).

Exterior checks

- Walk around the car and make sure that it is not leaning to one side, a result of worn shock absorbers and springs.
- Examine the tyres, including the spare. The tread should be legal and the walls free of cracks, bulges, and tears. Check that all tyres are wearing equally – uneven wear may indicate that the wheels are out of alignment. Alloy wheels which have been severely scuffed by parking too close to the kerb can suffer fractures which might cause them to disintegrate while driving.
- Badly fitting body panels indicate repaired accident damage. Gaps between body panels could mean that the vehicle has been assembled from the remains of two or more wrecked cars.
- Look for paintwork that doesn't match and signs of overspray on the door and window seals, handles and lights. Bubbles in the paintwork are a sign of rust.
- Use a magnet to check the bodywork, including the roof,

for filler. This indicates serious accident damage or corrosion which has been patched up. Don't buy if the magnet won't cling to the surface.
- Check for signs of rust, especially around the wings, door bottoms, sills, around wheel arches and along the bottom of the tailgate on hatchbacks. Bulges in the paintwork are an early sign of corrosion.
- Closely inspect the alignment of both the front and rear bumpers. If the brackets underneath have been damaged in a shunt, you could face an expensive repair bill.
- Check the windscreen for scratches and stone chips.
- Make sure all lights and indicators are functioning, and that exterior mirrors are fitted.
- Try out the keys to ensure they fit the doors, boot, and petrol filler cap.

Now use your torch to take a look underneath the car for signs of corrosion or leaking fluids. In particular, keep an eye out for oil leaks from the engine, gear box and axles; fluid leaks from the brakes, cylinders and pipes; water leaks from the radiator and hoses; holes in the exhaust system; and rips in the rubber seals over the front or rear axles. Test the amount of play in the steering, wheel bearings, drive shafts, spring shackles and shock absorbers. Probe any suspect areas with a screwdriver to check for signs of corrosion. Look closely at areas smothered with underseal – it may be there to conceal defects or corrosion.

Engine compartment checks

A clean engine compartment provides confirmation that the car has been well looked after. Any leaks or wear can be easily spotted. Check to see if any parts have been replaced.

Be cautious when the engine is smothered in oil and the bonnet and wings are filthy. Underseal is a sure sign of trouble – it's there to conceal damage or a dodgy repair.

- Check the dipstick for oil level and colour, and run it through the fingers to feel the texture of the oil. If the level is low, or the oil is thick, black, and gritty, or full of water bubbles, the car has been poorly serviced and maintained – which means there's a strong possibility of engine problems in the future.

- Open the oil filler cap. Creamy white deposits here indicate a leaking cylinder head gasket, which could prove expensive if the engine has been damaged as a result.
- Check the tension and wear of all belts and pulleys.
- While the engine is cold, remove the radiator cap and check the water level. A low level is a sure sign of a leak. Check all hoses and connections. Make sure it is green or blue – clear fluid means there is no antifreeze in the mixture. Brown liquid, or bluish orange stains, indicate rust.
- Make sure the battery is secure, the terminals firm, lightly greased, and free of corrosion, and that each cell is filled to the correct level with distilled water.
- Inspect the chassis and look at the top of the wings where the front suspension is fixed. Corrosion here can be very dangerous. Note the VIN number so you can compare it to the seller's vehicle documentation and ensure that the car has not been 'ringed' (stolen and given a false number plate).

Interior checks

You can tell a well-maintained car by its interior. Worn seats, shiny controls (particularly the pedals, gear knob and steering wheel), torn upholstery, damaged carpets are all signs of heavy wear. Look under carpets for signs of damage.

- Make sure there's enough leg and headroom to accommodate your passengers in the back, and check that the boot is big enough for your needs.
- Test all electrical components are functioning: the heater, front and rear wipers, lights, indicators, heated windows, etc. When you turn the ignition, make sure the appropriate warning lights are working and that they go out after a few seconds. An oil pressure warning light that fails to light may have been disconnected to hide a fault; if it stays illuminated there's a problem with the oil pump. DON'T BUY.
- Find out whether the stereo is included in the purchase price. Check that it's working and that the aerial is in satisfactory condition.
- Check the speedometer (see panel).
- Test the seat belts by pulling them out and letting the reel spool the belt back in. Look for fraying and other signs of wear.

SPEEDOMETER CHECKS

The amount of mileage on the clock is a major factor in determining the price of a vehicle. Which is why around a million cars a year are 'clocked' – unscrupulous sellers rigging the speedometer so that it shows a lower mileage than the car has actually covered.

On average, a car can be expected to travel 10,000 miles (16,000 km) per year. Cars which have covered higher than average mileage are cheaper to buy, but can be a risky proposition. What looks to be a bargain could end up costing you a fortune in repairs. Much will depend on the treatment the car has received in the past, so look for a full service history. Steer clear of vehicles previously owned by rental companies and driving schools because of the wide range of driving styles and skills they are subjected to (remember how rough you were on the clutch when you were a learner?). But a car which has been serviced regularly and maintained in good condition by a careful owner will still give good service after 80,000 miles (129,000 km) and may be a better bet than a car which has low mileage because it has been used exclusively for short urban journeys.

If the mileage seems suspiciously low for the car's age, check the service history very carefully. On a car with a five-digit mileometers, the reading shows zero when the car reaches 100,000 miles – so a car which has covered 139,000 miles will only show 39,000.

Signs of clocking include:

- Digits that don't line up
- Scratches and digs around the speedometer where a screwdriver may have slipped
- Damage to the heads of screws holding the mileometer

If you suspect that there has been tampering, telephone the previous owner (whose name will appear on the registration document) and ask what the mileage was when the car was sold.

Ask the seller to provide a written guarantee that the mileage shown is genuine. This will help you to claim compensation if the speedometer turns out to have been clocked.

TEST DRIVE

Now it's time to start the engine and look for leaks or smoke emissions. Listen for any unusual sounds such as rattles and clunks as these could signal expensive repairs to camshaft bearings. It should be quiet, regular, and responsive to more throttle. While someone revs the engine for you, go to the rear of the car and check the exhaust for blue smoke (an indication of worn engine parts).

For a test drive to show up any defects, it needs to last at least 20 minutes. It's no use sitting alongside the previous owner watching them drive – you must be permitted to take the wheel yourself. Before setting off, make sure you are covered by insurance and that the vehicle is road legal. There should be no problem with a car on a dealer's forecourt, but when buying privately make sure the vehicle is taxed, has its MOT certificate, and that you are covered by either the owner's or your own insurance.

Adjust the driver's seat and head rest. Familiarize yourself with the position of the controls and make sure they are comfortably within reach. Check out the all-round visibility. Use your rear-view mirror to check for smoke billowing out of the exhaust. Listen to the engine the whole time and keep checking the warning lights and gauges on the dashboard as you drive. Be suspicious of lights or gauges that seem not to be working – they may have been disabled deliberately to hide a serious fault.

Test the clutch while stationary by applying the handbrake and selecting second gear; now try to move off against the handbrake. The car should stall; if it doesn't, the clutch is slipping. You shouldn't have to lift the clutch too high before the biting point is reached. Rushing, hissing noises are a sign of trouble.

Accelerate and decelerate a few times to make sure the car stays in gear. If the car is unresponsive when you try accelerating quickly from a low gear there may be a problem with the carburettor. Gear changes should feel smooth and should not be accompanied by crunching noises. Test all gears, including reverse. If you have to force the gear lever, expensive repairs lie ahead. Climb a steep hill, allowing the engine to labour in as high a gear as possible. Look for power loss, clouds of exhaust smoke, and a rising temperature gauge. While you're on a gradient, test the handbrake and try a hill start.

Find a stretch of road with no camber and where there is not too much traffic. Take your hands off the wheel for a few moments to make sure that the car doesn't pull to one side.

The steering should feel precise, without too much play before the driving wheels respond. Turn from lock to lock, ensuring that the wheels turn freely and are not obstructed. A juddering steering wheel or one which clunks or clicks as you turn the wheel suggests problems with the steering or suspension components.

If the car pulls to one side or the steering wheel judders when you apply the brakes, get the braking and steering systems checked. See how the car responds to an emergency stop, and if the car is fitted with ABS make sure it kicks in to prevent the wheels locking. If the ABS light on the dashboard fails to illuminate, there is a fault in the system which could prove expensive. The brakes should not feel spongy – if you are not happy with the way they respond, don't buy.

Select a bumpy route which will test the suspension. You will soon notice any irregularities and hear the suspension bottoming out. A very rocky ride or noisy suspension is a sign of high mileage. Be very suspicious if the mileometer tells you otherwise.

After the test drive check the engine compartment and underbody again for leaks.

DOCUMENTATION CHECKS

It is vital that you examine the vehicle registration documents and service history to make sure everything is in order. This is especially important if you are buying privately. Check that the name the seller has given you appears on the registration document. You need to be able to track them down if something is seriously wrong with the car, so make sure you view the car at their home (be suspicious if they're standing by the car when you arrive; if you don't see them going in or out of the house, you have no way of knowing that it's not a false address). Don't be embarrassed to ask for verification of the seller's name and address if you are suspicious – there's a lot of your money at stake here.

Compare the details listed – colour; VIN (vehicle identity number); engine number, size and type; and date of registration – against the car itself. Any alterations to these details must be notified, so if what you see does not correspond to the registration document there is something amiss. The chassis number is usually stamped on the fire wall. The engine number is stamped on the engine block. The transmission number appears on a label on top of the transmission (do not confuse this with the engine number). Previous owners and the date the car was first registered also appear on this log. Where there are indications that the documents have been falsified or amended, contact the vehicle licensing authority to check the details given are genuine.

The service book should be up-to-date and stamped to give proof of services carried out. If it looks at all suspect, don't buy until you have been able to contact a previous owner and confirm the details. Ask to see service receipts, bills for new components (especially large items such as reconditioned engines) and repairs, together with roadworthiness (MOT) certificates, so that you can confirm that the mileage is genuine. No matter how low the price, don't buy a car with a suspect or non-existent service history.

BEWARE: STOLEN CARS

Buy a stolen car, and you are buying trouble. If the police can prove that you knew it was stolen you will be charged with dishonestly handling stolen goods. If you bought it in good faith, you may escape a prison sentence but you will lose the car. Because the car was not the thief's to sell, the money you handed over gives you no legal claim to the car; it remains the property of the person it was stolen from.

To avoid purchasing a stolen car:

NEVER hand over your money until you have been allowed to examine the registration documents.

ALWAYS make sure the seller's name appears on the registration document.

CHECK the VIN or chassis number and the registration against the vehicle's documents. If the windows have been security etched, make sure that the number corresponds with the registration or VIN number.

Warranties and guarantees

When buying from a dealer, demand a guarantee. On a new car, you should get at least three years' mechanical warranty. Read the small print to find out exactly what the guarantee

RULES FOR BUYING

1 Don't buy the first car you see, and don't become too attached to any one car. Keep your options open.

2 Even if it is the car of your dreams, don't let the seller know how you feel. Tell them the colour is wrong; that there are too many/too few doors; the engine's the wrong size, etc.

3 Don't let yourself be taken in by pointless frills like go-faster stripes, or GT badges.

4 When buying privately, it's never safe to assume that extras such as the radio or alarm/immobilizer are included in the purchase price. If it's not stated in writing (in the advertisement, for example), ask the owner to put it in writing. Make sure these items are in working order when you inspect the car. Ask for the handbook, and check that the spare tyre and tool kit are in place.

5 Have the car inspected by an expert if you are not yourself competent to judge potential mechanical faults.

6 Always haggle over the price. Make an offer which falls short of the asking price without being ridiculously low. If you find faults during the inspection and test drive, ask for a reduction to take account of the cost of repairs. When buying a new car, press for a substantial discount.

7 When buying from a dealer, establish the lowest price for the vehicle before discussing a part-exchange deal for your old car.

8 Check the tax disc and if the car is over three years old, find out when the last MOT or roadworthiness check was carried out. The MOT needs to be recent – if it's more than three months' old, strike a deal with the seller for the car to be tested again: you pay if it passes, they pay if it fails.

9 Get a receipt. At the bottom of the Vehicle Registration Document is a 'Notification of Sale or Transfer' which you will need to send off for the vehicle to be registered in your name.

10 Make sure you are given copies of any warranties or guarantees. Read the terms carefully – you could invalidate the guarantee if you fail to comply.

essentials

covers, and any terms you must abide by – such as having the car serviced by the dealer who sold it to you.

You may have to buy a warranty for a secondhand car. Before you write a cheque, make sure the cover offered is worth having.

Legal Paperwork

You've passed your driving test and bought a car – what more do you need? Before you can legally drive it on public highways, you need to make sure you have the following documents:

- A signed, valid driving licence (which will show the categories of vehicles you are permitted to drive). To drive overseas, you may also require an International Driving Permit.
- Vehicle Registration Document or logbook to prove that you are the registered keeper of the vehicle.
- A current vehicle excise licence (tax disc) to prove that you have paid your road tax, unless exempt.
- A current Vehicle Test Certificate (known in Britain as the MOT) to prove that the vehicle meets the minimum legal requirements for roadworthiness. All vehicles over three years old must be tested annually. Without a certificate you will not be able to renew your excise licence, so the car cannot legally be driven. (For details of what the MOT test covers, see Maintenance.)
- A valid certificate of insurance.

The police may require to see these documents if you are stopped while driving, though you have the option of taking them along to a police station within seven days of being asked to produce them (photocopies will not be accepted). Carry them on your person if you wish, but NEVER leave them in the glove compartment or elsewhere inside the car because a thief can use them to sell your stolen car. It's better by far to keep your registration document, insurance certificate and MOT in a safe place at home.

INSURANCE

It is against the law to drive your car or allow anyone else to drive it without insurance to cover damage or injuries to others and their property. The minimum (and cheapest) level of motor insurance is known as 'third party'. It will allow you to meet the claims of others who are injured or whose property is damaged as a result of your driving, but your own injuries and repair bills will not be covered. Work out whether you can afford to meet those bills yourself – if you can't, you might find yourself with no transport.

The next level of insurance cover is 'third party, fire and theft'. This extends the cover to include fire damage to your vehicle or compensation if your car is stolen. 'Comprehensive' cover will meet your own and other's claims for damage and injury, and will pay out if your car is stolen – but read the terms carefully, because cover varies from insurer to insurer. If you can afford the extra charge, it's worth having a policy that covers your legal expenses, because you might need to pursue a claim through the courts and that can be very costly.

There is fierce competition in the motoring insurance business, with rival companies desperate to win your business by undercutting one another. Turn this to your advantage by taking a few hours to ring around getting as many quotes as possible – you could save yourself up to 50 per cent. Some categories of driver, such as women and older, more experienced drivers – are eligible for special discounts. Don't just go for the cheapest quote, though. Choose one that provides all the cover you need at the best price.

No one is uninsurable, but some drivers will find themselves charged more for cover because insurance companies judge them to fall into a high-risk category. A young driver who owns a high-performance vehicle, lives in an urban area where crime is high, and works unsociable hours in a very well-paid profession, will pay the maximum premium. Penalty points on the licence for drink driving or speeding will make some insurers turn you away, while others may impose special restrictions. But never be tempted to falsify details, such as your address or profession, or by saying that the car is garaged overnight when it isn't, because your insurance policy will be invalidated if you are found out.

If you need to bring down the cost of your premium, do it

Although it's illegal to drive without insurance, many motorists take the risk because the cost of a fine can be less than the price of cover. If you are involved in an accident with a driver who has no insurance, your only recourse will be to take them to court – and there's no guarantee that you'll get the money you're entitled to even then.

This is one more reason to drive safely and calmly. When some lunatic in the grip of road rage challenges you to vehicular combat, bear in mind that they may be uninsured, leaving you to foot the bill.

legally. Ask if you can get a reduction for limiting your annual mileage, or for having an alarm or immobilizer fitted to improve security. Some insurers will give a discount for paying your premium in full rather than by instalments. (Before arranging to pay by instalments, find out what the interest charge is – there are some companies who will charge almost 50 per cent!) Safe driving pays, too, because the longer you go without making a claim on your insurance, the bigger your no-claims discount. After five years, this could add up to 65 per cent off your insurance bill.

It may cost more for a young driver to insure their own car than to have their parents insure it, but in the long run it pays. There's a danger that the policy will be invalidated if the insurer finds out that the youngster is the main driver. Also, with a policy of their own, your son or daughter can be building up a no-claims bonus.

Survival Kits

To save space in the vehicle, the survival pack has been divided into three kits. The aim of these kits is to get you out of any trouble, regardless of conditions, and help in any situation that you are likely to face while motoring.

The general and medical survival kits should be carried all the time, while the winter kit will be needed when weather conditions are poor.

GENERAL KIT

The car survival kit is a collection of useful items that make life safer and more comfortable in an emergency. These items will also help you to repair the car and get you home. Stow this kit securely in the boot. Make sure that items are replaced after use, and check the kit from time to time to make sure it's complete.

Waterproof coat and wellington boots

Reflective band – the kind cyclists wear

Protective gloves

Torch or free-standing lamp and spare batteries

Screenwash fluid and distilled water for topping up the coolant system or battery

Can of damp-repellent spray – also known as de-watering fluid (DWF) or WD40.

Warning triangle (this is a legal requirement in some countries)

Can of spare fuel – get a container with a built-in nozzle. Explo-safe cans are ideal.

Jump leads

Tow rope: get one with fixings that you can connect easily to the towing eyes on the car

Tool box containing:
• adjustable wrench
• pliers
• screwdrivers (one flat-head, one cross-head)
• small socket wrench set
• Allen keys
• plumber's tape (PTFE)
• masking tape
• handyman's knife

essentials

Reflective band – the kind cyclists wear

Torch or free-standing lamp and spare batteries

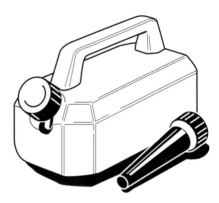

Can of spare fuel –with a built-in nozzle.

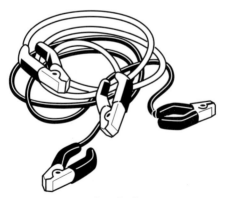

Jump leads

Warning triangle

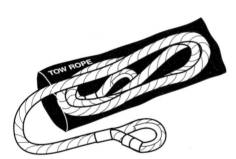

Tow rope: with fixings that connect easily to the towing eyes on the car

essentials

- coil of flexible copper/brass wire
- an assortment of self-tapping screws
- an assortment of nuts and bolts with washers
- haemostats. Used in the medical profession, in a breakdown these can help you retrieve small components such as nuts and bolts which have fallen into inaccessible places. You can also clamp them on to cables to secure them
- strong rubber bands
- radiator sealant

In addition, you should carry the following spares:
- light bulbs and fuses: buy a set which includes all types used in your car
- fan belt
- plug lead: carry the longest size
- HT lead: a duplicate of the one fitted
- spark plug: just one will help you check the system – it's unlikely that all would fail at one time
- hose: buy a long length that can be cut as required
- emergency windscreen: this one-size plastic screen can be fitted as a temporary measure to get you home

It's also advisable to carry an air compressor or foot pump, if you have room. And overalls to keep your clothes clean while you work.

How many of the tools and spares you carry will depend on whether you are likely to attempt any DIY repairs to get yourself home in an emergency. Anyone is capable of carrying out the basic repairs described under *Breakdowns* in **Emergency!**, but if you are not prepared to try, make sure you enrol in a motoring organization with a rescue service, and carry your membership card whenever you drive.

MEDICAL KIT
This should be packed in a soft container so it can be carried inside the car without fear of causing damage in an accident. The best type of pack is one that doubles as a cushion. It can then be left on the back seat where it will always be at hand. Don't stowing the medical kit in the luggage compartment – in an emergency you want it to be immediately accessible.

Typical travellers' ailments include motion sickness, upset stomach, and headaches. Bee stings and sunburn are common summer-time problems. Cuts and burns can easily occur when you're having a go at fixing the car, and fingers, especially those of children, too frequently get trapped in doors. To cover all of these emergencies pack:

Motion tablets (travel sickness)
Immodium (upset stomach)
Analgesic (aches and pains)
Antihistamine ointment (stings)
Flamazine (burns including sunburn)
Scissors
Tape
Burn sheet
Plasters (minor cuts/abrasions)
Assorted bandages
Large sterile dressings
Lip balm to prevent chapped lips

COLD WEATHER KIT
In cold weather add sleeping bags, food, thermos flask, extra clothing, shovel, wellington boots, snow chains, sacking, matches and candles. See *Winter Motoring Survival Kit* in **Bad-Weather Driving** for a full listing of items to help you when driving in freezing conditions.

OTHER NECESSITIES
In addition to the survival kit, every vehicle should have as many as possible of the following:

- road atlas
- handbook for the make and model of vehicle
- fire extinguisher (can be stowed conveniently under a seat)
- blanket to keep you warm in emergencies (can be laid over the back seat)
- mobile phone – a life saver, especially for vulnerable drivers travelling alone
- a card listing emergency numbers – such as your garage, insurance company, motoring organization helpline, etc – can be tucked away behind a sun visor.
- sunglasses – useful in winter, too, for reducing the sun's dazzle
- packet of mints, chewing gum, or boiled sweets – these not

essentials

only help to pass the time, but can sharpen concentration also

- bottle of water – to quench thirst, wash wounds, or clean sticky fingers
- small change for parking or tolls – keep in an accessible place to prevent delays or embarrassment. There is nothing worse than finding out too late that you have no cash
- clean chamois leather and window scraper
- a large piece of card, blank on one side, with 'PLEASE CALL POLICE' on the other. You can then place this in the rear window as a sun shade when the car is parked in sun, and to alert other drivers to summon help in an emergency.
- a pen and paper to take down details in the event of an accident

As time goes by, you will think of other essential items to add to this list. But remember, a survival kit is only of use if you can find everything in an emergency. Keep it organized!

Six accidents occur every minute on our roads, resulting in injury, loss of life and 3.2 million insurance claims a year. It's no wonder that safety features get top billing in car manufacturers' advertising campaigns. But over 90 per cent of road accidents are down to driver error – so look into ways of improving your own safety rating as well as your car's.

safe driving

SAFE CAR Accident prevention: Mirrors • Lights • Horn • Anti-lock brakes • Stability • Four-wheel drive • Crash protection: Seat belts • Child restraints • Airbags • Steering wheels and columns • Head restraints • Side-impact bars • Bull bars • Load restraints

SAFE DRIVER Alertness: Alcohol • Drugs • Medical conditions • Stress • Fatigue • Distractions • Awareness • Attitude: Road rage • Speeding • Tailgating • Anticipation

SURVIVAL KITS

SAFETY CHECKS

SAFETY IN THE GARAGE

safe car

Almost 50 per cent of accidental deaths occur on the roads. Dangerous driving and unhealthy attitudes to other road users are the main causes of these accidents, but since we can't change the way others drive – and of course it's always the other driver who's at fault – the next best thing is to choose a car that will keep us safe in the event of an accident.

So what makes a car safe? Advertisements for new cars make much of features like airbags, side impact bars, roll cages and seatbelt pre-tensioners, designed to minimize the risk of injury. But more mundane items like mirrors, wipers, demisters and lights are every bit as important to safety, because when used properly they can help you to avoid accidents in the first place.

Accident Prevention

Safety regulations ensure that all cars come equipped with a range of features designed to allow the motorist to see hazards and avoid them. Mirrors, headlights, wipers and demisters give the driver a clear view of the road. Lights and reflectors make the vehicle visible to other road users even in poor conditions. Indicators, brake lights, the horn and head-lights allow the driver to give others advance warning of his or her manoeuvres, while the brakes and tyres enable the car to be brought to a swift halt.

It's easy to take such features for granted when choosing a car – after all, they come as standard, the car wouldn't be allowed on the road if it didn't have mirrors, lights, brakes, etc. But test drive a few different makes and models and you will soon become aware that leg-room can vary dramatically from car to car, some feel cramped while others are impossible for anyone of below average height to drive safely. Some cars provide a clearer all-round view of the road by doing away with wide front and rear pillars. New innovations include dashboard warning lights to tell you when there's ice on the road, and some high-performance cars are equipped with traction control to give better grip in slippery conditions.

Even colour can make a difference to your safety. A light- or bright-coloured car stands out more than a dark one. Statistics show that dark blue cars are top of the league table where accidents are concerned, because blue blends into the background more easily than any other colour. Of course, if you live in a snowy wasteland, white would be the colour to avoid. Bright red, yellow and silver show up well in most conditions.

MIRRORS
You cannot drive safely unless your vehicle is fitted with at least two clean, correctly adjusted rear-view mirrors, at least one of which must be mounted on the outside of the vehicle.

The police have the authority to bring prosecutions against drivers who do not meet these requirements, and in some countries they can impose on-the-spot fines for a dirty or cracked mirror.

LIGHTS

It is vital that all lights and reflectors on your vehicle are kept clean and in good working order so that you can see and be seen, and signal your intentions to other road users.

Make sure that the beam of your dipped headlights is correctly adjusted so as not to dazzle other road users, while at the same time offering you a clear view of the road ahead. When the vehicle is loaded, or towing a heavy trailer, the headlights usually require adjusting; on some cars this can be done from the driver's seat. If in doubt, ask your garage to reset the headlights.

Always check when you start the car that the rear fog

 Most countries have laws requiring all vehicles to be fitted with two headlights to the front of white (or yellow – see *Travelling Abroad* in Long Journeys), which must be permanently dipped or fitted with a dipping device. Headlights must be switched off when the vehicle is stationary, except at traffic lights or other temporary stops. Always use your headlights when driving after lighting-up time (unless street lights are less than 200 metres apart) and in poor daytime visibility. In addition, vehicles must have two side lamps at the front, showing white through frosted glass. It is illegal to have a red light showing at the front.

At the rear you must have two red tail lights, two red reflectors (which on some cars are combined with the tail lights). Cars registered after 1971 must have brake or stop lights which display a non-flashing red light when the foot brake is applied. The only white lights permitted at the back of the car are the number plate lamp and the reversing lights.

Amber direction indicators which flash between 60 and 120 times a minute are required on vehicles registered after 1965. Rear fog lamps are compulsory on all cars registered after 1980. These must only be used during adverse weather conditions where visibility is less than 100 metres – it is illegal to turn them on at other times.

lights have not been left on by mistake. These can temporarily blind other motorists with their glare, causing accidents. They are for use in very poor visibility only.

Brake lights provide a useful signal to following drivers, so use the brakes rather than changing down the gears to lose speed.

Headlights can be flashed to warn others of your presence. Many drivers flash their lights to signal a pedestrian to cross the road, or another driver to emerge from a side road, but this can lead to accidents. It's all too easy to misinterpret what is intended by the signal, and in any case it is up to other road users to use their own judgement as to when it is safe for them to proceed – there may be hazards you cannot see which would place them in jeopardy.

HORN

The horn allows you to warn other road users of your presence. A brief toot should be sufficient to alert a driver or pedestrian about to embark on a collision course because they haven't noticed you are there. A long horn note should be used when approaching a blind spot like the crest of a hill, a sharp bend in a country lane, or a hump-backed bridge.

Remember that using the horn does not give you the right of way. For a start, there's no guarantee that it will be heard. Pedestrians who are hard of hearing or drivers of noisy heavy goods vehicles may not hear your horn. If a pedestrian doesn't look round at the sound of the horn, assume they haven't heard you. Use your headlights to signal to other drivers where noise may drown out the horn. When approaching a blind bend or other hazard, slow down and be prepared to stop if necessary. NEVER use the horn to rebuke other road users – that's a recipe for road rage.

In most countries there are laws prohibiting sounding your horn if your vehicle is stationary (except when another moving vehicle presents a danger to you).

There are also laws governing when a horn can be sounded in built-up areas (usually defined as areas where the street lights are less than 200 yards/metres apart). The time span varies from country to country, but as a general rule you should never use the horn at night unless it's an emergency.

ANTI-LOCK BRAKE SYSTEM

An increasing number of new cars, especially high-specification models, are now fitted with an anti-lock brake system (ABS). This sophisticated form of braking can be extremely useful in an emergency as it helps to maintain traction under severe braking by preventing the wheels from locking and skidding.

A sensor control attached to each wheel detects when the wheel is about to lock and responds by automatically releasing the brake and then re-applying it several times a second. You can feel this happening through the brake pedal, which pulsates up and down. There's no need for you to pump the brakes – in fact, pumping the brake pedal will interfere with the ABS's operation. And, whereas with ordinary brakes you have to take great care when braking in slippery conditions for fear of causing a skid, ABS allows you to brake as hard as you can on wet and slippery surfaces without losing control of the steering.

However, ABS has its limitations. If you try dangerous stunts like taking a corner too fast or braking at the very last minute, it can't prevent accidents occurring. And on loose gravel or snow, where all four wheels may lose traction, anti-lock brakes may actually take longer to stop the car than a conventional braking system.

Cars fitted with ABS have a light on the dashboard which tells you when there's a fault in the system. Don't try to investigate yourself – see an expert. Should a malfunction with the ABS occur, the ordinary brakes will take over.

STABILITY

Vehicles which are low to the ground with a wheel close to each corner offer greater stability than those designed for off-road use, which tend to be taller, with a high centre of gravity. When using off-road vehicles on normal roads, take care – especially when turning corners or changing direction – as the handling is not the same as for a front-wheel drive. Special courses are available – see advertisements in specialist motoring magazines, or consult your dealer for advice.

FOUR-WHEEL DRIVE (4WD)

In slippery conditions or on rough terrain, 4WD improves the grip that the tyres have on the road. It is now available in some conventional cars, as well as models designed specifically for off-road use. Ideal if you need a vehicle that can work in all weather and cope with difficult surfaces, but bear in mind that conventional-style cars with low ground clearance cannot cope with soft mud or sandy surfaces in the way that true off-road vehicles can.

Crash Protection

The real test of a car's crashworthiness is whether it can succeed in making severe accidents survivable. And if there's a single factor which gives car occupants a better chance of walking away from a crash than any other it's the integrity of the car's structure. A passenger compartment which suffers major distortion on impact (doors crumpling inward in a side-on collision; pillars that collapse and instruments that intrude in a head-on collision) will offer little protection to those inside.

Crash tests are the best means of measuring how well a car will withstand impact. Dummies packed with sensors occupy the driver's and passengers' seats, and the car is rammed into a concrete block. By analysing the wreck and the readings from the dummies, scientists can calculate the risk of injury to different parts of the body. Some of the results of these tests are published in consumer magazines, and if you're buying a car it's worth finding out how well that model performed in crash tests relative to other cars in the same class. You may find that the much-hyped new car of your dreams, fully equipped with state-of-the-art airbags, power steering and ABS, fares less well than a frumpy, no-frills rival.

Safest of all, structurally, are big, heavy cars. In a collision between a large car and a supermini, the bigger car's size and weight advantage will tell in its favour, and the supermini will come off worse every time. On the other hand, big cars cost more to buy, insure and run – so safety is not the only consideration to take into account. It is, however, an important factor, so once you decide which type of car will best suit your needs, check out the safety options on offer within that class.

SEAT BELTS

When a car travelling at 30 mph collides with a solid object, any occupants not wearing a seatbelt will be thrown forward at about the speed the car was travelling. When their bodies hit the windscreen or dashboard (or, in the case of back seat passengers, when they hit the seats or the people in front of them) the force of the impact will be three and a half tons – roughly the weight of an elephant. It goes without saying that the human body cannot withstand that sort of impact. Death or serious injury is the inevitable outcome.

All new cars are fitted with front and rear seat belts and in most countries it is now law that everyone in the vehicle must wear a belt where one is available. There are still many older cars which do not have rear seat belts, but most cars built since 1981 have mounting points located under the seat cushion and in the rear pillar so that it is easy to have rear belts fitted.

REMEMBER

Belting up has been proved to reduce injuries and save lives, so where there is a belt fitted, use it. The advantages far outweigh the disadvantages. Passengers who don't wear belts are not just risking their own lives – the effect of a back-seat passenger hitting the person in front at 30 mph is the equivalent of their jumping off a 30-foot building and landing on someone. Bear that in mind next time you have a passenger who doesn't want to wear a seatbelt.

It's also worth noting that insurance companies do not look kindly on people who don't wear seat belts. If you are injured in an accident as a result of failing to wear a seatbelt, that will count against you when your claim for compensation is assessed.

Types of seatbelt

Inertia reels

Most cars are fitted with inertia-reel belts on their front seats. These adjust easily and allow you some leeway for movement until the vehicle brakes suddenly or crashes, at which point inertia causes the reels to lock. To test the belt, give it a sharp tug; it should lock. Make sure the belt is

HOW TO WEAR A SEATBELT

Seat belts are designed so that, in the event of an accident, the webbing is in contact with bony areas such as the shoulders, ribs and pelvis, thus minimizing the risk of injury to delicate fleshy tissue. **Serious injury can result if the belt is not worn correctly.**

Seat belts are most effective when the wearer is sitting up straight and well back in the seat. First adjust the seat to a comfortable upright position (the further a seat is reclined, the greater the risk of your sliding out from under the belt in a crash). If your car has height-adjustable belts, position the diagonal band so that it rests midway across your shoulder. It should not be in contact with your neck, and the diagonal should never be worn under the arm. If it is not possible to adjust the height of the belt, boost your height by sitting on a cushion. Making sure that the belt is not twisted or caught on anything, pull it across your body.

Position the lap belt across the pelvis, NOT over the stomach or waist. Always place the buckle to one side to reduce the risk of injury.

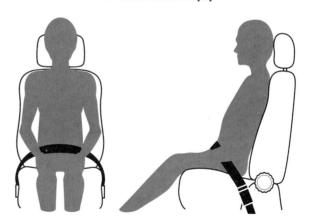

Pregnant women must take special care to keep the belt as low as possible over the hips. If in doubt consult your doctor.

It's a good idea to get into the habit of always checking the belt's release mechanism – in an emergency such as a fire, you may need to leave the vehicle in a hurry.

adjusted so that it fits snugly. In an accident a slack belt will give little protection, because by the time the slack is taken up your head will have made contact with the dashboard.

Pre-tensioners and web locking devices
A pre-tensioner fitted to the buckle will tighten the belt in the moment of impact, cutting down on your forward movement. A web lock or grabber acts on the reel, preventing the belt being pulled through the spool.

Lap belts
Most lap belts are simple devices, little more than pieces of webbing attached to an anchor point on the car's chassis. Because there's no inertia reel, they need to be adjusted to minimize slackness.

SEAT BELT MAINTENANCE
Check all belts regularly to make sure that they are in good working order and free of damage. If the webbing becomes frayed, contaminated or damaged the belt should be replaced.

Always keep seat belts fastened when not in use – in an accident a flying belt buckle can cause serious injuries. This will also prevent stray belt straps from getting caught in the car doors, or tripping up passengers as they leave the vehicle.

Keep all seat belts clean – dirty belts can leave marks on clothing. Never use bleach or chemical solvents as this will weaken the webbing, and NEVER dismantle the assembly to clean the belts. Use a cloth moistened with a mild detergent for cleaning, then fully extend the belts to allow them to dry thoroughly. A wet belt can cause rewinding problems. Keep the buckle and retractor free of obstructions.

SEAT BELT REGULATIONS

 In Britain and most European countries seat belts must be worn by the driver and all passengers (provided a seat belt is available), unless an exemption has been granted. Exemptions can be given for medical reasons (your doctor will issue you with a certificate). Drivers making local deliveries in a vehicle designed or adapted for that purpose are also exempt, and you are allowed to remove your belt while carrying out reversing manoeuvres – though you must put it back on afterwards.

Even if you are not involved in an accident, you can be fined for not wearing a seatbelt. All occupants over the age of 14 are personally responsible for making sure they wear a belt (and liable for the fine if they don't).

It is the driver's legal responsibility to see that any children under 14 wear a belt or, preferably, a restraint suited to their size and weight (a baby or child seat for infants, booster seats for bigger children). You could be fined or have your licence endorsed if you fail to ensure that children use seat belts or restraints where available.

Most European countries will not allow children to be carried in the front passenger seat. This is because the safest place for them is in the back seat. In Britain, the rules on carrying children are as follows:

Children under 3 years of age: must *always* wear a child restraint (an adult seatbelt will not do) when travelling in the front seat. In the back seat a child restraint must be used if one is available. There's nothing in the law to stop you carrying a baby or toddler in a back seat which is not fitted with a child restraint.

Children from 3 to 11 years of age and less than 1.5 metres (5 feet) tall: must wear an appropriate child restraint if one is available. If not, an adult seatbelt should be worn.

Children aged 12 and above or younger children over 1.5 metres tall: must wear an adult belt if one is fitted, whether they sit in the front or the rear of the car.

In Britain there's no law against carrying more passengers than there are seat belts available, or against carrying children in a car which has no appropriate child restraints whatsoever. But the fact that it's not illegal doesn't make it safe. Heavy passengers will pose a danger to those sitting in front of them if they don't wear a belt, and children have a much better chance of surviving an accident if they are secured by a child seat or other restraint rather than an adult seatbelt which they might slide out of. Don't stop at complying with the legal requirements – follow the recommendations set out below (see *Child Restraints*).

CHILD RESTRAINTS

Children who are left unrestrained in cars have accidents – even when the car is stationary. Try not to leave them unsupervised, and NEVER leave them alone in the car with the keys in the ignition. It's well worth fitting childproof locks so that the rear doors can only be opened from outside the car. And if you have electric windows, ask if a device can be installed which will allow you to override the rear-window switches so that they can only be operated from the driver's seat.

The only safe way for children to travel by car is strapped into a child restraint which is suited to their weight and size, and which conforms to approved safety standards (look for United Nations, European Community or British Standards labels signifying that the product has been tested and approved). The alternatives don't bear thinking about:

Holding an infant in your arms. Even if you are wearing a seatbelt, in the event of a collision the force of the impact will probably cause the child to be torn from your arms and hurled at the windscreen.

Putting your seatbelt round a child being carried on your lap. In a collision, you will be thrown forward exerting some three and a half tons of force on that child's body. If the child isn't crushed to death outright, horrific injuries will be inflicted.

Leaving the baby in a carrycot on the back seat. Even if the carrycot is strapped in, it's the cot which is restrained, not the baby. In a violent collision the baby could be thrown out.

Using an adult seatbelt to restrain the child. In a crash, a small child wearing an adult seatbelt will most likely 'submarine' out from under it. There's also a risk that the belt will bear upon the child's neck, damaging the thorax.

Using an adult seatbelt to restrain two children. The same dangers as above, multiplied by two.

Allowing the child to travel unrestrained: Even when an accident occurs at speeds as low as 12 mph children can suffer serious injury being thrown out of the car or through the windscreen.

Sitting on the floor of the luggage space of an estate car: Unless rear-facing seats with harnesses have been fitted in the luggage compartment, it is not safe for children to travel in this area.

If you are going to carry children in your car and you care about their safety, have a proper child restraint fitted for each child. Check before you buy that the restraint will fit both your child and your vehicle. Follow the manufacturer's instructions for installation and use in every detail. If in any doubt, consult your garage or dealer. Most child seats are designed to make use of an adult seatbelt to hold them in place, so it should be a straightforward process. Make sure that the car's seat-belt buckle does not rest on the frame of the child restraint, and that the restraint is anchored securely.

The safest place for children is in the back seat, so if your car doesn't have rear seat belts, buy a child seat which comes with it's own fastening straps and, if necessary, get a mechanic to fit it for you.

Many parents prefer to have young babies in a rear-facing baby carrier fitted to the front passenger seat. This has the advantage that you can see the baby clearly, but in the event of a collision baby would be much safer in the back seat. To keep an eye on children in the back seat, fit a second rear-view mirror angled to give you a good view of them without losing sight of the road ahead.

If for any reason you have to transport your child in a car where no child restraint is available, it is better for them to wear an adult belt alone in the back seat than no restraint at all.

TYPES OF CHILD RESTRAINT

The choice of restraint is governed by the child's size and weight rather than its age. Expensive as these restraints are, never buy a secondhand child restraint unless it comes with the manufacturer's fitting instructions and you are 100 per cent certain that it has never been used in an accident. If any signs of wear and tear are visible, DON'T buy.

> In summer, metal and plastic surfaces of child restraints left inside closed vehicles can get hot enough to cause burns. Check before placing your child in the seat that the buckle and other surfaces will not pose a danger.

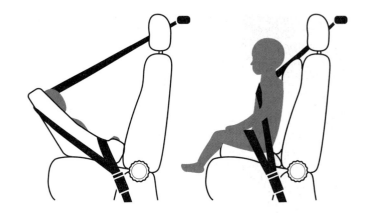

Baby seat

For babies up to nine months old, weighing up to 10 kg, a rearward-facing baby seat is the safest type of restraint. These can be fitted in the front or (preferably) the rear seat of a car using an adult seatbelt. A built-in harness with a crotch strap holds the infant in place. A sleeping baby can be carried from car to house in the seat, making it very convenient to use.

It's possible to buy a baby seat that will hold the infant in a rear-facing position until it's old enough to sit up, then convert into a forward-facing child seat which can be used until the child reaches 18 kg (at around 4 years of age).

Child seat

For children weighing between 9 and 18 kg (approximately 6 months to 4 years of age) an upright child seat (forward- or rear-facing) secured by an adult safety belt or by its own straps. A built-in harness holds the child in place.

Booster seats and cushions

Bigger children (weighing between 15 and 36 kg) can use a booster seat to lift them so that the adult lap and diagonal belt fits properly. The diagonal section must rest midway between the neck and shoulder, the lap section must sit low on the pelvis – NOT across the stomach. Booster seats are not suitable for use with a lap belt.

AIR BAGS

Airbags are designed to minimize the risk of facial and head injuries caused by crashing into the steering column or dashboard. In the event of a severe head-on collision, sensors trigger a small explosive charge and the airbag breaks through the cover. Within a fraction of a second the airbag will fully inflate to cushion the driver as he is thrown forward. Having absorbed the impact the bag deflates instantly.

You may hear a bang and see a puff of smoke when the charge detonates, but don't be alarmed – there's no risk of fire. The gas used to inflate airbags is non-poisonous.

Many new cars are fitted with a driver's airbag as standard equipment, and some also offer front passenger airbags. In Europe, where seat belts are compulsory, the airbag is designed to supplement the protection given by the diagonal part of the seatbelt. In the USA, on the other hand, not all states have a mandatory seatbelt requirement and so American cars tend to be fitted with 'full-size bags' to compensate. But an airbag is no substitute for a seatbelt. For a start, an airbag is not designed to inflate and protect you when your vehicle is hit from the side or rear, or if it

rolls over. So always belt up, even in a car equipped with airbags.

STEERING WHEELS AND COLUMNS
In a frontal collision, where no airbag is fitted, there is a risk that the driver's head will hit the steering wheel. A well-padded steering wheel will absorb the impact and do less damage than one which is hard and metallic. Raised switches or bolts in the wheel centre can cause nasty cuts and eye injuries. Metal rims and spokes may look stylish – but your face won't after it's been in a collision with them. For the same reason, look for a car that offers some degree of padding in the door panels to cushion your body on impact. Make sure there are no exposed metal bolts and fittings to cause injury.

You are less likely to suffer steering wheel injuries if you position yourself correctly. Sit at arm's length from the wheel rather than leaning over it with your arms bent.

HEAD RESTRAINTS
When your car is hit from behind (and rear-end collisions are one of the most common forms of accident) your body is thrown forward while your head and neck, if unsupported,

are jerked violently back, resulting in 'whiplash' injuries. Although not life-threatening, whiplash can be very painful and its effects can last a long time.

Head restraints are designed not to provide comfort but to prevent whiplash. They will also protect your head from being hit by back-seat passengers in a frontal collision.

To be effective, the head restraint must be strong, stable, and positioned correctly. One that is too low can do more harm than having no head restraint at all. Adjustable restraints are preferable to fixed ones, particularly for those who are above average height. If you share the driving with someone else, make sure you check the position of the head restraint every time you get in the car.

If a glance in the mirror tells you that you are about to be hit from behind:

• Remain facing forward. Resist the impulse to turn around

safe driving

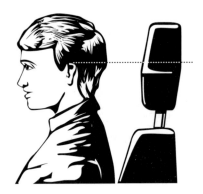

The padded section should be above the tops of your ears. The seat back should be upright to minimize the distance between your head and the restraint.

because having your head and spine at an angle increases the risk of whiplash injuries.

• Press your back against the seat and your head against the restraint.

SIDE-IMPACT BARS

Side-impact bars are installed in the door panels of the vehicle to prevent the door being pushed into the passenger compartment in a side-on collision.

There's some debate amongst safety experts as to how much protection these bars offer. If the oncoming vehicle strikes you only a glancing blow the damage may be minimized, but where it hits you full-on the chances of your escaping serious injury are slim. Even with bars fitted, the fact is that very little stands between your side and car that's smashing into you.

BULL BARS

In Australia these rigid bars are known as 'roo bars', because they are fitted to vehicles in the outback to protect them in the event of collisions with kangaroos. Where pedestrians and cyclists are more likely collision partners than kangaroos, bull bars give cause for concern because they maximize the risk and extent of injury to vulnerable road users. Whereas a child has a good chance of surviving when hit by a normal car travelling at 20 mph, a vehicle with bull bars fitted can kill at 10 mph.

There is a campaign under way to outlaw bull bars in Britain and elsewhere. In the meantime, if your car has bull bars or if you insist on having some fitted, make sure you

notify your insurer. To reflect the greater scale of damage and injury caused by bull bars, insurance companies may charge a higher premium. Failure to notify your insurer could result in your policy being invalidated.

LOAD RESTRAINTS

If you intend to use your car to transport heavy objects, tie-down eyes attached to the floor or side panels are essential. These small loops provide an anchor whereby heavy items can be secured to the chassis so that they won't be hurled forward in a collision. It is not safe to carry loose heavy items in the back of an estate or hatchback with split or folding rear seats, as the structure is not strong enough to restrain the load in a crash. There have been cases of children carried in the rear seat being paralysed by support struts being driven into their spines by the force of the load shifting forward. If you don't have tie-downs, use a load separator to prevent objects shifting forward. Alternatively, carry suitcases and other large items secured to a roof rack. (See *Loading the Car* and *Towing* in **Long Journeys** for further advice on carrying heavy loads, fitting roof racks, and towing trailers and caravans.)

It will assist the car's stability if you spread your load evenly – and that includes passengers. Don't have all the heaviest passengers on one side of the car, or all in the back. Too much weight in the rear causes light steering, and if one side is carrying a much heavier load than the other you could have problems when cornering.

> **Never allow passengers to travel in the luggage area or on a folded down rear seat.**

Inside the passenger compartment, keep things stowed away securely. Avoid having sharp or solid objects like glass bottles or hard-edged toys in the car, as these can cause serious injuries if the brakes are applied sharply. Keep the parcel shelf clear of packages to eliminate the risk of flying objects and to ensure good rear vision. Clear the driver's footwell of loose objects, too, as these can easily get under the pedals and cause an accident.

If you need to hang suits or dresses in the car, use the hooks provided, and make sure they do not swing around or interfere with rear vision.

safe driver

Car manufacturers are making safer cars than ever before, and yet the number of accidents continues to rise. It's possible that improvements in technology actually make matters worse. Some motorists seem to think that because their vehicle is equipped with anti-locking brakes and airbags it gives them the freedom to go even faster without getting hurt. But even the best technology cannot save you from the consequences of taking stupid risks.

So what makes a safe driver? Is it quick reaction time? The ability to handle a high-performance car well at high speed? Skill at the controls? Years of experience? Training in skills such as controlling a skid?

Ironically, the more skill and accuracy with which you handle the controls, the more confident you are that your speedy reaction times allow you to cope with high speeds, the more you believe that you are a good driver... the greater the statistical chance of your being involved in an accident. The reality is that few drivers are anywhere near as good as they think they are.

> **The key to being a safe driver is to remember the four As:**
>
> **ALERTNESS**
> **AWARENESS**
> **ATTITUDE**
> **ANTICIPATION**

Alertness

About a third of all accidents are rear-end shunts, where one vehicle collides with the back of another. This is a classic example of what happens when a motorist is not paying sufficient attention. Being alert means being on the look out for hazards, anticipating problems before they occur and responding quickly. It is an offence to drive without due care and attention, or to drive while under the influence of substances which are likely to impair your ability to perceive risks and take action to avoid them.

Careless driving is punishable by law. While the vehicle is moving, it is illegal to use a hand-held telephone, read a newspaper or map, tune a car radio or change a CD or cassette – or anything else that causes the driver not to be in a position to respond in the event of an emergency.

In Britain, careless driving can lead to fines, disqualification or endorsement of your licence. The police can prosecute for careless driving even if there has not been an accident. It's no use pleading that you were careless because you were tired–the law takes a dim view of motorists who drive when they're not fit to do so.

A number of factors can interfere with your ability to remain alert, among them: drink and drugs, medical conditions (such as hay fever and sight disorders), stress, fatigue, and allowing yourself to be distracted by things going on inside the car.

ALCOHOL
Around 20 per cent of all road traffic deaths are drink-related. Alcohol is a powerful drug which slows down the processes occurring in the brain, so that you take longer to react to unexpected situations. It inspires a false sense of confidence, affects your judgement of speed, distance and risk, and

reduces your co-ordination – turning avoidable hazards into potentially lethal ones.

Just one drink will impair your driving to some extent. And because the effects can be quite subtle to begin with, you may feel as though you're perfectly sober. It's almost impossible to calculate with any accuracy how much you can drink and be safe to drive, because everyone absorbs alcohol at a different rate, depending on sex, weight, metabolism, age, the type of drink consumed, and how much you've had to eat. Some people can be seriously affected even though they're well below the legal limit.

And don't let anyone tell you that you'll be all right if you stick to beer or cider rather than spirits. The amount of alcohol in half a pint of beer is roughly equivalent to the alcohol content of a glass of wine or a pub measure of spirits – more, if you're drinking extra-strength beer or cider. Even alcoholic sodas, which look and taste like soft drinks, can push you over the limit; at 4.2–5.5 per cent proof, they contain as much alcohol as many lagers.

Once you have alcohol in your bloodstream it takes time for the liver to break it down. The average person's liver can

 Legal limits for the amount of alcohol allowed in your bloodstream vary, depending on which country you're driving in. In Britain it is 80 milligrams per 100 millilitres of blood. The amount of drink required to reach this level varies from person to person.

The police have the right to demand a breath test even if you have not committed any traffic offence or been involved in an accident. All the law requires is that they have 'reasonable suspicion' that you may have been drinking.

The penalties for driving over the legal limit are severe. You risk being disqualified from driving, fined or imprisoned (if you kill or injure someone as a result of driving under the influence, the fine or prison sentence increases to match the seriousness of the offence).

When planning to drive abroad, check out the motoring regulations before you go. Some countries have much stricter blood alcohol levels, and there may be regulations prohibiting you from carrying (let alone drinking from) open bottles of beer, wine or spirits in the car.

only cope with one unit (that's about half a pint of beer or a glass of wine) per hour. You can drink all the black coffee you like, swim or exercise, take vitamins or hangover cures – it won't reduce the level of alcohol in your system. So if you've been out for an evening's drinking, it may be that the following morning, or even lunchtime the next day, will still find you over the limit. Police in some countries set up checkpoints to breathalyse drivers on their way to work and catch out the drinkers. Unless you have your own personal breathalyser kit, there's no way of telling for sure whether you will pass the test. So take public transport the next day and get a good night's sleep before driving again.

> **REMEMBER**
> Even if the accident is someone else's fault, when you're over the limit, you'll come out the loser. The pedestrian who steps out into the path of your car may be twice as drunk as you – but you will be the one who is breathalysed and prosecuted.

The consequences of drinking and driving don't end with legal action. Drivers with drink driving convictions face higher insurance premiums. Disqualification means inconvenience and the expense of extra travel costs, and if your job involves driving you could find yourself out of work. And if you kill or maim someone, you'll have to live with your guilt and the disapproval of your friends and relations. Of course it may just as easily be you who is killed or injured.

Rather than risk the consequences, avoid the problem: DON'T drink and drive. Leave the car at home and take public transport or a taxi instead, or arrange for someone who has spent the evening drinking non-alcoholic beverages to drive you home.

DRUGS
Drugs vary in their effect on the body, according to whether they are depressants or stimulants. Some substances remain in your system for two weeks or more. Like alcohol, they impair control and co-ordination; some have more extreme effects, playing tricks with your vision and perception. Illegal drugs are also suspected of being a factor in a number of road rage attacks.

If anything, the stigma attached to a drug-related motoring offence is worse than for drink driving. Even if your line of work doesn't involve driving, your employment prospects will suffer when it becomes known that you have a criminal record as the result of drug taking.

MEDICAL CONDITIONS

If you don't feel well, don't drive – especially when taking medication. Many drugs cause drowsiness, either when taken on their own or when mixed with other drugs or drink. Some medications cause the pupils to dilate, making the eyes extremely sensitive to strong light. Always ask your doctor whether prescribed drugs will impair your driving performance, and check the label or ask the pharmacist about over-the-counter remedies.

Even without the influence of drugs, your powers of concentration and the speed of your responses are reduced by illness. Something as mundane as a common cold can be dangerous at the wheel. A violent sneeze makes your eyes close and your body jerk, with potentially disastrous consequences if you swerve as a result – and at 70 mph you will cover well over a hundred feet in that second your eyes are closed.

Any injury which impedes the movement of your arms or legs will diminish your control of the vehicle and make driving difficult. Bandages, plasters, and splints will get in the way, sprains or heavy bruising will slow you down. If you suffer discomfort in the muscles or joints when driving, make sure that the mirrors are adjusted to keep head movement to a minimum. Install larger mirrors if need be. Use a cushion or back rest to give more support while driving.

Diseases of the ear can affect your balance as well as your hearing. Two-wheel transport like motorcycles and pedal cycles are out of the question while you're in this condition. Motorists, too, should exercise caution. If you find that turning your head leaves you giddy and disoriented, you will not be able to look over your shoulder to check your blind spots – which means you are not safe to drive. Consult your doctor.

As we get older, our hearing deteriorates. The high-pitched tones are often the first to go – which means that it can be difficult to hear horns and emergency vehicle sirens. To compensate for a hearing impairment, keep the radio low and check the mirrors more frequently (every three seconds). Have your hearing tested regularly, and if you are issued with a hearing aid, wear it.

HAYFEVER

One in ten drivers suffer from hay fever. When the pollen count is high the eyes swell and become sore and itchy. Even with the windows and sunroof closed, pollen-saturated air comes in through the vents. In addition to the sneezing fits and the difficulty of seeing when your eyes are watering, hay fever sufferers are likely to have trouble staying awake. It can be difficult to get a good night's sleep when the symptoms are at their worst, and antihistamines taken to ease the condition can cause drowsiness.

If you are badly affected by hay fever it is safer not to drive. When you have no choice but to drive, take precautions. Use non-sedative antihistamines, following the instructions on the label carefully (do not mix with other drugs without first checking with your pharmacist what the consequences will be). There are a number of non-sedative antihistamines available over the counter at pharmacies that will not make you sleepy. Cortisone drugs can help to suppress a ticklish nose. Don't wait until you have an attack, take preventive measures: ask your chemist about eye drops or nasal sprays which prevent the pollen getting to sensitive membranes. Wearing sunglasses to protect your eyes from irritating bright sunlight may also help.

Some new cars have filters that stop pollen spores from passing through the vents. If your car is not equipped with these, close all windows, turn off fans and close air vents.

STRESS

It's important to be mentally as well as physically fit when you drive. Driving is a stressful task at the best of times, because you have to be constantly alert for hazards posed by road conditions and other road users. Any motorist who feels no anxiety whatsoever when behind the wheel is obviously not awake to the potential dangers. But too high a level of anxiety overloads the brain and prevents you from making calm, rational decisions. If your mind is full of the blazing row you've just had with a partner or colleague, or if you let yourself get worked up about being late for an appointment because you've been stuck in a traffic jam for the last half-hour, you're going to get distracted from the job in hand. This often results in late decision-making and violent braking.

Try to find ways of coping with stress and combating aggression (see the section on *Attitude* below). Research has

SIGHT DEFECTS

Sight is critical to safe driving. If you cannot see properly you cannot assess traffic conditions and hazards. Some countries require drivers to undergo eye tests as part of the licence renewal procedure, but in Britain and elsewhere there is only one compulsory sight check, which forms part of the driving test. Having passed the test and gained a licence, a driver could, if he or she chose, go for 50 years without having their eyes tested again. It is estimated that 50 per cent of drivers on Britain's roads have some form of sight defect, and as many as 25 per cent fall below the minimum legal requirement.

Eyesight can deteriorate with age or as a result of disorders like glaucoma. Symptoms may develop so gradually that you will not even be aware there is a problem until an eye test reveals it. This is why it is essential to have your eyes checked once a year until you are 60, and every six months after that. Sophisticated machines can detect early warning signs of problems like cataracts and glaucoma, and will also reveal defects such as poor depth perception due to long-sightedness or near-sightedness, colour blindness, tunnel vision, and night blindness:

• **Hypermetropia** (longsightedness) and myopia (short-sightedness) are common problems which can be rectified by wearing contact lenses or glasses.

• **Colour blindness** is for the most part a hereditary condition (about 8 per cent of men are affected and less than 1 per cent of women), though some cases do result from eye disease or injury.

• **Tunnel vision** means that only objects which lie straight ahead can be seen clearly. Peripheral vision (the view to the sides) is gradu-ally lost. The most common cause is glaucoma, but brain tumours and degeneration of the retina can have the same result.

• **Night blindness** occurs when the cells of the retina (a light-sensitive membrane at the back of the eye) malfunction. There are a number of possible causes for this condition, including vitamin A deficiency. Sufferers will find driving at night difficult because they will have trouble judging and estimating distances, and the speed of other vehicles. Another problem which may be experienced in dark or low light conditions is over-sensitivity to glare. To compensate for poor light conditions, the pupil of the eye dilates to allow more light to enter. Some people are more affected by glare from oncoming headlights than others, and find driving at night difficult for this reason. But the solution is to see an optician – don't try using tinted glasses, lenses or visors when driving at night or in poor visibility.

For the majority of motorists, the most dangerous time is not night but dusk. As the light decreases, shapes lose their definition and objects seem to blend into their surroundings, making them difficult to see. Switch on your dipped beam headlights as soon as the light begins to fail.

If an optician prescribes glasses or contact lenses, be sure to wear them. Leaving them off out of negligence or vanity puts yourself and others at risk. Keep a spare pair of glasses in the glove compartment, so that you won't be stranded if you lose your contact lenses or break the glasses you're wearing.

shown that the risk of being involved in an accident increases when you are under the kind of severe stress that follows a bereavement or the break-up of a relationship. After receiving bad news, it can be very difficult to concentrate on driving. Switch to public transport for a while, or get a friend to chauffeur you until you recover.

FATIGUE

Falling asleep at the wheel happens all too often on motorways, with terrifying consequences. And even if you don't go so far as to actually fall asleep, driving when you are tired means that your concentration and risk perception are impaired, so you're more likely to have an accident.

One of the most common causes of fatigue is lack of stimulation. On a motorway or a road that you travel every day and know like the back of your hand, driving gets to be monotonous. Fog, rain and darkness make matters worse because there's even less to see. Because you're not getting any visual or physical stimulation, your senses become dulled, your levels of awareness and alertness decrease. And the longer you drive, the worse it gets. A driver who is tired before getting into the car – after a hard day's work or a sleepless night – is particularly at risk. Be careful if you have to drive at times when you would normally be asleep – more fatigue-related accidents occur between midnight and 8 a.m. than at any other time.

Try to reduce the risk of fatigue by taking precautions:

- A light meal like a salad, is best when you're about to set out on a long journey. A heavy meal will make you sluggish and tired, whether it's a roast lunch or a three-course evening meal.
- Don't take any medications that may induce drowsiness. Remember that drugs and alcohol can stay in your system for a long time.
- Driving at night is difficult enough, but if you are suffering from any sight defect or disorder it can be very stressful and tiring. Have your eyes tested and wear glasses or contact lenses if prescribed.
- If you know you have a long overnight journey ahead of you, try to sleep during the day. Prepare the car and do all the necessary packing and route planning, then rest. Avoid last-minute running around at all costs.
- Rattles and squeaks can be irritating, so do what you can to reduce noise in the vehicle. Make sure any luggage in the back is packed securely and that you don't have items rattling round on the floor of the car.
- Make yourself comfortable. Bad posture causes aches and pains which lead to fatigue setting in. It's particularly important when driving a hire car or a vehicle you're not familiar with to take time adjusting the seat and steering before you set off.
- Wear comfortable clothing that doesn't restrict body movement or steering. Layers of light, loose-fitting garments are best, that way you can stop and add or subtract a layer to achieve the right temperature. NEVER try to get dressed or undressed at the wheel – you need both hands on the wheel and both eyes on the road.
- Wear lightweight, flat shoes with enclosed or covered heels, and make sure that the soles grip the pedals. Nothing is worse than shoes which slip off the pedals when you're trying to control the car (check that the pedal rubbers themselves are not worn and slippery).
- Keep a window slightly ajar so that fresh air can circulate.
- Wipers can be very hypnotic. If it's raining and the wipers are on, don't stare at them – the effect can be very hypnotic and you'll slip into a trance-like state.
- When planning your route for a long journey, pick out a few places where you can take a break en route. Aim to stop at least every three hours for a 20-minute break. If weather conditions are poor, you may need to stop more frequently. Mature drivers need more frequent and longer breaks to relieve fatigue.

If you start to feel drowsy at the wheel, or if you're driving at night and lights start to blur, it's time to take a break. Pull into a layby or service area as soon as you can. In the meantime, do something to fight off the fatigue. Open the window and take deep breaths of fresh air. If you have a passenger, get them to have a conversation with you If you are alone, turn on the radio and sing along, or try giving a running commentary as you drive. Flex your fingers and toes, and stretch each arm and leg in turn while sitting at the controls. Don't stare fixedly at one point. Look as far ahead as possible then check the mirrors left and right, then look ahead again. By focusing on objects close at hand and then in the distance, you will work the optic muscles and help to keep yourself alert.

When you are able to stop the car, get out and stretch your legs. Go for a walk if it's safe to do so. If not, do a few gentle exercises in the car. Try rolling your head gently, first one way and then the other. Make circular movements with your shoulders to release some of the tension in your neck and spine. Pour yourself a refreshing non-alcoholic drink before you set off again – dehydration can make you feel lethargic on long journeys.

DISTRACTIONS

Safe driving means giving the road your full attention. Being distracted by something going on in the car, even for a split second, can have terrible consequences when you are travelling at speed. By the time you become aware of the hazard on the road ahead, violent braking or swerving may be your only option – which can have repercussions for the vehicles following along behind you. And even if you do have your eyes on the road, poor concentration slows your reaction times.

Eliminate distractions wherever possible. Physical discomfort can take your mind off the road, so dress in loose-fitting clothes, wear sensible footwear, adjust your seat to a comfortable position, and visit the toilet before you depart. Tidy up the interior so that there are no loose items to fall about when you accelerate, brake or corner. Make sure that the driver's footwell is kept clear, because if something were to roll under the pedals it could prevent you from applying the brakes in an emergency.

The correct way to maintain safe control of the vehicle is to have *both* hands on the wheel, positioned at two o'clock and ten o'clock or three o'clock and nine o'clock.

This is why it is illegal to use a hand-held mobile telephone while driving (there are phones that can be operated safely without taking your hands off the wheel, so if you must use make or receive calls in the car, use one of these). One of the most common causes of accidents is tuning the radio or changing a cassette while driving. Don't get too engrossed in a radio programme or telephone conversation – your hazard perception and response times will suffer. If you

---

DON'T SMOKE AND DRIVE

 Smoking can seriously damage your health in the long term – smoking while driving can kill you in seconds. For as long as that cigarette lasts, it is placing you and your passengers in jeopardy.

To start with, concentration is lost while you search for the cigarette packet and lighter. To light up you have to take one hand off the wheel (two hands are needed to light a match). Once the cigarette is lit, you need one hand to hold it or remove it from your lips. The ash has to be flicked somewhere, which means using the ashtray or flicking it out of the open window (with a risk of it being blown back into your eyes). Sometimes when the smoker tries to take the cigarette from their mouth it sticks to the lips, so that the hand slides down, nipping off the hot tip which drops into the lap causing your attention to be diverted yet again.

When the cigarette is finished it must be extinguished and disposed of. Using the ashtray involves taking a hand off the wheel, throwing the cigarette out of the window could injure cyclists or pedestrians, or cause grass fires.

Some insurance companies now charge smokers a higher premium to reflect the risks they run. Why run risks when you don't have to? If you must smoke, wait until you stop for a break and then light up.

---

have passengers, keep your eyes on the road while you talk to them – and avoid getting into an argument or having a stressful heart-to-heart with the one you love.

NEVER allow pets to roam free in the car – they can become excited and cause a major distraction. The majority of dogs love travelling and like nothing better than sticking their heads out of the window. This can be dangerous; have the windows open just enough for ventilation, but not enough for the dog to get its head out. If your dog is a poor traveller, don't sit him on your lap to make him feel better, seek the advice of a vet before you travel. For a long journey, some nervous pets may need to be prescribed tranquillizers. Keep all pets in the rear of the car, either in purpose-built carriers or behind a wire screen. It's a good idea to see they get exercise before the journey to make them a little calmer. Take along a supply of food and water for them on the journey and stop frequently to monitor their condition.

Dogs should be put on a lead when you let them out as they will be excited and want to run. Don't let them in fields where there are livestock, and don't let them foul public areas. If you have to leave an animal alone in the car, leave them with adequate ventilation and water. On a hot day, park in the shade and leave the rear windows open at least 4 inches. Do not leave them unattended for hours on end – as the sun moves across the sky the shadow will disappear and the car will turn into an oven. Every year there are reports of dogs dying a terrible death in parked cars because of their owners' thoughtlessness.

Insects like wasps, bees or hornets, can cause pandemonium when they get themselves trapped inside a moving vehicle.

STAY CALM. Keep your eyes on the road. Don't swipe at the insect – you will only make things worse. Wind a window down so that it can fly out. If that doesn't work, pull over when it is safe and legal to do so, open the door and coax it to leave.

Children can be a major source of distraction on long journeys. As the miles mount up their enthusiasm gives way to boredom. Don't allow children to slip their shoulders from seat belt in order to get a better view of the surroundings. Take along a supply of colouring books and favourite soft toys to help pass the time. Be careful what you give the children to eat before and during the journey, especially if they are prone to travel sickness. Sweets may add to the pleasure of the trip, but avoid large boiled sweets which they might choke on, and sticky sweets which will mark the interior of the vehicle. Crisps will make them dry so have a drink handy. This will lead to them requiring to relieve themselves, so be prepared for plenty of short halts.

Frequent rest stops are essential. Stop at a designated picnic or parking area and supervise the children, preventing their pent-up energy from placing them in danger. Keep them off the road and don't let them play ball games where cars are parked. An open field is ideal for letting them stretch their limbs in safety. Don't climb fences to gain access – honour the country code.

As it gets dark encourage the children to sleep. Cushions and blankets will make this easier.

Awareness

A safe driver is one who thinks about their driving and looks for ways to improve it. The majority of motorists consider themselves to be good drivers, but the fact that driver error plays a part in over 90 per cent of accidents means that a lot of people are kidding themselves.

An important aspect of driving safely is developing an awareness of your limitations and those of your vehicle. We all have limitations, though many of us fail to recognize them. When there's an accident or near-miss, we tend automatically to hold the other driver responsible rather than accepting our own portion of the blame. That means we come away without learning anything from the experience. So it's no wonder that drivers who have been in an accident are twice as likely to have another one, while drivers who are at least partly to blame for an accident are four times more likely to be involved in a similar accident within the next year.

All too often when we take risks, we try to justify them instead of taking a critical look at our attitude and driving practices. That needs to change if you want to be a safe driver, because otherwise you will go on repeating those risks and having accidents or narrowly avoiding them.

CAR GAMES FOR KIDS

• Each child in turn adds up the number plate of the car coming in the opposite direction. The highest score wins.

• Each child picks a colour. Every time they spot a car of that colour they score a point. The winner is the first one to 30.

• Play 'first one to spot...' Before setting off on the journey give each child a list of objects which they must spot – bridge, church, canal, types of animals, trees, road sign, etc. Each of these can be a point of discussion and explanation.

Start by making an adjustment in the way you assess your own performance as a driver. Recognize your limitations. If you are middle-aged, don't think that because you are experienced you cannot be involved in an accident. If you are a mature driver, adapt your driving habits to fit your physical abilities. Drive shorter distances, stay out of heavy traffic, and try to stick to familiar routes. Drivers of all ages should review their driving from a safety angle. Do you routinely leave for work at the last minute and use aggressive tactics to get you through rush-hour traffic regardless of the risks? Can you honestly say that you always match your speed to your vision and the prevailing road surface conditions? Do you enjoy the thrill of danger? Do you think that your fast cornering, rapid acceleration and breathtaking manoeuvres impress others? In safety terms, you're a disaster. It's definitely luck rather than judgement that has kept you alive thus far.

The more routine an action becomes, the harder it can be to change. Advanced driving lessons can help you to re-evaluate your driving and improve your standards, and there's the added incentive of a reduction in insurance premiums if you pass the advanced driving test at the end.

Attitude

No driving test can assess attitude – for the duration of the test all candidates are on their very best behaviour, suppressing negative tendencies like aggressive behaviour and risk-taking. Unfortunately, once the test is over, there's a tendency to forget about the rules of the road and the need for courtesy to other road users. Getting there in a hurry becomes all important, and drivers will risk their lives to gain a few seconds. As traffic grinds to a halt on congested roads and motorways, stress levels can reach the point where drivers show no tolerance for one another and 'road rage' breaks out.

ROAD RAGE

Why do otherwise normal, law-abiding people turn into violent maniacs when they get behind the wheel? Research surveys show that most road-rage offenders believe themselves to be the victims of someone else's bad driving. They interpret some simple incident like being overtaken or cut in on as a threat, and respond aggressively. Or they react to antisocial behaviour, such as driving too slowly or hogging the overtaking lane, by setting out to teach the other driver a lesson. This leads to headlight flashing, horn tooting, obscene gestures and verbal abuse, which can in turn escalate into tailgating or deliberately obstructing the other vehicle's progress. While this sort of activity is going on, those involved get so caught up in the battle that they lose sight of the risks they are taking. They ignore the traffic around them, the condition of the road surface, and the rules of the road, particularly the speed limit.

To combat road rage:

STAY CALM. Avoid letting yourself get stressed. Concentrate on your driving. Don't get into the car fuming over a row you've just had – that's giving road rage a head start. Don't set yourself an impossible deadline which the traffic won't allow you to keep – leave plenty of time for your journey, plan for delays. Play soothing music, think calmly and logically about the task in hand – giving a running commentary on your driving may help to focus the mind. When you feel the stress mounting, try counting to ten or deep breathing exercises, or pull over when safe to do so and take a break. If you know you are overwrought and having difficulty controlling your emotions, don't drive. Seek counselling or take steps to sort yourself out before you do something you'll regret.

BE TOLERANT. You're not a mind reader, so why assume that the other driver is deliberately trying to annoy you? Chances are it's a genuine mistake, so let it go. And when you make a mistake yourself, take an apologetic and courteous attitude. Most people respond in kind, so courtesy will smooth over a potentially explosive situation, while abuse will make it worse.

CONCENTRATE on your driving. Remember, safety is paramount. Think of the consequences dangerous driving can have.

DISENGAGE. Don't let it get personal – even if you're certain the other driver's action was deliberate, do not retaliate or engage in vehicle combat. It's not your place to teach anyone a lesson. Sooner or later, dangerous drivers get their just deserts with no help from you. When someone drives like an accident waiting to happen, your priority should be to get out of the disaster zone before it's too late. Even though it's galling to let them have their own way, in the interests of self-preservation you must resist the impulse to take up their challenge. Let them think you're a coward – better that than to be pronounced dead.

For further tips on what to do if you become a victim of someone else's road rage, see **Under Attack**.

SPEEDING

Drivers don't only take risks when aggression and stress cause them to lose all sense of caution. Some do it for the thrill of danger, or to impress others, or because they enjoy the illusion of being in control of a powerful car at high speeds. Young male drivers are particularly at risk. Often they think that the speed of their reactions is fast enough to cope, but in many cases a fast reaction will be the wrong reaction, because they haven't allowed themselves time to consider all the possible implications. Even on an empty road, with no other traffic to contend with, speeding kills. In nearly 20 per cent of accidents, no other vehicle is involved.

In many countries it is illegal to use devices which detect or jam radar frequencies in an attempt to defeat police speed traps. You can be prosecuted for using these devices.
Penalties for speeding include substantial fines, licence endorsements and/or disqualification.

Driving too fast causes thousands of avoidable deaths and injuries every year. The risk of your having an accident increases the faster you go, while the chances of survival for you and road users in your path decreases as the needle on the speedometer climbs. Nine out of ten pedestrians will survive being hit by a car travelling at 10 mph, but at 40 mph nine out of ten is the death toll.

Obeying the speed limit is not necessarily the same thing as travelling at a safe speed. The speed limit represents the maximum permissible speed in optimum conditions. A safe speed is one which allows you to stop safely within the distance you can see to be clear.

When assessing what would be a safe speed, you need to take into account:

Weather: It takes much longer to stop on wet or icy surfaces. ABS brakes help prevent skids, they don't reduce your stopping distance.

Visibility: At night or in fog you won't be able to see far ahead.

Road conditions: Bends and hills mean blind spots. Stopping distances increase when travelling downhill. In densely populated areas there's a danger of pedestrians stepping off the pavement into your path.

Traffic: heavy traffic means more hazards to watch for.

Driver: High speeds require total concentration, excellent vision (to scan the horizon), and the ability to evaluate hazards and take appropriate action. This level of concentration cannot be sustained over long periods, even by the most experienced driver. Know your limitations, the speed you are safe and comfortable with, and drive accordingly.

Vehicle: The power of the engine and braking characteristics will determine how fast it can travel in safety. Worn brakes, worn tyres, and poor suspension make it more difficult to stop in a hurry.

It's easy to speed unintentionally when your speed perception gets distorted, as happens in poor visibility or after you've been travelling at high speed on a motorway. Keep checking your speedometer.

TAILGATING

Driving too close to the vehicle in front is so common that many drivers aren't even aware of the risk they're taking. At least 10 per cent of accidents occur as a result of this practice, and it's one of the things most likely to incite road rage in others.

safe driving

The following distances are based on a vehicle in optimum condition on a flat, straight road in good, dry conditions, with an alert driver:

STOPPING DISTANCES

speed	thinking distance*	braking distance	overall stopping distance
20 mph	6 m/20 ft	6 m/20 ft	12 m /40 ft (3 car lengths)
30 mph	9 m/30 ft	14 m/45 ft	23 m /75 ft (6 car lengths)
40 mph	12 m/40 ft	24 m/80 ft	36 m /120 ft (9 car lengths)
50 mph	15 m/50 ft	38 m/125 ft	53 m /175 ft (13 car lengths)
60 mph	18 m/60 ft	55 m/180 ft	73 m /240 ft (18 car lengths)
70 mph	21 m/70 ft	75 m/245 ft	96 m /315 ft (24 car lengths)

*Thinking distance is the time it takes for the driver to recognize the need to brake and apply pressure to the pedal.

Allow yourself time to react to hazards by leaving a safe gap between your car and the vehicle in front. If someone behind you draws too close, increase the gap in front of you to compensate. That way you won't find yourself sandwiched between other vehicles in the event of a crash.

ANTICIPATION

The old motto, 'Be prepared!' applies as much on the roads as in the Boy Scouts. Develop your ability to read the road and identify potential dangers early on, so that you can respond in good time should the need arise. Remain constantly alert to the changing road conditions, even when you're certain you know the road like the back of your hand – most accidents happen within 10 miles of the driver's home. Never be complacent in your driving; other road users can make mistakes or take reckless chances. Drive at a speed which allows you time to evaluate and act upon any hazards which may arise.

By anticipating problems you can avoid having to slam on the brakes at the last moment, with the risk that entails of a following car slamming into you. Slow down gradually by applying the brakes, so that following drivers can see your brake lights and adjust their speed accordingly.

Other common accident scenarios and techniques for avoiding hazards are dealt with in **Defensive Driving**

DEADLY MOTORWAY DEBRIS

Thousands of tons of debris are cleared from motorways every year, much of it potentially lethal. Vehicle parts account for most of the rubbish, though items as large as garage doors and gas cookers have been retrieved from traffic lanes by police. Even relatively small items can kill: a sheet of newspaper, if it lands across the windscreen or wraps itself round a motorcyclist's head, can cause a fatal accident.

Motorists, when faced with a piece of debris on the road ahead and a split second in which to decide what action to take, will, in most cases, swerve suddenly to avoid the debris – creating a further hazard for following drivers.

To minimize the dangers of road debris, give yourself time and space in which to react:

• Keep a safe distance from the vehicle in front. If it is carrying a load which appears unstable, allow an even greater gap. Should another car fill the gap, ease off again to maintain that safety margin. Remember that the shortest stopping distance at 70 mph is the equivalent of 24 car lengths.

• Read the road ahead. Keep an eye on what cars in the distance are doing. If you see them taking avoiding action, prepare to react. Watch out for drivers way ahead of you using their brake lights, hazard warning lights or indicators. Give yourself time to slow down to a halt – braking suddenly will most likely result in your car being shunted by the vehicle behind.

When carrying a load of any description, make absolutely sure it is secure before you set off. The slipstream at 70 mph exerts considerable force.

If you see a dangerous obstruction in the road, find a safe place to stop and telephone the police. Your warning could save lives.

Safety Checks

Safety demands that you and your car need to be in tip-top condition. Before driving off, always carry out a quick inspection to ensure that there are no signs of forced entry and that the car is serviceable (see *First Parade* in **Maintenance**), and that your survival kit(s) are stowed correctly. This check will only take a few minutes and yet it could save you hours of misery.

A quick way to remember the items which need checking is to think **POWER:**

P etrol (oil or diesel)
O il
W ater (screenwash, coolant)
E lectrics (lights)
R ubber (tyres and wipers)

Next, check underneath the vehicle for potential hazards or obstructions. Make sure no animals or children are at risk of being run over when you reverse.

DRIVER CHECKLIST

- Do you have a hangover?
- Are you taking medication that makes you drowsy?
- Suffering from any ailments or injuries, dental problems, sight defects?
- Feeling stressed after receiving bad news or having a row?

If the answer is yes, find some other form of transport, or stay indoors.

COCKPIT DRILL

Doors: Make sure all doors, including the hatchback or boot, are closed securely.

Seat: Adjust the driver's seat to suit your height, making sure that the angle and distance from the wheel are comfortable. Adjust the head restraint so that it is level with the tops of your ears and close to the back of your head.

Steering: On some models the steering wheel can be adjusted. This is done by pulling a lever. Make sure it is securely engaged once you have made an adjustment. NEVER adjust the wheel when driving.

Seat belts: Make sure everyone is wearing a seat belt.

Mirrors: Adjust the interior mirror so as to give maximum all-round vision with minimum head movement. Check the exterior mirrors: you should be able to see one-third car and two-thirds road. A passenger can assist with this, otherwise it may be necessary to hop in and out of the car until you're happy with the angle. The height of both mirrors is important: too high and you'll create a dangerous blind spot; too low and you won't see cars in the distance preparing to overtake. There are small inserts which can be stuck on to the wing mirrors giving a wider angle and eliminating blind spots.

Ensure the car is in neutral and the handbrake is applied. Switch on the ignition and check that all warning lights and gauges are functioning. On vehicles with a manual choke, set the choke (new cars are fitted with an automatic choke) and start the engine. Depress clutch pedal and select gear. Don't touch the accelerator pedal when starting, it will only flood the engine.

Never race a cold engine. Let it warm up until it reaches normal operating temperature. This is when the temperature needle reaches normal and the choke is not required. While the engine is warming up, test the indicators, main beam, dip, and side lights, also hazard warning lights, and horn.

REMEMBER
NEVER leave an engine running unattended, especially with children or pets in the vehicle.

Check your mirrors, look over your shoulder to check your blindspot (if reversing, be especially wary of children or animals behind the car), release the handbrake and move off gradually. For the first few miles, be gentle on the brakes and take time changing gears – this will save wear and tear on the car.

safe driving

Safety in the Garage

Too many garages end up being used as a storage space for unsafe equipment and dangerous chemicals. If you intend to carry out car repairs or other work in the garage, make sure that it is a safe, well-lit and well-ventilated environment. Have a fire extinguisher and a first-aid kit on hand.

Having invested in good quality tools, look after them. Store them in a tool box when not in use. Stow away tools, garden implements and other items on shelves or stout hooks.

DON'T store large quantities of petrol, paraffin and other flammable substances. In some countries there are legal limits on the amount of petrol you are allowed to store in a domestic environment.

Make it a rule that children are NEVER allowed into the garage unsupervised. It is not a suitable play area.

Store hazardous chemicals out of the reach of children – locked away if possible. Research has shown that most accidents occur when dangerous substances are stored less than four feet from ground level without being locked away.

Study the manufacturer's instructions on the label. It's all too easy, when you use a product regularly, to ignore the warnings on the label. Almost any chemical can be dangerous when used carelessly.

Hazardous items typically found in the garage include:

Petrol: Highly flammable/explosive. NEVER allow petrol fumes to build up – make sure the area is well ventilated. Do not smoke or permit any naked flames or sparks in the area. NEVER syphon fuel by sucking on a tube. If swallowed, petrol can cause severe gastrointestinal irritation. Inhaling the fumes can damage the lungs and cause pneumonia-like disorders. **NEVER induce vomiting as further lung damage will occur. Seek medical attention immediately.** Wear protective clothing and goggles to prevent contact with skin or eyes. If petrol gets on to the skin, rinse for several minutes under running water. Eye contact should be treated by irrigating the eyes with tepid water under a mixer tap or shower attachment for a minimum of 20 minutes, then seek medical assistance as soon as possible.

Antifreeze and de-icer: Antifreeze may contain ethylene glycol. If swallowed it can damage the kidneys, brain and heart. De-icers often contain methanol, which if inhaled can cause dizziness and nausea. If swallowed, damage to the eyesight may occur. Do not induce vomiting. Seek medical help without delay. To treat cases of skin and eye contact, follow the procedure described under Petrol, above.

Engine oil: Prolonged skin contact can cause serious skin disorders and cancer. Always wear gloves and protective clothing, and wash away any oil that comes in contact with the skin. Take care when disposing of used oil.

Car batteries: Give off highly explosive hydrogen gas and contain caustic acid. For a full list of safety precautions, see **Maintenance**.

Brush cleaners and paint strippers: May contain methanol. Some contain dichloro-methane, which can be absorbed through the skin or by inhalation, causing damage to the central nervous system. Rinse thoroughly for at least 20 minutes and then seek medical attention as soon as possible.

Solvents, adhesives and sealants: Highly flammable and give off toxic vapours which can quickly cause dizziness and nausea. Over-exposure can lead to headaches, vomiting, stupor and hallucinations. Long-term exposure can cause liver and kidney damage. Extreme exertion after inhaling may put the heart at risk. **Do not induce vomiting. Seek medical attention immediately.** Avoid skin contact. Wash off as soon as possible with soap and warm water. Don't scrub – try to peel the glue away gently.

Rust removers: These are both highly poisonous and highly corrosive. Avoid all skin and eye contact. If any is swallowed, call an ambulance. Do not induce vomiting.

Carbon monoxide: Inhalation causes sickness, chronic tiredness, muscular weakness. Victims should be helped outdoors or where there is a plentiful supply of fresh air, such as by an open window. Loosen restrictive clothing, especially around the neck and chest, and check that the victim is breathing. Administer artificial respiration and/or cardiac compression if necessary. Even if the victim claims to feel better afterwards, insist that they seek medical attention.

Your car is one of your most valuable possessions. Even if it's just an old banger, when someone steals or vandalizes your vehicle you suffer in cash terms (insurance excesses, loss of no-claims bonus), and, even worse, you're deprived of your usual means of transport, having to rely instead on public transport – which may mean walking home from the nearest station or bus stop late at night – or cadging lifts from friends.

vehicle security

CAR CRIME

ANTI-THEFT DEVICES Alarms • Immobilizers • Tracking/recovery systems • Mechanical devices • Locks

DETERRENTS Etching • Vehicle watch

BASIC PRECAUTIONS

PARKING

VANDALIZED!

STOLEN!

SECURITY CHECKLIST

car crime

Car crime is big business. Every year hundreds of thousands of cars are stolen or vandalized, forcing up insurance premiums and costing taxpayers millions in criminal justice costs. In the UK alone, a car is stolen every 60 seconds. Of these, around a third are stolen for 'one-off use', such as 'joy riding', or as a getaway vehicle after committing another crime, or just as a means for the thief to get home after missing the last bus. There's a good chance that these cars will be recovered, because the thieves tend to dump them after a few hours, but more often than not they're burned-out wrecks by that time – either damaged in a crash or vandalized.

A few years ago joy riding accounted for two-thirds of stolen cars, but now that honour goes to cars stolen by professional thieves. This is because of a boom in the market for secondhand parts – thieves steal popular makes and strip them down for spares. Old cars are possibly even more at risk than new ones (top of the thieves' hit list in Britain is a 10-year-old Ford Escort 1.3), partly because the owners think that no one will be interested in stealing their old banger. New models and high-performance cars are likely to be 'ringed' – given a change of identity and sold on (possibly to an unsuspecting buyer). Whether it's been ringed or stripped, once it's been stolen there's little chance of getting your car back.

And car crime doesn't end with vehicle theft: in Britain a car is broken into and something stolen from it every 20 seconds. The cost of repairing the damage, let alone replacing the items stolen, can be considerable – so it's well worth investing in the best security devices you can afford to protect your car. Some insurance companies will reduce premiums (by as much as 50 per cent in some cases) when an approved electronic security system is fitted.

Anti-Theft Devices

It's almost impossible to make a car totally thief-proof. What a security device can do, however, is to make access as difficult and time-consuming as possible to deter thieves. Most car thieves are opportunists, seizing upon easy targets – it takes only a matter of seconds and little effort to break into an unprotected car, and the chances of being caught are slim. A device that takes several minutes to disarm, and which sounds a piercing alarm the whole while, will make your car a much less attractive prospect.

There are hundreds of anti-theft devices on the market, ranging from inexpensive mechanical immobilizers such as steering wheel clamps to sophisticated (and costly) electronic systems. In deciding how much to spend you will need to think about the level of risk for your car (is it a high-performance car, attractive to thieves and a target for vandals), whether any security features have been incorporated by the manufacturer (such as built-in immobilizers or alarms), and the sort of areas you use your car in (do you have no choice but to park in the street or use high-risk inner-city car parks?).

Before buying any product, seek an unbiased opinion of its performance. It's a good idea to check out reviews in motoring or consumer magazines – often a range of comparable devices will be put to the test and the results published. Or ask friends and colleagues what they use and whether they can recommend it.

Whichever security device you opt for, make sure it is as visible as possible to act as a deterrent. The idea is to let the thief know that breaking into your car will be more trouble than it's worth, so that hopefully he'll give up on the idea and move on to the next easy target. Use window stickers supplied by the manufacturer to advertise the fact that you've got a state-of-the-art electronic immobilizer/alarm fitted, because if the thief has to break in to find out it's there you'll be faced with an expensive bill for damage. (The downside of these stickers is that they alert professionals to what they can expect, but a determined pro will probably find his way round any security device if it's worth his while, so settle for deterring the opportunist amateurs.) Electronic alarms usually have a flashing LED light display which can be seen from the side window. Mechanical devices tend to have neon yellow parts to catch the eye of the would-be thief.

ALARMS

An alarm should have a siren loud enough to warn you if anyone is tampering with your car and, hopefully, frighten off the would-be thief. In a recent official survey, convicted thieves were asked whether they would try to steal a car if they knew it was equipped with an alarm; 83 per cent said they would be deterred from tampering with the car, and that if an alarm sounded while they were trying to gain entry they would run away.

On the other hand, another survey aimed at members of the public found that the majority tend to ignore car alarms, assuming that it's a false alarm. It's important when selecting a car alarm to make sure that it is not going to be set off by a strong breeze or a passing car. In some countries, including Britain, local authorities have the power to prosecute owners of vehicles whose false alarms cause a nuisance. And thieves have been known to use the alarm to work to their advantage, by rocking a parked car to set off the alarm in the middle of the night and then hiding. Once the owner has reset the alarm and gone back to the house, the thieves emerge and rock the car again until the alarm sounds. By doing this several times, they fool the owner into thinking that the alarm is faulty. The owner then disconnects the alarm and the thieves can make off with the car in peace.

Many car manufacturers now offer built-in car alarms as an option. This is worth having, because even though a factory-fitted alarm may not be the most advanced system money can buy, it should offer a good level of protection and will have been tested and approved for your model of car.

If your car did not come with an alarm fitted, you need to decide whether you are going to buy a simple system that you can fit yourself, or pay an expert to fit something more sophisticated. Be warned, the cheaper and simpler it is to fit,

the easier it will be for a thief to get around. For example, air-pressure-sensitive devices which you lock over the steering wheel are advertised as having a siren so piercing that the thief will be unable to drive because of the noise – in fact, thieves can rip these off and throw them out of the window in a matter of seconds. Alarms which use the car's horn are also a doddle for thieves: the wires are usually fitted behind the engine grille – snip them and the alarm stops. If you're on a tight budget, it's probably best to opt for an alarm which can be expanded; buy the basic unit to start with and add the rest as and when your finances allow.

Go for the noisiest siren you can get. To make sure that thieves can't silence the alarm by getting under the car and cutting the battery cable, get a system with a back-up battery. The method whereby you can switch off the alarm, should the need arise, varies: some use a hidden switch or a key in the siren unit, but the best are operated by remote control (which may also operate the car's central locking). But be warned: these remote locking devices are not without risk. Illegal receivers, known as 'grabbers' can be used by thieves to copy your code as you lock the car; the code is then copied on to their own remote and transmitted to open your car. A grabber's range is limited, so be suspicious of anyone standing close by holding a small box when you lock the car. The best remote control systems foil grabbers by automatically changing their code each time they are operated.

Remember to change the batteries of your remote control as often as the manufacturer recommends, or you won't be able to deactivate the alarm.

Alarms can detect an intruder in a variety of ways, depending on which sensors they are fitted with:

Direct contact sensor. Electronic sensors in the doors, boot/hatch, bonnet trigger an alarm when forced open. This system won't be activated if thieves smash a window to steal your radio.

Current and voltage-drop sensors detect changes in the car's electrical system. If your vehicle is fitted with a cooling fan which runs even when the engine has been switched off, this system cannot be fitted. Again, there is no protection against a thief smashing the window.

Ultrasonic sensors detect changes in air pressure within the car and will trigger the alarm if someone smashes a window or gets in the car. The downside is that if it's windy outside or if a passing vehicle creates a strong breeze, air coming through the vents can set off the alarm, so you have to remember to close all interior vents, windows and sunroof when you park the car (if you have a convertible with a soft roof, opt for another type of alarm altogether). Some sensors can be switched off, or the sensitivity adjusted – but don't turn it down too far or the alarm may not go off when someone tries to break in.

Microwave sensors detect solid objects which pass through beams directed past all points of entry. Microwave systems are expensive, but less prone to false alarms. They are also suitable for convertibles, as even with the roof down the beams will trigger the alarm if anyone reaches inside the car.

Shock sensors detect sudden shocks, like someone trying to smash their way in or vandalize the car. The sensitivity needs to be adjusted to avoid false alarms every time another vehicle passes by.

Tilt sensors react to the car being lifted, thus preventing anyone loading the car on to another vehicle or towing it away.

Other features worth having include a panic button, so that if you are attacked when in or near your car the alarm will sound; a status monitor, to notify you (usually by means of the LED display) that the alarm has been activated while you were away from the car; and finally, perhaps the most useful secondary feature of all, engine immobilization to disable the electrics and prevent the car starting when the alarm goes off.

The latest innovation in alarms is the use of specially formulated, non-toxic smoke. In the event of an attempted car-jacking or attack, there is a 35-second countdown. If the owner does not reset the system, the engine starts to misfire and progressive immobilization begins: lights flash, the horn

sounds and the engine stops completely. Finally a dense smokescreen is pumped into the car. The car remains immobilized until the correct PIN number is entered.

Whichever system you choose, make sure there is a good visual deterrent such as a flashing light visible from outside the car. And, most important of all, **remember to switch your alarm on** – even if you're only leaving the car for a couple of minutes.

IMMOBILIZERS

There are two main types of immobilizer: mechanical (for example, crook locks and clamps which physically prevent the operation of controls such as the steering wheel or gear lever) and electronic. An electronic immobilizer is wired into the car's electrics to prevent the engine from being started. (A third form of immobilizer is the steering column lock, fitted as standard in all cars built since 1972. This operates when the key is removed from the ignition, and the steering wheel is turned until it clicks.) Of these, the electronic immobilizer is the most difficult for thieves to get around, because the wiring is designed to be as complicated and confusing as possible – making it no easy matter to snip the wires or re-route the circuit.

The most basic electronic immobilizers work by breaking the starter motor circuit. More sophisticated (and therefore more difficult to bypass) versions are connected to the ignition system. Some systems switch themselves on automatically whenever the car is left, which saves you having to remember. The device used to override the immobilizer varies from a key which you insert into a socket in the dashboard, or a remote control handset, or a key pad which you use to type in a secret code number.

It is possible to buy a combined alarm/immobilizer system which prevents the engine being started when the alarm is activated – this is the best system to go for, because an immobilizer by itself will not protect your cars from smash-and-grab thieves or vandals, or from being loaded on to another vehicle or towed away.

Check out which system is best for you with a dealer – don't buy secondhand, because a manufacturer's warranty is well worth having, and with a dealer you can find out exactly what features the system has and arrange for it to be professionally fitted. It can be very dangerous if an immobilizer activates when the car is moving, so ask your dealer what safeguards are built in to prevent this.

Most immobilizers are invisible, so remember to place the manufacturer's stickers in the window to warn potential thieves that the car is protected.

TRACKING/RECOVERY SYSTEMS

For a top-of-the-range high-performance or luxury car (or caravan) thieves are prepared to put in a lot of effort. Organized gangs have equipped themselves with tow trucks so that they can transport stolen vehicles to a workshop where immobilizers and alarms can be deactivated out of the public gaze. Once the car is in their hands there is little hope of recovering it – unless you have it fitted with an electronic tracking system.

As soon as you report the car or caravan stolen, a high-powered transmitter will send a coded message to activate a small transponder unit concealed within your car, which then broadcasts a silent homing signal. These signals can be picked up by the police (there are control units throughout the country equipped with Tracker detectors, especially at ports and on major motorways). Even if the car is hidden away in a garage, the police can locate it.

Tracker systems are expensive, so it's really only worth considering for a valuable car. Contact one of the major motoring organizations or your insurance company for further details (your insurance premiums may be reduced because of the chances of recovering the vehicle are dramatically improved with a tracker system).

MECHANICAL DEVICES

If your car is old and low in value, it's not worth spending a fortune on an electronic immobilizer or alarm system. But don't assume that thieves won't give it a second glance – unprotected old cars are favourite targets. Fit a mechanical immobilizer to make it as hard and time-consuming as possible for the thief to drive your car away.

Most of these devices are made of hacksaw-resistant metal with a heavy lock to prevent use of one or more of the car's controls. You can fit them yourself and transfer them from car to car, because they are universal in design. They should

be highly visual, because the first line of defence is to force the potential crook to look elsewhere for easier pickings. None of these devices can protect your car from a determined thief – the most they will do is slow him down. And they can't protect the car from vandals or smash-and-grab

Steering wheel clamps to prevent the wheel being rotated more than a few degrees

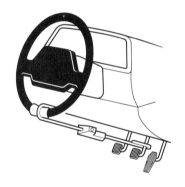

Steering wheel to pedal locks, to prevent the clutch and/or brake pedal from operating

Gear lever and gear-to-handbrake locks, to prevent movement of the gear lever. (If your car has a gear lever which can be unscrewed, a thief can easily bypass this.)

vehicle security

raids on the contents. So if you've got an expensive car or if you have to leave valuable items in the car, only use a mechanical immobilizer in conjunction with a more sophisticated alarm or immobilizer.

LOCKS

It's all to easy when you're in a hurry to forget to lock all the doors, especially when you're carrying passengers and need to ensure that their doors are locked as well. With central locking, the only door you need to remember to lock is the driver's door, because then all the other doors will be locked automatically. Many new cars come with central locking as standard, but if yours is not equipped there are kits available for most makes and models. These kits can operate two or four doors – and on some cars the boot or hatch, too.

> When buying a kit or a car fitted with central locking, check with the dealer that in the event of a serious collision the locks will pop open so that rescuers can get you out of the car. In some countries this is a legal requirement.

Deadlocks

Deadlocks (or 'double locks') are the most effective form of lock. Whereas ordinary locks can be opened by smashing a window and using the interior control, or by using a coathanger or special tool to tamper with the lock mechanism, deadlocks cannot be opened from inside or outside without the key. This means that the prospective car thief would have to climb in through a broken window, making him very conspicuous.

Most deadlocks have a normal position and a high-security position. When leaving the car unattended you should always use the high-security position (which means giving the key an extra turn) to ensure that your car is protected. If you have to leave children locked in the car while you run a quick errand, use the normal locking position so that rescuers can free them in case of an emergency.

Locking wheel nuts

Alloy wheels are expensive and an easy target for thieves, so fit lockable wheel nuts or bolts to prevent them from being stolen. These usually come in sets of four – one per wheel –

and you can fit them yourself. Always carry the key in case you have a puncture.

Locking fuel cap

Fit a locking fuel cap to prevent thieves from siphoning your petrol/diesel, or from filling up when the tank runs dry. The cap should take a different key to the doors and ignition, because otherwise thieves can steal the cap and use it to make a copy of your car keys.

 If you can't afford a shop-bought immobilizer, or if you want some additional security, try one of the following measures when leaving the car in a dubious area:

- Use a stout chain padlocked from the steering wheel to the clutch pedal, preventing the clutch from being depressed.

- Leave the minimum amount of fuel in the car, so if it gets stolen it can't be driven far. A valve on the fuel line which can be closed to prevent fuel entering the carburettor is probably more effective. This can be discreetly hidden under the bonnet.

- Remove the HT lead. This is a push fit lead which clips in between the coil and the distributor.

- On older cars the rotor arm can be removed. Unclip the distributor and lift out the rotor arm.

- On some models it is possible to remove the gear lever by unscrewing it.

- Some people have even removed the steering wheel when parking their car.

If you do remove any component, to save carrying it around, lock it in the boot. You are less likely to lose it or misplace it if you do this. Hide it away so even the most determined of car thieves will not detect it. In the boot lid there are channels that can be used for this purpose.

Deterrents

If the manufacturer hasn't already done so, have the registration number or VIN (see panel below) etched on to all glass surfaces – windscreen, sunroof, wing mirrors, lights and windows. This will deter thieves who 'ring' stolen cars, because instead of simply changing the number plates to give it a new identity they will have to replace all the marked glass – an expensive process.

Some insurance companies will security-etch your windows for free. Alternatively, you can buy a do-it-yourself kit from an accessory shop or consult your local Crime Prevention Officer for a list of garages and specialists who provide the service.

Of course, security etching won't deter joy riders or thieves who smash a side window to steal your radio. You can make life more difficult for these opportunists by having the side windows covered with a transparent laminated polyester film. This sticks to the inside of the window and prevents the glass from breaking when struck with a brick or other blunt instrument. It will also mean that in the event of an accident the glass will craze rather than showering you with sharp fragments. You will still be able to escape through the window, if necessary, by pushing the whole window out.

Vehicle Identification Number (VIN)

Every car has its own VIN displayed in the engine compartment. A new innovation, at the moment restricted to luxury cars, is to have the VIN printed on lots of tiny microdots the size of a pin head and scattered throughout the car during manufacture. By examining the car with a special detector it is possible to check that the VIN microdots tally with the number displayed in the engine compartment. Since luxury cars have the greatest risk of being 'ringed', these microdot VINs are a feature worth having.

VEHICLE WATCH

This is a scheme operated by some police forces (so far, mostly in urban areas). It works like this: few people make a habit of driving in the middle of the night (except shiftworkers, who may seldom use their cars in the middle of the day), so the local police will fit stickers to the front and rear windows of the car advertising the hours when it is unlikely to be in use. When a police officer sees a car with a night-time sticker being driven between 12.30–5.30 a.m. (or 10 a.m.–4.30 p.m. in the case of a day-time sticker), the car will be flagged down as a matter of course and the driver questioned and asked to confirm their identity.

CARAVAN SECURITY

There is a thriving market in stolen caravans. They're more difficult to trace and therefore easier to sell than cars. Don't trust to luck – take precautions to protect your caravan:

• Keep a note of the chassis number and put it in a safe place together with the registration documents (DON'T leave these documents in the caravan itself). It's a good idea to take a photograph of the caravan for insurance purposes, and to draw up a list of any distinguishing features, marks, scratches – for identification purposes in the event that the stolen caravan is recovered.

• Etch the chassis number on all glass surfaces, and use an ultra-violet pen to mark it on a few other surfaces in the interior.

• Fit a security device to immobilize the caravan or sound an alarm when it is moved. Activate the security system whenever the caravan is left unattended, even for a short period. Make sure there is a reliable power source that cannot be easily interrupted by a thief, so that the alarm will sound in the event of interference.

• Do not leave valuable items inside. It's best to leave the curtains open so that potential thieves can see that there is nothing of value to tempt them – drawn curtains may lead them to suspect that there's something worth stealing hidden within.

• Check out the site security before you leave it in a commercial caravan site. A good site will have insurance cover. If the caravan is going to be left on site for some time, remove the wheels.

vehicle security

Basic Precautions

Around 60 per cent of car-related theft is carried out not by professionals but by casual thieves who take advantage of an easy opportunity such as an unlocked door, boot, or rear hatch, or an open window. A recent survey of motorists found that 29 per cent admitted to leaving their vehicles unlocked at some time. Most would say they only leave the car unattended for a few minutes while popping into the newsagent or filling up with petrol, or when it's in their garage – but it takes only a matter of minutes for a car to be stolen.

It's all very well investing in anti-theft devices and deterrents, but you have to make a habit of using them every time you leave the car. Where fitted, ensure that deadlocks, immobilizers and alarms are engaged before leaving the car and lock the fuel filler cap. Always make sure all doors and windows (including the sunroof) are secure by physically checking each one. This applies even when the car is parked in your own garage or driveway. On cold mornings it may be tempting to start the car and go back indoors to finish your tea while the engine warms up. This is an open invitation to thieves. Always remove the ignition key. Filling station forecourts are a favourite hunting ground for thieves – so many trusting owners go in to pay for their fuel leaving the car unattended and the key in the ignition. When removing the keys engage the steering lock by turning the wheel till it clicks. (Never attempt to move a car without the keys in the ignition, as the steering lock will still be engaged, preventing the wheel from turning.)

> Never leave a child or an animal alone in a car. Thieves won't be deterred by their presence – they may even make your car a more attractive target. Children have been abducted from cars, and they can suffer injury when left alone, locked inside a parked vehicle. To keep them safe, take them with you.

Keep your car keys secure at all times and never have the make, number, or your address on the key fob – this will only make life easier for thieves. Just the logo or the manufacturer's name on a key fob is a breach of security: anyone finding the key can tour the car park trying it in every car of that make until they find yours.

Your spare set of keys are best kept at home. But it's a good idea to have another spare key somewhere more accessible in case you manage to lock your keys in the vehicle. There are plenty of hiding places on the vehicle where a key can be secured, like a recess under a bumper or wing. Special magnetic holders are available for this, but don't rely on the magnet – tape them on as an extra precaution.

DON'T ADVERTISE

Make your car as anonymous and unattractive to thieves as possible. Remove temptation: before getting out of the car make sure that no valuables are on display. Never leave a coat, even an old one, lying on the seat – a thief may break in to see whether you have left any money or credit cards in the pockets. The coat may be worthless and the pockets empty, but you'll find yourself with a hefty bill for replacing the window.

Lock everything that you cannot carry with you out of sight in the boot. This is particularly important around Christmas time, when you're rushing back and forth to dump one load of shopping in the car before going off to buy some more. No matter how much of a hurry you're in, take the time to lock everything in the boot. Mobile phones are a prime target, so make a note of the serial number and keep it in a safe place so a stolen phone can be identified if recovered by the police, and mark your phone and battery with your postcode.

When going on holiday (or on your return), don't leave the car unattended while it's loaded with your luggage. No matter how early a start you're making, don't load the car the night before (and when you get back from holiday, regardless how tired you are, make it a priority to unload). It's all too easy for a thief to do the unloading for you overnight. If you have a garage, load the car indoors and out of sight – you don't want to advertise the fact that the house is going to be left empty for a couple of weeks. While loading, lock the car behind you and activate the alarm if you have to go back into the house to fetch more items.

If you have only basic insurance cover for your car, extend your household insurance to cover coats, cameras, luggage, etc in case they are stolen from the car.

51

> NEVER leave cheque or credit cards in the car, even out of sight in the glove box.
>
> NEVER leave your driving licence, registration document, MOT or insurance certificates in the car. And remove any personal correspondence or other items with your name and address on. These documents can be used to provide the thief with a cover story if stopped by the police, and they make it easier to sell your car (all the thief has to do is get the car re-registered in his name and sell it on to an unsuspecting buyer).

RADIOS

Car stereo systems are the target in a third of all thefts from cars. You may have a pretty average radio, but the sight of it sitting there in the dashboard can still be enough to tempt a thief to steal it – and the resulting damage to your car may cost a lot more than the radio did.

There are a number of ways to protect your radio, the main ones being removal of the unit or front panel, or fitting a radio protected by security coding.

A removable stereo system is designed to be slid out of the dashboard and either taken with you or hidden in the car. (Some cars have a flap that covers the radio, leaving a space so that to the casual observer it looks as though the radio has been removed.) Most radios are too heavy to carry around all day, so the majority of drivers put them under the front seat or in the boot. The majority of thieves know this, and if they see a gap in the dashboard where the radio should be they may break in to see if they can find where you've hidden it.

To get round this, car audio manufacturers have come up with removable control panels. Instead of taking out the entire unit, you just unclip a panel the size of a pocket calculator and put it in your pocket or handbag. It's possible to buy a replacement panel, but so expensive that it defeats the object of stealing the unit.

Security coding ensures that the radio will not work if the power is cut (for example, by removing the radio from the car) unless the correct four-digit code is typed in. There are over 10,000 possible combinations, so the chances of anyone cracking the code are slim. Some systems refuse to accept more than half a dozen tries at the number, shutting down if the wrong code is typed in several times in a row.

A recent innovation from car manufacturers is the unique stereo, which is designed to fit only one model of car. Since all other cars of the same model will be fitted with a radio already, there's no point in stealing the radio.

Whichever method you decide to opt for, apply a little common sense as well: don't display manufacturers' window stickers advertising what a great stereo system you've got, and don't leave speakers sitting on your rear shelf. Use a UV (ultra-violet) pen to mark your stereo with your postcode or registration number to help identify the equipment in the event that it is stolen. Keep a note of the serial number in a safe place at home (not in the car!).

Parking

For the thief, car parks offer a wide selection of cars to choose from. Unattended railway station car parks which are virtually deserted outside the rush hour are especially popular with criminals, but there are easy targets available in shopper's car parks too, as car owners distracted by their kids or in a hurry to get to the shops forget to lock all the doors and secure the windows before leaving the car.

Eliminate that last-minute rush. Always allow time for parking when planning a journey. In a large city the search for a parking space can take as long as the journey itself. It's tempting to park illegally when you've been driving round and round in circles with not a space to be seen. DON'T DO IT! It can be very costly, and it could leave you vulnerable to attack – if your car gets clamped you could have to wait in the car for hours until the unclamping team turns up. You may even have to abandon the car and find alternative means of getting home, especially late at night. Look at the signs to see if parking is legal and a time limit imposed. Some areas are for permit-holders only and the signs are few and far between. Wait until you find a legal parking place.

Don't park the car on waste ground, in isolated rundown areas, and if it's likely that you won't be returning until it's dark, bear in mind what your parking place will be like by then. Choose somewhere that's well lit. In station and airport car parks, find a spot as near to the exit or a courtesy bus stop as possible. If you have to park in the street, choose a busy shopping street or somewhere your car is overlooked by offices by day and houses by night, not a dark, dingy alley. Retract the aerial fully to stop it being vandalized. When leaving the car parked in a narrow road, if you have spring-loaded wing mirrors tuck them in to avoid them being broken off by passing vehicles. Don't park in a place where the car obstructs other vehicles. Park as close to your final destination as possible. Always try to park under a street lamp if the car is to be left unattended after dark. Be especially careful where you park a soft-top convertible.

Organized gangs target car parks with poor security, as do sex offenders seeking to prey on unaccompanied females. Whenever possible use attended and secure car parks.

AT HOME
Your car is as vulnerable at home as anywhere else and the same precautions (locking all doors, fastening windows, activating alarms, removing all valuables, etc) need to be carried out. More than half of all thefts from cars occur when the car is parked at or near the owner's home, so don't be complacent, be vigilant. If you don't have a garage, park as close to your home as possible, preferably in a well-lit spot where you can see it.

If you have a garage, use it. Fit the best locks available to secure the garage door and keep it locked. If your car is stolen from an unlocked garage your insurance company may refuse to meet the claim in full. You'll be protecting your home, too – garages often double as workshops and are full of valuable tools which can be used to gain entry to your house. Keep the car and garage keys in a secure place. Don't leave them on display where anyone can see them; put them in an ornament or some other regular hiding place. If you don't want to forget something which you must take with you the next day, leave the keys with this item. No way can you then go without it.

When you drive out of the garage, park on the drive and secure the garage door behind you. An open garage is an open invitation to the criminal element, signalling that there's no one at home. Deny thieves this information.

Be suspicious if you find another car blocking your drive-

way. An old trick used by thieves is to park across a private entrance in the hope that the owner will leave his or her car unlocked while they go looking for the driver of the other vehicle.

Always reverse into the garage. It makes leaving easier, and in the event of a house fire the car can be removed faster (but if the fire has already reached the garage, stay well clear – DON'T risk your life to save a heap of metal on four wheels).

See *Garage Hazards* in **Safety** for guidelines on making your garage a safer place.

Vandalized!

If you see someone tampering with your car, resist the impulse to challenge them. They may be armed, or there could be a lookout close by who will join in any attack on you. Call the police immediately and give them a description of the villain. Keep out of sight and don't block the thieves' escape route – it's self-preservation, not cowardice. Damage to the car can be put right, but if you try playing the hero and get kicked to a pulp by the thieves the damage may be irreparable.

The same rules apply if you return to the car to find that the alarm has been activated. Be cautious; observe from a vantage point for a few minutes to make sure that the coast is clear before moving in. If the car has been broken into or vandalized, check what damage has been done before you get in and attempt to drive away. In the course of ripping out your radio or smashing their way in, the thieves may have damaged vital safety components or disconnected wires in the electrical system. The best course of action is to notify the police; they will tell you whether the car is safe and legal to drive.

Make a note of any items that have been stolen. The theft of credit cards, cheque books and cheque-guarantee cards should be reported immediately to the relevant banks and card companies so that a stop can be put on the cards' use. In the event of your mobile telephone being taken, notify your air-time supplier so that the phone can be cut off before expensive calls are logged up. Ask them whether any calls have been made since you last used the phone – all calls are logged automatically, and the numbers dialled may provide the police with a clue to the thief's identity.

If the keys to your house have been stolen you will need to get the locks changed as soon as possible. Inform the police immediately if there is any possibility that the thief could have found your address from anything left in the car. The neighbours are unlikely to suspect anything amiss if they see someone gaining entry to your house with a set of keys, so you should phone someone you can trust and get them to watch the house, or ask the police to send someone round.

Notify your insurance company of items stolen and any damage which has been done. Glass can often be replaced without affecting your no-claims bonus. Check the small print of your policy to see exactly what is covered and what view of the insurance company takes of your protecting the no-claims discount by failing to report a theft or accident. There have been cases of insurance companies declaring a policy invalid after discovering that the motorist concerned had failed to report a theft or act of vandalism.

Stolen!

The first thing to do is to make absolutely certain that you are looking in the right place. The police estimate that 10 per cent of cars reported stolen are false alarms – in reality the owner has simply forgotten where they parked the vehicle, or they have parked illegally and as a result their car has been towed away. So before you panic, check that you've got the right floor of the multi-storey, or the right side street, and that no parking restrictions were infringed by leaving the car where you did. If the car has been towed away there should be warning signs giving details of who to call to get your car back – upon payment of a hefty fine.

Only when you are certain that the car has been stolen should you call the police. They will need a full description of the vehicle, including the registration number, and a list items left in the car. It will be helpful if you can tell them how much fuel was left in the tank – when the tank is almost empty there's a good chance that the car will be dumped as soon as the fuel runs out. It's particularly important to let the

police know if you left your mobile phone, credit cards, house keys, vehicle documentation or anything bearing your home address inside the car. Thieves can use registration and other documents to sell the car to an unsuspecting buyer who will have no idea it's been stolen. Take the name and number of the police officer for insurance purposes. Notify banks, credit card companies, mobile phone operators, as appropriate. And if the house keys have been taken let your family know – the thief could drive up in your car and let himself in. The house will need to be secured and the locks changed.

As soon as possible, report the theft to your insurance company. It can take months for the claim to go through, but in the meantime you may be entitled to a hire car. Some of the more expensive alarm/immobilizer systems come with a theft warranty – provided the system was switched on at the time of the theft, you should receive a compensation payment.

Security Checklist

Before leaving your vehicle unattended, check the following:

- The place where you have parked should be safe (well-lit, in a busy area, where it will not cause an obstruction to other vehicles or pedestrians – see *Parking* above) and legal.
- Credit cards, cheque cards and books, house keys, vehicle documentation (including your driver's licence), should be on your person NOT left in the car.
- Valuable items should be removed from the car or placed out of sight in the luggage compartment. This includes removable stereo systems or those with removable front panels.
- Keys must be removed from ignition no matter how briefly the car will be left unattended.
- Steering lock should be engaged.
- All doors and windows must be secured (except in the event that an animal has been left in the car, in which case the windows should be left ajar – see **Safety**)
- All alarm/immobilizer systems and anti-theft devices should be set before leaving the car.
- Retract the aerial and tuck in spring-loaded wing mirrors.

vehicle security

PARKING DOs AND DON'Ts

Put some thought into where you park – follow these guidelines to stay safe:

Do look for an authorized car park that is well lit, supervised either by attendants or closed-circuit television cameras, with restricted entry and exit points.

Do make sure the car park will be open when you plan to return.

Do park as close as you can to the pay booth, to a CCTV camera or to a ramp where there are more likely to be other drivers. Try to park at ground level if you expect to be returning to your car late or when the car park is not busy – the top and bottom floors tend to be deserted outside peak hours. Avoid parking near pillars or large objects which someone could hide behind.

Always park near an exit to minimize the amount of time you spend walking around in the car park. Before leaving the safety of your locked car, take a look around. Don't take risks – stay inside the car until you are certain it is safe to leave.

Do reverse into the parking space – that way you can make a quick getaway should the need arise.

Do leave plenty of room between cars so you don't get scratched by a carelessly managed door (be careful as you open your own doors), and so that it won't be easy for an assailant to trap you.

Don't park next to a beaten-up looking car covered in dents and scratches. This may indicate the driver's lack of concern for not only their vehicle but yours also.

It's a good idea to note the number of the car next to you. That way, if you come back and find your car has been damaged you'll have some hope of tracking down a witness, or even the culprit.

Be suspicious of anyone loitering nearby who seems to be paying close attention to your movements, they may be planning to steal the car or mug you.

Make a note of where you have parked the vehicle. Write down the level, bay, and exact spot.

Engage the steering lock, activate any security devices and secure all doors and windows. Have your belongings ready before you unlock the door and step out of the car. You're at your most vulnerable while you're leaning into an open doorway, intent on picking up items from the seat or dashboard. Someone can sneak up behind, give you a hefty shove which sends you sprawling into the seat, and steal your bag or briefcase.

In pay-as-you-leave car parks, always take your ticket with you. Should a thief steal your car, he will be challenged by staff at the barrier for not having a ticket.

Don't loiter. When walking to and from the car, keep to the centre of the 'road', avoiding dark areas where someone could be hiding. Walk quickly and purposefully, and keep looking about you. Check over your shoulder occasionally to see what's going on behind. Listen for suspicious noises.

If something or someone strikes you as suspicious, don't continue walking into danger – if there is an attendant to hand make for their booth, or go where there are other people (even if it's in the opposite direction to your destination), where no other options are available make your way quickly back to your car. (See Personal Security for more detailed advice on how to ensure your safety in these situations.)

Don't let children loose in a car park. Hold their hands so they don't run out into someone's blindspot and get hurt.

When you come back to your car have your keys in hand, ready to open the door and get in quickly. A car key can also make an effective weapon in the event that you are attacked (see Under Attack in Personal Security). If you are nervous, let the car park attendant know that you going to collect your car.

Check your car for signs of forced entry before getting in. If you see something suspicious, don't get in the car – get help.

Don't take your time getting into the car. Toss your bags in quickly and then get in, keeping your back to the car. By facing outwards you can see anyone approaching and avoid being taken by surprise. Once in the car, lock the door and get underway as soon as possible.

Don't follow too fixed a routine – if you regularly park in the same place for the same length of time, a thief could monitor your movements and plan to steal your car when he knows you won't be there. Vary your habits.

If you have to park your car in dodgy areas on a regular basis, it might be as well to downgrade alloy wheels for steel ones and take whatever other precautions you can to make your car blend in to the surroundings. Strip it of any flashy exterior accessories that might attract thieves and remove badges which give away the fact that it's got a high-performance engine. Make it look as anonymous and boring as possible.

Bad weather puts your skills and your vehicle's capabilities to the test – a test which all too many motorists fail by driving inappropriately for the conditions. Slippery road surfaces and poor visibility demand total concentration. To maintain control of your vehicle, you need to understand the risks and adjust your driving accordingly.

bad-weather driving

ADVERSE CONDITIONS Be prepared! • See and be seen

FOG

NIGHT Dazzle

BRIGHT SUNSHINE Hot-weather hazards

VEHICLE HANDLING

SKIDDING Why skids occur • Skid prevention • Correcting skids • Skid pans

SNOW AND ICE Preparing for winter • Winter motoring survival kit • Stuck in snow • Stranded!

RAIN Driving in rain • Aquaplaning

FLOODS Driving through flood water

HIGH WINDS Coping with crosswinds

RULES FOR BAD-WEATHER DRIVING

adverse conditions

As a driver, you cannot afford to ignore the weather. Though you may be warm and dry inside your car, the miserable conditions on the outside will dictate how far you can see and how well your vehicle responds to the controls. Braking distances can be as much as ten times greater than normal – depending on the severity of the weather. If you're travelling too fast you won't see a hazard until it's too late, and slamming on the brakes will only cause the car to skid out of control.

Although bad weather gets the blame for all those motorway pile-ups, the real responsibility lies with bad drivers. When you take to the road in dense fog, freezing cold or heavy rain, you need to be aware of the dangers those conditions pose. You must be prepared for the worst – and remember, the worst that can happen is not arriving at your destination later than planned, but failing to reach your destination because you've become another statistic in the annual count of accident victims.

Be Prepared!

It pays to check out the weather forecast before getting in the car – especially if you're setting out on a long journey. That way you will be prepared for adverse conditions along the way, and you can check your equipment and load any extra gear you may need. Plan your route carefully, taking account of the weather. If it's icy, avoid steep hills where possible; in very heavy rain there will be a risk of flooding in low-lying areas near rivers; in high winds some bridges may be closed to traffic and high, open places will be particularly exposed. Having chosen a route, memorize it as best you can. In poor visibility you may not be able to see road signs and landmarks, so it's easy to get lost. You should also adjust your estimate of how long the journey will take – allowing extra time for rest periods after all that intense concentration behind the wheel. Telephone ahead to warn whoever is expecting you that there's a strong possibility you will be late; this way you won't feel that you have to rush.

Safety, not speed, should be top of the agenda. Most accidents happen because drivers do not allow themselves the time and space in which to react to emergencies, and then have to resort to harsh braking, harsh acceleration or harsh steering – the primary causes of skidding. You need to drive at a speed which allows you to read the road and take in vital information such as the condition of the road surface ahead of you, the presence of obstacles in your path, and the actions of other road users. Bear in mind that stopping distances increase dramatically on slippery roads, so the gap between you and the vehicle in front will need to be increased to match the conditions. The golden rule is to make sure that you can stop on your own side of the road within the distance you can see to be clear. If the driver behind you is too close, the only safe response is to increase the space in front of you even more to allow room for manoeuvre in an emergency.

Your understanding and command of your vehicle is more crucial than ever in bad weather. The middle of a heavy downpour is no time to discover that you don't know how to switch on the rear wipers or de-mister without taking your eyes off the road. And you certainly won't want to discover that there's insufficient antifreeze in your screenwash by having your windscreen turn to ice on a freezing winter's day. Take the time to carry out a quick maintenance check on your tyres, wipers, battery, oil, fuel level, lights, indicators, screenwash reservoir(s) – front and rear – and coolant reservoir (see Maintenance). Start gently, and test your brakes to make sure they're working before you pick up speed.

SEE AND BE SEEN

 Your safety depends on being able to see and be seen. If you can't see the road clearly, you cannot assess the hazards ahead. And if other road users cannot see your vehicle, there's a real danger that they will set themselves on a collision course, unaware of your presence until it's too late.

Using your lights will not drain the battery – it's recharging the whole time you're driving – and they cost nothing to run. So turn them on as soon as daylight begins to fade or whenever you switch on the windscreen wipers. In bad weather, windscreens get obscured by rain and condensation, so even in broad daylight you should use dipped headlights to make sure that other drivers can see you.

Some drivers try to make do with using their side or parking lights in these bad-weather situations, but these are too dim to be of any real use. They don't throw any light on the road to help you see more clearly, and they don't make your presence obvious to other drivers. They are intended to be used when the vehicle is parked on an unlit road at night.

Main-beam headlights are so bright that they will dazzle other road users, and in fog, snow or heavy rain there's a real risk that the dense vapour cloud in front of you will reflect the glare of your headlights straight back at you, making visibility worse instead of better. Use main-beam lights on unlit roads for the best possible view of the road ahead, but dip them whenever you encounter another vehicle. Time it so that you dip them just before the beam of your lights reaches the other vehicle, and always dip your lights when going round a bend or reaching the summit of a hill or hump-backed bridge. Return to main beam when you are sure that there's no risk of dazzling anyone; for example, when overtaking, you can return to main beam as soon as you draw level with the other car; when being overtaken, dip your headlights as the overtaking vehicle draws alongside you and keep them dipped until the other driver is beyond the reach of the beams.

When you find yourself being dazzled by someone else's lights, reduce your speed. Don't look directly at the lights. If necessary, prepare to stop by looking for a safe place to pull over. Whenever you adjust your mirrors to avoid glare from drivers behind, make sure you put them back to the original position as soon as possible.

Remember that main-beam lights, though offering a much clearer view of the road than dipped lights, still leave blind spots. They can only show you what lies straight ahead, not what's happening on either side of you, behind you, or around the next bend. Reduce your speed accordingly.

Dipped headlights increase your visibility without dazzling other road users, and are therefore the best choice for most situations. Their maximum range on a straight road is only about 16 metres/17 yards (compared to 83 metres for main-beam lights), so whenever you have to rely on dipped lights to see the road ahead, make sure that you are driving at a speed that will allow you to stop within 16 metres – in optimum conditions that means approximately 16 mph, but if the road is slippery you should come down to 10 mph or less.

Low-mounted high-intensity fog lamps are designed to penetrate dense mist and falling snow. When visibility falls below 100 metres (108 yards) you should switch on front and rear fog lights where fitted (if your car is not equipped with fog lamps you can buy them from car accessory shops, and it's possible to fit them yourself). Where a single fog lamp is fitted, make sure your dipped headlights are switched on as well to prevent other drivers assuming they're looking at a motorbike.

Always switch your fog lights off when visibility improves – in most countries it is an offence to use fog lights when visibility is not below 100 metres, because of the risk of dazzling other road users. On motorways there are marker posts at 100 metre intervals on the verge, so you can use those as a guide. There's a warning light on the dashboard to remind you when the fog lights are in use – get into the habit of checking that it is not illuminated when it shouldn't be. This can easily happen if you drive home in a heavy mist and forget to switch off the fog lights before taking the key out of the ignition. Next morning you set off in bright sunshine – and get stopped by the police

SEE AND BE SEEN (continued)

for using fog lights when you shouldn't.

Even when visibility is poor enough to warrant using your fog lights, if you're crawling along in traffic with another vehicle close behind, you should turn off your rear fog lights. Provided the other driver is close enough for you to see, your tail lights will be enough to let them know you are there. Dazzling other road users serves no purpose and can be dangerous. In patchy, drifting fog you will need to change your lights to fit the circumstances.

There are occasions when it's useful to turn on hazard warning lights to inform following vehicles of danger ahead. Although these are primarily for use when the vehicle is stationary, on a motorway or dual carriageway it's permissible to use them while the car is moving – provided you turn them off again once the traffic behind has had time to take notice. (Hazard lights also come in handy if your car has no reversing lights: when reversing on an unlit road, use them to illuminate the road to your rear.)

Whichever lights you use, the lenses must be clean or the intensity of the beam will be reduced. Follow the First Parade routine described in **Maintenance** and make sure your lights are clean and operational before you set off on a journey. Carry at least one spare bulb of each

type in the car. When the back of the car is weighed down with luggage or heavy passengers, check the angle of the dipped beam; you may need to adjust it to compensate for the load.

To reduce the risk of being dazzled by other vehicles' lights – and to make sure that you can see unlit vehicles, cyclists and pedestrians – make sure that your windows are clean. To prevent the interior misting up, use your de-misters or heated windscreen. Warm air from the vents can be directed at the windows once the car is under way, but until the engine has warmed up you will have to make do with a clean dry cloth or chamois leather.

The screenwash reservoir should be kept filled (with an appropriate antifreeze added in winter) and the wiper blades checked for signs of wear. If the wiper blades have frozen to the window, don't try to rip them off as you will damage the rubber. In winter, allow plenty of time to clear the windows of snow and ice. It's illegal to drive along peering through a porthole of cleared windscreen. Use warm water or a proprietary de-icer to get rid of the ice. In a snow storm, stop as often as necessary en route to clear the windows, lights and mirrors (not forgetting your number plate). It may be cold, unpleasant work, but your life could depend on it.

Fog

Of all the bad-weather hazards, fog is the most dangerous. Dense fog is invariably followed by news headlines about motorway pile-ups caused by drivers ignoring the speed restrictions. No matter how experienced and how good a driver you are, there will be other road users who drive like maniacs, endangering your life as well as their own. These reckless drivers seem to think that what they can't see won't hurt them, and so they pose a far greater hazard to you than the fog does. On motorways this madness goes on at higher speeds, hence the pile-ups. You need to be alert to the risks and to give serious consideration to whether your journey is really necessary.

Part of the problem is that fog not only reduces visibility, it distorts the things you can see and muffles sound. Because

your view of the road is limited, you can't evaluate hazards as you normally would. Usually we judge speed by how fast the landscape goes whizzing by, but you can't do that in fog. Some drivers think the safest thing to do is to tuck themselves in close behind the vehicle in front and follow blindly – a recipe for disaster.

Freezing fog makes matters even worse. The road will be slippery, increasing braking distances still further. The windscreen gets misted on the inside and can freeze over on the outside. And then there's the unpredictability of drifting or patchy fog. You can be in the clear one moment and smothered in a blanket of the stuff the next. Many drivers, when they get into the clear, assume that it's safe to pick up speed – then all of a sudden the road dips to a low-lying area and visibility is severely reduced again.

The level of concentration required is very difficult to keep up for any length of time. Your eyes soon tire of scanning the road for obstacles and fellow road users – not to mention road signs and landmarks. It's easy to miss your turning when you can't make out where you are until the last minute. Always allow extra time for your journey. If you're running late, find somewhere safe to stop and make a phone call. NEVER try to drive faster to make up lost time. As the old saying goes: Better to be late in this life than early into the next.

DRIVING IN FOG

The surest way to keep yourself safe in fog is to decide not to go out in it. But if your journey cannot be put off, set about minimizing the risks. Check out the weather forecast or contact one of the big motoring organizations to see whether by changing your route you can avoid the fog. If there's no way of bypassing it, stick to a route that you know well. That way you won't have the added worry of getting lost with no road signs to guide you. When on the motorway, obey all speed restrictions and warning signs. Keep a look out for accidents ahead, and for fire engines, police cars, and ambulances answering emergency calls – these vehicles may be forced to use the hard shoulder if the motorway is congested, so be prepared when you see them coming up from behind. If you are uncomfortable with the speed of traffic, or if conditions deteriorate, leave the motorway.

Follow the guidelines listed under *See and Be Seen*, above, and use your dipped headlights. The main beam will be reflected by the fog and will only dazzle you. When visibility falls below 100 metres (325 feet) turn on your high-intensity fog lamps as well. Rear fog lights are so bright that they make it difficult to see the brake lights, so it will be difficult to judge when the driver in front is braking. Allow plenty of space and keep your speed low so that you can brake in the distance you can see to be clear. Remember that the driver behind you will be experiencing the same difficulty, so turn your rear fog lights off when the driver behind is close enough to see your tail lights. You can be prosecuted for driving with fog lights switched on when it's possible to see further than 100 metres ahead, so turn the fog lights off as soon as visibility improves.

Keep the windscreen clear. Condensation builds up outside the car as well as inside, so use your wipers and your de-mister (or a clean cloth). When you stop to take a break and give your eyes a rest, clean your windows, lights, mirrors and reflectors. In freezing fog you will need a screenwash containing antifreeze to keep the windows clear. Make use of your heated windscreen, too.

Most important of all, keep your speed down to allow you plenty of reaction time. The majority of motorists drive far too fast for the conditions. Check your speedometer at regular intervals – fog can be deceptive and you may be surprised to see how fast you are going. Whatever the normal speed limit for the stretch of road you are using, in fog you should drop to a speed which will allow you to stop within the limit of your vision. Dipped headlights may allow you to see only 16 metres ahead of the car. That means you need to be going slow enough to stop in 16 metres or less, certainly no more. An easy way to calculate the maximum speed for the conditions is to apply the rule: 1 mph = 1 metre of visibility. So when your view of the road is limited to 16 metres ahead, you should travel at 16 mph. This is based on the stopping distance for a good car with good brakes and tyres travelling on a dry road; if the road is slippery, or your tyres or brakes are worn, you will need to drive slower still.

One of the worst things you can do in fog is to get sucked into following the tail lights of the vehicle in front. When travelling on the motorway in heavy fog, unless traffic is at a complete crawl, you should be far enough back that you can only see the rear fog lights of the vehicle in front. If you can see the car itself, you're too close. There's a danger that your eyes will focus on the tail lights, drawing you closer without your even realizing it. Should the other car stop suddenly, you'll rear-end it, and if the other driver runs into a ditch or an obstruction at the side of the road, you'll be in there behind him.

Never underestimate how deceptive fog can be. When vehicles are inadequately lit, it can be hard to tell whether they are stationary or moving slowly. You can't see junctions up ahead, let alone the vehicles waiting to pull out of them, until you are on top of them. Even when you can see them, you can't rely on those vehicles staying where they are – they may not have seen you. For this reason it's best not to overtake in fog, especially on a two-lane road. Even on a motorway it is best avoided unless absolutely necessary, and you should never follow the car that overtakes you.

bad-weather driving

Your best option is to drive in the left-hand lane, staying well back from the car in front. There's every likelihood that the driver behind will get impatient when you maintain a snail's pace, but don't be pressured into going faster and closing the gap between you and the vehicle in front. The closer that car behind gets to your bumper, the bigger the gap in front of you needs to be. Imagine what would happen if the car in front were to brake suddenly: the closer you are to that car, the harder you have to brake – and if the driver behind has left a gap of only 3 metres he has no hope of reacting in time, so he's going to slam straight into the back of you. If, on the other hand, you have maintained a safe gap between yourself and the vehicle in front (that is, one which takes into account the stopping distance for the prevailing conditions), you can brake more gradually, giving the car behind more time to react.

Very often another vehicle will overtake and fill the gap in front of you. Your response must be to drop back so that the safe distance is maintained. It's vital to stay calm in these situations. NEVER retaliate or take it upon yourself to teach a bad driver a lesson, because that will only make things worse. Count to ten, breathe deeply – whatever it takes to keep your cool – and don't lose sight of the fact that it's not a race or a battle; your prime objective is to arrive safely at your destination. Some drivers lose all self-control when they don't get their own way, and they will do everything they can to challenge you to make it a duel: obscene gestures, flashing lights, overtaking and then braking to force you to lose speed suddenly. It's called road rage. Don't let yourself be a victim. Keep your own aggression under tight control, however infuriating their behaviour may be. And make sure your driving betrays no signs of aggression: when you need to expand the space in front of you, do it in a gradual, subtle way, by gradually easing off the accelerator rather than using your brakes. (Normally it's good practice to use the brakes so that your brake lights provide a useful signal for the driver behind, but in these circumstances the red light will be like a red flag to a bull, and is therefore best avoided.) For further advice on dealing with road rage and aggressive drivers, see **Personal Security**.

As dangerous as following another vehicle's tail lights is the practice of following the Catseyes or centre lines of the road. When you straddle the centre of the road, you run the risk of colliding head-on with an oncoming car doing the same thing. It's much better to follow the inside kerb, while keeping an eye out for parked vehicles. Focus on what you can see, scanning your eyes back and forth to fight the hypnotic effects of fog. Think about and question what your eyes tell you, to keep yourself alert.

Making a right turn in fog is especially hazardous, so exercise maximum caution. Turn off the in-car stereo, wind your window down, and listen out for other traffic. You will probably hear oncoming vehicles before you see them. While waiting to turn, keep your foot on the brake pedal so that your brake lights provide a warning to cars coming up from behind. Use your horn to warn others of your presence, and listen for other drivers using their horns. Remember that fog muffles sounds, making it unusually quiet. Don't be lured into a false sense of security. Turn only when you are absolutely certain it is safe to do so.

In the countryside it's best to keep your window open the whole time. It's easy to get lost on country lanes, so look and listen for clues. You may hear running water that will help position you. Look for roadside landmarks like a church gate.

Driving in fog is extremely tiring. The level of concentra-

RULES FOR DRIVING IN FOG

- Clean all lights, windows, mirrors and reflectors so you can see and be seen
- Use dipped headlights
- Switch on fog lamps if visibility falls below 100 metres
- Use windscreen wipers to clear condensation
- Direct warm air from vents at windscreen or wipe the glass with a clean cloth
- Keep your speed down – remember that stopping distances double or treble in fog
- Maintain a safe gap between your car and the vehicle in front
- Don't overtake
- Drive in the left-hand lane and follow the inside kerb
- Open the window and listen before turning
- Before setting out, ask yourself whether your journey is really necessary.

tion required is difficult to sustain for long periods and eye strain gets to be a problem. At the first sign of fatigue, start looking for a safe place to pull over and take a rest. On a motorway, that means turning off at the next service station or junction – NOT pulling over to the hard shoulder. Try to relax while driving. Instead of sitting hunched over the wheel, sit well back in your seat.

In fog you should always park your vehicle off the road. Having parked, check on foot to make sure it is in a safe position and not causing an obstruction. When you have no choice but to park on the road, leave your sidelights on. NEVER park facing against the direction of the traffic flow in fog. If you've broken down or been involved in an accident, switch on hazard lights and set up a warning triangle 50 metres (54 yards) behind the car. On a motorway you should aim for the hard shoulder, getting as close to the grass verge as possible; switch on your hazard lights and set up the warning triangle 150 metres (164 yards) away. See Emergency! for further advice on what to do in the event of a breakdown.

Night

There are many advantages to driving at night, especially if you have a long journey ahead of you – for example, at the start of your holidays. By night the roads are clearer, reducing travelling time; and instead of having to make a detour round big towns you can drive straight through them, allowing you to choose the most direct route. In summer, it's much cooler and there's less risk of the car overheating under the strain of towing a caravan. It's easier to get the children to sleep through the journey, making the ride less stressful for everyone. But night travel has its downside too.

Unlit roads can be very disorientating, with the view of the road restricted to the length of your headlight beams. You have to be constantly alert to the risk of unlit obstructions blocking the road, such as a fallen tree, or a broken-down vehicle. There are more blind spots to worry about than in daytime: trees and buildings throw shadows,

and cyclists or pedestrians can appear from nowhere, dressed from head to toe in dark clothing with complete disregard for their own safety. Navigation is more difficult in the dark and if the route is unfamiliar extra care must be taken. It's hard on the eyes (especially if you suffer from night blindness). And most of all, it's a real strain staying awake at a time when you would usually be asleep.

DRIVING AT NIGHT

To overcome the hazards of night driving you need to make careful preparations for your journey. Give all windows, mirrors, and headlight lenses a good clean – the slightest film of grease or dirt on the glass will increase glare and reduce visibility. Make sure all your lights are working, that dipped beams are adjusted to compensate for a heavy load in the back, and that de-misters, windscreen washers and wipers are all fully operational. (See **Maintenance** for a full list of the checks you should run before a long journey and details of how to carry them out.) Make sure the fuel tank is full, especially if your route takes you off the beaten track, as service stations will be scarce. Pack a fluorescent or reflective band (the kind cyclists wear), or a bright jacket that will show up in the dark – if you have a breakdown and have to walk to get help, you'll need to be seen.

It's a good idea for the driver to undergo a maintenance check, too. If you are on medications, check with your doctor to make sure they won't interfere with your driving. Ask your optician whether your night vision is up to scratch. Clean your glasses to remove smears. Don't wear tinted glasses unless your optician has prescribed them and told you that it's safe to use them for night driving.

Try to sleep as much as possible during the day before you travel, but don't drink alcohol or take sleeping tablets or other medications to help you sleep, as these stay in your system a long time and may impair judgement (see **Safety**: *Safe Driver*). Eat a light meal rather than a hearty feast which will leave you sluggish and tired. Plan your route well (you won't want to get lost in the dark) and allow for more frequent rest stops than you would on a day trip. Older drivers need longer breaks to allow time for their eyes to recover from glare, and young, inexperienced drivers need extra time to unwind after concentrating hard behind the wheel. Check the map for service areas where you can park in safety, and aim to stop once every couple of hundred miles.

Spend your breaks dozing or relaxing with a hot drink, then take a little gentle exercise to wake you up again. If it's safe to do so, you can get out and walk or jog for a little while. Alternatively, you can remain in the car and exercise. Roll the head gently, first one way then the next – a lot of tension builds up here when you're driving. Circle the arms to relax the shoulders, and twist from the waist up, turning from side to side in your seat. Stretch your arms and legs, relax and stretch some more.

While driving, listen to the radio or a tape to keep you

> When driving at night it's important to keep the car doors locked to prevent any potential robbers or rapists letting themselves in when you draw up at traffic lights or get caught in a motorway traffic jam.
>
> Remember to lock the car behind you and activate any security devices whenever you leave the car – even if you will only be gone for a few minutes. You don't want to find yourself stranded because a car thief has made off with it.
>
> When parking at night, remember also that it is illegal to leave a vehicle facing against the direction of the traffic flow.

alert and pass the time. Or, better still, have a passenger stay awake to navigate for you and encourage you to talk. This will ensure that you don't nod off. Keep your eyes moving rather than fixed on one point. Look as far ahead as possible then check the mirrors left and right, then look ahead again. By focusing the eyes at different distances you will keep the optic muscles working. If it's raining and the wipers are on, avoid staring at them – the effect is like a stage hypnotist swinging a pendulum back and forth before his subject's eyes.

Keep the car on the cool side, with a window ajar so that fresh air can enter. Whenever you start to feel drowsy, it's time to stop. Look for a lay-by or service area where you can take a break, and in the meantime open the window further, get someone to talk to you – or talk to yourself, if you have to – to stay awake.

Apart from staying awake at the wheel, the most important thing is to make sure you can see and be seen. Even on well-lit city streets you should use your dipped headlights, as

the next turning could take you into a street where there are no lights. On unlit roads, use your main beam lights provided there is no danger of dazzling other road users.

Remember that it's illegal to sound your horn in a built-up area between 11.30 p.m. and 7.00 a.m. – and at night most drivers have their windows closed and the radio on, so they won't hear you in any case. To remind other road users of your presence, flash your headlights instead. It's a good idea to do this when approaching a bend or junction, to warn other vehicles of your approach.

Make use of the information given by other vehicles' front and rear lights. Judge the sharpness of a bend by the angle of the lights as they sweep around it, watch for a succession of drivers up ahead putting on their brake lights or swerving around some obstacle in the road, and plan your driving accordingly. Roadside markers, reflective studs and road markings are also useful indicators of bends in the road and junctions – on motorways the reflective studs are colour-coded, with green studs marking exit and entry roads, and amber studs running alongside the central reservation. Use the white studs which separate the lanes to help you steer a straight course.

As always, your speed should be dictated by the distance you can see to be clear. At 60 mph the shortest stopping distance in optimum conditions is 73 metres (240 feet). If you can only see as far as the beam of your headlights, reduce your speed accordingly. On a straight stretch of motorway with your main-beam lights on, you may be able to travel safely at 60 mph, but where there are bends in the road your lights cannot show you what lies ahead and you will have to reduce speed accordingly. Allow a maximum of 1 mph per metre of visibility for a well-maintained vehicle on a dry road surface.

Overtaking at night should be restricted to straight stretches of road, where you can see beyond the car you wish to overtake and be certain that it is all clear ahead. Dip your lights until you are parallel with the vehicle you are overtaking, then return to main beam. In bad weather, when the road is wet or icy, you will not be able to judge the state of the road surface ahead – overtaking could send you aquaplaning through a puddle or skidding on black ice – so do not overtake when the conditions make it inadvisable.

When leaving a brightly lit area, reduce your speed and allow time for your eyes to adjust to the dark. The same rule applies at dusk or dawn; it takes time to for your eyes to grow accustomed to the contrast, and in the meantime shapes merge into one another. You won't see the drunk staggering off the pavement, or the child about to run out into the road, unless you give yourself time to react by driving more slowly.

DAZZLE

It is inevitable that you will be dazzled by oncoming lights while driving at night. Sometimes this happens because other motorists are inconsiderate and have left their lights on main beam, but even with dipped lights there is a degree of dazzle when the vehicle is travelling uphill or the rear is loaded down, or when a caravan/trailer is in tow. NEVER retaliate by switching your own main-beam lights on.

When you see an oncoming car, prepare to be dazzled. Picture the road ahead and remember it, so that if you get dazzled you have a reference and some idea of what to expect. Bear in mind that in the glare of the lights you won't be able to see debris in the road, cars parked by the kerb, cyclists or pedestrians in your path, so slow down.

Headlights from behind can dazzle you by shining in your rear-view mirror. Adjust the mirror to prevent the light reflecting into your eyes, but correct the angle as soon as the car behind has gone.

The way to avoid being dazzled is never to look directly at the lights. On dip, your beam should illuminate the nearside kerb; this is where your eyes should be also. Use your peripheral vision to judge the path of the oncoming car.

If you are dazzled, your night vision will be lost, leaving you blind for a few minutes. You may need to pull over and stop to give your eyes time to recover.

Lights inside the car can also cause dazzle and destroy night vision, so it's best not to switch on a torch or the interior light while the car is moving, and don't use cigarette lighters or matches while at the wheel. For map-reading by night, buy a hooded light designed for the purpose. These can be obtained from any car accessory shop – the light plugs into the car's lighter socket, so you won't even need batteries. Always stop to study the map, and give your eyes time to adjust to the darkness before moving off again.

Bright Sunshine

Bright sunshine may seem an odd subject for a chapter on bad-weather driving, but dazzle can be a hazard by day as well as by night. Strong sunshine will impair your vision – especially when you emerge from a shaded area into dazzling brightness. Apart from temporarily blinding you, it can make it difficult to judge distances. Things seem nearer in bright light. Until your eyes recover, you are at risk because you can't read the road and evaluate the hazards ahead.

When the sun is low on the horizon in the early morning and late evening, it can cause all sorts of problems for drivers. I live to the west of London, so any early start forces me to drive into the sun, and returning home it will be there in my eyes again. The glare is worse still when the roads are wet, because the sun will be reflected up off the ground. And when travelling up hill into the sun there's no escape from its dazzling effects.

Even when the sun is behind you it can cause problems by shining in your mirrors, preventing you seeing what following traffic is doing. And oncoming drivers, facing into the sun, may fail to see you and think they can use your side of the road to overtake another vehicle. Be prepared for anything! Sunny mornings are also the time when birds and animals take to the road. Drive sensibly to avoid wildlife but never swerve violently as you risk losing control of the car and endangering yourself and other road users.

Slow down, and if you are blinded by the light, pull in somewhere safe and wait until you can see clearly again. Adjust your mirrors to reduce glare (remembering to put them back to give the best view of the road behind once the sun has moved in the sky).

Most cars have sun visors fitted to deflect the glare, some have a tinted area at the top of the windscreen (or you can buy an adhesive filter to stick to the glass), but when the sun is low on the horizon these may be of little use. Sunglasses are a better option, so keep a pair handy even in winter.

HOT WEATHER HAZARDS

The sun brings heat as well as light, another source of trouble for motorists:

- Tempers boil. Keep cool when you're stuck in a jam or involved in an accident. Getting into a fight is not the answer.
- Engines overheat. Stop the car and allow the engine to cool. If for some reason you cannot stop immediately, switch on the heater. Insane as this may sound, turning on the heater lends volume to the engine-cooling system. The interior of the car may turn into a furnace, but the engine will cool. As soon as it's safe and convenient, stop the car and open the bonnet – first protecting your hands against the heat of the metal so that it won't burn your skin. Wait until the temperature drops before undoing the radiator cap, other-

wise a jet of scalding steam will shoot out.

- Drivers can get sluggish and lethargic, especially if they allow themselves to become dehydrated. Take regular breaks, and drink plenty of liquids.
- Road surfaces get sticky and clog tyres, reducing their grip. Always check your tyres and clear the tread of obstructions.
- Children and animals can die if left in a parked car with insufficient ventilation and water. NEVER leave a child or animal in the car in hot weather for more than a few minutes. Open the window to allow ventilation without allowing enough room for the child or animal to wriggle out or a thief to break in. Fit roll-down sun blinds for side and rear windows. Return to the car as soon as you possibly can.

vehicle handling

In addition to reducing visibility, adverse weather conditions can affect vehicle performance. At times it can seem that the driver is battling against the elements for control of the car, as strong winds cause the steering wheel to jerk in your hands, and water or ice on the road diminish the tyres' grip. If not handled correctly, the car is liable to skid or aquaplane – a nightmarish experience for any driver, but especially for those who have no idea how to regain control safely.

Skidding

Learner drivers are given no practical tuition in the art of controlling a skid. In studying for the driving test they may pick up a little theoretical knowledge – 'To correct a skid you should steer into it' – but when faced with the terrifying

reality, chances are their reaction will be instinctive: slam on the brakes and steer as hard as possible away from whatever obstacle the skid is carrying you towards. After all, if steering into the skid is going to put you on a collision course with an oncoming juggernaut, you're not going to be too keen on putting the theory to the test. Unfortunately, there's every likelihood that you will hit that juggernaut, because the harder you brake and the more harsh your steering, the less likely you are to regain control of the vehicle.

WHY SKIDS OCCUR

Skids happen when the tyres lose their grip on the road surface. Even at the best of times (travelling in a straight line on a good road surface at a constant speed with tyres of the correct pressure and tread depth), the area of tyre in contact with the road is not much bigger than the palm of your hand, which means that the amount of traction available is limited. When the car turns a corner, accelerates or brakes, a redistribution of weight occurs and some tyres end up bearing more of the load than others. A lighter load on the

EXCESSIVE STEERING
Cornering forces throw weight of car and passengers sideways.

EXCESSIVE ACCELERATION
Weight is thrown to the rear, making the front of the car light. Front wheels may lose traction.

EXCESSIVE BRAKING
Weight is thrown forwards, making the back of the car light. Rear wheels lose their grip on the road.

tyre means less pressure bearing down, and therefore less grip. If the car is travelling too fast for the prevailing conditions, this loss of tyre grip will result in a skid.

The odds in favour of a skid can be improved still further by trying to adjust your speed and change direction at the same time. This is why so many skids occur on bends: drivers approach the bend too fast, realize the error of their ways as they steer into the corner and the tyres start to slip, so they try to lose speed by applying the brakes. Of course, this only serves to lock the wheels, so the driver ends up with no steering control and a car that won't stop.

A skid can occur in any conditions, but where the tyres are worn or the road is slippery, tyre grip will be reduced to the point where skids happen more easily and at much lower speeds. Be on the lookout for hazardous road surfaces at all times of year.

SKID PREVENTION

Prevention is better than cure where skids are concerned, so do as much as you can to minimize the risks. Avoid jerky handling of the controls: apply steering, braking and acceleration as smoothly and gently as you can. Slow down and change gear before taking a bend, so that your foot comes off the brake while the car is still travelling in a straight line. Maintain a constant speed as you turn the corner, then accel-

erate gently once you have cleared the bend.

Anticipate potential hazards by reading the road. Look well ahead, checking for danger signs, and considering what action you will take if necessary. Pay attention to weather conditions and the road surface, and then modify your speed to suit the prevailing conditions.

On icy roads stopping distances can be trebled, quadrupled, or multiplied by ten, depending on the severity of the conditions, so harsh braking must be avoided at all costs. When you apply the brakes it must be done gently and progressively. This means that you need much more room in which to bring the car to a halt. If you're travelling at 60 or 70 mph, with a gap of 10 metres between you and the vehicle in front, you haven't a prayer of stopping in time (even in good conditions it can't be done: the shortest achievable stopping distance at 60 mph is 73 metres or 240 feet). What's more, if there's a heavy goods vehicle behind, it will take even longer to stop than you will, the momentum of its load carrying it forward for some distance after the brakes have been applied. This is why it is so crucial to maintain a gap which reflects the stopping distance for the prevailing conditions and to travel at a speed which allows you time to react.

Keep your car in good working order – your life depends on it. Defective brakes and suspension, worn tyres, or tyres

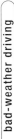
bad-weather driving

SLIPPERY ROADS

The condition of roads can vary, even in the best of weather conditions. Always study the road ahead, noting the camber and changes in road surface, especially when approaching a bend, junction, or bridge.

• When well-maintained, tarmac or asphalt dressed with stones or chips provide a good skid-resistant surface, but constant wear and tear can result in their becoming polished smooth.

• Concrete roads may hold water, which freezes in cold weather and creates icy patches.

• Cobblestones are extremely slippery when wet.

• Slow down when you have to drive over potholes, drain covers, and other bumps in the road. Alternatively, provided you can do so without posing a danger to other traffic, adjust your course so as to avoid them.

• Spilt fuel, especially diesel, will make the ground very slippery, so exercise extreme caution where a heavy goods vehicle has lost a significant amount of fuel. Small patches of spilt fuel are often found at or near service stations.

• Snow and ice are dealt with in detail later in this chapter. Remember that ice can be patchy, forming first in exposed areas and lingering longest in shaded areas. You cannot always see ice, so learn to detect its presence in other ways: the steering will feel light and the tyres cannot be heard when running on icy ground.

• Soft mud and sand pose similar problems to driving in deep snow, and so the same driving technique applies. Avoid wheel-spin, which will cause the vehicle to dig itself in deeper.

• Fallen leaves provide no traction for tyres, especially when wet, and damp patches under trees can be slippery with blossom and other deposits.

• Loose gravel or shale provides little purchase for tyres. If the wheels spin, chips will be thrown at the bodywork, damaging the paint.

• Deposits of oil and tyre rubber accumulate on road surfaces during long dry periods. A summer shower will slicken the surface of this coating, turning the road into a skid-pan.

Remember: road conditions may be a contributing factor, but the cause of skids is bad driving. To eliminate the risks: look well ahead, read the road, and match your speed to the prevailing conditions.

---

which have been over- or under-inflated, all help to increase the risk of skidding. Learn as much as you can about your car so that you understand it's capabilities, but never push it to the limit of those capabilities – always preserve a safety margin in case of emergencies. Don't assume that because it is fitted with safety features such as an anti-lock braking system (ABS), you can get away with driving recklessly. ABS cannot prevent skidding or make it possible for you to stop within a shorter distance than normal brakes. The power to prevent skidding rests solely with you, the driver – not the car.

CORRECTING SKIDS

To correct a skid you must remove the cause. This sounds simple enough, but it goes against the instinctive reaction, which is to brake hard or wrestle with the steering wheel in an effort to avoid a collision. Like a rabbit petrified by oncoming headlights, most drivers will fix on the object they are afraid of colliding with. Even though the brakes and steering will not respond because the wheels are locked, they keep their foot on the pedal. And as a result, they crash.

So you must fight the urge to panic. Focus your mind – you need to take action NOW. What caused the skid? Your first priority is to remove that cause. Only then, when you have regained control of the car, can you set about taking evasive action.

Cause: excessive braking

Braking hard, in a vehicle not fitted with ABS, causes the wheels to lock. If you feel the car start to skid after applying the brakes harshly, ease off the brake pedal to allow the wheels to start turning again. The tyres will then regain some grip on the road, restoring steering control.

What you do next depends on the circumstances and condition of the road surface. Where there are no obstacles in the way and your goal is to lose speed or bring the car to a halt while continuing in a straight line, use pulse braking. If you are sliding across an icy surface towards another vehicle or a brick wall, you need to take evasive action: use cadence braking to prevent the wheels locking. Steering will be restored sufficiently for you to gently steer into the skid for a few seconds (if the rear of the car is sliding to the right, steer to the right – and vice versa), then, equally gently, steer back in the direction you want the car to go. Don't over-correct with the steering wheel as this can start a skid in the opposite direction.

> ## Pulse and Cadence Braking
> If your car is equipped with ABS, you can skip this section. Anti-lock brakes sense when the wheels are locking and automatically release and reapply the brakes several times a second. All the driver has to do is keep braking hard.
>
> Pulse and cadence braking are the DIY alternative to ABS. The objective is the same, whichever method you adopt: to bring the car to a halt without causing the wheels to lock.
>
> *Pulse braking:* pump the brakes rhythmically, in short pulses. Don't 'bounce' on and off the pedal, keep your foot steady and apply pressure – on–off, on–off, on–off – until the car can be stopped without further skidding.
>
> *Cadence braking:* this takes longer because you hold the brake pedal down until the moment you sense that the wheels are on the point of locking, then ease off and steer for a few seconds. Brake again until you sense wheel-lock, then release the brake and steer some more. Repeat until you have brought both steering and braking under control.

Cause: excessive acceleration

Harsh acceleration can cause the wheels to spin even when you're just trying to start the car. At high speed it's a sure-fire way to cause a skid. The cure is to take your foot off the accelerator, which should be sufficient to cure the skid. Don't slam your foot on the brakes or jerk the steering wheel as that will only start a fresh skid.

Cause: excessive steering

If you take a corner too sharply, the car will start to slide. Excessive speed is generally the underlying cause of the skid, so to restore the tyres' grip on the road, reduce the speed by taking your foot off the accelerator. If your foot was on the brake – because you left it until too late before trying to reduce speed for the bend – release the brake pedal and reapply it (see cadence braking, above). To regain steering control, steer momentarily into the skid to straighten the wheels, then smoothly point the vehicle in the direction you want it to go. Don't jerk the steering wheel or over-correct the steering: you will only start to skid in a different direction.

Understeer (front-wheel skid)

A front-wheel skid can be caused by accelerating too fast round a bend. Instead of turning in the direction steered, the front wheels lose their grip leaving the car to continue in a straight line. This is most common in front-wheel drive cars, though it can also occur in rear-wheel drive vehicles. There are a variety of techniques for curing a front-wheel skid, depending on the vehicle you are driving.

If your car is rear-wheel drive, take your foot off the accelerator and momentarily turn the steering wheel to straighten the wheels. Once the car is travelling in a straight line, apply the brakes smoothly if you are off-line, or accelerate gently and smoothly if the way is clear.

In a vehicle with front-wheel drive, provided the skid was not caused by the car speeding into the bend, you may be able to regain control by smoothly turning the steering wheel in the opposite direction to the slide. Thus if the car is travelling at about 30 mph, keep a light pressure on the accelerator – if you release the accelerator as the slide occurs, the car will be thrown further off-line – and steer in the direction you want the car to go.

If, on the other hand, your front-wheel-drive car has skidded because of excessive speed, remove the cause by releasing the accelerator. Steer smoothly and briefly in the direction of the skid, and once the tyres have straightened, steer the vehicle back on course. Only then should you gently accelerate.

Oversteer (rear-wheel skid)

In a rear-wheel skid the back of the car slides away from the corner; if this skid is unchecked the car could spin full circle. Once again, the causes are excessive speed, acceleration or braking when steering round a bend – especially where the camber of the road slopes into the curve.

Remove the cause by taking your foot off the accelerator or brake. Briefly and smoothly turn the steering wheel in the direction of the skid. In other words, if the rear wheels are sliding to the right, steer to the right. Don't leave it too late, and don't over-steer, or the car may skid in the opposite direction. When the rear wheels are realigned and the car is back on course, it is safe to accelerate gently.

Four-wheel skid

On ice all four wheels may lose adhesion, leaving the car sliding out of control in whatever direction it was heading in when the skid started. Harsh braking by a driver who has been travelling too fast for the conditions is the usual cause.

If your car is equipped with ABS, brake hard and let the anti-lock brakes kick in. Drivers of vehicles not fitted with ABS should use cadence braking to allow them to brake and steer. A car that is skidding sideways may change direction when the wheels unlock, so prepare to straighten the wheels the moment steering control is restored, then pump the brake again until the wheels are about to lock, release the brake and steer smoothly in the direction you want the vehicle to go. Once full control has been regained, accelerate gently.

SKID PANS

Theory is no substitute for first-hand experience gained in controlled conditions. Practising on a skid pan will give you untold confidence. And once you know what to expect from a skid, you will have a better chance of controlling it.

Ask your local Road Safety Officer about organizations offering courses in skid control. Some schools use a skid pan (an open, flat area such as a disused airfield or car park which has been treated to make the surface slippery), others use skid vehicles. These are cars which have been adapted to simulate the effects of different types of skids. They are an excellent training facility, allowing you to master the techniques in complete safety. By recreating the mechanics of a skid at slow speed, simulators help you to recognize each

stage of the skid and learn the appropriate action to deal with it.

Whether you're a new driver or an old hand, as little as half an hour's skid tuition will prove to be invaluable if you are ever foolish enough to allow your car to skid for real. Instead of being panicked into taking all the wrong decisions, you will find yourself confidently regaining control before any damage has been done. You might even have a little fun along the way.

Snow and Ice

 Winter brings with it many dangers for the motorist, not least of which is the changeability of the weather. You can set off in clear blue skies and a couple of hours down the road find yourself in the middle of a blizzard. So the first rule is to check out the weather forecasts for a few clues as to what you can expect, and to be prepared for the worst.

When temperatures are low, icy roads are a distinct possibility. Don't be deceived by the fact that some roads may be completely free of ice; conditions vary greatly depending on the location and the amount of traffic the road carries. Ice will linger on roads which are seldom used and in places which are sheltered from the sun – for example, on valley bottoms, or where shadows are cast by tall buildings, trees or bridges. Exposed areas such as bridges or north-facing gradients will also be slow to thaw. Motorways are generally the first roads to be treated with grit or salt, and what ice does form tends to be dispersed by the constant flow of traffic. But there remains the danger of patches of black ice, so you cannot afford to be complacent. Black ice is notoriously difficult to spot, so the first indication of its presence will be the behaviour of vehicles up ahead or a sudden silence as the tyres stop making any sound, accompanied by a sensation of lightness in the steering.

Snow, sleet, hail and freezing fog bring a deadly combination of slippery road surfaces and reduced visibility. Not only will the view through your windows be obscured, but the road surface is hidden under a blanket which may conceal black ice or potholes. Road markings and signposts may be completely covered, too, so you won't know where you are or whether you have priority over oncoming vehicles. As if that weren't enough to contend with, there's a good chance of other road users skidding out of control and colliding with you.

Where the snow is falling heavily and laying deep on the ground, it can build up around the wheels and brakes, packing them solid and affecting their operation. Caution must be exercised in high, exposed areas where the snow lies in deep drifts across the road, or you could find yourself stuck.

PREPARING FOR WINTER

Cold weather places a lot of extra demands on a vehicle, and the more you can do to maintain it's condition, the less chance there is of your ending up stranded by the roadside waiting for a mechanic. At the onset of winter, carry out the Winter Maintenance programme described in **Maintenance**, or if you don't feel confident of your ability to perform service checks yourself, ask your garage to give it a pre-winter once-over. Ask them to change the battery if it's nearing the end of its life span. Throughout the winter months, run through the additional checks listed below on a regular basis. Take care, though: in sub-zero temperatures you must not allow your skin to come in contact with metal or petrol, as either will cause your flesh to freeze. (If your fingers do get stuck to metal, don't try to rip your hand away as the skin will tear. Pour warm water over your fingers to free them.) Wear gloves and try to keep them dry.

- If you have to top up the cooling system, make sure to add antifreeze. The colder the weather, the greater strength of antifreeze solution required – check the label on the bottle for the correct ratio of antifreeze to water.
- Similarly, when topping up with screenwash, use one of the brands which contain a freezing inhibitor. Do not add coolant antifreeze, as this will strip the paint off the car!
- Check the condition of the windscreen wipers and replace the blades if they are showing signs of wear.
- Cold weather and long hours of darkness place a lot more strain on the battery, which has to cope with the demands of parking lights, heaters, and wipers. It's therefore not surprising that flat batteries are one of the prime causes of

winter breakdowns. See Maintenance for details of how to maintain your battery in good working order.

In addition, carry out the following routine every time you take the car out in winter:

- Frozen locks can be thawed either by using an aerosol spray available from car accessory shops, or by using a match or cigarette lighter to heat the key before putting it into the lock. NEVER force the lock, as the key could break off in your hand.
- Make sure your tyres and brakes are free of compacted snow.
- Check all the lights, including the brake lights, reversing lights, indicators, and fog lights. Wash the lenses free of dirt and grime. Clean all mirrors and reflectors, too.
- Before setting off you will need to clear all windows of snow and ice. It is not enough to clear just a small patch in front of the driver's seat, and the wipers could be damaged if you try using them to shift the snow, so there's no alternative but to allow time to do the job properly. If you have front or rear heated windows, you can defrost the easy way. Simply start the engine and flick the appropriate switches. Alternatively, you can use the car's heater to help by directing the vents so that they point at the windscreen. In the meantime, set to work with a soft plastic scraper to clear the ice or snow. If you haven't a scraper, a credit card can be used, but avoid anything that will scratch the screen – and don't use metal scrapers on heated windows because the filaments could be damaged. Aerosol de-icing sprays are quick and convenient to use, but wipe any splashes off the paintwork. NEVER be tempted to throw a basin of hot water at the windscreen – you could crack the windscreen. If you must use water, be very careful. Make sure the water temperature is not too high; you should be able to immerse your hands in it without discomfort. Pour the water on the metal above the windscreen, and let it trickle gently down over the glass.
- Check that you have more than enough fuel to get you to your destination. If you get stuck in snow or have to make a long detour because of the weather, you will use extra fuel. Service stations may be forced to close if conditions

are very bad, especially in rural areas, so fill up at the first opportunity rather than hoping you'll find somewhere cheaper or with the right kind of coupons later on.

- In addition to the usual survival kit, pack appropriate items for cold-weather emergencies.

DRIVING IN WINTER

Before you set off, take the time to plan your journey. Listen to weather forecasts and traffic bulletins on the radio, or contact one of the major motoring organizations to check that roads are passable. Stick to major routes – these are

WINTER MOTORING SURVIVAL KIT

Be prepared for the worst and carry the following equipment in your car (not the boot – every time you open the doors all the warm air will escape, so put the gear where you can get at it) when there is any possibility of blizzard conditions:

Extra clothing
Sleeping bag(s) or blanket(s)
Wellington boots
Thermos flask containing a hot drink
Food, e.g. chocolate bars
Candles and a box of matches
Mobile phone
Battery-operated radio to monitor news and weather reports
Shovel
Sacking/old doormats or a bag of grit
Spare can of fuel

The warm clothing should include a fleece or wool hat and a thermal fleece jacket or thick woollen sweater. Ski gear, like those padded over-trousers which come up to the chest – is ideal for this purpose. Stuff a pair of extra thick socks into the wellingtons. And make sure to include a pair of gloves, preferably the kind which are waterproof on the outside with a thermal lining; your hands will need protection when shovelling snow or clearing windscreens.

Cold-weather emergency food rations need to be high in fat and sugar, like chocolate or bread thickly buttered and coated with honey. Fill the thermos flask with a soup or a sweetened drink such as hot chocolate.

Two candles can create sufficient heat to warm a car interior and save running the engine. Store them in an old coffee tin, which can then be used as a holder for the burning candle.

Sacking or old doormats can be pushed under the wheels to provide traction if you get stuck in deep snow. (A bag of sharp sand or grit – or cat litter, which doesn't freeze – will serve the same purpose.) Tie long strings to the mats so you can retrieve them without having to stop and get out of the car.

SNOW CHAINS AND WINTER TYRES

In an area prone to hard winters, you should carry snow chains. In some countries, like Norway, the law demands that snow chains be fitted and without them you would not be permitted on mountainous routes. Buy the kind that can be slipped on to the tyre without having to take the wheel off the car; simply lie them on the ground and gently drive forward so that the wheels are in position. Fit chains to all four tyres for the best results, but if for some reason you only have one pair fit them to the driving wheels (front, if you have front-wheel drive; back wheels for rear-wheel drive). Remove the chains when travelling on road surfaces which are not coated with snow and ice.

It's possible to buy winter tyres, which have deep patterned treads, or even studded treads, to cope with cold climate driving. These are ideal for use in regions where snow is guaranteed for months on end, but because they are not suitable for roads which are free of snow and ice those who live in areas where winter conditions come and go will have little use for them.

Stopping distances at 20 mph for various types of tyres (allowing for a reaction distance of 6.5 metres/22 feet):

Regular tyres	on snow	25 metres (82 feet)
	on ice	52.5 metres (172 feet)
Snow tyres	on snow	22.5 metres (74 feet)
	on ice	53 metres (173 feet)
with snow chains	on snow	18 metres (60 feet)
	on ice	29.5 metres (97 feet)

more likely to be gritted and snowploughed than minor roads – and travel by daylight. Tell someone the route you are intending to take and what time you expect to arrive (allow two or three times as long as you would in good conditions; chances are you'll run into delays and will need rest stops to recover from the strain).

The next step is to prepare the car by clearing away all snow. The priority is obviously to make sure the windows, lights, mirrors and number plate are not obscured, but it's worth shifting snow off the roof, too. Otherwise, when you apply the brakes all the snow could slide forward on to the windscreen, blocking your view. Make sure your wheel arches are free of compacted snow and that the brakes are not hindered in any way.

A cold engine will take a while to warm up, and this is especially true of older cars. That does not mean that you should sit revving the engine in an attempt to force it to heat up quicker, and neither should you allow it to idle for ages before driving off – 30 seconds should be enough to get the cold, sluggish oil pumping. Just make sure you start off gently, keeping your speed low and taking it easy with the controls for the first few miles – which you would need to do anyway on icy roads – so that the engine warms gradually, bringing the oil and coolant to a temperature where they will flow freely throughout the system.

When you're finally on the road, use your de-misters, heated windows, etc to help keep the windows clear and free of condensation. But don't let the car get too warm and snug, or you could end up falling asleep at the wheel. In heavy snowfalls, you may need to stop at regular intervals along the way to wipe snow off the windows, lights, brakes, etc. Find a safe, level place to park, out of the way of passing traffic. Remember that cars can skid on icy roads, so don't take chances by working on your car in close proximity to moving vehicles.

Headlights not only enable you to see in poor conditions, they help you to be seen. Switch on your dipped headlights as soon as the light starts to fade. Driving at night in a snow-storm is very demanding. The snow reflects your headlights straight back at you, so main-beam and fog lights may cause too much glare, and even dipped headlights may prove too dazzling. Side lights will cause less glare, but there's little

chance of other drivers realizing you're there if the car isn't adequately lit. Rest as often as you can to allow your eyes time to recover from the strain.

Some vehicles are designed to perform better in icy conditions than others: four-wheel drive, for example, offers better road-holding capabilities than front- or rear-wheel. But no matter how well-equipped your car, it will skid unless you adjust your driving to suit the conditions. Smooth and easy does it, is the golden rule. When driving on snow or ice the secret to avoiding skids is to drive in as high a gear as possible at a constant, slow speed, keeping the steering wheel steady and braking gently and seldom. Jerky movements, whether braking, steering or accelerating, should be eliminated. Avoid changing gear, braking or accelerating while steering round a corner; reduce your speed and change gear on the approach, while travelling in a straight line, so that when you reach the bend all you have to do is steer.

To prevent the wheels spinning when pulling away or manoeuvring, use the highest gear that your car will tolerate (consult the manufacturer's handbook for your particular make and model). Don't race the engine by bearing down on the accelerator: keep it light. You want the wheels to turn, not spin. If you're in deep snow, wheel-spin will only dig you in deeper, on ice it deprives you of steering control. Change up a gear earlier than you normally would. The trick is to select a gear which will allow you to maintain a low speed without stalling, but with room for a little acceleration should conditions permit. Once you're underway, keep gear changes to a minimum because of the risk of skidding.

Conditions vary on winter roads, the road surface will be fine one moment and a sheet of ice the next, so focus on the feedback you get from the car. You can't see black ice, so the first indication will be when the steering feels light and the noise from the tyres stops. Tune your senses in to detect these warning signs. Black ice tends to form in patches the size of a large puddle, so if you slide forwards on a straight stretch of road there's every chance that you'll be back on tarmac within the space of a few feet.

If you do start to slide, follow the standard procedures for controlling a skid: first remove the cause of the skid (take your foot off the brake pedal if the skid was brought about by harsh braking, ease off the accelerator if speed was the

bad-weather driving

problem), steer briefly and smoothly into the skid to straighten the wheels, then steer to a safety line position when you have regained control of the car. Soft banks of snow by the side of the road can provide an emergency safety barrier – steering into deep snow will slow the car and stop the skid. But remember there's no way of knowing what lies beneath a snow drift: you could hit a solid object or, then again, you could end up stuck in a ditch.

Take care when there are winter maintenance vehicles about. Salting vehicles travel at about 35 mph spreading rock salt across all lanes of the road as a precaution against ice. Be patient and DON'T try to overtake. The same applies to snowploughs. Stay well back, and use only the part of the road that has been cleared. Snowploughs can leave drifts in partially cleared lanes, and you risk getting stuck if you try to overtake the plough by driving through an uncleared or semi-cleared section.

Keep to the areas of road that others have used and, in deep snow, aim to drive in their tyre tracks whenever possible. Where the tracks have formed deep ruts in frozen snow, turning off can be tricky if you allow the car to lose too much momentum or stop altogether. Keep going at a slow, steady speed and you should have no trouble.

The same principle applies when climbing a hill. Before starting the ascent, assess which gear will be needed to take you to the top. Change gear on the approach and then remain in that gear, maintaining a steady speed until you reach the summit. Don't try to take the hill at too high a speed – you will only cause the wheels to spin. Avoid stopping en route, because it can be a real struggle to get going again. Leave as much space as possible between your car and the vehicle in front, so that if it runs into trouble on the hill you will be able to manoeuvre round it rather than having to stop when it stops. If necessary, wait at the bottom of the hill until you can see that you will have a clear run to the top.

Going down a steep, icy hill requires maximum caution. Change to bottom gear at the summit (if you drive an automatic, select 'hold' so that you can maintain a low gear throughout the descent). Far from slowing you down, standing on the brake pedal will only lock the wheels and cause a skid. Let the engine control the car's speed. Start slow and hopefully the car will continue slowly down the hill. If you absolutely have to brake, keep it smooth and gentle. Come off the brake when you feel the wheels lock.

 STUCK IN SNOW
It can be difficult to restart the car when you stop in deep snow. The most common mistake is to rev the engine hard; this creates wheel-spin which will dig the car in deeper than ever.

- Choose the highest gear the car will tolerate – usually second – and apply gentle pressure on the accelerator pedal.
- Turn the wheels from side to side a few times to push the snow out of the way. Then straighten the wheels, angling them so as to follow the ruts created by other road users.
- Place something under the drive wheels to aid traction. Your winter motoring survival kit should include sacking, old doormats, or a bag of grit (alternatively, use cardboard, twigs, an old blanket, or a plank of wood). Dig or scrape away as much snow as possible, then place your sacking or grit under the wheels. Your piece of sacking or doormat should have strings attached so that once the car is free it can be towed along until you reach a piece of ground where you can stop without fear of getting stuck again.
- If necessary, traction can be increased by adding weight over the drive wheels. On a rear-wheel drive vehicle heavy items in the boot will help, or have your passengers sit on the rear end or stand on the rear bumper. On a front-wheel drive vehicle, ask them to sit on the front wings.
- Passengers can also help by pushing. But make sure they are in a safe position where they won't slip under a wheel and there's no chance of the car rolling back on them. Once the car is moving, drive on until you reach firmer ground or a favourable gradient before picking up the passengers.
- If you're on your own, try gently rocking the car by selecting a low gear (or reverse, if you need to back out) and alternately applying light pressure on the accelerator to go as far forward as you can and then slipping the clutch. Each time the car will move a fraction further forward, until you arrive at a point where you can drive away. In some situations you may need to switch between forward and reverse gears (on an automatic, switch quickly from D

STRANDED!

If your vehicle breaks down or conditions deteriorate to the point where the road ahead and behind is impassable, it is vital that you know how to survive until the emergency services can reach you. Don't panic – being stranded in snow is not immediately life-threatening provided you take appropriate action.

• Maintain a positive mental attitude. If you are on a regular traffic route, someone will come along to rescue you.

• STAY WITH THE CAR. Never wander off in an attempt to seek help unless you can see a house with its lights on close at hand. It's easy to get lost in a blizzard, and walking in deep snow is very tiring. As well as running the risk of getting hypothermia, you will make it more difficult for rescuers to find you. In the car you can survive for several days, especially if you have packed your winter survival kit. In the open you won't last the night.

• In cold weather the seals around the doors and windows will freeze up, making the car airtight. This will happen sooner if the engine is run frequently and there are a number of people in the car. Check every so often to make sure that at least one window can be opened – this will ventilate the car and prevent the window from freezing shut.

• Clear an area around the exhaust pipe and the exterior heater vents (these are normally located under the windshield) so you can run the engine and heater without risking carbon monoxide poisoning. If the car gets completely buried it is essential to poke a breathing hole in the snow using an umbrella or stick. Check continually that it is not blocked.

• Many people die in these situations from carbon monoxide poisoning because the warmth from the heater makes them drowsy and they fall asleep with the engine running. As they sleep, the car fills up with toxic fumes which slowly kill. To conserve fuel and prevent the risk of inhaling carbon monoxide, run the engine every now and then for about 10 minutes, so that it warms up the interior and keeps the battery charged, but DON'T leave it running constantly. When you feel drowsy, stop the engine and open a window.

• Take the tin of candles and matches from your winter survival kit. Light a candle and, using the tin as a candle-holder, place it on the floor. This will increase the temperature in the car and, more importantly, will alert you should carbon monoxide fumes build up. If the candle starts flickering and dying, ventilate the car immediately.

It may seem dangerous to permit a naked flame inside a vehicle – and where you suspect the possibility of a leak or where there is a strong smell of fuel, lighting a candle would constitute an unacceptable risk and should therefore be avoided. However, in cold-weather emergency situations where the vehicle is immobile and there are no fuel leaks, lighting a candle is safe and can save lives.

• Gentle exercise will prevent stiffness and help to maintain body warmth, but bear in mind the need to conserve energy and don't overdo it.

• To keep warm without the engine running, everyone should wrap up in the extra clothing and sleeping bags from the survival kit. If you have minimal kit, insulate yourselves with newspaper, maps, carpet, or seat covers. These items should be wrapped around the body under your clothing. Much of your body heat will be lost if you fail to cover your head – a head-rest cover makes an ideal improvised hat. Huddle together for warmth.

• If there are other motorists trapped, get together in one car. The extra bodies will raise the temperature inside the car. Maintain ventilation, though, because the air will get stale quicker.

• Take it in turns to sleep, so that at least one person is always awake to act as a lookout for approaching rescuers. When a vehicle comes in range, signal by sounding your horn or flashing your lights.

• If you are alone, try to stay awake. Use a battery-operated radio, if you have one, to monitor news and weather broadcasts (don't use the car radio, as it will drain the battery). If it's very cold you will only doze for short periods.

• If you have to leave the car, wear adequate clothing and avoid getting wet – keep sweating and contact with water to a minimum. Knock snow off your clothes before re-entering the vehicle.

• Ration yourself with the food and drink – it may have to last for a long time.

///////////////////////////////////////

DON'T DRINK

Alcohol will lower your body temperature. That warm glow you feel after a drink occurs because the surface blood vessels dilate, allowing the blood flowing through them to cool.

Alcohol also impairs judgement – after a few nips you may feel as though you can wade through the snow to safety – and promotes drowsiness.

Drink and driving don't go together, so make it a rule never to carry alcohol in the car.

bad-weather driving

to R), driving a few inches at a time, to rock the car out. A word of warning: this may damage some transmissions, so check the manufacturer's handbook before you try it.

- If the car is well and truly stuck, digging it out is the only solution. Dig around each wheel and clear a track to a firmer surface. Clear the snow from around the chassis and sump so the wheels can get a good grip. A greater distance will need to be cleared when travelling uphill, because you'll need to get enough traction to gain momentum.
- Provided you carry a foot pump, you could let most of the air out of the tyres – an under-inflated tyre will give you more grip. But stop as soon as you come to firmer ground or a favourable incline and re-inflate the tyres.

Rain

Most people are alert to the dangers of winter weather; they expect to encounter icy roads and drive accordingly. But countless unwary drivers get caught out whenever a light shower ends a long spell of dry weather. The rain mixes with oil and rubber deposits which have built up on the road surface to create a slick film as lethal as any black ice.

Heavy rain can cause flooding, or leave large puddles which will have you aquaplaning if you hit them at speed. Visibility will be reduced, too. In a real downpour, the wipers may not be able to cope. Spray thrown up by large vehicles can obscure your windows completely. At night a wet screen reflects and intensifies all light sources. Each raindrop acts as a prism; every streetlight, every car, and every illuminated advertising hoarding will add to the general dazzle, making it very difficult to see. Never stare at oncoming lights. Memorize the road before the lights reach you, then look towards the kerb while using your peripheral vision to monitor the road.

And on top of everything else, there's the psychological effect of rain. Everyone seems to be in a mad rush to get out of the wet as quick as they can. Drivers are much more likely to lock their keys in the car when it's raining. Even with remote locking this can happen: you use the remote to lock the car, then realize that you need an umbrella or raincoat from the boot. In the ensuing confusion of testing the umbrella or slipping on the coat, the boot is slammed with the keys left inside.

Pedestrians, too, are in more of a hurry. Instead of waiting to cross the road safely they may run out unexpectedly, especially if they are improperly dressed for the conditions. Those who are dressed for the weather, with a hood covering their ears, may not be able to hear oncoming traffic. Their gaze is directed at the ground as they focus on dodging puddles rather than vehicles. An umbrella will also limit vision, especially if it's held at an angle to block the wind. As a driver, you must make allowances for unexpected behaviour and show consideration by not driving through puddles at speed and splashing passers-by.

DRIVING IN RAIN

Make sure that your vehicle is maintained in a condition that will allow it to cope with whatever the weather throws at it. Modern disk brakes can usually cope with puddles and heavy rain, but drum brakes may get waterlogged. When the road is clear and you can do so safely, test your brakes to make sure they are operating effectively.

A clean windshield is vital at all times, but especially important in wet weather. A dirty screen encrusted with flies and other debris will prevent the wipers from keeping the screen clear.

- At least once a month, thoroughly clean the windscreen with a solvent that removes all road grime and grease. Either buy a proprietary cleaner from a car accessory shop, or save money by using clean water and vinegar.
- Check your wipers regularly for splits or other signs of wear. If necessary, change the blades to maintain maximum efficiency.
- Keep the screenwash reservoir topped up. Often when you switch on the wipers they will end up smearing the windscreen, and if there's no screenwash in the bottle you won't be able to clean the glass.

Use your wipers to clear any build-up of condensation from the windscreen. Condensation will also form on the interior windows, especially if you are carrying passengers. Use de-misters to blow warm air on to the windscreen, or keep a window ajar to prevent a mist forming on the glass. Have a clean, dry cloth within easy reach of the driver's seat so that you can wipe the windows when you stop at lights or get held up in traffic.

To aid visibility and help others to see you, switch on your dipped headlights whenever you turn on the windscreen wipers. Main-beam lights will dazzle other road users (and may reflect back off a curtain of falling rain into your own eyes), and fog lights should only be used when visibility is reduced to below 100 metres (328 feet). Give your headlight lenses a wipe over every time you stop for a break – filthy spray from the road will soon create a film which substantially reduces the amount of light given off.

Because both visibility and road-handling are impaired in heavy rain, reduce your speed. The less you can see, the slower you will have to go. Sometimes a thunderstorm can bring such a torrential downpour that the windscreen wipers will not clear the glass no matter how fast they go. If that is the case, find a safe place to pull over and wait out the storm. The lightning is not a threat, unless you have a phobia that reduces you to a nervous wreck. If that is the case, don't drive until you have recovered sufficiently to allow you to concentrate on your driving.

Tyre adhesion is reduced when the roads are wet, and it can take you twice as long to stop as it would on a dry surface. You will therefore need to maintain a gap between your vehicle and the one in front which reflects the greater stopping distance. Cyclists must be given an extra wide berth in case they swerve to avoid a puddle or get blown off course. Bear in mind that they may not hear you approaching, and a hood or rain-spattered glasses may obscure their vision.

Follow the precautions for avoiding a skid and be smooth and gentle when steering, braking and accelerating. Failing to adjust your driving to the conditions can end in grief, especially when cornering or overtaking. Don't swerve to avoid a puddle – you could lose control. If oncoming traffic will have to pass through a sheet of water on the road, be alert to the risk of vehicles skidding into your lane, and prepare yourself, too, for a large splash that might temporarily obscure your view of the road. Make sure your windows are closed! If you have to stop to ask for directions, wind the windows up again afterwards.

SPRAY

In heavy rain, large commercial vehicles throw out a wall of spray which can obliterate your view of the road for as long as it takes to overtake or be overtaken. Driving behind an 18-wheeler while its tyres send gallons of filthy water raining down upon your windscreen faster than your wipers can clear it is obviously dangerous. Stay well back, waiting for an opportunity to overtake safely. You need to be certain that the road is clear for some distance ahead of the truck before you commit yourself to overtaking. If you cannot see what is going on beyond the truck, it is too dangerous to attempt overtaking. Besides, there's every likelihood that when you do overtake you will only find yourself stuck behind yet another heavy vehicle spewing out water.

AQUAPLANING

When a car travels along a wet road at speeds of over 50 mph (80 kph) there is a danger of the tyres skating over the water's surface instead of maintaining contact with the road. This phenomenon is known as aquaplaning.

At low speeds, water that is picked up by the tyre treads gets dispersed as the wheel turns. But the faster the wheels turn – and the thinner the tread depth – the more difficult it is for the tyres to cope with a high volume of water. Excess water, instead of being centrifuged away from the tyres, is pushed forward, forming a barrier between the tyres and the road surface.

From the driver's seat you can't see this happening – but you will certainly feel it. There may be some kickback from the steering wheel as the front wheels take to the water, then the steering will feel light, just like driving on ice. Suddenly you find yourself skidding sideways at speed, the car behaving as though it has a mind of its own.

Frightening as this sensation is, don't panic. As with other varieties of skid, the instinctive reaction – to brake or steer with all your might – is the wrong one. Braking and steering will not stop the car aquaplaning – that will only happen when you are clear of the puddle of water and the tyres' grip on the road is restored – but rough handling of the controls will cause a skid.

The correct course of action is to reduce speed by easing off the accelerator. Keep both hands on the steering wheel (the quarter-to-three hold is best), but do not turn the wheel hard one way or the other as this will cause the car to lurch suddenly in that direction when the tyres come in contact with the road again. If the car is aquaplaning sideways and there's a risk of running off the road, steer very slightly into the slide then smoothly and gently in the opposite direction when you feel the tyres gripping the road.

This technique is difficult to master even with the benefit of skid-pan tuition, so you should do everything within your power to prevent aquaplaning occurring:

- Make sure that your tyres are properly inflated with a tread depth well above the minimum of 1.6 mm.
- Slow down when you see a sheet of water ahead, or when visibility is poor enough to prevent you seeing any such hazards in time to react.
- In heavy rain study the camber of the road and anticipate where surface water will collect. On most roads water will form pools by the kerbside, so move to the crown of the road where possible.
- Leave a gap between your car and the vehicle in front which takes into account the wet-weather stopping distance (which may be double or treble the usual distance required to bring the car to a halt).

It's worth signing up for a skid-training course, which will give you the opportunity to experience a skid in controlled conditions. In a situation where split-second decision-making is crucial, the more confidence you have in your abilities the better.

Floods

After heavy rain, floods are most likely to occur in low-lying areas near rivers and lakes, and at dips in the road where the drainage is poor. But even on high ground you may turn a corner to find a torrential current of water washing across the road. Fords and places where a river floods its banks on a regular basis may have marked posts to indicate the depth of the water. Where no such depth gauge exists it can be difficult to estimate whether the flood can be negotiated safely by car. And at night it can be difficult to distinguish between a road surface that is merely wet and one that is flooded.

When you drive through a flooded part of the road there is a danger not only of aquaplaning but of damage to your vehicle. If the puddle is deep, water can be picked up by the cooling fan and sprayed over the engine, causing the electrical system to short circuit. You won't be able to restart the engine until the ignition has had a chance to dry out – but provided the car has been running long enough to get hot, the heat radiated by the engine should be sufficient to dry the electrical components in 15 minutes or so.

A more serious problem occurs when water is sucked into the engine through the air intake of the exhaust. Once water enters the cylinders it can cause a hydraulic lock which will wreck the pistons, con rods, and crankshaft, leaving you with a very expensive repair bill.

Wherever possible, you should avoid driving through deep water. You should know where flooding is likely to occur in your local region. When it has been raining heavily, plan a route that avoids these areas. This may increase the mileage, but it will prove quicker (and possibly cheaper) in the long run.

DRIVING THROUGH FLOOD WATER

When you see a large puddle or flood ahead, slow down. If part of the road is free of water, drive round the puddle – but don't swerve into the path of oncoming traffic or create a hazard to other vehicles. When you cannot drive round the water or turn back and take an alternative route, proceed as follows:

- If you are at all uncertain how deep the water is, stop the car in a safe place and try to gauge the depth. Where there are no depth-marker posts to help you, use adjacent trees, lampposts, fences or hedgerows to help you identify the shallowest point. Check for underwater obstructions such as branches or other debris.
- Watch another vehicle negotiating the flood. Keep well

away from the water until the other car has passed through. You don't want to get drenched by the spray or swamped by the bow wave, and if the other car were to stall mid-way through you wouldn't want to find yourself stranded in there too.

- Even if the other car makes it through safely, there's no guarantee that you will, too. The position of the air intake for the exhaust is lower on some cars than others. Check how high it is off the ground on your car and watch the other car to give you a reference as to how far the water comes up the wheels. If you can be sure that your air intake will be well clear of the water, proceed. If in doubt, find another route.
- Enter the flood using the shallowest route. Depending on the camber of the road, the water is usually deepest near the kerb and shallowest at the crown.
- Select first gear in a manual gearbox or use lock-up to maintain a low gear if you drive an automatic. Proceed slowly; slip the clutch so you can keep the revs up without picking up speed. This will stop the car from stalling and prevent water from entering the exhaust. Stay in the same gear throughout and don't let the revs die down.
- Keep your speed down. If you go fast you will create a wave. Where a solid object like a tree or wall stands in the path of a wave, it will send the water bouncing straight back at you.

Having made it through the water, test your brakes before picking up speed. When waterlogged, brakes will not function properly. Drum brakes, in particular, are useless when soaking wet.

TESTING YOUR BRAKES

Having checked your mirrors to make sure you won't endanger other traffic, drive slowly for 100 metres or so, keeping your right foot gently on the accelerator and depressing the brake lightly with your left foot. The friction will dry the brakes. (This is also a good practice before parking the vehicle as it dries out the drums and disks preventing water corrosion and rust.)

High Winds

Strong winds can drastically affect the handling of your vehicle. High-sided trucks and caravans are particularly unstable, veering sideways with no warning whatsoever, and for this reason they may be subject to diversion from routes featuring exposed bridges or stretches of motorway when the winds reach gale force. But small cars, too, can be blown off course, especially when emerging from a sheltered area where they have been screened against the effects of the wind and the driver has relaxed his or her hold on the steering wheel.

During a violent storm there is the risk of trees or advertising hoardings being brought down directly on top of vehicles or in the path of oncoming traffic. Even the gentler blustery breezes can reduce visibility. Dust storms frequently occur in farming areas during a hot summer, as the dry particles of top soil are picked up and carried on the wind. In more populated areas the major problem is litter: a sheet of newspaper can be swept across a windscreen by a sudden gust, totally obscuring the driver's vision. It can also block the cooling vents, causing the vehicle to overheat.

COPING WITH CROSSWINDS

Always be prepared for strong gusts of wind when travelling along exposed roads such as elevated sections of motorways or open dales, and when crossing viaducts or bridges. That means taking into consideration the effect the wind may have on larger vehicles, and on pedestrians, cyclists and motorcyclists – give them as much room as you can when overtaking in case the wind causes them to swerve.

When overtaking larger vehicles such as trucks or coaches, and when emerging from a cutting or underneath a bridge, keep a firm grip on the steering wheel using both hands in the 'quarter-to-three' position. Often you won't be aware that you've been compensating for the crosswind by applying a few degrees of steering lock until you pull into the lee of a high-sided vehicle or embankment, at which point the car starts to veer because the wind resistance has dropped. It's almost as though you're being sucked into the slipstream of the other vehicle. Then, when you emerge on the other side, the wind strikes again, forcing you out wide. Over-compensating can lead to loss of control, so don't let yourself be panicked into violently correcting your steering. Watch your speed, because the faster you're going, the more extreme the effects will be.

Debris can be scattered far and wide in high winds. With smaller objects like traffic cones it's better to run them over rather than swerving into the path of another vehicle. Large objects such as trees, fences, advertising hoardings, and other tall structures which get torn loose by the wind are more difficult to deal with. If a warning of gale-force winds has been broadcast on television or radio forecasts, the best plan by far

is to stay at home. If you must go out, choose a route where there are as few trees as possible. Falling branches do considerable damage when they strike a car or force it to swerve, and you will have little or no warning.

Overhead power cables are another hazard: if you come across a power line that has been blown down over a road, keep well away from it. Within the car you are insulated, but if you step outside of the car on to a wet road surface you could be electrocuted. Reverse back down the road to a safe point, stop oncoming traffic from proceeding into the danger area, and if you have a mobile phone call the emergency services. It will not be safe to proceed until the road has been cleared, so you should either wait or take another route.

RULES FOR BAD-WEATHER DRIVING

• Always check the weather forecast before setting out, particularly on a long journey or one which will take you through treacherous terrain.

• If the weather is really bad – gale-force winds, heavy snow, torrential rain, thick fog – don't go out unless there is absolutely no alternative. In addition to battling against the elements, you will have to contend with reckless or inexperienced drivers who have no idea how to cope with the conditions.

• If you have no alternative but to drive in bad weather, make sure that your vehicle is up to the journey. Take the time to run through the 'First Parade' or winter maintenance checks, paying particular attention to lights, windows, battery, tyres, oil, wipers and water. Carry vital spares and a survival kit in case of emergencies. If you live in a region where the winters are long and hard, consider investing in a four-wheel

drive vehicle or one with ABS. Snow chains may also prove useful.

• Make sure you are prepared for the arduous task ahead. Try to get some rest before and during the journey so that you can maintain the higher levels of concentration required. Take the safest route rather than the quickest one. Let someone know your route and estimated time of arrival.

• Adjust your driving to suit the conditions. Reduce your speed and maintain a gap between yourself and other vehicles which reflects the increased stopping distances. To reduce the risk of skidding, brake, accelerate and steer smoothly, and never speed up or apply the brakes on a bend.

• Practise the techniques for controlling a skid on a skid pan, so that you won't be gripped by panic if one should ever happen to you for real.

Each year, defective cars claim the lives of drivers, their families, and other road users. And even where there is no loss of life, broken-down vehicles are a source of grief, bringing traffic on our gridlocked roads to a standstill. Yet many of these accidents and break-downs – and the expensive repairs which follow – are avoidable. Regular maintenance is the key to running a car that is safe, reliable and legal.

5

maintenance

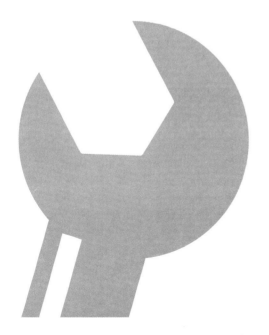

ROUTINE MAINTENANCE Your car • Vehicle components •Service intervals

FIRST PARADE

WEEKLY SERVICE Tool kit • Exterior checks • Engine compartment checks • Winter maintenance

KEEPING IT CLEAN Automatic car washes • Manual car wash • Chips and scratches • Waxing • Rust prevention

PERIODIC MAINTENANCE Choosing a garage • DIY servicing • Preparing for the MOT

FAULT FINDING Diagnosing faults

routine maintenance

Running a car is expensive, and sometimes keeping up a regular servicing schedule may seem like a luxury you just can't afford. But scrimping on maintenance is a false economy: sooner or later the vehicle will let you down, costing you a fortune in repairs – and in fines, if you should be prosecuted for failing to maintain government-imposed safety standards. The car will decrease in value more rapidly than if it were cared for, it will burn more fuel, and emit more pollutant gases. Tests have shown that poorly maintained vehicles account for 50% of the pollutant gases in the atmosphere.

If you want to save money, the most effective way is to learn the basics of car maintenance and put them into practice by checking your vehicle over for potential faults on a regular basis. That way you will reduce running costs and ensure that minor problems are dealt with before they get too serious or expensive to put right. Even if you prefer to let a garage carry out any necessary repairs or major services, a knowledge of what the job involves – and the ability to check whether it has been done – will prevent you from being ripped off by unscrupulous mechanics.

Take care of your car and it will provide reliable, economical transportation for years to come. Neglect it and you're taking the fast lane to the breaker's yard, risking prosecution and injury along the way.

Your Car

VEHICLE COMPONENTS

Detailed mechanical knowledge is not required to carry out general maintenance checks, but it will help if you have some grasp of how the essential components of a car function.

The chassis

This is the frame that gives the vehicle rigidity. Because it holds the engine and provides a mounting for the suspension and steering, it is important that the chassis retains its shape and is not weakened by damage. Any accident that distorts the chassis will affect the handling of the vehicle.

The engine

The engine's main functions are:

- Lubrication - oil is forced at high pressure through a system of pipes and hoses to lubricate moving parts and prevent them overheating.
- Fuel – the fuel system pumps a mixture of fuel (be it petrol or diesel) and air through a series of fuel lines to the engine's cylinders.
- Ignition – the ignition system ignites the fuel-and-air in the combustion chamber (see Ignition system below)
- Cooling – the cooling system removes excess heat from the engine
- Exhaust – the exhaust system expels used fuel

The capacity of the engine is expressed in litres; the higher the capacity the more powerful the car. Most cars have four-cylinder engines. The fuel-and-air mix is sucked into the cylinders through a system of valves. Once inside, the burning gases expand and contract, forcing the pistons up and down. The crankshaft translates this up and down motion into a rotary motion which turns the wheels.

To prevent the engine overheating, coolant fluid is pumped through a series of channels around the engine. The cooling system is driven by a fan belt, which also operates the radiator fan.

Ignition system

The battery emits a low voltage charge which is then transformed by the coil into a high voltage which is transmitted to the distributor. As the pistons drive the engine, the rotor arm revolves inside the distributor, bringing about a sequence of contacts with the spark plugs. When the high-voltage spark jumps across the spark plugs it ignites the fuel-and-air mixture. It is possible to immobilize the vehicle by removing the rotor arm.

Once the engine is running, it generates its own power and thus recharges the battery.

Transmission system

The transmission connects the engine to the wheels via the clutch (in non-automatic cars) and gearbox. The purpose of the clutch is to provide a means of temporarily disconnecting the transmission from the engine so that it's possible to leave the engine idling; it also permits the gradual application of engine power and assists in gear changing. In automatic cars there is no clutch pedal; instead, the clutch is an integral part of the gearbox.

The gearbox allows you to adjust the engine's power to match your road speed. Most cars have four or five forward gears and a reverse gear; some four-wheel drive vehicles have a double gearbox with eight to ten gears to cope with off-road driving.

The final part of the transmission system is known as the differential. This allows two wheels on the same axle to turn at different speeds: for example, when you go round a corner the inner wheel has less ground to cover and therefore rotates more slowly than the outer wheel. The majority of cars are front-wheel drive, but some larger cars are driven by the rear wheels while the front wheels are used for steering. Off-road vehicles have four-wheel drive for maximum grip on uneven surfaces.

The gearbox is connected to the differential via the propeller shaft (prop shaft). To allow for movement in the rear suspension, the prop shaft is fitted with universal joints.

Suspension

The suspension isolates the vehicle from road shocks. It helps keep the vehicle on the road and prevents pitching and rolling when travelling over uneven surfaces.

Braking system

When the brake pedal is pressed it forces the brake fluid through a hydraulic system which applies pressure to push the brake pad on to the metal disc or drum that rotates with each of the four wheels. Drum brakes are shielded against dirt and spray, but if the vehicle is driven through deep water the linings will get soaked. Disc brakes are less affected by water.

The handbrake, which prevents the car moving when parked, operates on two wheels only.

SERVICE INTERVALS

Some components are subject to more wear and tear than others, and should therefore be inspected on a regular basis. The tyres, lights, and windscreen wipers, for example, need to be replaced from time to time. Fluids such as engine oil, coolant, brake fluid and battery electrolyte need to be kept at optimum levels if the car is to function properly. For safety's sake, it is recommended that routine maintenance on these items should be carried out every week. The checks are very simple to carry out and shouldn't take very long, so this minor service is one you can do yourself.

Other items (such as filters, engine oil and spark plugs) get less efficient with age, and manufacturers recommend that they are replaced after a certain period. Safety-related equipment such as the braking system needs a thorough overhaul from time to time. Work of this nature may require specialized equipment and skills, and is therefore best left to the professionals. A major service can comprise as many as sixty different checks and routine replacements – a good garage will provide you with an itemized list showing exactly what has been done.

If you buy new, your car will come with a warranty of between one and three years, which specifies the service intervals, what work is required, and, in many cases, where

maintenance

the work must be carried out. For the duration of the warranty you should obey its terms. If it is specified that the car should be serviced by a franchised dealer, don't try to save money by servicing the car yourself or taking it to an independent garage; and don't over-run the service schedules, even by a few hundred kilometres – you run the risk of having the warranty declared null and void if something does go wrong.

Don't leave it until the day before the warranty expires to take the car in for a major service. Allow a month's leeway, so that if the labour proves unsatisfactory or any replacement parts fail to bed in properly, you still have the safety net of the warranty. The same advice applies if you are taking the car abroad or on a long journey; have it serviced weeks rather than days in advance of the trip.

Most manufacturers' recommended service intervals fall somewhere between every 5,000–12,000 miles. However, the age of the vehicle, the use it is put to and its performance may dictate that servicing be carried out at more frequent intervals. Older cars – especially those which have been neglected in the past – will need more frequent servicing, as will vehicles used mainly for short journeys; in exceptionally dusty or humid conditions; in mountainous regions; in severe cold weather; on rough and/or muddy roads; or to tow trailers. Poor driving habits such as leaving the engine idling too often or excessive braking will also necessitate more frequent services. Regular DIY maintenance checks, on the other hand, can result in longer service intervals and fewer replacement parts being required.

First Parade

There is no such thing as a maintenance-free car. Even though manufacturers are designing new cars with longer and longer service intervals, some day-to-day maintenance is still required to keep the car in good condition. It is your legal responsibility as a vehicle owner to ensure that your car is roadworthy.

A good habit to adopt is that of carrying out a series of simple checks the first time the car is used each day. In the

military this was called first parade. The procedure only takes a few minutes and could save you a lot of inconvenience and expense.

- As you approach the vehicle look for signs of coolant, oil, fuel or other leaks. If you see an unusual pool under the car, it may mean that something is leaking. Green or yellow fluids suggest a radiator leak. Red could be hydraulic fluid. Clear liquid might be water or petrol – your sense of smell will tell you which. Oil is dark and sticky. Check the relevant fluid levels. It can be difficult to identify the source of the leak; if it looks to be a serious leak or if you suspect even a slight brake fluid or petrol leak, don't drive the car until the problem has been investigated by someone suitably qualified.
- Check the tyres for signs of excessive wear or damage. Clean off any patches of oil or grease using water and a little mild detergent. Remove any embedded debris, such as small stones or broken glass, using a screwdriver. Do not try to remove larger items, such as nails, which have penetrated the surface as the tyre may deflate. Leave them in the tread (to identify the location of the damage) and remove the tyre for repair. (See *Changing a Wheel* in **Emergency!**).
- Make sure that the windscreen, windows, mirrors, lights, reflectors and number plates are all clean and clear. It is against the law to drive with any of these obscured.
- Check that the seat belts are in working order: that they are securely anchored, that the buckles function, and that the webbing is not frayed.
- When you start the car, keep an eye on the warning lights on the dashboard. These vary from car to car, so study the handbook and identify what each one means. The warning lights should all come on briefly when you turn the igni-

> **REMEMBER**
> A full service history (or, in the case of a used car, a continuous record from the time you bought it), will help to determine the price you get for your car when you come to sell or trade it in. A vehicle with a service history is always worth more than one without.

tion key. If any light fails to come on, it may indicate a burned out bulb or a fault in the electrical system. Should one of the lights come on when the engine is running, do not ignore it. Never assume that the light itself must be faulty – check that the relevant part of the system is operating correctly.

The daily maintenance checks don't end when you leave your garage. As you drive, get into the habit of paying attention to the sounds and smells made by the engine – any unusual noises, vibrations or odours could be your first indication of a fault. For example, a regular clicking noise as you drive might be caused by a nail stuck in the tread of one of your tyres. Should that nail work itself loose at high speed, it could make the tyre explode, causing you to lose control of your car.

Keep an eye on the dashboard gauges, especially the temperature gauge. This warns you if the water level in the radiator has fallen, or the system has sprung a leak, and the engine is overheating. Driving the car in this condition will seriously damage the engine.

Weekly Services

Set aside time once a week (or, failing that, every 500 miles) to run through the following maintenance routine. The best time to do the work is in the morning, after the car has been parked overnight. That way you can be sure that the engine will be cold and there will be no risk of burns and scalds.

If DIY maintenance is to save rather than cost you money, you have to know what you're doing. So, when carrying out general maintenance checks, there is one vital piece of equipment you should not be without: a manufacturer's handbook. If you bought your car secondhand and were not supplied with a handbook, purchase a workshop manual from a spares supplier or car accessory shop. For older or more unusual cars, you may have to scour secondhand bookshops and car boot sales. Alternatively, check the small ads in one of the many vintage car magazines – virtually every make and model has its own enthusiasts' club which will help you track down service manuals and parts suppliers for your car.

WARNING LIGHTS

This light warns that the oil pressure is low. Stop the car as soon as possible. Check the oil with the dipstick after the car has been standing on a level surface for a few minutes, and if necessary top up the engine oil (for instructions, see Weekly Service below). If the light is still illuminated when you restart the engine, stop the engine immediately. Running the car when the oil pressure warning light is on could seriously damage the engine.

If the warning light flickers on and off as you drive, it probably means that the oil level is low. What little oil remains in the sump is sloshing from one side to the other, causing the warning light to operate.

This light warns that the brake fluid level is low. The handbook will show you where the brake fluid reservoir is located, and how to check the level. If the level is below the minimum mark, do not drive the car. If the light comes on while you are driving, it may mean that one of the brake circuits

has failed, leaving you with inadequate braking. Find somewhere safe to stop – leaving plenty of space between you and any other vehicles, because it will take you longer to come to a halt. Do not drive the car until the fault has been rectified.

Always check that this light comes on when you switch on the electrical circuits. It should go off as soon as you start the engine. If the light remains on while the engine is running, it means that the battery is not charging. Turn the engine off and look for the source of the problem – the most likely culprits are loose electrical wires or connections, or the fan belt could be loose or broken.

Fuel is running low. Find a service station as soon as possible.

The tasks involved are all relatively easy and require no specialist skills, but read the safety guidelines set out on the facing page before undertaking any inspection or maintenance work. The manufacturer's handbook for your vehicle will feature diagrams showing the engine layout, and these will enable you to identify and locate the various parts and components.

TOOL KIT

The items listed here will enable you to tackle a range of maintenance projects. Before you invest in a set of tools, check the manufacturer's handbook or a workshop manual to find out whether you need metric or AF sizes.

1   spanners
2   pliers
3   screwdrivers (one flat head and one for cross-head or Phillips type screws)
4   oil filter wrench
5   oil can
6   oil funnel
7   containers for draining engine oil and coolant
8   tyre pressure gauge
9   tyre tread depth gauge
10   electric test lamp
11   handyman knife
12   ball-pein hammer
13   wire brush
14   tool box
15   clean rags
16   coolant solution
17   screenwash
18   distilled water - for batteries which require topping-up

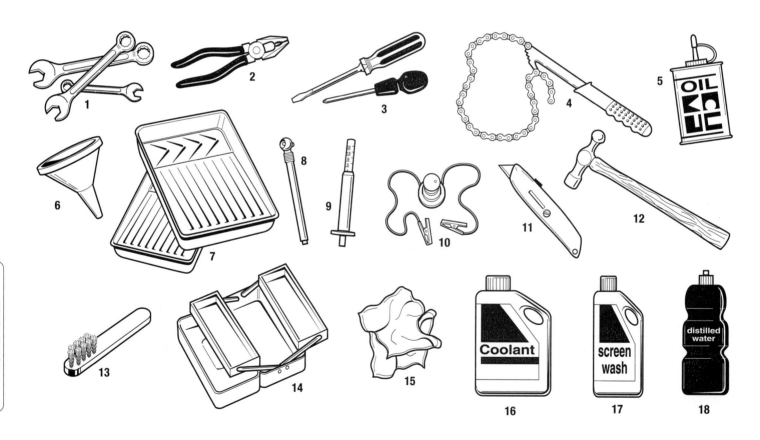

SAFETY FIRST

To prevent injury to yourself or damage to the vehicle, the following precautions should always be observed:

DON'T rush. Be methodical. Make sure everything is correctly assembled and tightened. Take a break when you feel yourself getting tired or else your concentration will suffer.

ALWAYS keep loose clothing and long hair well out of the way of any moving parts. Many cars have electric engine fans that switch on automatically, even when the engine has been turned off. If your tie or hair got caught in the fan it could prove fatal.

REMOVE jewellery – rings, watches, etc – before working on a vehicle. Metal jewellery can cause injury if it touches a high-voltage part of the engine such as the battery.

DO use a barrier cream on your hands to protect against infection or damage to skin, and to make the grime easier to remove afterwards; but make sure your hands are not left slippery. Long term or regular contact with used oils and fuel can be a health hazard.

DON'T SMOKE. Keep naked flame and sparks away from fuel and the battery.

DON'T wear oil-soaked clothing or keep oily rags in your pockets.

ALWAYS keep a fire extinguisher of a type suitable for liquid fires in the garage. Extinguishers are colour coded; blue (dry powder), black (carbon dioxide), and green (halon) are best for dealing with burning fuel. Direct the extinguisher at the base of the fire to put out the flames. Never try to extinguish a fuel or electrical fire with water.

ALWAYS keep your work area tidy. Wipe up spilt oil or grease before someone slips on it, and don't leave things lying around where people can trip over them.

NEVER allow children and animals into the work area. Keep them away from unattended cars.

ALWAYS park the vehicle on a level surface, apply the hand brake securely and chock the wheels to stop the vehicle from moving. The transmission control lever should be in neutral (or 'park' for automatics).

ALWAYS park cars with catalytic converters away from materials which catch fire easily, such as dry grass, oily rags, etc.

NEVER touch any part of the engine, exhaust or catalytic converter while it is hot. Turn off the engine and wait until it cools down.

NEVER work underneath a vehicle which is supported only by a jack. A number of deaths have resulted from cars slipping off jacks, or piles of bricks disintegrating under the strain. Use axle stands or ramps with a load-rating sufficient for the job. Make sure you locate the supports in such a way that the car won't collapse and where they can't slip.

NEVER attempt to tighten or loosen tough nuts while the vehicle is on a jack; it may slip and fall off. Try to loosen wheel nuts and other tight fastenings before the vehicle is raised off the ground.

ALWAYS get help when lifting very heavy items – don't risk injury by trying to do it alone.

NEVER connect or disconnect the battery while the ignition is on.

NEVER touch any part of the ignition system when it is switched on. If the insulation is worn or the components are damp or dirty, the resulting electrical shock could be severe enough to kill you.

NEVER use electrical equipment in damp conditions or while standing on wet ground. Make sure that electrical appliances which run on mains electricity are properly wired and, if necessary, earthed. It is also advisable to use a circuit breaker.

DON'T allow brake fluid or antifreeze to come in contact with the car's paintwork as it may damage the finish (or remove the paint altogether).

NEVER siphon toxic liquids such as fuel, brake fluid or antifreeze by mouth, and avoid contact with the skin or eyes.

NEVER run the engine in an enclosed space, and especially not over an inspection pit. Carbon monoxide, which is present in exhaust fumes, is a killer. Even cars fitted with catalytic converters can give off this toxic gas. Move the car into the open, or at least make sure the rear end is pointing outside the workplace.

ALWAYS get someone to check on you from time to time when working alone on the vehicle, just to make sure that all is well.

In the event of an accident, seek medical attention as soon as possible.

maintenance

GARAGE HAZARDS

FIRE
Petrol is extremely volatile. If vapour is allowed to build up, the slightest spark can cause it to ignite. If you smell strong petrol fumes – petrol vapour is heavy and will be densest near the floor or in an inspection pit – DON'T SMOKE or allow any kind of naked flame in the area. Stop work on the car: careless use of tools could lead to sparks. Don't turn electric lights on or off – it could cause a spark. Get everyone out and ventilate the area immediately.

TOXIC FUMES
In addition to being highly inflammable, petrol vapour and the fumes given off by various solvent-based glues and paint strippers are highly toxic. Inhalation can result in unconsciousness, damage to the lungs, pneumonia-like disorders, and even death. Always follow the manufacturer's instructions when using toxic products and make sure the garage or workshop is well ventilated. Never use cleaning solvents or adhesives from unmarked containers.

If you are affected by fumes, get to fresh air immediately. Loosen restrictive clothing. It is advisable to seek medical attention even if the dizziness wears off.

Spanners
It's possible to get by with only an adjustable spanner, but you would do better to invest in a set of spanners. Should an ill-fitting spanner slip, it could end up injuring you and damaging the car.

Open-ended spanners can tackle most nuts and bolts, but you'll get a more positive grip using a socket spanner. Sockets can be bought with useful extras like extension bars (to reach into recesses) ratchet handles and plug sockets, but never improvise an extension to the handle of a spanner not designed for this purpose. Combination spanners (socket one end, open-ended the other) give the advantages of both types. Assemble a set to cover a reasonable range of sizes (say 7 mm to 17 mm).

An adjustable spanner does come in handy when you need a duplicate size – to hold a bolt while turning a nut, for example. A self-grip wrench will lock on to a nut or bolt,

leaving your hands free for other tasks.

Buy the best you can afford: spanners made of poor-quality metal have a tendency to snap. Nickel-coated versions should last a lifetime.

Pliers
Standard combination or 'engineers' pliers will cope with most gripping and holding jobs, while long-nosed pliers come in useful for fiddly work. Buy a pair with cutting edges for stripping cable insulation.

Screwdrivers
A set of cross-point and straight-blade screwdrivers in assorted sizes will enable you to deal with the variety of screw sizes on every car. Those with rubber-coated handles are the safest, just in case you accidentally touch a high-voltage electric lead.

Oil-change equipment
To change your engine oil yourself you will need an oil filter wrench, a funnel, and a container large enough to drain the oil into.

Tyre pressure gauge
Most car accessory shops stock a variety of pressure gauges displaying readings in a number of different ways. Choose the display you find simplest to read.

Electric test lamp
Using a test lamp with a 12-volt test bulb or LED display inside a probe handle will reduce the risk of damage both to you and to the car's sensitive electronic circuitry. Simply connect the crocodile clip to clean body metal and touch the probe on the electrical terminal that you want to test. If the bulb lights, the terminal is live.

Ball-pein hammer
A 1 lb ball-pein engineering hammer, or one that has interchangeable heads for various types of work, is ideal.

Wire brush
For removing rust, dirt or flaky paint from the underbody.

Specialist tools

If you're planning to undertake more ambitious projects, you will need to invest in a good trolley jack, preferably one with a fail-safe locking device in the event of hydraulic failure. The jack supplied with the car is suitable only for roadside wheel changes. You should NEVER work beneath a car supported only by a jack. To support the car safely and securely you will need axle stands or wheel ramps. An inspection lamp which operates from the car battery will allow you to see what you're doing.

A purpose-made spanner for unscrewing spark plugs may come in handy, but make sure you buy the right size (check the handbook or workshop manual). Get one with a rubber insert, to prevent damage to the insulating porcelain, and a short handle to guard against over tightening. If the fit is too tight you could snap a plug – and there's nothing worse than trying to get a damaged plug out of the engine block.

Tool care

Having invested in a set of tools, take the trouble to look after them. After work, clean spanners by wiping them with a clean dry cloth to get rid of grease and dirt. Non-stainless tools, except files, may be wiped with an oily cloth from time to time, to prevent them from going rusty.

Never leave tools lying around. Store them safely, out of the reach of children. A tool box is the ideal way to keep everything together.

EXTERIOR CHECKS

Tyres

The condition of the tyres will affect the steering and general handling of the car, so careful checking is vital. Don't forget to check the spare – you could need it in an emergency.

First make sure that the tyres are properly inflated by using a pressure gauge (the handbook will tell you the recommended pressure for your front and rear tyres according to use, load, type and size of tyre fitted). For the reading to be accurate, the tyres must be cold. Tyres that have just completed a long journey or that have been standing in the hot sun – especially if one side of the car has been in sun and the other in shadow – will register a higher pressure than the handbook specifies.

- Unscrew the dust cap from the valve on the tyre.
- Press the gauge firmly on to the valve and read the pressure.
- Use a tyre pump to inflate any under-inflated tyres to the manufacturer's recommended pressure. If you don't have a tyre pump at home, use a pump at a service station as short a distance as possible from your home. Driving heats the tyres up, so let the tyres cool before testing for pressure.
- When you have finished checking and inflating, replace each dust cap otherwise dirt and snow can deflate the tyre.

NEVER over-inflate your car's tyres. Too much pressure gives a bumpy ride and light steering, reduces the car's grip on the road (because there is less tread in contact with the road), and can cause the tyres to explode at high speed or when cornering.

Under-inflated tyres can be equally dangerous: the steering will feel heavy, the tyre walls will flex too much and overheat – making them less stable on bends and at high speeds, and you will use more fuel to compensate for the increased rolling resistance.

Both over- and under-inflation will reduce a tyre's life. A correctly inflated tyre will last 26 per cent longer than one which is 20 per cent below the recommended pressure.

A tyre that loses more than 0.28 kg per sq. cm of pressure each week is defective. Have a tyre specialist investigate the cause.

Once the tyres have been properly inflated, run your fingers around the edge of each one to check for cuts and bulges in the sidewalls. Bulges are usually the result of knocking the wheels against the kerb when parking. This distorts the steel wires inside radial tyres, destroying the tyre's rigidity and strength.

Once a month (or every 1500 miles) you should also check the tread using a tread depth gauge to make sure it complies with the legal minimum. This varies from country to country – if you plan to take your car abroad, check out the regulations for places you plan to visit. UK law requires all tyres - including the spare - to have a tread depth of at least 1.6 mm throughout a continuous band comprising the central three-quarters of the width of the tyre tread, around the full circumference of the tyre. New tyres have a depth of about 7 mm. On wet and icy roads, the difference between the grip of a new tyre and that of one which just manages to satisfy the legal minimum could mean the difference between life and death.

Tyres fall into two categories: cross-ply and radial-ply. Modern cars tend to be fitted with radial-ply, which are longer lasting and more flexible than cross-ply tyres, and give a better grip – especially when cornering. It's best to have the same type of tyre on all four wheels so that the braking and cornering characteristics are uniform throughout. In Britain it is against the law to fit radial- and cross-ply on the same axle, or to have radials on the front and cross-ply on the rear.

Don't let the fact that tyres are expensive dissuade you from replacing any excessively worn or damaged tyres as soon as possible. Remember – driving on four worn tyres could cost you your driving licence.

Spare Wheel

Don't leave it until you have a roadside puncture to discover that you can't undo the wheel nuts. Have at least one practice session to make sure that you can get the spare out and fit it using the tools provided. Whenever you have a new tyre fitted, make sure you can loosen the wheel nuts – it may help to spray them with a penetrating lubricant. Retighten them securely afterwards.

Lights

It is illegal to drive with defective lights. Switch on all the lights in turn and check that they're working. Make sure your checks include all the following:

PATTERNS OF WEAR

Excessive and uneven tyre wear can be caused by faults in the braking system, the suspension, poor wheel alignment, under- and over-inflation of the tyres:

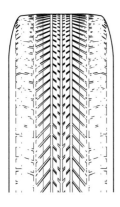 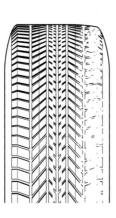 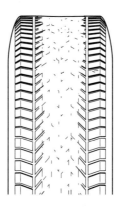 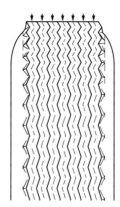 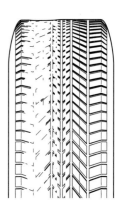

Wear on both sides: the tyre is under-inflated.

Wear on one side: damage caused by hard cornering or incorrect wheel camber.

Wear down the middle: the tyre is over-inflated.

Feathered edge: poor wheel alignment.

Uneven wear: due to poor wheel alignment, malfunctioning suspension, incorrect camber, disc/drum in need of renewing.

Where poor alignment or balancing of the wheels is at fault, you should consult a tyre agent or dealer. While rarely dangerous, this will wear the tyres very quickly.

- headlights
- tail lights
- indicator lights
- number plate lights
- reversing lights
- brake lights
- fog lights

Brake lights pose something of a problem because they will work only when the brake pedal is depressed. If you have no one to help you by operating the pedal while you watch from behind the car, check your rear lights are working by looking for the reflection in a window or glass door. Failing that, try backing up close to a wall at night. When you brake, look in your mirrors to see if both red lamps are lighting up the wall. You can also use this method to see if your rear fog lights and the direction indicators, are working.

• Buy from a tyre specialist rather than an ordinary garage. Price wars between quick fit companies can result in savings for you.

• Buy retread or remould tyres. These are used tyres which have had their outer layers replaced. Technology has improved standards to such a degree that most aircraft tyres are now retreads. Choose a reputable brand which conforms to industry safety standards and carries a speed rating on the sidewall.

• NEVER buy part-worn (secondhand) tyres. Although they may have enough tread to be legal, they may have sustained internal damage that you won't find out about until the tyre explodes at high speed.

• Make your tyres last longer: tyres wear out twice as fast at 70 mph (112 kph) as they do at 35 mph (56 kph).

• Have a specialist tyre fitter swap the wheels at the front (which suffer more wear and tear) for those at the back. Rotating your tyres in this way ensures you get the maximum life out of all four tyres.

Check that the direction indicators work with the brake lights on and that the brake lights work with the tail lights on. Some faults may cause the various rear lights to interact, with possible dangerous consequences for other drivers behind you.

If a bulb is not functioning, check first for corrosion on the bulb holder and connections. Fitments and means of access vary between different models of cars, but replacing a bulb is an easy task – it's simply a matter of removing the cover with a screwdriver or by undoing the spring release, and installing the new bulb. Do not leave the bulb out of the headlight reflector for any length of time as dust, moisture and smoke may enter the headlight body and reduce its performance.

REMEMBER

Never touch a halogen bulb with your fingers – even the tiniest amount of grease from your skin will shorten the bulb's life. Wrap the bulb in tissue paper before handling it. (If your fingers do come in contact with the bulb, clean it with a tissue dipped in methylated spirit.)

Consult the handbook for precise details of what bulb to buy and how to go about fitting it. Most manufacturers now supply bulb-and-fuse sets in plastic kits for emergencies. Always make sure the new bulb has the same wattage as the old:

Headlights, main and dipped	60/55W
Front direction indicator lights	5W
Side direction indicator lights	5W
Rear direction indicator lights	5W
Brake lights	21W
Tail lights	5W
Front fog lights	55W
Rear fog lights	21W
Reverse lights	21W
Number plate light	5W
Interior light	10W
Luggage compartment light	5W

Having made sure that the bulbs are functioning, clean all the lamp lenses. Up to 50% of light can be lost if the glass is dirty.

maintenance

Hinges and latches
Check that all door, bonnet and hatchback hinges operate properly and that all latches lock securely. Smear a little grease on door catches and lubricate all hinges.

It may be necessary from time to time to lubricate locks by putting a spot of oil on the key, inserting it into the lock and turning it. Do this several times.

Windscreen wipers
Examine both front and rear wiper blades for tears or signs of wear. Clean the blade by wiping it with a cloth soaked in an alcohol based cleaning solution or methylated spirit, then rinse with clear water. If the blade needs to be replaced, either check the handbook for the specifications or measure the length. It's best to measure both blades (i.e. the driver's and passenger's sides) as on some cars they are different lengths. Replacement blades come with fitting instructions on the pack. They can be tricky to fit – sometimes a drop of washing-up liquid in water will help them to slide in.

Windscreen washers
If the windscreen washer isn't squirting out as it should, try using a pin to clear any blockages in the washer jet, or to redirect the spray. Aim them fairly high on the windscreen, because when the car is moving the airflow will usually deflect the spray down.

Horn
Check that the horn is working. A short toot should be enough to prove that it works but it's a good idea – when you find yourself in unpopulated surroundings - to check its operation over a few seconds.

ENGINE COMPARTMENT CHECKS

Engine oil level
Engine oil is the lifeblood of your vehicle, so make sure you put some thought into what you buy. There are a wide variety of oils on the market, all graded by their viscosity (thickness) at various temperatures. The small print on the label will tell you how the oil performs in cold and hot cli-

mates. Always refer to the handbook for guidelines on which oil to buy. It's not necessary to buy the brand recommended – but you must get the right grade. Using a thicker-than-recommended oil can cause sludge to build up, reducing the engine's performance; oil that is too thin will lead to premature wear on the engine.

To check the oil level, park the car on level ground – if you're parked on a slope, you'll get a false reading – and leave it standing for a while so that the oil can drain back into the sump. Your handbook will tell you where to locate the dipstick (if not, look for a 'ring pull' stick emerging from a tube or whole at the side of the engine). Remove the dipstick and wipe it clean on a piece of lint-free cloth. Re-insert it fully, then withdraw again. The oil level should be visible between the maximum and minimum marks.

Droplets of water on the dipstick are a sign of water getting into the oil. This is usually the result of a worn engine head gasket, which can eventually cause more serious engine problems.

If the oil level is low, remove the oil filler cap and top up, a little at a time. Use a clean, grit-free funnel for this to avoid any spillage. Wrap a cloth around the filler hole to soak up any spills, and always wipe around the engine afterwards.

Do not overfill – too much oil can lead to burnt-out valves and spark plugs, gasket and oil-seal failures.

If the oil needs to be topped-up regularly, check for leaks and, if necessary, seek expert advice.

 NEVER pour engine oil down the drain or bury it in the ground – you will be breaking the law. The used oil from one car can cover an area of water the size of two football pitches. If it seeps underground or via a drain into a river or stream it will endanger fish, birds and other river life. Pour the discarded oil into an empty can and take it to an oil recycling bank – contact your local council for details of disposal sites in your area. Remember that oil containers, filters and oily rags should also be disposed of at an approved site.

Coolant level
Some modern cars have sealed systems, which means that you do not need to top up the radiator. Instead you should

CHANGING THE ENGINE AND OIL FILTER

You will need the following items:

- the correct grade and quantity of engine oil for your car (see the manufacturer's handbook)
- oil filter wrench
- clean, lint-free rags
- a container large enough to hold the drained oil but shallow enough to fit under the car (a large washing-up bowl will do)
- a new washer for the drain plug

Warm up the engine by taking the car for a short drive, then switch the engine off. Place the empty container in position under the engine. Remove the oil filler cap from the top of the engine to allow the oil to drain faster. Now undo the drain plug. Don't worry if the drain plug falls into the bowl – you can retrieve it later. It will need to be cleaned up in any case and the washer will probably need replacing.

While the oil is draining you can set about replacing the filter. Most new cars are fitted with all-in-one canister filters which you unscrew (by hand, if you can, or using the oil filter wrench if it's difficult to

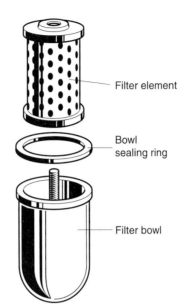

Filter element

Bowl sealing ring

Filter bowl

Older cars have a bowl-type filter. Unscrew the fixing bolt, lift the bowl away and gently tip out the contents into a suitable container. Note how any springs and washers are arranged and make sure they go back in the same order. Discard the old filter element and rinse the bowl with paraffin. Dry the bowl inside and out with a clean lint-free cloth and insert the new element. Remove the old rubber sealing ring from its groove in the filter head on the engine. Clean and dry the filter head and insert the new sealing ring. Position the bowl against the sealing ring and hold it in place while you hand-tighten the bolt.

budge); once the filter is removed, clean the mount, apply a little oil to the seal of the new canister and screw in by hand.

By the time the new filter is in place, the oil should have finished draining. Wipe clean the drain plug hole and replace the plug securely. Slowly pour in the fresh oil until it reaches the correct level – use the dipstick to check. Wipe away any spillages and then run the engine for a few moments to check for leaks from the drain plug and new filter. Switch off the engine and allow time for the oil to settle before using the dipstick to recheck the level.

have the system checked annually by the dealer. VW Beetles and Citroën 2CVs have air-cooled systems, so their owners can skip this section. For the majority of cars, however, a weekly check on the coolant level is a must.

It is best to check the coolant level at the start of the day, before the engine has been run.

Modern cars have a coolant reservoir tank showing minimum and maximum levels; in older cars the coolant level should be just below the radiator filler neck. Rock the car gently when checking the water level, just in case there's an air-lock in the system. This can happen if the car has been standing for some time in hot weather.

If there is insufficient coolant in the radiator, top up with the water/antifreeze mix recommended in the manufacturer's handbook. When replacing the cap, make sure that it is tightened down fully, not just to the first stop.

A system which requires frequent top-ups has probably sprung a leak from the radiator or one of the various hoses. Look for softening caused by oil spills, splits in the hoses, or loose clips. If no leaks can be found, it's possible that there's

maintenance

an internal fault in the engine, such as a crack in the cylinder head or a blown cylinder head gasket. Seek specialist advice.

Dirty brown water in the radiator indicates corrosion in the cooling system. Have the system drained and then refill with fresh water/anti-freeze mix to prevent further corrosion.

Whatever the time of year, don't just top up with water – you will dilute the coolant solution, which could result in corrosion damage, or a frozen engine come the winter. Always check the label before buying anti-freeze: some cheaper brands are highly flammable – if your engine gets too hot in the summer the anti-freeze may ignite and set fire to the engine.

WARNING

 Antifreeze and brake fluid contain dangerous chemicals. Take precautions to prevent contact with the skin or eyes. If this should happen, rinse the skin for several minutes until all traces are removed. If the area of skin affected is large or becomes sore or a rash develops, seek medical attention. The eyes should be irrigated under running water (preferably at blood temperature) for 20 minutes. Then hold a soft cotton pad gently over the affected eye and seek medical attention.

Unfortunately, being a bright colour and sweet-tasting, antifreeze is attractive to children – and deadly. If swallowed, it can damage the kidneys, brain and heart. DO NOT induce vomiting. Keep the casualty calm and seek urgent medical attention.

Prevention being better than cure, keep antifreeze, brake fluid, and other dangerous chemicals locked away where they can't pose a hazard.

Screenwash

The handbook will tell you where the reservoir is located. If your car has a rear wash-wipe or headlight washer system, there may be separate reservoirs for these. Remove the reservoir cap and top-up as required, leaving an air space of about 25 mm below the filler neck. Car accessory shops stock screenwash additives which assist in removing mud and flies, and keep the glass free from smears. In winter, add a specially formulated screenwash anti-freeze solution. NEVER use coolant anti-freeze as this will damage the washer system and paintwork.

Clutch fluid level

Cars with a hydraulic clutch may need topping up occasionally using the manufacturer's recommended fluid. Check the reservoir regularly, though you should seldom need to add fluid. If the level repeatedly falls below the mark you have a leak in the system. Have the car checked out by an expert.

Brake fluid level

Check the fluid level in the reservoir. Modern cars have minimum and maximum markings to guide you, on older cars the filler should come up to the bottom of the filler neck. NEVER top-up the system using brake fluid which has been stored in an opened container – moisture from the air can damage the system. When you have finished, wipe the cap clean before you replace it: dirt in the system can cause brake failure.

Brake fluid is toxic (see Warning panel for advice on what to do in the event of an accident). Always handle containers with care and follow the manufacturer's instructions. Keep out of the reach of children.

A sound brake circuit will rarely need topping-up. As the brake pads become worn you can expect the fluid level will fall slightly, but if it frequently drops below the minimum level there must be a leak in the system. Do not drive the car until it has been thoroughly examined by a qualified mechanic. Never take risks where brakes are concerned.

Battery

Batteries contain acid and give off a highly explosive gas. Read the safety guidelines below and make sure you follow them carefully.

Make sure the battery connections are secure and free of corrosion. Remove any corrosion with soapy water and then smear the terminals with petroleum jelly before tightening the leads. Check that the earth lead or strap is in good condition and secure, and that the clamp is holding the battery firmly in position so it doesn't rattle the whole time you're on the move.

New cars tend to be fitted with batteries which are 'sealed

SAFETY FIRST

NEVER expose a battery to naked flame or electrical sparks. DON'T smoke. If working in the dark, DON'T use a match or a lighter to see what you're doing. DON'T allow a metal tool to touch the battery terminals or connecting straps as this will short the battery and cause sparks.

NEVER disconnect the battery while the cell caps are removed. Sparking could occur.

ALWAYS check the manufacturer's warnings on the label before charging or attempting to jump start the battery. Batteries which are sealed for life require special precautions.

TAKE CARE when using a battery charger. Disconnect both battery leads before connecting the charger. Switch off the power supply before the charger leads are connected or disconnected. Allow plenty of time for recharging and opt for a low-rate trickle charge. DON'T top up with water immediately after recharging – wait at least 30 minutes or else the corrosive liquid may overflow.

NEVER allow battery fluid to come in contact with your skin, eyes or clothes. The corrosive chemical inside the battery will burn. Deposits around the terminals may also be harmful.

ALWAYS wear gloves and eye protection when handling or checking the battery. After touching any part of the battery wash your hands thoroughly. DON'T touch or rub your eyes.

If the acid comes in contact with your skin, rinse the affected area for at least 20 minutes under running water until all traces of the chemical are removed. Don't scrub. You may suffer caustic burns: seek medical attention.

In the event of the eyes being affected, irrigate under a tap for at least 20 minutes. DON'T use hot water. If you have a mixer tap or a shower attachment, get a gentle flow of water at about blood temperature. If you can't get to a tap, a bowl of clean water splashed into the eye for a while will bring some relief. Do the best you can with what's available and get medical assistance as soon as possible.

Remove contaminated clothing – the acid will continue to burn as long as it is in contact with the skin. Rinse affected skin thoroughly.

for life' and require no maintenance. Unlike old-style batteries, these have no removable cell caps. To check the electrolyte level and battery condition, simply look at the indicator on top of the battery and that will tell you whether the time has come for the battery to be replaced.

Batteries with removable cell caps may need topping up occasionally in order to make them last longer. Because electrolyte expands with heat, it's best to check the fluid level when the battery is warm. A cold battery may look as though it needs topping up, but there's a danger that if you add

water to bring it up to the mark the liquid will overflow when it gets warm, corroding the terminals.

- Turn off the ignition.
- Remove the cell caps.
- Use natural light or a torch to check the level.
- If the fluid level is below the maximum mark, add sufficient distilled water to bring the level back up to maximum or to just above the tops of the battery plates, as applicable (see handbook or the label on the battery). Do not overfill.
- Replace the cell caps, making sure that they are securely fastened.
- Wipe up any spilt water.

Distilled water can be purchased from most garages and car accessory shops. NEVER use ordinary tap water, which will damage the plates and almost immediately cause the battery to malfunction. And don't substitute water collected while defrosting your refrigerator – it's bound to contain impurities and could shorten the life of the battery.

Batteries will need checking more frequently in hot weather and as they get older. If you find the battery needs topping up virtually every week, have it checked by a qualified car-electrician – there could be a fault in the charging circuit.

maintenance

94

WINTER MAINTENANCE

Extra care is needed in winter to cope with the cold, damp conditions. The following precautions are advisable:

• Check the level of anti-freeze in your cooling system. Insufficient anti-freeze in the mix can lead to the engine over-heating because the liquid lies frozen at the bottom of the radiator instead of circulating as it should.

• In extreme cold you should change to a light viscosity oil which will make starting easier and relieve the strain on the battery.

• Keep the battery fully charged, especially in diesel engine cars.

• Check your windscreen washer fluid level and add a screenwash anti-freeze.

• Check the labels of anti-freezes and de-icers – some cheaper brands contain corrosive chemicals which will damage the paintwork.

• If leaving the car parked in the open, a newspaper or a sheet of plastic placed against the windscreen will keep it from icing up.

• Check that front and rear windscreen wipers are not frozen to the screen before you switch them on – you could burn out the motor.

• Use a de-watering spray to protect the engine and ignition.

• Smear a thin layer of petroleum jelly over the headlights to prevent snow collecting on the lenses.

• Road salt is corrosive. It coats the underbody, finding its way into crevices and gaps in the underseal. Wash the bodywork frequently and use a hose to direct a jet of water at the underside. Leave time for the water to sink in, then hose again to flush away accumulated salt and grit.

If you have a hydraulic jack and a set of axle stands or wheel ramps, it's a good idea to give the underside a thorough clean when spring arrives. Wear a mask and goggles for protection as you scrape off loose dirt with a plastic scraper (DON'T use a knife, you might wreck the underbody sealant). Rinse away remaining dirt with a hose spraying tepid water. Check for any leaks and damage to pipes, cables, seals and joints. Make sure the exhaust system is secure and shows no signs of corrosion.

One more reason to check that exhaust: a corroded or damaged exhaust system will be noisy – and in some countries you can be prosecuted for running a vehicle that causes a noise nuisance.

maintenance

Keeping It Clean

Cleaning the car may be a chore you could do without, but there's more at stake than appearances. Beneath that layer of grime, various scratches, dents and blemishes can go unde-tected. If neglected, further damage will occur as the film of dirt traps moisture, encouraging corrosion. The areas where the most dirt accumulates – around the wheel arches, for example – are particularly susceptible to rust. Left unpro-tected against the elements, the paintwork will discolour. When the time comes to sell or trade in your car, you'll pay a heavy price for your neglect. And while we're on the subject of financial incentives, there is a fuel saving of up to 1% to be had by keeping your car shiny (cars coated in a thick layer of dirt suffer friction drag).

Giving the car a wash and polish allows you to monitor the condition of the bodywork. Defects can be repaired and the development of rust arrested before it has a chance to take hold. Some wear and tear to door seals, interior trim and seat covers is inevitable, but regular maintenance will keep the car looking in showroom condition.

AUTOMATIC CAR WASHES
The quickest way to get your car clean is to use an automatic car wash. Most large service stations offer some form of car

wash, whether it be the drive-through variety with revolving brushes, or a 'jet wash' where you operate a hand-held lance to hose the car down.

Drive-in washes have improved a great deal in recent years. Provided you follow the instructions (which should be prominently displayed at the entrance to the car wash), and ensure all windows are shut, all doors properly closed, that the sun-roof is secure and the aerial retracted, your vehicle should emerge intact. Roof-mounted aerials should be unscrewed – if the aerial is laid flat against the roof, there's a risk that it will be ripped off and get tangled in the brushes, where it could cause some nasty scratches to the paintwork. It's a good idea to check beforehand whether the wipers should be stowed horizontally or vertically. Temporary roof racks may have to be removed, especially if they are not 100 per cent secure.

The machines offer a variety of different programmes, ranging from a basic wash using water with a mild detergent additive to shift grime, to a deluxe service whereby the car will be shampooed and rinsed, the wheels and underbody scrubbed by contra-rotating brushes, and then a coating of wax will be applied before the car is hot-air dried to a shine.

However, even the best drive-through car wash cannot get into every nook and cranny, and you miss the opportunity that a hand wash offers to inspect the bodywork. Worse still, if the brushes have been allowed to become worn, you could find tell-tale swirling marks on your paintwork where the car has been 'flayed'.

Jet washes are usually a cheaper alternative because you do all the work yourself. Again there are various options available. The basic model offers a hand-held lance with a control which allows you to adjust the water pressure or spray pattern. More sophisticated models have two hoses: one sprays water, the other has a brush on the end and applies shampoo or wax, according to which programme you have selected. The range of programmes will be displayed at the service station cash desk; simply select the one you want – shampoo and rinse/hi-foam and rinse/shampoo and rinse and wax/hot shampoo and rinse and hot wax – and pay the cashier. You will then be issued with a token to operate the machine. The automatic wash runs through a timed sequence, with audible warnings to tell you when it's time to switch from the brush to the jet hose.

Dress for the job: wellington boots are essential. Do not use the high-pressure jet to blast away dirt. It may be quick, but the force of the water will get behind the grit and cause tiny scratches to the paintwork. Use a gentle spray to thoroughly soak and loosen dirt, starting from the roof and working your way down so that the water can start penetrating those areas on the lower bodywork where the dirt is thickest.

The high-pressure jet can then be used to clean the wheel arches and underbody. (Jet washes are ideal for removing the salt residue which accumulates in winter.) It is all too easy to soak the brakes, so before driving back on to the road apply your foot brake several times to dry out the brake shoes.

MANUAL CAR WASH

Washing the car yourself is good exercise – and cheap. All the equipment you need is a garden hose, a bucket, two large sponges, a soft-bristled brush and a chamois leather.

To prevent the car ending up with a smeared finish, make sure it is parked out of direct sunlight and that the bonnet is cool.

 In some countries it is an offence to wash your car in the street in a built-up area. Check with your local authority to make sure no such rules apply where you live!

Cleaning the Interior

Some people prefer to start by cleaning the interior, because this prevents dirt from inside getting spread all over the freshly cleaned exterior. However, if the interior is not too dirty, you may prefer to attend to this job while the exterior is drying off after its shampoo.

Start by collecting up all the sweet wrappers, used pay-and-display tickets, and rubbish from the floors, interior pockets, glove compartment and ashtrays. Remove all loose mats or carpets to be beaten and brushed, or gone over with a vacuum cleaner. The inside of the car can then be vacuumed. It's possible to buy a small, 12-volt vacuum cleaner which plugs into the car's cigarette lighter. These have a thin nozzle which is excellent for getting into all the tricky places like between seats and into door pockets. Alternatively you could wait until you next visit a service station and pay to use the powerful commercial vacuum cleaner on the forecourt.

Wipe vinyl surfaces using a cloth moistened with a mild soap solution, then wipe clean with a dry soft cloth. NEVER use solvents, they are toxic and inflammable and will give off fumes, causing headaches and nausea on long journeys. To remove ingrained dirt, use an old toothbrush. Don't use any product which might leave the steering wheel slippery – this could cause an accident.

Never allow water or liquid cleaning agents to come in contact with electrical components.

Wipe interior windows with a glass cleaner intended for use in cars – other cleaning agents can leave smears. It's surprising how dirty these can get, even if you're a non-smoker.

Open all of the doors and clean around them. Check for rips and tears in the interior trim and upholstery. Car accessory shops stock various repair kits and stain removers to put right any damage, but never use petroleum or spirit-based solutions. And finally, don't overlook the inside of the boot or luggage compartment. Clean and vacuum – and check the spare wheel and tool set while you're at it.

Glass Surfaces

Be careful what you use to clean the windows, inside and out. Anything which causes smears – shampoos containing silicone or wax, washing-up liquid – will reduce visibility, particularly at night or in wet weather. Clean the glass inside and out with a glass cleaner, preferably one specially made for use in cars, or a mixture of ten parts of water to one of white vinegar. But DON'T put this solution into the screen-wash bottle as it could affect the pump.

Certain petrol-based cleaning agents can damage rubber wiper blades. Clean the blades gently with a damp cloth. Take special care with heated rear windows. The insides should be wiped gently with a soft cloth or damp chamois leather. Clean along the wires not across them, and NEVER use solvents or sharp objects (such as window scrapers) to clean the glass.

Don't forget to clean the various lamp lenses and mirrors. When cleaning mirrors, take care not to scratch the glass.

Rinse off dirt before wiping with a chamois leather, and never use abrasive cleaning agents.

Bodywork

First close all the windows, doors and the sunroof, then soak the body with a gentle spray from a hose or by pouring several buckets of lukewarm water over it. This will remove all the loose dirt and soften the more persistent grime. NEVER direct a high-pressure jet of water against the body at full force – grit will be driven into the paintwork, causing scratches. For the same reason, don't go to work with a sponge until the worst of the dirt has been rinsed away: the sponge will trap grit and scour the paint.

Next, fill a bucket with tepid water containing a little car shampoo. Don't use boiling water, or washing-up liquid – this will get rid of grime, but will cause smears when it rains. Starting at the roof, work your way down to the bonnet, and then the top half of all the doors. By leaving the really dirty areas to last, the water will stay clean longer. Change the water in the bucket when it gets mucky, otherwise you'll only be redistributing the dirt. Clean a small area at a time

> At certain times of year when rainfall is low, there may be a hosepipe ban in force. A car can be cleaned with just two buckets of water.

and then rinse. This will prevent smearing and water marks.

Some blemishes can prove difficult to remove. Certain trees give off a sticky sap that discolours the car. Bird droppings, especially those from seagulls, have a high acid content and will remove paint if left on for long periods. Insects on the windscreen are difficult to remove and extra help maybe needed here. Remove oil, tar, and stubborn stains by gently rubbing with a cloth moistened with a proprietary car-cleaning fluid or turpentine – use only a small amount because too much will take the shine off the paintwork, leaving it patchy. Rinse the affected area thoroughly afterwards.

Clean the grille crevices and wheel rims using a soft brush dipped in your bucket. A soft brush may be required to clean the wheels; leave these till last as they are invariably the dirtiest part of the car.

Never use a harsh cleaning agent on a vinyl-covered roof. Brush away dirt and then sponge with tepid water containing a mild detergent. Chrome and aluminium surfaces can be cleaned with car shampoo, though it will take a special proprietary cleaner to remove serious tarnishing. Be careful when cleaning aluminium alloy wheels. Some are coated with a protective finish and will be scratched by a stiff brush.

After you've finished shampooing, rinse thoroughly with clean water. If you have a hose, flush that coating of mud (and winter road salt) away from the underbody.

Finally, dip a chamois leather in a bucket of clean water, wring it out and use it to dry the car.

CHIPS AND SCRATCHES

Once the paintwork is clean it will be possible to see any small blemishes like scratches and stone chips (caused by stones thrown up from the road surface). These should be dealt with immediately to prevent rust taking hold.

Provided the damage is superficial, clean the area with a drop of methylated spirits on a clean, lint-free rag. Then use a paint stick with added rust inhibitor (obtainable from any good car accessory shop in a wide range of colours) to conceal the damage. These have an integral brush in the lid, ideal for delicately applying paint to small areas. It's important to shake the stick well, so the paint is mixed to the correct shade.

Deep scratches where rust has already set in should be cleaned by scraping off surface rust with a knife. Next, treat with a rust neutralizer, then apply a primer and finish with a coat of paint. If a large area has been affected, obtain the correct shade of paint by contacting a franchise dealer (you will need to quote the car's VIN number to get a perfect match). Follow the manufacturer's instructions, allowing each coat of paint to dry completely before applying the next. Rub the surface down with wet-and-dry abrasive paper between coats. Allow at least two weeks for the new paint to harden, then blend it into the surrounding area by rubbing with a paintwork renovator.

WAXING

An occasional waxing protects the paintwork from the elements (and is an essential part of winter preparations), but you should NEVER apply polish to paintwork which has recently been resprayed or to a new car. Paint takes time to develop a protective outer layer, and until that has hardened polish will do more harm than good.

There are several types of polish available. Soft and liquid wax contain cutting compounds which remove traffic grime – and some of the paint from the car. Hard wax gives a high gloss and is recommended for metallic paint finishes. Whichever variety you use, follow the manufacturer's guidelines.

Make sure you wash away all the dirt and grit before using polish, as it will seal in any blemishes. Allow the bodywork to dry; water can get trapped in door handles, seams, and around fittings, making polishing difficult. Pour the polish on to a damp cloth and not the car. Do a small area at a time, allowing the polish just long enough to dry so that it can be removed easily. If left for too long it will take more effort.

Avoid getting polish on bumpers and spoilers, as it tends to leave a stain. Chrome parts should be polished with a cleaner intended for that purpose.

RUST PREVENTION

Corrosion thrives on moisture. Most preventative measures are therefore directed at removing moisture-retaining dirt from cavities and joints, keeping drainholes clear and ensuring that protective coatings are not damaged, allowing rust to set in.

Environmental factors affecting the rate of corrosion include high humidity, industrial pollution, and salty sea breezes. Salt, used on the roads in icy/snowy conditions, will cause paintwork to deteriorate and will accelerate the onset of rust. If your car is subject to any of these environmental factors, you should be especially rigorous in cleaning and inspecting the bodywork.

To protect your car against rust:

- Check for damage to the paintwork and get it repaired promptly
- Remove wet floor coverings from the car and dry them thoroughly before replacing
- Check drain holes in the sunroof, doors, and body panels for blockages. One way of doing this is to pour water into

the gullies, watching to see that it runs free.

- Clear the underbody of accumulated mud, sand and road salt, using a high-pressure washer. Wash inside wheel arches, suspension mounts, and under front and rear bumpers. Be careful when removing mud from the underside of vehicles fitted with anti lock brakes: they may have sensors fitted in the wheel arches.
- After washing your car, check the interior for leaks. Lift the mats and inspect for signs of water seeping in and collecting there. Remove the floor cover in the boot and inspect this area.
- Clean inside the engine compartment. Use a penetrating oil to clean the engine, then apply a de-watering fluid, using a paintbrush to work it into all springs, pipes, screw and nut heads. This will both clean and protect engine parts, repelling moisture and rust. A clean engine is easier to work on, and you can see at a glance what is wrong with the engine should it malfunction.

periodic maintenance

 Most car owners prefer to leave the complicated procedures involved in a major service to the experts. But all too many hand over the keys with a sinking feeling that they're about to be ripped off and there's nothing they can do about it but trust to luck.

CHOOSING A GARAGE

Owners of new cars may risk invalidating the manufacturer's warranty if they have the vehicle serviced by anyone other than the franchised dealer. Where no warranty applies, you can choose between franchised dealers, independent garages, quick-fit outlets and doing it yourself.

Price isn't the only factor to be taken into consideration: a main agent service history is considered essential for luxury and specialist cars – opt for a cheaper form of servicing and you'll knock a large chunk off the secondhand value. Franchised dealers are familiar with the manufacturer's specifications and the service they carry out has been devised to accommodate special features peculiar to that make, which is why a service book showing that all work has been carried out on their premises will enhance the resale value.

However, the fact that a garage has been awarded a manufacturer's franchise is not in itself a guarantee that you will get value for money. Don't let those smart premises lull you into a false sense of security. Never assume that price is an assurance of quality: garages can give a very poor service and yet charge you a fortune. The only way to ensure that you get value for money is to follow these rules:

- Know your car. Unscrupulous mechanics determine how much they can get away with overcharging by the level of ignorance you show when asked: 'What did you say is wrong with it?' The more clueless you seem, the more they'll try to blind you with jargon and rip you off. See Fault Diagnosis below for a guide to some of the most common problems and their symptoms.
- Ask friends to recommend a garage which they have found to be trustworthy.
- Make a list of specific items or problems you would like checked or repaired, then phone around for quotations. Make sure all quotes cover parts, labour and VAT. Once you've got a handful of quotes you can set about negotiating to bring the price of repairs down.
- Be wary of fixed-price special offers on servicing. Find out what is included in the price. All too often these services are limited in what they cover and you'll get a nasty surprise when they phone you midway through the service to say

that additional work is required at a vastly inflated price.

- Franchised dealers should quote a price based upon the manufacturer's recommended service schedule. To get a comparable service from an independent garage, show them the schedule in the service handbook, and ask for a quote based on this.
- It's a good idea with independents to ask to speak to the mechanic who will carry out the service. Use the opportunity to find out how much he knows about your make and model.
- Having accepted a quote, put it into writing that if any problems are diagnosed which will take the cost above the price quoted, the garage must get your authorization before proceeding. Get a quote for parts, labour and VAT before deciding whether to sanction it. If in doubt, get a second opinion – it may be possible to get the relevant parts cheaper elsewhere.
- Insist that the invoice is accompanied by a complete breakdown of the work carried out. Check it to ensure that you have not been charged for things you did not want
- Any old parts which have been replaced are your property. If you want to be certain that the work has been carried out, ask to see the old components.
- If the repair proves faulty or a new part fails, the garage should put it right free of charge. If they refuse, you are entitled to have the work done elsewhere and at the garage's expense. The garage is also responsible for any damage the car sustains while in their possession.

SERVICE CHECKLIST

To carry out a DIY 12,000 mile service, you will need to be able to perform the following tasks (in addition to those listed under Weekly Service in Routine Maintenance):

Engine compartment
- Renew engine oil and filter
- Adjust valve clearances
- Renew and gap spark plugs
- Renew air filter element
- Adjust or renew contact-breaker points
- Check ignition timing
- Check idle speed
- Check condition and tension of fanbelt(s)
- Renew camshaft belt
- Lubricate throttle and manual choke
- Check cooling system for condition and leaks
- Inspect brake pads and renew if necessary
- Automatic cars: check transmission fluid level

If the vehicle has power steering, fuel injection, air conditioning, these will also need checking.

Under the car
- Check transmission, differential and transfer box

- Check driveshafts
- Check steering gear/linkage
- Check suspension, shock absorbers, etc.
- Check exhaust system for security and good condition
- Lubricate grease points on steering, suspension, etc.
- Check brake and clutch systems for condition, security and leaks
- Check thickness of brake pads, discs, and linings
- Inspect and lubricate handbrake cable, adjust if needed
- Check wheel bearings
- Check tightness of wheel bolts
- Inspect tyres thoroughly

Around the car
- Check headlamp alignment
- Check foot brake, handbrake, and clutch for free play, stroke and operation
- Check operation of heater controls and heated rear window
- Check operation of wipers and washers
- Check operation of locks and hinges

Road test
- Check instruments
- Check brakes and steering
- Check handbrake function

DIY SERVICING

Labour costs account for over 50 per cent of the average garage bill, so there are huge savings to be made by doing it yourself. But remember, you will only save money if you do the job properly. Incompetent workmanship could prove lethal, and it may cost a fortune to put right. Know your limitations, and, when in doubt, DON'T DIY – seek expert advice. It is not advisable for amateurs to tackle safety-related equipment such as the steering and braking systems.

Many local authorities run evening classes taught by qualified mechanics. A course in car maintenance will improve your mechanical skills and help build your confidence; it will also acquaint you with all the necessary safety procedures. Invest in a workshop manual and a set of tools which can cope with every project you intend to tackle.

It's possible to pick up secondhand manuals, tools and car accessories at car boot sales, but NEVER buy safety-related items such as brake and steering components on the cheap. Make sure any spare parts you buy come from a reputable source and conform to European safety-standards, that they come with a warranty, and that they are suitable for your particular car. To be certain of buying the correct part for your car, you will need to be able to tell the dealer the model, engine size, year of manufacture and the Vehicle Identification Number (VIN) which appears on the vehicle registration document.

PREPARING FOR THE MOT

In Britain, all cars over three years old must undergo an annual check known as the MOT which is carried out at an authorized test centre to ensure that the vehicle complies with legal safety standards. Without a valid MOT certificate you cannot obtain road tax or insurance, which means that the car cannot be driven on any public highway.

One in four cars fail the test, the majority because of faulty lights. Defective windscreen wipers or washers are the next most common cause for failure, with tyres and exhaust emissions not far behind. A car that fails its MOT may not be used except to drive it to a place where the necessary repairs can be carried out. Having been repaired, it will have to undergo a second MOT.

The best way to avoid the expense of a re-test is to run a few checks at home before taking your car to a test centre. Any defects can then be repaired ahead of the MOT.

- Check that all the lights are working, that the lenses are clean (replace any that are missing, cracked or discoloured) and that headlamps are angled so they don't dazzle oncoming traffic.
- Check that the windscreen wiper blades aren't damaged or worn. Washer jets must be correctly aimed and free of blockages.
- Check that the horn works.
- Check the exhaust for leaks. Excessive smoke will probably lead to failure of the emission tests.
- Check that the tyres are at the correct pressure, that the tread depth is above the legal minimum, and that there are no cuts or bulges in the side walls.
- Check the steering. The road wheels should move instantaneously when the steering wheel is turned.
- Check the operation of the brakes (carry out an emergency stop on a clear road with no traffic behind you; the car should stop quickly and in a straight line) and the handbrake.
- Check the windscreen for cracks and stone chip damage. Remove any dangling ornaments with obscure vision, such as furry dice.
- Check that all mirrors are present and in good condition.
- Check that front and rear number-plates are clear.
- Make sure there are no leaks from the underbody. Fuel tanks and pipes must be secure.
- Check the bodywork for damage or corrosion.
- Check that all seats are safe and secure.
- Inspect door hinges, locks and latches.

All test centres have a viewing area which overlooks the workspace where the tests are carried out. If you want to see how the professionals go about performing these checks, go along and watch an MOT inspection in progress .

fault finding

Regular maintenance and servicing should go a long way towards ensuring that your car is reliable. Components that are checked frequently, and replaced when they show signs of wear and tear, should not suddenly fail. Parts which are nearing the end of their life will usually display warning symptoms, so don't ignore unusual noises, smells or vibrations. Instead of just driving on, listen to what your car is telling you: pull over when it is safe to do so and investigate.

Diagnosing Faults

The key to diagnosing faults is to remain calm, take note of all the symptoms, and then work your way logically through the possible causes. Never leap to conclusions – eliminate the alternatives before you start making adjustments or fitting replacement parts. Never assume that because a component is new it cannot be faulty. And remember that when a component such as a fuse or spark plug fails, some other fault may have caused it to fail. Always investigate the possibility of an underlying fault.

Weather-related symptoms
Take into account the prevailing weather conditions. In heavy rain or dense fog, water can get into the engine compartment, dampening the ignition system and causing the engine to misfire. Extremely hot weather can lead to a slackening of the fan belt, which prevents the water pump and cooling system from operating efficiently. Winter brings with it all kinds of problems: the battery may have trouble stirring a cold stiff engine into life; the fan belt may slip because the water in the pump has frozen (listen for a tell-tale screeching noise when the engine is started from cold); the handbrake may freeze in position; and, worst of all, if temperatures get low enough, the cylinder block could crack.

SMELLS AND SOUNDS THAT SPELL TROUBLE

- A burning smell can have a number of causes, from a cigarette smouldering on the carpet to a slipping clutch, a burnt out wiper motor, or a handbrake that has accidentally been left on. Or it could be that a careless mechanic has left a scrap of rag in contact with a hot part of the engine.
- An acrid smell of burning accompanied by smoke could mean a short circuit in the electrical wiring.
- A strong smell of petrol might indicate a leaking pipe or fuel tank. Did you overfill the tank or spill petrol down the side of the car?
- Oil fumes could warn of a leaking pipe or valve.
- A rhythmic crackling noise may indicate a cracked distributor cap. The high-tension current takes the least line of resistance and jumps the crack instead of the spark plug gap (if it is dark, you will be able to see it happen). Carbon deposits in the crack must be cleaned out before repairing. Remove the cap and clean away burnt deposits using a sharp object like a screwdriver or nail file. Seal the crack with either oil, using the dipstick from the engine, or nail polish if available.
- Heavy, rhythmic knocking sounds are a sign that the big-end bearings are worn.
- Rumbling noises could signal worn crankshaft bearings.
- Tapping noises might be caused by worn piston bearings, a worn camshaft, valves in need of adjustment,
- Fan belts screech when they slip or slacken.
- Gaskets and hoses which have sprung a leak may hiss as gases escape.

It's worth taking the time to identify the fault even if you intend having a garage do any necessary repairs. The more specific you are, the less time the mechanic will have to spend investigating – and the lower your bill for labour costs.

maintenance

- Rattling noises from the engine could have a number of causes, including worn chains, loose generator or fan mountings, worn crankshaft bearings.
- Grinding or screeching when the clutch pedal is depressed suggests a worn or misaligned part in the clutch system. Seek expert help.
- A whirring noise which occurs every time a gear change is made is a sign that the clutch release bearing is on the way out.
- Grinding or screeching from the brakes could be a sign of worn brake pads, or corrosion. Seek expert help.
- A high whining noise indicates that the universal joints are wearing out.

ENGINE FAULTS

Symptom: Starter motor doesn't turn
Possible causes:
- Flat battery
- Corroded or loose battery terminals/connections
- Electrical or wiring fault
- Ignition/starter switch faulty

Action: Check the battery. If it is flat, change or recharge it. Follow emergency starting procedure described in **Breakdowns and Emergencies**. Inspect the terminals; clean and tighten if necessary. Check for loose electrical connections. Faults in the ignition system, such as a defective starter switch, require expert assistance.

Symptom: Starter motor clicks
Possible causes:
- Starter motor is jammed
- Loose electrical connections

Action: You may need a new starter motor. Rocking the car backwards and forwards in gear with the ignition off might solve the problem. Some starter motors have a square end which can be rotated to release the mechanism. Check for loose connections.

Symptom: Starter motor turns slowly
Possible causes:
- Battery low or defective
- Battery terminals corroded or loose
- Starter motor faulty

Action: Recharge battery. Check terminals; tighten and clean. If the starter motor makes a harsh, grinding noise it could mean that the securing bolts are loose, or that parts of the mechanism are worn or broken. Seek expert assistance.

Symptom: Poor acceleration, misfiring or lack of power
Possible causes:
- Engine is overheating
- Blocked or dirty air cleaner filter element
- Slipped fan belt
- Blocked or damaged exhaust system.
- Fuel system fault
- Ignition system fault
- Electrical fault

Actions: Check the oil temperature gauge – it may be that low oil pressure is causing the engine to overheat. Check the dipstick – BE CAREFUL AS IT MAY BE VERY HOT.

If the engine has not overheated, the problem may lie in the ignition system (check that the spark plugs are clean and correctly gapped) or the fuel system. Seek expert advice.

Symptom: Engine overheats or temperature gauge reads too high
Possible causes:
- Blockage in radiator airflow
- Blockage in coolant system
- Coolant or engine oil level low
- Faulty thermostat
- Faulty water pump
- Slack or worn fanbelt
- Faulty electric cooling fan or switch

Actions: Check coolant hoses for signs of leaks or damage.

The fanbelt may have slipped or snapped (see Breakdowns and Emergencies for repair techniques), or the electric cooling fan's fuse may have blown (see the section on fuses in Electrical Faults below).

Symptom: Oil pressure warning light comes on when engine is running
Possible causes:
- Oil level low
- Oil leak
- Faulty oil pressure switch
- Badly worn engine components

Actions: Check oil level with dipstick. If oil level is correct, get expert help.

FUEL SYSTEM FAULTS

Generally there is prior warning to a fuel problem. The engine will lose power and misfire.

DANGER!

Vehicles with a fuel-injected engine should be left to the experts. The system is pressurized and it is therefore extremely hazardous to tamper with fuel pipes and hoses.
Take special care even when checking for fuel leaks on non-fuel injected engines:

- Do not smoke or allow flames or sparks near fuel.
- Do not allow fuel to come into contact with hot exhaust or engine systems.
- Wear protective clothing and goggles to prevent exposure to fuel. If any does come in contact with your skin, wash it off immediately. Irrigate eyes with running water for 20 minutes and seek medical help.
- Beware of the toxic fumes given off by petrol (see the safety tips which precede the Weekly Service at the beginning of this chapter).

SAFETY FIRST

If your car has electronic ignition, DO NOT carry out any further tests. Seek expert advice – the high voltage from an electronic system can KILL. Never touch any ignition system that is switched on, or while the engine is running.

Check that there is fuel in the tank. To be certain that the gauge is not faulty, rock the car and listen for the fuel sloshing about in the tank. Have the gauge repaired by a professional mechanic.

Repairs to the fuel system are best left to the experts.

IGNITION FAULTS

Symptom: Starter turns briskly but engine won't start
Possible causes:
- Check that you have not run out of fuel
- Check for dirty or damp high tension leads and distributor cap
- Dirty or incorrectly gapped distributor points
- Excessive choke (hot engine) or insufficient choke (cold engine)
- Fouled or incorrectly gapped spark plugs (remove, clean and re-gap, using a feeler gauge)
- Dirty battery connections
- Other ignition system fault
- Other fuel system fault
- Poor compression
- Major mechanical failure (e.g. camshaft drive)

Actions: Having confirmed that there is fuel in the tank, check whether there is a spark. To do this, remove a plug and prop it up so that the threads rest on bare metal (e.g. the cylinder block). DO NOT touch the plug or the lead while you operate the starter to check for a spark.

The following checks should NOT be carried out on electronic ignition systems:

If there is a spark from the plug, clean and dry or renew

the plugs, check the gap and replace. If the engine still won't start the problem may lie in the fuel system.

If there is no spark from the plug, look for a spark at the contact breaker points when the ignition is switched on. No spark here could indicate dirty or damp high tension (HT) leads are to blame. Once they have been cleaned and dried, try again.

If there is a spark at the contact breaker points, proceed to check the following items (you are looking for signs of damp or damage; check for a spark then clean/dry/replace as necessary before checking again – once you get a spark, move on to the next item):

- the 'king lead' (the central HT lead)
- the distributor cap and rotor arm
- the HT leads and connections.

If there is no spark at the contact breaker points, check the low tension circuit connections. If these seem sound, check the capacitor, then the HT leads and connections and finally the coil.

A de-watering fluid or spray may help if damp is the problem. If cleaning and drying does not solve the problem, seek professional help.

DRYING OUT THE IGNITION SYSTEM

If the ignition system gets wet the engine will stop. This is prone to happen after driving through deep water. The fan throws water over the engine, soaking the distributor, coil, leads, and plugs.

Wipe all parts, including the plugs, with a dry cloth. Spray a de-watering fluid over components to dry them out.

Symptom: Ignition warning light not illuminated
Possible causes:
- Coolant loss due to internal or external leak
- Low oil level
- Brake binding
- Blockage in radiator
- Electric cooling fan faulty
- Ignition timing malfunctioning

Actions: Check for leaks in hoses and pipes. Fuse for electric fan may need replacing. Check oil level. Seek expert advice.

Symptom: Ignition warning light comes on when engine is running
Possible causes:
- Fanbelt slipped, slack or broken
- Faulty alternator
- Other electrical or wiring fault

Actions: Check fanbelt. Burnt-out brushes in the alternator, loose electrical wires or connections may be to blame.

ELECTRICAL FAULTS

The electrical system is protected by a series of fuses which provide a safety valve when a malfunction occurs. Always check the fuses before stripping down the component. In most cars the fuse box is located beneath the dashboard (check the handbook if you have difficulty locating it). Bear in mind that you may one day have to replace a fuse at night with no lights, so it pays to familiarize yourself with the procedure and to know what spares you carry in the fuse box.

Before renewing a fuse or a relay, always make sure that the ignition and the relevant circuit are switched off.

To replace a fuse, you will need to know its rating and which circuits it protects. In most cars fuses are colour-coded as follows:

Colour	Rating (amps)
Red	10
Yellow	20
Green	30

In older vehicles the fuses may consist of a piece of wire wrapped round a ceramic strip, or enclosed in a glass tube.

As a general rule, in newer cars fuses plug into sockets in the fuse box. Pull out the suspect fuse and examine it. A blown fuse can be recognized by a break in the wire connection between the two terminals. Replace a blown fuse with one of the same rating. Never use wire or any other material to bridge the gap where a fuse should be. If the fuse blows on a vital component and you do not have a spare, use a fuse of equivalent or lower value from a non-essential circuit, like the radio or heater. NEVER substitute a higher value fuse, as this can damage the component or even start a fire. Remember to replace the borrowed fuse and restock with spares.

A blown fuse is an indication that some other electrical component in the car's electrical system may be faulty. This can be difficult to trace, so if a fuse blows, get the car checked over by an expert as soon as possible.

A relay is an electro-magnetic switch used in circuits which control operations such as the heated rear window, intermittent wiper, indicator/hazard flasher system, and the horn. To check whether a faulty relay is responsible for a malfunction, remove the relay (most plug into a socket) and substitute a relay which you know is functioning.

Having eliminated a blown fuse or faulty relay as the cause of an electrical malfunction, check for loose, dirty or corroded connections. Make sure that the battery is not flat. All electrical components are connected to earth, either by a lead or through their mountings. Check that these earth connections are not faulty.

TRANSMISSION SYSTEM FAULTS

Symptom: Difficulty in engaging gear (manual gearbox)
Possible causes:
- Worn gearbox components
- Oil leak from the gearbox
- Worn clutch plates
- Engine idle speed too high
Action: Consult a qualified mechanic.

DANGER
Brake pads and linings, clutch linings and underseals may contain asbestos. Inhaling asbestos brake dust can cause permanent scarring of the lung tissue and cancer. Wear a mask when doing any dusty work or spraying.

Symptom: Gear changes are sluggish
Possible causes:
- Low transmission fluid level (automatic transmission)
- Transmission fault

Action: Consult a qualified mechanic.

BRAKE FAULT
For all brake faults the recommended course of action is the same: seek help from a qualified mechanic immediately.

Symptom: Brakes feel spongy
Possible causes:
- Air in brake system
- Brake fluid leaking from system

Symptom: Car pulls to one side
Possible causes:
- Faulty brake components
- Incorrect wheel alignment
- Incorrect tyre pressure
- Faulty suspension components

Symptom: Brakes squeal or judder
Possible causes:
- Worn or corroded brake components
- Contaminated brake fluid
- Faulty suspension

STEERING FAULTS
As with braking faults, the course of action in each case is to seek expert advice as soon as possible.

Symptom: Vibration in steering
Possible causes:
- Wheels need balancing
- Worn or damaged driveshaft
- Faulty suspension
- Worn steering components

maintenance

REMEMBER

Prevention is better than cure. Stick to a regular maintenance schedule so that worn components can be replaced and faults nipped in the bud. That way you'll save on expensive repairs.

Symptom: Heavy or erratic steering
Possible causes:

- A punctured tyre
- Low tyre pressure or uneven tyre wear
- Incorrect wheel alignment
- Worn steering components
- Car unevenly loaded
- Faulty suspension
- Failure of power-assisted steering (where fitted)

The best antidote for panic is an effective strategy. If you know what action to take, you'll find it easier to cope – whatever the emergency. Hopefully you will never need to put these strategies into practice, but familiarize yourself with the correct procedures, just in case.

emergency!

BREAKDOWNS Vital equipment • Action plan • Parking in a safe place • Motorway breakdowns

ROADSIDE REPAIRS Fuel system • Overheating • Low oil pressure • Punctures • Changing a wheel

EMERGENCY STARTING Jump leads • Push start • Towing

EMERGENCIES Brake failure • Jammed accelerator • Windscreen shattering • Fire • Submerged in water • Stuck on a level crossing

ACCIDENTS

FIRST AID

INSURANCE CLAIMS

breakdowns

A vehicle that is well maintained and serviced regularly should be reliable, but still breakdowns can happen from time to time. Carry the survival kit, spares and tools listed in Essentials, and you will be prepared for just about anything. It also pays to be observant: keep an eye on the gauges and warning lights, listen to the car, note any strange sounds or smells. If something doesn't seem right, start looking for a safe place where you can pull over and investigate. Don't drive off into remote, sparsely populated areas or join a motorway with the engine clanking or wheezing or giving off fumes. Get into the habit of mentally recording the locations of garages and phone boxes by the roadside – this information could be vital in an emergency.

Vital Equipment

Probably one of the most useful items to have in an emergency is a mobile phone. For long journeys, especially in isolated rural areas, a car phone can be a lifesaver – how else are you going to summon the emergency services in the event of an accident? By the time you find your way to the nearest habitation it could be too late to save some casualties. And if you break down while driving alone, it will give you great peace of mind to know that a qualified mechanic is on the way without your having to walk many miles along lonely roads in search of a phone. Your friends and family, will benefit, too, because you'll be able to tell them that you're running late and not to worry. If you don't own a mobile phone, it can be worth hiring one short-term to take on holiday or for a long journey.

It is illegal to use a mobile telephone while driving. Always pull over to a safe place before making or receiving a call.

Just in case the phone should ever fail you, make sure that you always carry some money and a phone card, as well as waterproof clothing, a reflective band and torch (for times when visibility is poor) so that you can walk to the nearest payphone.

Situations can arise which will prevent you leaving the car to summon assistance – for example, if you are travelling with young children who cannot manage the walk to a telephone and cannot safely be left alone in the car, leaving you no option but to stay near the car with them; or if the car breaks down on the motorway and you cannot get across to the hard shoulder. For these occasions (and for disabled drivers at all times) it's a good idea to carry signs which alert passers-by to your predicament. It's possible to buy sets of signs which include messages such as PLEASE HELP, RUN OUT OF PETROL, INFORM POLICE.

In many countries it is compulsory to carry a warning triangle which can be set up to warn other drivers that there is a broken-down vehicle ahead. Even in countries where it's not required by law, it makes sense to keep one of these in the boot at all times.

Having a first-aid kit and fire extinguisher could mean the difference between life and death in an emergency situation – especially if you take the trouble to learn how to use them. The best type of extinguisher for in-car use is a dry powder (blue) or Halon/BCF (green). A water-filled extinguisher (the red variety) would be fine if the upholstery caught fire, but should NEVER be used on burning liquids or electrical fires. Car accessory shops sell small, dashboard-mounted extinguishers, or you could rig up a sling so that the extinguisher fits over the back of the driver's seat. Always keep the extinguisher in the car, not in the boot – each second is precious when dealing with fire, so you need to be able to lay hands on the extinguisher in an instant.

Make sure that your spare tyre is in good condition and that you carry a wheel brace and jack. With a little knowledge and the correct spares a lot of anxiety and time can be saved, especially if you do a lot of driving in rural areas where garages and public telephones are few and far between. The older your vehicle and the poorer its condition, the more spares you should carry – especially if it is a rare or unusual model.

But carrying tools is a waste of time if you don't know how to use them. If you haven't already done so, study the manufacturer's handbook and acquaint yourself with where everything is and how it works. Don't wait until the car breaks down to try to find out where the distributor or the fuel filter is.

If a major component fails there will be little you can do, especially if your car is a fairly recent model. More and more manufacturers are fitting components with tamper-proof seals to prevent you from making repairs or adjustments. But many mechanical failures can still be repaired at the roadside, so that with a little ingenuity you can nurse the car home or to a garage.

For those who are not technically-minded, the most useful piece of equipment to carry is probably a membership card for one of the national motoring organizations offering a breakdown repair and recovery service. The cost of membership is nothing compared with the fees charged by private garages when summoned to rescue a broken-down vehicle. Vulnerable drivers – women, the elderly, and disabled drivers – are strongly advised to join.

It pays to shop around, as prices vary depending on the level of service you want. Collect brochures from the market leaders and compare services and prices before committing yourself.

Even if you're not a member of an organization, it may be worth phoning them when you break down and asking whether they will come out if you agree to take out membership. Some will come to the aid of non-members in return for a small call-out fee in addition to the parts and labour charges.

BREAKDOWN ACTION PLAN

- If possible, park safely

- Get passengers to a place of safety

- If the car is causing an obstruction, warn approaching traffic:
    Switch on hazard warning lights
    Set up warning triangle

- Phone for assistance. Inform the police if the car is blocking the road.

emergency

Parking in a Safe Place

Often there are warning signs when a vehicle malfunctions. Use this time to pull off the road and park safely. Whenever a vehicle stops on the road it becomes a hazard to traffic and there is a risk of another vehicle running into yours. Unless the car is completely immobilized by an engine failure and cannot be driven, make it your priority to get to the kerb, a layby, or an emergency telephone if you are on the motorway – even if it means driving another hundred metres on a punctured wheel. The risk of making the damage worse is nothing compared to the risks you face when parked in a dangerous position, and there's no way you can work on the car while it's blocking traffic.

Switch on the hazard warning lights and steer smoothly to the kerb or hard shoulder. If the engine does not respond, try coasting out of gear to the roadside.

DON'T open offside doors. Get passengers out through the nearside doors and make sure they move well away from the car to a place where oncoming traffic will not endanger them. At night, make sure no one stands behind the car where they might obscure the rear lights. When pushing the car, helpers should position themselves so that the lights will still be visible to approaching vehicles.

In the event that mechanical failure does stop the car dead on a normal road, you will need help from passengers, other motorists or pedestrians to block the lane while the car is pushed to a safe spot – provided this can be managed without placing anyone in danger. (See below for what to do if your car breaks down on a motorway or autoroute.) If the car cannot be moved, the police must be informed immediately. Leave the car with the steering wheel turned towards the nearside kerb, so that if it is hit by a passing vehicle the impact will send it towards the kerb rather than into oncoming traffic.

Do your best to warn approaching vehicles of the obstruction. Place your warning triangle in a prominent position at least 50 metres (164 feet) ahead of your car, in the same lane (or on the grass verge, if it's a narrow country road). On motorways the triangle should be placed 150 metres (492 feet) before the car on the hard shoulder. If possible, send someone to direct traffic around the obstacle – but make sure they are wearing something bright or reflective that will show up well in poor visibility.

Only when the car is in a safe position off the highway can you set about trying to identify the problem. Don't attempt a repair unless it's something you know you can handle. If the repair would involve working on the offside of the car in close proximity to passing traffic, or if it's something that will take you hours, call a breakdown service.

PHONES

A mobile phone will enable you to call for assistance without leaving your car. If you haven't got a carphone or a Citizens' Band radio, you will either need to walk in search of a telephone or place a PLEASE CALL POLICE sign in your rear window and hope that a passing motorist will comply.

If you're travelling with young children and there isn't a public telephone in sight, you face having to take them with you on what could be a long walk in search of a phone, or remaining in the car with them and hoping that help will find you. Only you can decide the best course of action for the circumstances.

Before setting off in search of a pay phone, put on warm clothes, the reflective band from your survival kit, and flat shoes or boots if you have them. Take a torch in case it gets dark. Make sure you've got your phone card, loose change, a note of your motoring organization membership details and your car's registration number, make and model. Jot down a few notes on what you think the fault may be or, if you're not sure, the symptoms which led up to the breakdown. Make a note, too, of your location – if there are no street signs to go by, look for distinctive landmarks which will help the breakdown service to find you. Where you've been lucky enough to stop within sight of a public telephone, all you need do is look at the location details posted inside the call box.

Once you have phoned for assistance, return to the car and find a safe place to wait. If the car is parked safely, you can sit inside with the doors locked. Where the car is causing an obstruction, wait somewhere close by. If you can't find shelter within sight of the car, or if you go into a nearby house or shop, leave a note in the car telling the breakdown service where you can be found – they won't do a thing to the car if you're not around to authorize it.

Motorway Breakdowns

 The speed and volume of traffic on motorways makes breakdowns all the more dangerous. Do whatever you can to avoid breaking down in the first place: constantly monitor the gauges for temperature, fuel, oil pressure, etc. Listen for unusual noises.

If you detect something amiss, signal your intention to move over to the inside lane, then slow down, and turn off at the next junction or service area.

If the car is behaving erratically, switch on the hazard warning lights to alert other drivers as you steer towards the hard shoulder. Try to keep going until you reach an emergency phone (these are dotted along the hard shoulder at one-mile intervals). When you stop the car, pull way over to the far side of the hard shoulder. Turn the steering wheel away from the motorway, so that if another car does hit yours it won't be shunted into the path of oncoming vehicles. Leave your hazard lights on (and your sidelights too, if visibility is poor).

You are not out of danger on the hard shoulder, so evacuate the vehicle (leave pets inside the car with the window ajar) using the nearside doors (the ones furthest from the traffic). The safest place to wait for help is on the embankment or grass verge. When it's pouring with rain or there's a freezing fog, you may feel tempted to wait in the car where it's warm and dry. DON'T. In poor visibility the risk of another vehicle running into a car parked on the hard shoulder increases. Put on the waterproof clothing from your survival kit and huddle together for shelter on the embankment.

Hold on to children at all times and prevent them playing or running about. Don't let the anyone mill around the vehicle – even simple repairs should not be attempted alongside the motorway. Make sure no one stands behind the car, obscuring the rear lights.

STAY SAFE!

- Keep calm.

- If you can, park under a streetlight, near a telephone, or outside a house or building that looks occupied.

- Lock the car doors and take the keys with you when leaving the car.

- DON'T hitch a lift.

- Helpful strangers may have sinister motives. Beware! If someone approaches, get into the car, lock the doors and open the window just enough to speak through. A genuine Samaritan will understand your caution and be happy to call the police for you. But if someone makes you feel uneasy or suspicious, tell them help is already on the way. Sound the horn and turn on all your lights to attract attention if you feel threatened.

- Decline offers from amateur mechanics – they may do more harm than good despite having the best of intentions.

- Once you've called for assistance, find a safe place to wait.

- Provided the car is parked where there is no danger of it being hit by passing vehicles, a vulnerable driver such as a lone woman will be safest inside with the doors locked. If you are travelling alone, sit in the passenger seat to create the impression that you're waiting for the driver to return.

- When the recovery vehicle arrives, make sure it is from the organization you called and that they have your name. Refuse help from private firms looking for trade – they'll charge a high price for their services.

If the car stops dead in the middle of a lane and you can't coax it on to the hard shoulder, switch on your hazard warning lights and display a CALL FOR HELP sign if you have one. Remain in the vehicle with your seatbelt on until the

> To warn oncoming traffic that you have stopped on the hard shoulder, position your warning triangle at least 150 metres (492 feet) from the rear of the car.

road is completely clear and you can be certain of getting across to the hard shoulder. When a car is travelling at speed on the motorway it can be a dot on the horizon one moment and on top of you the next. If the road is busy, wait for the police to come to your aid. Some stretches of motorway are covered by closed circuit cameras, others are patrolled regularly by the police. Either way, help will get to you if you sit tight.

EMERGENCY TELEPHONES

Emergency telephones are located at one-mile or one-kilometre intervals. Marker posts situated at 100-metre/328-feet intervals behind the hard shoulder will point the way to the nearest phone.

> NEVER try crossing to a telephone on the far side of the motorway. NEVER cross the motorway for any reason whatsoever.

If you haven't managed to stop within sight of a telephone and have to walk along the hard shoulder to reach one, take a torch with you and wear the reflective band from your survival kit even in broad daylight. Remember the danger posed by passing traffic; someone who is dozing off at the wheel can easily veer on to the hard shoulder, so keep well over to the side furthest from traffic. In wet weather clouds of spray will be thrown up by heavy vehicles, and you may have to battle against cross winds. In fog sounds will be distorted, and you will be shrouded in mist with no hope of motorists seeing you until it's too late. That walk to the emergency telephone can be a terrifying experience in bad weather, but try to stay calm and keep as far away from the lanes of moving traffic as you can. If it's possible to walk along the embankment rather than the hard shoulder, do so.

If you belong to a motoring organization, take along your membership details as the operator will need these when calling out a recovery vehicle for you.

The emergency telephone will connect you, free of charge, to the police control centre. The operator will be able to tell exactly where you are calling from because each phone has it's own unique code. A list posted by the phone will tell you what information the operator needs from you, such as the make, model, registration and colour of your car, your name, and membership details if you belong to a motoring organization. Don't worry if you don't belong to any organization – the police will send for a locally-based recovery vehicle (though this will cost you far more than a motoring organization's services would).

Women travelling alone or with children will be given priority, so tell the operator immediately if that is the case.

Stand behind the telephone, facing approaching traffic so that you can see anyone coming towards you. If a car pulls over or you see someone walking towards you, describe them (and their vehicle and registration number) to the operator. Stay on the line if you feel threatened – it's unlikely that they will risk attacking you while the operator is listening in.

Provided there are no suspicious strangers in the vicinity, you will probably be advised to return to wait by your vehicle for the breakdown service.

Don't sit in the car while you wait for help. It's true that motorists have been attacked while stranded by the roadside, but far more have been killed by trucks hitting their stationary vehicle as they sat helpless inside. The safest thing to do is to sit on the embankment within easy reach of your car. Leave the doors on the passenger side unlocked so that you can hop back in and lock the doors if anyone approaches. Don't assume that a breakdown mechanic or police officer is genuine until you have seen their identification through the car window. If you've phoned for assistance, the mechanic should have been given your name. Only when you're certain that the person you are dealing with is who they say they are is it safe to unlock the doors and get out.

> If the emergency telephone is out of order, return to your car and wait close by. The police regularly patrol sections of motorway where telephones aren't functioning in case there are stranded motorists in need of assistance.

roadside repairs

The causes of breakdowns are often simple. Three of the most common are: running out of petrol, flat battery, and flat tyre. Provided the car is parked where you can work on it without the risk of being hit by passing traffic, it's worth investigating the cause of the problem and seeing whether you can effect a temporary repair which will get you to the nearest garage. Even if you are not capable of carrying out the repair yourself, it can save a lot of time and bother if you can describe the fault accurately to the operator when you telephone the breakdown service. Hopefully the mechanic will be able to bring the relevant spare part and send you on your way instead of having to tow the car to a garage.

The Fault Finding tips at the end of the previous chapter will give you some idea how to work out what's gone wrong, and on the following pages you will find a range of temporary repairs that will enable you to get home in the event of a breakdown. With a car that is still under warranty, you won't want to risk invalidating guarantees by carrying out improvised repairs, but with an old car there's probably not much to be lost by patching up broken components as best you can.

Follow the safety guidelines listed under Weekly Service in Maintenance and take precautions to ensure you are not injured while inspecting your car or carrying out roadside repairs.

Fuel System

When the engine turns over but refuses to fire, chances are you've got a fuel problem. Eliminate the most obvious problem first: check that there is fuel in the tank. Normally the fuel gauge will tell you when fuel is

NEVER allow naked flame or sparks anywhere near fuel. Do not smoke or permit anyone else to smoke nearby. It's also a good idea to disconnect the battery first. When checking out or repairing an electric fuel pump, be sure to turn off the ignition beforehand.

running low, but if you suspect the gauge is faulty, remove the filler cap and then rock the car. You should be able to hear the fuel sloshing around inside.

One problem with allowing the car to run out of petrol is that it can have a knock-on effect. The sediment that is present in most fuel tanks will get sucked into the fuel system, choking up filters and the main jet inside the carburettor. If you allow a diesel to run dry, it's not just a matter of pouring in fuel from a can: the system will have to be bled.

To avoid these problems, get into the habit of keeping an eye on the fuel gauge. Don't wait until you're running on fumes, fill up when the indicator hits the halfway mark. In a city where 24-hour service stations are thick on the ground you can afford to pass by one where the prices are too high because you won't go far before finding a cheaper alternative. But when driving in sparsely-populated areas, bear in mind that you may have difficulty finding a garage that sells the right fuel for your car. And because many rural service stations close on Sundays and public holidays, the few that remain open can get away with charging a fortune.

Your only alternative is to carry a can of fuel in the boot. Don't use any container. Buy a purpose-made fuel can from a car accessory shop. Get one with a pouring spout, as it makes the job of filling the tank much easier. Alternatively, carry a funnel. You can improvise a funnel from the top half of a large plastic drinks bottle, or, as a last resort, from newspaper. Simply fold the paper to make a cone, then tear off the bottom.

Replace the contents of your spare can every few months, as fuel deteriorates. Vapours can escape, so keep the spare can in the boot where there's no danger of you or your pas-

emergency

In some old cars the battery is located in the boot. It is not safe to carry a spare fuel container in the vicinity of the battery as a stray spark could ignite petrol fumes.

sengers inhaling poisonous fumes. If you drive a hatchback, make sure no one smokes in the car while there is a can of fuel in the luggage compartment. Have the windows open a little, and stop and check the can if you smell petrol fumes.

There is some warning when the car runs out of fuel. One cylinder will stop before the others, causing the car to splutter and lose power. Use this warning to pull off the road.

Hopefully you will notice that the tank is running low before it gets to this stage. If you are not carrying any spare fuel, conserve what little you have left by careful driving:

- Accelerate smoothly to get into top gear as soon as possible.
- Do not allow the engine to labour.
- Avoid stopping. Keep off the brakes as much as possible. If you see traffic lights in the distance, anticipate whether they're about to turn to red. Reduce speed on the approach so that by the time you arrive they're changing back to green.
- Make sure you have a clear run at any hills. Hang well back from vehicles in front – you don't want to get stuck behind them and have to waste fuel on a hill start.
- Don't be tempted to coast downhill out of gear. Stay in a high gear, and don't use the accelerator. If you switch off the ignition, the steering lock will come on, the brake servo will not function, and a great deal of extra pressure will be required on the brake pedal to slow the vehicle, making it unsafe.

FUEL CUT-OFF SWITCH

Some modern cars are fitted with a safety device which cuts off the fuel supply on impact. This cut-off switch can sometimes be activated by driving too fast over a bump or hitting a kerb.

If you think this may have been the case, there's no need to call out a mechanic. The handbook will tell you how to reset the switch.

FUEL LEAKS

Leaks from the tank are rare. A small hole can be temporarily blocked by pushing a shaped stick or rag into the opening. Chewing gum is also useful. A more efficient way is to use a self-tapping screw (if you don't carry these in your tool kit, borrow a 'non-essential' one from the interior trim) with a piece of leather as an improvised washer. A leak in the seam of the tank can be stemmed by rubbing soap into the crack.

If you are stranded in a remote area and have no choice but to make an emergency repair, a large hole can be stopped using a piece of hose. First place a bolt with a large washer into the hole. Push the hose in, then place another large washer over the end. Tighten the nut and the hose will expand, sealing the hole.

A leak from a fuel line will not stop a vehicle, but it does create a risk of fire. Fuel dripping on to a hot component like an exhaust pipe will ignite. To stop small leaks, wind a length of string coated with soap around the pipe.

DEFECTIVE FUEL PUMP

If you have a fuel-injected or diesel engine, do not attempt to inspect or repair a faulty pump yourself. Even when the engine is not running, pressure in the system remains high and specialist knowledge and tools are required to deal with this.

Fuel pumps come in two varieties: electrical and mechanical. An electrical pump should make a whirring noise when you switch on the ignition. If it doesn't make a sound, check the wires feeding the pump for loose connections. Next, detach the feed pipe or hose from the pump to the engine and place the end into a container. When you turn on the ignition, fuel should spray out of the pipe. If no fuel comes out, the pump is defective.

To check a mechanical fuel pump, detach the feed pipe and place it in a container, then get someone to operate the starter. Again, fuel should come out of the pipe if the pump is working. Check that the sealing ring on the filter cover is fitted properly.

A defective electrical pump can sometimes be started by turning the ignition on and then giving the body of the pump a light tap with a spanner. If all else fails, a petrol container can be used to gravity-feed the engine. Cut the fuel line where it leaves the pump and place the end in the bottom of a petrol can suspended above the carburettor. Gravity will feed fuel into the system.

VAPOUR LOCK

During hot weather fuel can turn to vapour inside the tank. The pump will then fail because there is not enough liquid for it to operate. This can also be caused by using too high a grade of petrol for your car.

To remedy this, soak a piece of rag in cold water and wrap it around the fuel lines. This will cool the pipes and return the fuel to its liquid state.

AIR LOCK

Sometimes an air lock can cause petrol starvation. If when you release the filler cap air can be heard escaping, you have probably cleared the problem.

Older vehicles often have a small air hole in the filler cap and if this gets blocked it can cause an airlock. Buy a replacement cap as soon as possible.

FLOODING

An excess of petrol in the fuel–air mixture can flood the engine. This is a common problem in cold weather, when full choke is required to start the engine. If you have a manual choke vehicle and forget to ease in the choke, or you pump away at the accelerator pedal with the choke full out, the engine will stall.

Flooding can also occur while the car is being driven. Watch out for blackish exhaust fumes or a strong smell of petrol. Another sign may be that the engine stops when left idling while halted at traffic lights.

To rectify this, push the manual choke in and slowly depress the accelerator pedal all the way down. Keep it down and turn the starter for a few seconds. This creates an increase in air flow and will help dry the plugs. If it doesn't do the trick first time, be patient and wait about 10 minutes before trying again.

Vehicles fitted with an automatic choke should be taken to a garage for repair when flooding occurs. You might be able to drive to the garage if you keep the revs high whenever you have to stop in traffic.

If the plugs have been soaked you may need to take them out and dry them. You will be able to see the petrol on the electrodes. Dry this off and use a piece of emery paper to clean the fouling from the gap.

DEFECTIVE CARBURETTOR

Modern cars tend to have fuel-injection systems in place of the carburettor. Those which do still have carburettors are fitted with tamper-proof seals to prevent DIY repairs. If this is the case, you have no choice but to leave it to the specialists. NEVER attempt roadside repairs.

On an old car, persistent flooding of the carburettor may occur as a result of the float being punctured or the needle valve becoming jammed open. Sometimes tapping the carburettor lightly can be enough to cure a stuck needle valve.

Another problem which can arise is a clogged air cleaner. This filter sits on top of the carburettor and prevents dirt and dust getting sucked into the system. Should this become choked with dirt it will seriously restrict the air supply.

To prevent this from happening, make sure you service the filter regularly – especially in dusty conditions. Strictly as a last resort, you can run the engine with the air filter removed – but this is purely a get-you-home measure. Install a new filter as soon as possible.

Overheating

Overheating is one of the commonest causes of breakdown, especially on a hot summer's day when the roads are congested with holiday-makers.

The temperature gauge or warning light should tell you that there is a problem. When you see the needle on the gauge climbing, slow down but remain in a high gear. Strange as it may sound, switching on the heater can help stabilize an engine that is overheating. Although the inside of the car will get hotter, the heater will give greater volume to the coolant, thereby making the engine cooler. Drive slowly until you can safely pull over. If you are not carrying a container of water, try to continue to the next garage or place where you can obtain water.

Should you fail to notice the warning indicators on the dashboard, or if the temperature gauge fails to operate because so much coolant has leaked away that there isn't enough left in the system to operate the gauge, the next sign could be steam escaping from under the bonnet, random banging or bubbling sounds from the engine, or a smell of burning oil or paint. Pull off the road immediately you notice any of these signs. Don't drive any further.

When safely parked, open the bonnet very cautiously as a cloud of scalding steam could escape. Leave the bonnet open, switch off the engine and wait for things to cool down before you do anything else.

NEVER attempt to remove the radiator cap until the engine has cooled down fully. Scalding steam will erupt from the radiator if the cap is removed too soon, and this can cause serious burns.

Allow at least 15 minutes for the engine to cool down, more if it's a very hot day. When you think the engine has cooled sufficiently, using a cloth or thick glove to protect your hand, turn the cap very slowly. DON'T lean over the engine, keep your body angled so that your face is well clear. At the first sign of hot water or steam escaping, screw the cap back on and leave it to cool some more.

Once the radiator cap can safely be removed, unscrew it slowly keeping your face well clear. Allow the pressure to escape, then check the water level inside the radiator. Do not immediately refill with cold water as the thermal shock may cause costly damage to the radiator or engine block. If you can, use hot water; otherwise wait another 10 minutes then trickle the cold water in slowly.

As you pour the water in, watch for leaks from hoses, the radiator and water pump. Small leaks can be temporarily repaired (see below) to allow you to continue your journey as far as the next garage. Where the leak cannot be repaired, however, the car should not be driven.

Apart from leaks in the system, other possible causes of overheating include:

- Leaves or other debris covering the radiator
- Burst or collapsed hose
- Broken fan

OVERHEATED BATTERY

Occasionally, where there is an electrical fault, the battery can overheat. Typical symptoms are a smell of rotten eggs coming from the battery (as opposed to the catalytic converter in the exhaust system of modern petrol-engined cars) and the contents of the battery may bubble.

There is a danger that the battery could explode so exercise extreme caution. DO NOT breathe the fumes as they are toxic.

The safest course of action is to call out a mechanic to put right the electrical fault which is causing the battery to overheat. However, if you have no alternative but to continue, drive very slowly and stop at regular intervals to allow the battery to cool off again. Proceed only as far as the nearest garage.

- Faulty thermostat
- Loose or broken fan belt
- Blown head gasket

One of the signs of a leak in the cylinder head gasket is the presence of air bubbles inside the radiator, so if you see bubbles floating to the top after you have refilled the radiator, this could be the cause. It's best to call out a breakdown service as to continue will risk further damage to the engine.

REPAIRING LEAKS

A flying stone can sometimes puncture the metal tubes which carry water round the engine, or the radiator tank itself. There are products on the market designed specifically to seal a leaking radiator. If you drive an old banger whose metalwork is growing weak with age, it's worth adding one of these to your emergency kit. It is intended purely as a get-you-home measure, so the radiator should be professionally repaired or replaced at the earliest opportunity.

Having repaired any form of leak in the cooling system, replace the radiator cap, but don't screw it on too tightly. If you tighten it all the way, the pressure could be more than your temporary repair can withstand.

To repair a hole in a tube, cut away the fins to expose the damage and snip through the part of the tube where the hole is. Seal the two open ends by using a pair of pliers to crush them flat, then bend each piece back on itself to form a seal.

Several tubes can be repaired this way with no serious affect on the engine, but bear in mind that such improvised repairs are best confined to vehicles whose warranties and guarantees have expired – you could risk invalidating the manufacturer's warranty by carrying out your own emergency repairs on a new car.

A small hole in the radiator tank may be plugged with a match, pencil or small piece of wood shaped to fit the hole. An egg broken into the radiator will help seal any gaps, as will tobacco – break up six cigarettes and put the tobacco in the radiator.

If a seam is leaking, chewing gum makes a handy repair material. Push this firmly into the seam while still malleable. Contact with water will harden the gum.

Split hose

Cooling water is carried between the engine and radiator in rubber pipes. As these age and deteriorate, leaks can occur. The introduction of antifreeze in readiness for winter tends to show up every weak spot, because it is oily. Check for cracks when you carry out your weekly service. The points where the jubilee clips are clamped on are particular weak spots.

If you find a leak near a hose clip, tighten the clip to reduce the flow of escaping coolant to an occasional drip. Be careful not to over-tighten the clip because you could make the leak worse. If you can't reduce the flow in this way, remove the hose and wrap a little tape around the joint, then reconnect the hose and refill the radiator.

The top radiator hose is the one most likely to split because it carries the hottest water. If a leak occurs, wait until the engine has cooled, then dry the outside of the hose, rub the area with an emery cloth if you have one, and wrap a waterproof tape tightly around the damaged area. Garages and accessory shops sell hose-repair kits containing tape designed for the purpose, but you can make do with carpet tape or plumber's tape, or other non-porous sticky-backed equivalents. Make sure the tape covers not just the damaged part but much of the surrounding area as well.

If the hose has a large split, cut a piece of tin to match the diameter of the hole and insert this plate so that it blocks the hole. Wrap the outside with wire to keep the metal plate in position.

Collapsed hose

If the lower hose gets soaked with oil it can become soft. This, combined with heat from the engine and the suction of the pump, can cause the hose to collapse.

To overcome this, insert a piece of heavy wire coiled to the same diameter as the hose.

BROKEN FAN

A minor accident, like rear-ending the car in front, can cause damage to the plastic blades of your cooling fan. To compensate for a broken blade, cut off the blade opposite so that balance is restored, otherwise the fan will vibrate excessively.

FAULTY THERMOSTAT

When the vehicle keeps overheating even though you cannot find any leaks in the cooling system, a faulty thermostat may be to blame. On some systems, water will not circulate or the electric fan will not operate until the thermostat reaches a certain temperature. When the temperature fails to register because the thermostat is sticking, the cooling system cannot function. Confirm the cause of the problem by switching on the heater. If it blows only cold air, the thermostat needs to be repaired.

A vehicle can be run – as an emergency measure – with the thermostat removed, but you risk doing serious damage to the engine in the process. If you have an expensive new car and don't want to end up with a very high repair bill, DON'T drive without the thermostat. With an old banger, however, it may be worth taking the risk. The handbook or workshop manual will tell you where it is located and how to remove it.

FAN BELT

The fan belt drives the water pump, so anything which prevents the fan belt operating will cause the engine to overheat. Check your fan belt regularly for signs of wear to avoid this problem occurring.

A loose belt can be tightened by adjusting the retaining nuts, or by binding the belt with tape to reduce the slack.

A broken belt should ideally be replaced with a replacement belt of the correct size or a universal belt which has to be cut to the right length. Fit the belt by hand – trying to lever it on with a screwdriver could cause damage. Make sure

emergency

you slacken off the pulleys as much as possible to make it go on easily.

Most improvised substitutes won't hold out against the kind of pressure a modern fan belt is subjected to. Since the generator requires high tension to make it work, it's best to run any temporary belt you improvise out of string or nylon rope (tights or stockings stretch too much) between the crankshaft and water pump pulleys only. Provided the battery is in good condition, the engine will run without the generator – but you will have to turn off the radio, heater and wipers to make the battery last as long as possible. You should be able to keep going for about an hour – less at night with the lights on – which will hopefully be enough to get you to a garage.

If all else fails, let the engine cool fully and clear away all broken bits of belt, then drive slowly in high gear with all unnecessary electrics switched off. This should enable you to travel about 5 km (3 miles). The engine is liable to overheat again, so be prepared to stop and let it cool down.

Low Oil Pressure

Oil is the lifeblood of the engine. Without lubrication, metal will rub against metal causing excessive wear until moving parts seize up. Monitor the dashboard warning lights constantly. When the oil pressure warning light comes on, or if you smell burning or hear rhythmic knocking sounds, slow down and park the car as soon as you can.

Hopefully the problem can be rectified by topping up the oil level. Drive on slowly, smoothly and gently, and keep monitoring the gauges. There may be an oil leak, in which case you will have to continue topping up the level until you get home.

If you have no oil, NEVER try to raise the level by adding water. Driving on will damage the engine beyond repair, so you may have no choice but to abandon your journey.

When the oil level is fine but the lubricant is not circulating because the pump has failed, you will need to call out a breakdown vehicle.

In the unlikely event that you were to find yourself in a remote area, far from civilization, where it was a matter of life and death to continue your journey at all costs, you could try letting the engine cool and then pouring in 6–8 pints of oil above the normal level. This will submerge the crankshaft and splash oil around the moving parts. But this is risky and could ruin your vehicle – save it for dire emergencies only.

Punctures

Many problems can be averted if you get in the habit of inspecting your tyres (including the spare) at frequent intervals as described in Maintenance. Check the tread for sharp objects like stones, nails, or glass embedded in the tyre. Before removing them, mark the spot so that if the tyre starts to deflate you will know where the air is escaping from. These types of puncture release air very slowly; it could take several hours before you're aware that you've got a flat tyre. Driving on a flat tyre is a little like running over Catseyes. When the ride gets suspiciously bumpy or the steering is affected, pull over to a safe place and check each

AVOIDING PUNCTURES

Some punctures are unavoidable, but you can minimize the risks by careful driving.

• Take care when parking not to damage the sidewall or rim of the wheel by striking the kerb.

• Try not to drive over debris or sharp objects in the road if you can avoid it. Reduce your speed and try to go round the debris, but NEVER endanger other road users by swerving violently.

• On the scene of an accident look out for broken glass. Road junctions and traffic lights are common places for this.

• Think twice before driving on a gravel or unpaved road or in long grass. Reduce your speed to lessen the risk of damage.

wheel. It may just be that you're on a badly worn stretch of road, but take a look to be on the safe side.

BLOWOUTS

A slow puncture is a hazard of everyday motoring and is rarely dangerous, but a blowout can be disasterous. This is a sudden, rapid deflation – the tyre doesn't so much leak air as burst. Fortunately improvements in tyre design and manufacture have made blowouts a rare occurrence, but they do still happen, especially when tyres are under-inflated or the car is driven at speed over a sharp object.

A driver who has taken one hand off the steering wheel to light a cigarette or change a cassette will find the wheel suddenly snatched from their grasp as the car swerves violently towards the side where the puncture has occurred. If a rear wheel has burst the back of the car may 'fishtail'. This is why it is so important to keep both hands on the wheel in either the quarter-to-three or the ten-to-two position and maintain a steady grip at all times.

It is vital that you stay calm in the event of a blowout. If you allow yourself to panic you might try to correct the sudden change of direction by slamming on the brakes and over-steering – which will cause the car to skid. The correct response is to:

- Avoid braking. The brakes can't slow a deflated tyre, so applying the brakes will only work on the good wheels, making the car weave even more.
- Come off the accelerator to lose speed. The aim is to roll gently to a safe stopping place.
- Counter the pull on the wheel by using both hands to steer smoothly but firmly in the opposite direction. The steering wheel will feel very heavy and it will take considerable effort to maintain control, so brace yourself.
- Look for a safe place to pull off the road or out of the main traffic flow. Signal your intentions and drive slowly, steering gently towards the kerb or hard shoulder when you see a gap in traffic.
- In the outside lane of a motorway in heavy traffic, you may have to settle for pulling in as close as you can to the central reservation. Follow the standard procedure for a motorway breakdown (above).

- There's no point worrying about damaging the tyre further by driving on it. Chances are it's been damaged beyond repair already.
- On a normal road, try to stop on firm, level ground to make changing the wheel easier.
- NEVER expose yourself to danger by trying to change a tyre on the offside with your back exposed to passing traffic. The damaged wheel must be positioned next to the kerb, so if the puncture is on the offside you must drive to a quiet street where you can turn the car around.
- The hard shoulder is NOT a safe place to change a tyre. You may have seen motorists doing it, and some get away with it and live to tell the tale – but a great many don't.

REPAIRING A PUNCTURE

Your tool kit (see Essentials) should include a can of tyre sealant. This is ideal for quick temporary repairs on slow punctures caused by driving over a small sharp object. But be warned: the tyre will be useless afterwards.

Simply screw the can's adaptor to the tyre valve and press the trigger. An air-and-sealant mix will squirt into the tyre, which will spread all around the tyre's interior as you drive (you need to cover about 40 km/20 miles to give it time to work).

CHANGING A WHEEL

Don't wait until you have a flat tyre to read through these instructions one stage at a time. You should have the whole procedure clear in your mind before you start the job. You will also need to study your vehicle's handbook because some cars have unusual features. For example, many Italian cars have wheel nuts that turn in the anti-clockwise to tighten and clockwise to loosen (the exact reverse of British wheel nuts). A quick look at the handbook might prevent you giving yourself a hernia trying to turn a nut in the wrong direction. You should also check where the jacking points are – positioning the jack in the wrong place could result in the metal of the underbelly giving way and the car crashing down.

It's a good idea, when you get a new car, to have a practice session. Wheel nuts are often tightened to the point where they can be impossible to shift with the flimsy tools provided with the car, so the best place to make that discovery is in

1

- Switch on the hazard warning lights and side lights if visibility is poor. Set up your warning triangle to warn approaching traffic.
- Check that the handbrake is applied and engage first or reverse gear. Using a block of wood or some large stones, chock the wheel diagonally opposite the puncture to prevent the car rolling when it is jacked up.
- Place the spare wheel flat on the floor just under the side of the car. This will prevent the car from falling to the ground, should it topple off the jack.

2

- Prise off the wheel trim.
- Loosen the wheel nuts a quarter turn each, using the wheel brace. If they are too tight, try pushing down with your foot on the long handle of the wheelbrace to get more leverage.

3

- Locate the jack at the correct jacking point (see manufacturer's handbook). It should lock securely into the jacking point. Now lift the car so that the puncture is clear of the ground.

4

- Finish unscrewing the wheel nuts, bottom ones first, and place them in your pocket or somewhere there's no risk of losing them. Pull the wheel off, making sure the car doesn't move on the jack.
- Take the spare wheel from under the car, and place the punctured wheel there instead.

5

- Align the bolt holes on the spare with the bolts in the hub before lifting the wheel and sliding it on. Wheels are very heavy, so it may help you to use a piece of wood to lever the spare into position.
- Hand-tighten the wheel nuts, working diagonally (i.e. first one corner, then the other). Slowly lower the jack so that the tyre touches the ground.
- Remove the jack and finish tightening the nuts using the wheelbrace. Don't use extra leverage to tighten them, as you could damage the threads. Make sure all are secure.

6

- Replace the wheel trim.
- Pack up all your gear and stow it back in the car. Remember to remove chocks from the wheels and pick up planks of wood, etc.
- Replace the punctured tyre as soon as possible. It is illegal to carry a spare which is not roadworthy.

your garage where you can lay hands on tools that will shift them.

The other thing to make sure of before you start is that you are parked in a safe place where the ground is firm and level. NEVER park on a bend or on a hill to change a wheel. Make sure the damaged wheel is positioned next to the kerb. If you have no choice but to park on soft ground, make sure you have a flat piece of wood to go underneath the jack and help spread the load, otherwise it will sink into the ground when you jack the car up.

The other essential items are the spare, wheelbrace and jack. And, where locking wheel nuts have been fitted, a device for removing them. Some wheel trims also need to be removed with a special device. If any of these are missing or not in a fit condition to be used, you cannot proceed any further. Place everything you will need on the ground beside

---

NEVER crawl or even reach under a car supported only by a jack. If the car wobbles on the jack it is not secure and you are not safe to proceed. Call out a breakdown service.

---

the car, because you won't want to reach into the car when it is jacked up.

Once you are satisfied that you have all the tools and can handle the job, it's time to begin. If you carry overalls and gloves for working, put them on.

LOOSE WHEELS

If you hear a rhythmic clunking coming from underneath the car, it could mean that the wheel nuts have worked loose. Slow down gently and check them. Tighten them using the wheelbrace, but be careful not to over-tighten.

emergency starting

When the engine won't start and the headlights appear very dim even on main beam, the most likely cause is a problem with the battery. Before lifting the bonnet to take a look, get out a pair of gloves to protect your skin.

It may be that the battery has plenty of life but the terminals are damp or corroded, preventing a good connection being made. This often happens in damp conditions when the battery is nearing the end of its life. See Maintenance for tips on checking and cleaning the terminals.

More usually, the lights or radio have been left on after the engine was switched off. This can drain a battery within a few hours. Or it may be that the car has been used for a series of short-hop journeys in winter with the lights, heater, radio, demister, wipers, etc all going strong. You need to drive for some distance, or keep the engine running at fast-idle

---

Batteries contain hazardous chemicals which should not be allowed to come into contact with the skin or eyes. They also give off an explosive gas, so NEVER use a match or lighter to illuminate the battery, don't smoke, and take precautions to ensure nothing shorts or sparks in the vicinity of the battery. ALWAYS read the manufacturer's warnings on the label before tampering with a battery. Follow any precautions they may advise in addition to the ones set out in this book.

---

speed, to charge the battery and compensate for all the demands you've placed on it.

Some new cars are fitted with maintenance-free batteries. These have a condition indicator, so you can tell at a glance whether the battery needs to be replaced or recharged. There will be a label on the battery (or a note in the car's handbook) telling you how to go about recharging it – follow the manufacturer's instructions to the letter.

emergency

Jump Leads

The most convenient way to start a car with a dead battery – provided you can find a friendly motorist who is willing to let you connect up to their fully charged battery – is by using jump leads. You should have a set in your tool kit. Buy a good-quality brand – it's a false economy to settle for a cheap set with puny jaws and thin cables because they could melt or you could get a shock from handling the uninsulated clamps. They need to be at least 4 metres (13 feet) long. Sometimes it is difficult to get another car close enough, so the longer the better.

Check that the battery you will be using to boost yours is of the same voltage and polarity. You cannot proceed if one is negative earth and the other is positive.

Make sure the flat battery has sufficient fluid; top up with

distilled water if necessary. Examine the terminals to make certain they are free of moisture, dirt and corrosion.

First of all, take the following precautions:

- Remove rings, bracelets, wristwatches and other jewellery. Tie back long hair and make sure that you're not wearing any loose clothing that could get fouled in moving parts of

the engine.

- Position the two cars so the jump leads will reach, but not so close that they are touching. There's a danger that if something goes wrong they could weld together.
- Make sure, if you are doing this in a garage, that the area is well ventilated and that the ground is clear of flammable liquids. Fuel vapour could ignite if there's any sparking. NEVER use a service station forecourt.
- Turn off all electrical equipment – lights, wipers, heater, radio, etc.– in both cars, unless you are working by the roadside at night, in which case the hazard warning lights will have to be left on. Switch off the ignition for the time being. Close all the doors.
- Apply the handbrake and select neutral gear for a manual transmission, park for an automatic.

Leads must be connected and removed in the exact sequence listed below. Throughout the procedure, keep your hands and the cables clear of moving parts such as fans and drivebelts.

If both batteries are POSITIVE EARTH:

- Connect the black cable first to the negative (-) terminal of the booster battery, and then attach the other end to the negative (-) terminal of the flat battery. The lead must not be allowed to touch any metal part of either car.
- Now connect one end of the red cable to the positive (+)

terminal of the booster battery and attach the other end to a good earthing point – such as a metal bolt or bracket – on the vehicle with the flat battery. This earthing point must be at least 45 cm (18 ins) from the battery, so that any sparking which occurs will not ignite gases from the battery. Make sure the leads are not touching each other.

If both batteries are NEGATIVE EARTH:

- Connect the red cable first to the positive (+) terminal of the booster battery, attaching the other end to the positive (+) terminal of the flat battery. The lead must not be allowed to touch any metal part of either car.
- Next, attach one end of the black cable to the negative (-) terminal of the booster battery and connect the other end to a good earthing point – such as a metal bolt or bracket on the engine block – at least 45 cm (18 ins) from the flat battery so that any sparking which occurs will not ignite gases from the battery. Make sure the leads are not touching each other.

Start the car with the booster battery and let it run at medium revs for a few minutes. Keep it running while trying to start the car with the flat battery. Run both engines for a few minutes until the one with the flat battery is going smoothly. If it doesn't work first time, have a couple more goes before giving up and looking for another cause of the problem.

Once the defective car is started successfully, stop the booster car's engine and remove the jump leads in the exact reverse order to which they were connected.

Having started the engine, you need to run the car for about 40 km (25 miles) to allow the battery to recharge properly. If you switch the engine off before it has time to recharge fully, the battery will probably die on you again.

Push Start

This method is not suitable for all vehicles. Push- or bump-starting can damage cars with automatic gearboxes, catalytic converters and diesel engines. Save yourself a fortune in

> ### DOs AND DON'Ts
> DO make sure the way ahead is clear.
>
> DON'T let a 'good Samaritan' steer while you push – if they turn out to be a car thief on the make, it might be the last you ever see of your car.
>
> DON'T push start while in reverse gear – you could wreck the transmission.
>
> DO run the car for a good distance once you've got it started, to give the battery time to recharge fully.

repair bills by checking the manufacturer's handbook before proceeding.

1 Switch on the ignition.
2 Turn off unnecessary electrical equipment (heater, radio, etc).
3 Select second or third gear.
4 Hold the clutch pedal down.
5 On cars with a manual choke, pull the choke out only if the engine is cold.
6 When the car is rolling at jogging speed, let the clutch out and the engine should fire.

When travelling alone, it may be tempting to try push-starting the car on a hill, steering with one hand through the open door while you trot alongside. BEWARE: there's a danger that on a steep incline the car will pick up speed very quickly, and you may not be able to hop back in. There's also a risk that you could trip and lose your grip on the steering wheel. Either way you could end up waving your car goodbye.

> ### TOW-STARTING A CAR
> This method works along the same lines as push-starting. First check the handbook to make sure you will not damage the car in the process, then read the section on Towing (below).
>
> Once you have hitched up the car and devised a system of communication with the driver who is towing you, simply follow the same procedure as for push-starting (points 1–6).
>
> Keep the tow rope taught until the engine fires then let it go slack as you stop so it can be undone.

emergency

Towing

When a car breaks down you may have no choice but to find someone to tow you home or to a garage. Some cars can be damaged by being pulled by a tow rope, and if this is the case you will have to wait for a professional breakdown service. Cars with power steering or servo-assisted brakes are especially problematic, because if the engine is not running these systems cannot function, making the steering heavier and the braking less efficient. Check the manufacturer's handbook – you may have to abandon the idea of towing or travel at snail's pace.

A recovery vehicle will come specially equipped either to transport or tow your car; all you have to do is follow instructions. But where you have to rely on another motorist many problems can arise, especially when you are armed with nothing more sophisticated than a length of rope. If available, a rigid tow-bar is much better than a rope, because there's no chance of the towed car suddenly rolling into the back of the towing vehicle.

LAWS GOVERNING TOWING

The first rule is to make sure that you're familiar with the legal requirements on towing for the country you are in.

- The maximum towing speed is invariably lower than the normal speed limit.
- There will be a legal restriction on the maxium length of tow rope between two vehicles. In most countries this is around 5 metres (16.5 feet).
- A bright piece of coloured cloth should be tied halfway along the rope to draw the attention of other road users to its presence.
- There may be a requirement to display an ON TOW sign on the vehicle to warn other road users.
- The towed vehicle's number plate should be covered with a sign displaying the number of towing vehicle.
- There may be prohibitions against towing on a motorway, or restrictions on how far you can go (in Britain towing would be allowed only as far as the next exit).
- Both vehicles should be taxed and insured.

Most vehicles are fitted with welded-on towing eyes which can be used to anchor a rope. In the absence of these, attach the rope to a bumper mounting point or an anti-roll bar mounting (DON'T tie it round a bumper or bodywork, as these cannot tolerate the strain).

Make sure the rope does not exceed the legal maximum length. Purpose-made tow ropes have metal clasps or fasteners at either end. When using an ordinary length of rope, secure it with a bowline.

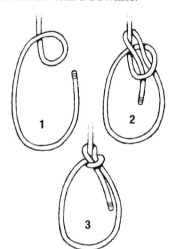

A bowline is ideal for towing because it will neither tighten nor slip when under strain, but will be easy to untie afterwards.

1. Make a small loop a little way along the rope.

2. Bring the end through the loop, feed it round on itself and then back down through the loop.

3. Pull on the end to tighten the knot.

Make sure that the rope will not foul the steering mechanism, bodywork, or number plate as it could cause damage. Where it passes over a sharp edge, use a piece of cloth to pad the area and prevent the rope being damaged. Position the rope so that it does not rest on hot components or receive the full heat of the exhaust pipe.

Where possible, turn the ignition on to the first position so that the hazard warning lights can be used to alert other road users. In the event of an electrical fault, however, the horn, lights and indicators on the car being towed will not function. The driver of the rear car should compensate for this by giving clear hand signals.

Make sure that the steering lock is not engaged. You must be able to steer the car if you are to follow the other vehicle round corners!

The two drivers must devise a route and a system of

signals for when you need to stop, turn off, slow down, etc. It's important that the towing driver signals early to warn the other driver of any manouevres he intends to make.

To move off, the towing vehicle should pull away very slowly to take up any slack. Keep to a slow, steady speed throughout, and drive smoothly so as to prevent the rope snatching. This places such strain on the rope that it could snap, with potentially disastrous consequences.

The rope needs to be kept taut – but not over-tight – the whole time. This poses a problem when travelling downhill, as there will be a tendency for the towed car to gain on the towing vehicle. To counter this, the driver of the towing vehicle should pick up speed a little, while the driver of the car being towed should apply the brakes.

At junctions, both cars should slow almost to a halt, so that the rope remains taut in readiness for moving off. The driver in front must wait for a sufficient gap to allow both cars to complete what will be a very slow manouevre. Keep an eye out for pedestrians who don't notice the rope and try to cross between the two vehicles.

Finally, keep your journey as brief as possible. It isn't only the rope that takes the strain when towing!

emergencies

No matter how skilled a driver you are, life-threatening situations may arise through no fault of your own which will severely test your abilities. A component failing while the car is travelling at speed can put lives in danger. Knowing what to do if this happens will give you a greater chance of survival.

Don't be a passive driver. For every emergency there is a proven counter-measure which will see you through, and the better prepared you are, the better the outcome. In a crisis things happen quickly. There's no time to weigh up the choices – you need to react fast. Those who have never mentally rehearsed what they would do in an emergency are prone to panic, and in many cases the panic reaction will be the wrong one. Familiarizing yourself with the following emergency strategies could mean the difference between life and death.

Brake Failure

Total brake failure is very rare with modern cars, most of which are fitted with a dual braking circuit, so that if one system fails the other should still operate.

In the unlikely event that your brakes do fail, there are a number of measures you can take to reduce the car's speed and bring it to a stop. Act quickly but calmly. You need to do several things at once to bring the car safely under control.

- Take your foot off the accelerator.
- Pump the footbrake repeatedly in case you can restore braking this way.
- Keep a firm grip on the steering wheel, but don't make any violent movements as you could cause a skid. Keep it smooth. If you need to take one hand off the wheel to work the handbrake or gear lever, try to time it so you are on a stretch of road where you can go straight and not have to worry about steering.
- Put your hazard warning lights on to warn other road users that the vehicle is behaving erratically.
- Try to apply the handbrake a little at a time. If you apply

emergency

maximum pressure it may well fail because the heat generated will cause the rear drums to expand. Give a series of short jerks instead.

- Change down through the gears, all the way to first. This may wreck the gear box, but that's a small price to pay if it prevents injury. With a manual gearbox changing down at speed is difficult, see Defensive Driving for some useful clutch techniques.
- Keep looking all the while for an escape route. Look for a soft bank, or a turning that leads to an uphill slope.
- Scraping the edges of your wheels along kerb will reduce speed, as will brushing along a hedge or wall.
- If you have to mount the kerb, take it at an angle rather than head on.
- Where there is no alternative, for example if you are picking up speed going down a steep hill, you may have to try running into the vehicle in front. Do everything within your power to warn the driver by sounding your horn and flashing your lights, and make the collision as gentle as you possibly can.

///////////////////////////////////

WARNING
NEVER try to jump out of a runway car unless it is heading over a cliff edge or an impact it cannot possibly survive. If this is the case, open the door, undo your seatbelt, tuck your chin into your chest, your arms into your sides, bring your feet and knees together, and bend at the waist to try and form a ball. Drop from the car and remain balled up as you roll along the ground.

Far more common than brake failure is the problem of a reduction in braking efficiency brought about by the brakes getting soaked or overheated. See Floods in Bad-Weather Driving for advice on how to dry out damp brakes.

When brakes overheat, as can happen if the footbrake is applied continuously while descending a steep hill, the fluid vaporizes and the brakes lose their stopping power. When you depress the pedal it will feel spongy and unresponsive. This condition is known as fading.

To prevent this occurring, engage a low gear when descending a steep incline and use engine power to slow the car. To cure fading, pump the brakes repeatedly. Stop and allow the brakes to cool for a while before continuing your journey.

Jammed Accelerator

The accelerator pedal relies on a series of springs to bring it back up when you remove your foot. Should the throttle return spring break while you are driving, the pedal will remain down.

Check the mirrors and start looking for a safe place to pull over, signalling to other traffic if necessary. Try hooking your toe under the pedal to bring it back to normal. Braking will be difficult if the revs are still high. You may have to change into neutral and switch off the ignition (leaving the ignition key in and taking care not to engage the steering lock), then coast to the side of the road.

Strictly as an emergency measure if you find yourself stranded far from help on quiet roads, a temporary repair may be effected by putting a small cushion or something soft under the pedal to hold it up. Drive slowly, applying minimal pressure to the accelerator, to the nearest garage or telephone. NEVER try this on a busy motorway.

Lights Failing

If the headlights cut out as you are driving along, slow down. Provided you can do so without endangering other road users, pull off the road immediately. Where the volume of traffic prevents this, use the hazard warning lights to drive slowly to a safe stopping place.

Windscreen Shattering

Stones thrown up by other vehicles when travelling at speed can hit the windscreen with enough force to shatter it. Always slow down on newly resurfaced roads. If loose chippings are being thrown up by a passing vehicle, press the fingertips of one hand against the glass. This will act as a shock absorber and prevent the windscreen shattering if it gets hit.

Be careful when driving behind vehicles with double

rear wheels. Large stones and even bricks can become lodged between the two wheels and fly out with no warning.

Laminated windscreens are made from interleaved layers of glass and plastic. Although the outer glass may crack on impact, your vision should not be impaired. You will still need to have the windscreen replaced, but it can wait until you get home or to your preferred garage.

Toughened glass windscreens, when struck with sufficient force, can fracture into hundreds of pieces. It can be virtually impossible to see through this crazed surface. Slow down and try to peer through an undamaged part of the windscreen, if there is one. Lean forward in your seat to help you see better, and pull over as soon as it is safe to do so. DON'T try to punch a hole as you drive unless there is no other option – you could cut your hand badly, and flying glass splinters will be blown straight into your face, possibly blinding you. If your vision is totally obscured and it's a choice between punching a hole or risking a collision, try to protect your hand by covering it with cloth, strike with the back of the hand, and turn your face to protect the eyes.

Once the car is parked in a safe place, spread a newspaper or cloth over the heating vents, radio speakers, and any other openings. Wearing gloves or having wrapped your hand in cloth to protect it, gently break away the remaining glass. Make sure there's nothing left that could fall out as you drive. Wrap the broken glass up in paper before disposing of it, to make it safe. Don't leave any fragments on the road where they might cause blowouts in other vehicles.

If your car survival kit includes an emergency windscreen, fit it according to the manufacturer's instructions. These are made of tough plastic and are usually held in place by the wipers and the front doors. Once fitted, this will get you home or to a garage where you can have a proper windscreen put in.

Many insurance policies include cover for windscreen replacement. This is well worth having, because it will allow you to call out a specialist windscreen fitter to attend to your car at the roadside at preferential rates. Keep the telephone number of your insurance company's windscreen replacement service in a place where you will be able to find it in an emergency.

Driving without a windscreen is extremely dangerous and therefore strictly a last resort. Put on a coat or thick sweater to protect you from the draught and wear sunglasses or prescription glasses to protect your eyes. Drive very slowly to the nearest garage.

Wiper Failure

If the windscreen-wiper motor burns out or refuses to work, causing the wipers to stop clearing the glass in a heavy downpour, slow down and place your face close to the windscreen to help you see better. Pull over and find a safe spot to park as soon as you can.

It may be possible to improvise a repair which will keep the wipers going. On the driver's side use something that will stretch – strong rubber bands, braces, a lycra band – and tie one end to the wipers and jam the other in the door or tie it to the door mirror. Now tie the wipers together with a piece of cord long enough to extend through the passenger's window. By pulling on this cord the wipers can be manually operated.

If the wiper blade on the driver's side should fly off suddenly, stop and replace it using the one from the passenger's side.

There are water-dispersant sprays available which will form a film on the windscreen to repel water, but this is no substitute for windscreen wipers in heavy rain. If vision is seriously impaired, abandon your journey until the rain stops.

Bonnet Flying Open

A faulty release mechanism could allow the bonnet to spring open suddenly as you are driving along. Normally there is a safeguard built into the system to prevent this: in addition to the manual release (located just under the dashboard) there is a secondary safety catch which will still secure the bonnet if the release catch is pulled accidentally.

To prevent the problem arising, when running through your First Parade checklist always make sure the bonnet is

emergency

secured. Press it down firmly, and if there are any problems with the mechanism get them fixed.

If the bonnet does fly open while you are on the road the impact could shatter the screen sending shards of glass into the passenger compartment. Try to keep steering on the same straight course, slowing down gradually. Look through the space between the hinges and the body for a view of the road ahead. Once you have reduced speed sufficiently you can wind down the driver's side window and stick your head out to check that the road is clear. Signal, and when safe to do so, pull over to the side of the road.

As a temporary repair to get you home (assuming the windscreen is still intact), rig up a temporary catch for the bonnet using wire or a length of tough cord.

Fire

Fire can spread through a vehicle in seconds. What looks like an insignificant outbreak can swiftly develop into something major. Petrol is highly volatile – once the vapour ignites the whole tank could explode.

The majority of vehicle fires are caused by accidents that rupture fuel lines and petrol tanks. Electrical faults and dropped cigarettes are among the other most common causes.

If you see smoke or flames coming from the vehicle while on the move ACT quickly. Pull over to the side of the road as soon as you can, because while the car is moving the slipstream is fanning the flames and feeding the fire.

- STOP the car
- SWITCH OFF the ignition
- EVACUATE everyone from the car by the nearside doors and direct them to a place of safety upwind and clear of traffic
- DON'T waste time unloading luggage and other belongings – your life could be at risk

Minor fires can be dealt with using a fire extinguisher, but the small extinguishers designed for cars are not large enough to tackle a serious blaze.

FIRE EXTINGUISHERS

All cars should carry an extinguisher. Invest in one weighing at least a kilo (2.5 lb) and filled with either dry powder (blue) or a liquid gas called Halon/BCF (green), both of which are suitable for liquid or electrical fires.

Because of the ozone-depleting potential of Halon, its future use and availability is likely to be restricted. For liquid fires – but NOT electrical – you can use aqueous film-forming foam (cream) which, as the name suggests, forms a film on the burning liquid to smother the flames.

NEVER use a water extinguisher (red) on liquid or electrical fires.

The substances within these extinguishers are toxic in confined spaces. Ventilate the area thoroughly once the fire has been extinguished.

Keep the extinguisher in an accessible place – NOT locked in the boot. Check it often and make sure you know how to use it.

NEVER attempt to fight a fire when it would mean your life or anyone else's at risk. Call the emergency services for assistance.

If you have no extinguisher, provided the fire is not too serious, try to smother the flames with any thick material (natural fibres rather than man-made, unless the fabric is labelled as flame retardant) you have to hand: a car rug, blanket, or coat.

When dealing with a cigarette that has dropped on to the upholstery, dowse the seat with any available liquid such as a soft drink, milk, or tea if you have a flask. Don't open all the doors as the increase in oxygen will only feed the fire. Once the fire has been extinguished, use gloves to remove smouldering seat cushions or other materials. Now open all the doors, sunroof, hatchback, etc to thoroughly ventilate the car.

A fire under the bonnet is much more unpredictable and dangerous. DON'T raise the bonnet as the rush of air will fan the flames and create a fireball. The aim is to starve the fire of air. If the heat is intense, get away from the car and call the emergency services. Only where the fire has yet to gain a hold have you any hope of putting it out with a car-size fire extinguisher. Without an extinguisher you have no option but to wait for the fire brigade.

Open the boot just enough so the extinguisher's nozzle

will fit through. Working with the extinguisher at arm's length, direct the jet of foam or gas at the base of the fire moving it from side to side until the flames are smothered.

When dealing with an electrical fire, never touch burning wires with your bare hands. Switch off the ignition. If you have an extinguisher which is suitable for electrical fires, direct it at the base of the flames, moving it from side to side until the fire is out.

Burnt-out cars can seriously damage your health!

Many modern cars have computerized engine-management systems. When consumed by fire, these components produce cancer-causing agents that can be absorbed by the skin.

NEVER touch anything under the bonnet of a burnt out car.

When visiting scrap yards in search of spares keep away from burnt-out vehicles.

Submerged in Water

Be extra careful when driving or parking near water, especially if the manouevre involves reversing. When possible, get someone to direct you. Park parallel with the bank, not running towards it. If you have no choice but to leave the front of the car facing water, leave it in reverse gear with the handbrake on (when facing in the opposite direction, leave the car in first gear with the handbrake on).

Never leave children unattended in a car parked on a jetty or by the waterside. A child playing at driving by mimicking your actions could release the handbrake and send the car rolling towards the water.

If you are in a car which somehow falls into deep water, KEEP CALM. In most cases the car will land the right way up, tilting at an angle as the heavy engine starts to sink first. How buoyant it remains will depend on a number of variables such as the load carried, the design of the car, the speed of impact, and how airtight the door and window seals are.

Often a vehicle will remain afloat long enough for the occupants to escape while still on the surface – but only if you have the presence of mind to act quickly. The shock of 'splash down' can be terrifying, and precious seconds may be lost while the occupants gather their wits.

To escape while the car is floating on the surface:

- Release your seat belt and instruct all passengers to do the same.
- Get all the passengers to move to one side of the car (making it sink lower) while you try opening the door on the opposite side as it rises clear of the water.
- If you can open the door, hold hands to form a human chain and get clear of the car quickly.
- Alternatively, you could try wriggling out through a window or, if the sunroof opening is big enough for passengers to get through, use this as your escape route.

Once the car starts sinking, water pressure will make it very difficult to open the doors. Undo all seatbelts, and turn on the lights. The internal light will help you see and the headlights will mark your position for rescuers. Release any automatic door locks or master locks, but do not try to get out yet. Quickly close all doors and windows, and the sunroof to prolong flotation time and allow the occupants to breathe. These air pockets will be near the roof, and most probably towards the rear of the car (assuming the vehicle is sinking nose-first), so hold babies clear of the water and get children to stand on seats.

Keep one hand on a door handle to help you remain oriented, but do not attempt to open doors until the interior of the car is almost filled with water. Only when the water pressure inside the car is almost equal to that outside will it be possible to open a door or window and swim to safety. Explain this to the passengers and keep them from panicking. The calmer and more confident you seem, the more likely they are to follow your lead.

At first the water will stream in, but when it gets around chin-height the car will settle. Tell everyone to take a deep breath then open the door and swim to the surface, blowing out through your mouth as you go. Link arms with children and help non-swimmers.

If the door won't open, try winding a window down, or kicking out a window (attack the corner for maximum effect).

///////////////////////////////////////

WARNING

Where doors and windows are operated electrically they may behave erratically when water floods the electrics. The doors could lock and windows may start going up and down randomly even though no one is touching the controls.

If you drive a car with electric windows, invest in a 'Life-hammer' – a tool with a chromium-plated head designed to break car windows in an emergency when the electrics fail and prevent your escape. It also has a sharp blade to cut through seat belts if necessary. Keep it in the glove compartment at all times. Once you've cracked a corner of the window with the Lifehammer, use your feet to push out the glass.

Having made your escape, stay together on the surface, making sure everyone is accounted for.

Stuck On a Level Crossing

 A level crossing is the last place you want to get stuck, but breakdowns have a way of happening at the least opportune moment and every year there are scores of accidents involving cars and trains. Many of these result from drivers ignoring the guidelines for crossing railway tracks:

• NEVER stop on a level crossing, and don't park near a crossing.
• WAIT until the car in front has cleared the crossing before you attempt to cross. If the road ahead is blocked, DON'T enter the crossing.
• NEVER ignore the flashing lights which warn of an approaching train or try to zigzag round the half barriers. Wait behind the barrier or white line until the signals show it is safe to proceed.

In rural areas you may come across unattended crossings with no signals. stop, look and listen to make sure no trains are approaching. Where there is a telephone-link to the signal operator, call and check that it is safe to proceed, then call again to let the operator know you have cleared the crossing.

If your car should break down or be involved in an accident on a level crossing, the first priority is to establish whether there is a train coming. If you can see or hear one approaching, or if the signal lights are flashing, the only thing you can do is to get everyone out of the car. Don't waste time trying to move the car or empty it of your belongings. For safety's sake you need to get about 50 metres (165 feet) clear of the track, because when a train travelling at speed hits a car, debris can be flung in all directions causing serious injuries.

Where there is no indication that a train is approaching, use the emergency telephone to inform the signal operator that your vehicle is causing an obstruction, and follow any instructions you are given. Provided there is time, try to move the car by using the starter motor to jerk it clear. Select a low gear and operate the starter in short bursts to jerk the car forward. This method will not work on an automatic car.

Alternatively, get someone to help push you clear – but abandon the car the moment you hear an approaching train or if the alarm or warning lights should come on.

accidents

The exact course of action to be taken after an accident will depend on how serious the damage is and whether there are any casualties, but the number one priority should always be to make sure that one accident does not lead to another.

If you witness an accident you must instantly decide whether you can do the most good by stopping to assist or driving to a telephone and summoning the emergency services. Don't dither – either park the car (see below for tips on how your vehicle can be used to shield the crash scene) or proceed. Many secondary accidents are caused by motorists slowing down for a better look at the crash, only to collide with other drivers who have allowed themselves to be similarly distracted.

REMEMBER

Accidents are very distressing. There could be people on the scene with terrible injuries, screaming in panic and terror. Others may be screaming abuse. If you are to help anyone, you need to remain calm and authoritative. Take a couple of deep breaths to steady yourself. Walk swiftly – don't run – to the scene, formulating a plan of action as you go, and then take it one step at a time.

Accident Procedure

If you are yourself involved in an accident, try to keep as calm as possible. The law requires you to take certain steps, and a successful insurance claim can depend on your ability to record essential details. You may be injured or in a state of shock, but try to compose yourself sufficiently to carry out the following procedures:

1 STOP! Failing to stop after being involved in an accident is an offence. You must remain on the scene if someone has been injured or if there is damage to any vehicle, property, or licensed animals.
2 Further collisions are a major risk, so if the crashed vehicles are causing an obstruction, warn oncoming traffic.
3 Make the accident scene safe by stabilizing vehicles, extinguishing cigarettes, and moving uninjured persons to a safe place at the roadside (DON'T move casualties unless there is a risk of fire or explosions endangering their life).
4 Administer first aid to the injured and send for an ambulance.
5 The police should be called to the scene where there is injury, traffic obstruction or damage to property.
6 Take photos or make a sketch-map of the scene before moving vehicles. Note any damage sustained. Record road conditions at the time of the accident, speed at which vehicles were travelling and actions taken by drivers which had a bearing on events.
7 Exchange details (names, addresses, car make and model, insurers, etc) with other drivers or passengers involved, and note all registration numbers. Take down names and addresses of witnesses.
8 DON'T get involved in an argument and NEVER admit liability.
9 After a major accident, the police will arrange for damaged vehicles to be towed away, but in a minor accident you will probably be left to make your own arrangements. The motoring organizations will send out a recovery vehicle if you are a member; alternatively, contact a local garage.

YOUR LEGAL OBLIGATIONS

All countries have legislation requiring you to stop in the event of an accident where a person has been injured or damage has been done to someone else's vehicle, property, or animal.

Even if your car is untouched and you do not consider the

emergency!

accident to have been in any way your fault, you must stop. The other driver might contend that he or she crashed because your lights dazzled them, or that your actions forced them to swerve into the path of another vehicle. These are contributing factors which involve you in the accident.

If you drive on, you can be reported to the police for failing to stop, and there's a danger that the courts will look upon this as an admission of your guilt and award the other driver damages. You would also incur a fine and your licence would be endorsed. And where there is evidence to suggest that you had been drinking beforehand, you could face disqualification.

You must give your name and address (and that of the vehicle owner), and the registration number of the vehicle to anyone having reasonable grounds for requiring them. Ask for their details in return. If someone refuses to give this information, make a note of their registration number and call the police immediately. You should also contact the police if the other driver is argumentative, or if you suspect that a criminal offence has been committed, such as driving under the influence of alcohol.

If for any reason it is not possible to give your name and address at the scene of the accident, report the accident to the police within the next 24 hours. You will also have to produce your insurance certificate.

It's a good idea to report the accident to the police even in cases where there seems to be no legal requirement to do so. It can happen that a driver will admit to being at fault, and then subsequently change his mind. Always try to get the name and address of an impartial witness at the scene of the accident, and pass these details on to the police. The more evidence you can amass (see the section on insurance claims below) the more chance there is of your claim being paid in full.

Don't get into any arguments and – callous as this may seem – don't say sorry even if it was all your fault. The golden rule is: NEVER admit liability. There may be factors you are not aware of – the other driver may have been drinking, their licence may have been revoked, they may have failed their driving test and taken to the road illegally – but if you take the blame you could end up paying damages even though they were breaking the law.

Accidents involving injuries

If someone is hurt in an accident, however, slightly, the police should be informed. As the driver, it is your responsibility to make a statement to a police officer at the scene or to call in at a police station within 24 hours.

Anything you say will be taken down and could be used as evidence, so think carefully and make sure you give an accurate account.

Accidents involving property

If you damage a parked car or knock down a roadside fence, you must try to find the owner and give them your insurance details. If you cannot do this, inform the police within 24 hours. Failing to report an accident is an offence – you could be fined and have your licence endorsed.

Accidents involving animals

So far as the law is concerned, you are obliged to stop and exchange details with the owner if you hit a dog, horse, mule, cow, sheep, goat, or pig. (Where the owner cannot be found, the police should be notified within 24 hours.) There is no such obligation in accidents involving other animals such as cats, deer, foxes, hedgehogs, badgers, etc.

Animals are unpredictable, so if you see one on or near the road, slow down. But NEVER swerve violently to avoid hitting an animal as you could cause a serious accident. A large animal like a cow or deer will damage the car in a collision. Where a collision seems inevitable, warn your passengers to prepare for impact and brake hard. It may not be possible for you to remove the heavy carcase from the road, in which case you should set up a warning triangle to alert oncoming traffic, and send for the police.

An animal that is injured and in pain may lash out at those who try to help it. A wild creature that is unused to human contact will be doubly terrified, and could inflict severe bites or scratches – badgers are particularly fierce, but even a deer can do a lot of damage with its flailing hooves. If you see an injured wild animal, the best course of action may be to contact a local animal charity, wildlife sanctuary or vet's surgery and report the animal's location. Someone equipped with the necessary protective gear will turn out to try and rescue the wounded animal.

CONTROLLING PETS

It is every pet-owner's responsibility to control their animals. If you have dogs, don't let them out alone, especially on busy streets. Some love chasing cars and cyclists.

Before taking a horse on to a road make sure it is controllable. Sometimes a well-trained horse will have a calming influence on a more nervous animal. Make sure the tack fits well and is in good condition – check for frayed straps and reins. For your own safety, wear an approved helmet and fasten it securely.

If you decide to help an injured animal, approach it slowly and cautiously, using a gentle, soothing voice. If you have someone with you, get them to cause a distraction while you try to restrain the animal by its head. Apply the same principles of first aid as you would with a human. Stop any bleeding and offer reassurance. Wrap a small animal like a cat or dog in a blanket, remove it from the road to a safe place, and then phone the police. They will either advise you or come and take over.

WARNING OTHERS

To prevent a bad situation from becoming worse, you need to warn oncoming traffic of the hazard that lies ahead. But before stepping out into the road, slip on a flourescent/reflective band or something light-coloured, or carry a torch – even in daylight – to make yourself visible.

Hazard warning lights or vehicle indicators should be switched on. At night, use the headlights of undamaged vehicles to illuminate the scene. Make sure no one stands where they would obscure approaching vehicles' view of the lights.

Set up a red warning triangle as you would for a breakdown. On a two-lane road, it's a good idea to use two triangles – one 50 metres (164 feet) behind the car in the same lane, the other 50 metres ahead of the car in the other lane – to warn traffic from both directions of the danger.

Passengers or bystanders can assist by directing traffic, but make sure they are wearing bright clothing or reflective strips. The aim is to slow traffic down before it reaches the scene of the accident – but keep it moving because if the approach roads are blocked the emergency services will not be able to get through.

If you stop to help out at an accident, park your vehicle so it provides a clearly visible shield for the crash site. Put your hazard warning lights on (and dipped-beam headlights at night). Leave the car with the front wheels pointing into the kerb, so that if the car is shunted it won't plough into the crashed vehicles.

MAKING THE VEHICLES SAFE

Damage to vehicles can result in fuel spillages and electrical components sparking, so you must take action immediately to reduce the risk of fire.

- Ask all drivers to switch off their ignition and apply the handbrake. Motorbikes and diesel vehicles need to have the the fuel supply switched off. Leave the keys in the ignition to prevent steering lock being engaged and to permit electric windows, lights, etc to operate.
- Stabilize damaged vehicles. Where the vehicle is upright, apply the handbrake. Don't try to right vehicles that have landed on their sides or upside down, but do what you can to stop them from falling over.
- Warn everyone to extinguish their cigarettes – the crash scene must be a strictly no-smoking area.
- Check for tankers and haulage vehicles displaying hazchem (hazardous chemical) warning signs.

It's very important that, when phoning the police or fire brigade, as much information as possible is given about the hazardous cargo. If the driver is still conscious, get a detailed description of the load. If not, quote everything that's written on the hazchem plate.

Evacuate the area quickly. If the cargo is leaking, avoid breathing in the fumes. Take everone upwind and stop all traffic in both directions at least 100 metres (328 feet) from the site.

TELEPHONING FOR HELP

If anyone is injured, or the road is blocked, the police must be informed. The fire brigade and ambulance service may also be required. Make sure that the emergency services are called immediately. Hopefully, someone on the scene will have a mobile phone, otherwise it will be necessary to find a

HAZARDOUS CHEMICALS

Vehicles carrying toxic, corrosive, or other dangerous cargo must by law display an orange hazard warning sign. The symbols and codes on these panels tell the fire brigade what sort of substance is on board, and what measure should be taken to deal with it.

The emergency operator will require the following information:

- Your telephone number.
- The location of the accident. Be as precise as you can. If you don't know the name of the road, gives as many clues as possible by describing landmarks, junctions, etc.
- How many vehicles are involved and whether the road is blocked.
- The number of casualties, and any details you can give of their injuries. Let them know if there are any children, pregnant women or elderly victims.
- Whether any vehicles carrying hazardous chemicals are involved. Make a note of all information on the hazchem placard and read it to the operator.
- Other relevant details, such as whether there are people trapped, fuel leaks, fire hazards, black ice, fog, etc.

The operator may have further questions, so do not hang up until they tell you to.

telephone. On motorways, emergency telephones are located alongside the hard shoulder at mile or kilometre intervals.

Calls to the emergency services are free, but the three-digit telephone number varies according to where you are in the world. Before driving abroad, find out the emergency phone numbers for police, fire and ambulance for each of the countries you intend to visit, write them on a piece of card and place it behind the visor or somewhere you'll be able to lay hands on it in an emergency. In some countries, like Britain and the USA, one number will connect you to all three emergency services. The operator will ask whether you require the police, fire brigade or ambulance service. If there are casualties, ask for the ambulance service; if there are people trapped, ask for the fire brigade; where wrecked cars are blocking the road, ask for the police. Where all three services are required, ask to be put through to the ambulance service and the control officer you speak to will pass on details to the police and fire brigade.

GAINING ACCESS TO CASUALTIES

Once the traffic is under control, the emergency services have been sent for, and damaged vehicles have been stabilized, it's time to turn your attention to treating any casualties. Make a rapid assessment of their injuries and administer first-aid (giving priority to those most seriously hurt).

Motorcyclists and children travelling unrestrained in cars are especially vulnerable – often they will be thrown clear of the wreckage, so you will need to conduct a search of the area, looking over hedges and amongst tall foliage for victims. DO NOT remove a crash helmet or riding hat unless your medical training tells you that it is absolutely necessary to do so in order to give artificial ventilation or clear the airway. Untrained persons should never attempt to remove a casualty's helmet.

Those who are badly shaken but otherwise uninjured can be moved to a place of safety; those who are injured should be left where they are until the emergency services arrive – unless fire or other hazards put them in imminent danger. Do what you can to make them comfortable and keep them warm, but DON'T give food or drink in case they have suffered internal injuries.

Where the impact of collision has left vehicles crumpled

and distorted, it can be difficult to gain access to casualties. Broken glass will hinder rescuers' efforts, so avoid breaking windows unless absolutely necessary. Try prising the door open with a lever such as a jackhandle. Once the door starts to open, wrap a seat belt round the window frame and pull on this.

When someone has been crushed or impaled in an accident, you can worsen their injuries by freeing them. Having gained access to a trapped casualty, administer first aid (see the section on First Aid which follows) but do not try to remove them from the vehicle unless their life is endangered by fire or other hazards.

If fire makes it necessary to free a trapped motorist, try to find a lever which will lift the wreckage clear of the casualty's body. Where the driver's feet are trapped by the pedals, tie a length of seat belt to the pedal using a clove hitch (see below). Attach the other end to the frame of a door which is almost closed. Opening the door should provide sufficient leverage to force the pedal away from the driver's foot. (Either door can be used, depending which foot is trapped.)

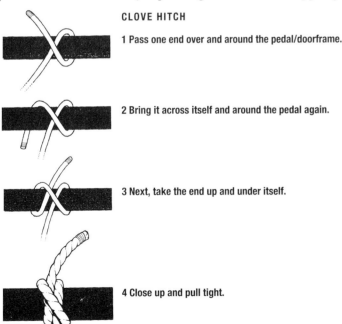

CLOVE HITCH

1 Pass one end over and around the pedal/doorframe.

2 Bring it across itself and around the pedal again.

3 Next, take the end up and under itself.

4 Close up and pull tight.

MOVING A VEHICLE
Where possible, don't move any vehicles or disturb the evidence until it has been officially recorded. If the vehicles must be moved for safety reasons, get someone to photograph or quickly sketch the position of each vehicle, and use chalk to mark the place where they stood, or scratch the road surface with a sharp instrument such as a screwdriver.

To move a car, put the gear in neutral and take off the handbrake. Leave the keys in the ignition to prevent steering lock, as you will need to steer the vehicle while pushing the car clear. When it is no longer causing an obstruction, reapply the handbrake and switch off the ignition.

MOTORWAY ACCIDENTS
Motorways have the best safety record for the ratio of accidents to the amount of traffic, but it is here that many of the worst crashes occur – the high-speed pile-ups which result in serious injuries and fatalities.

If you witness an accident on your side of the motorway, decide instantly whether to pull over and assist (bearing in mind that it may be difficult to stop in heavy, fast-moving

emergency!

traffic) or proceed to an emergency telephone. Put on your hazard warning lights to let drivers behind know there is a problem, and give your full concentration to your driving. Craning your neck for a better view, or using your mobile phone while you are at the wheel, will put you on course for a collision.

When the accident is on the other carriageway, pull up by the next emergency telephone and call for help. If you call on your mobile the operator may have difficulty pinpointing the location of the accident, but the coded number of the emergency telephone will tell them exactly where you are.

NEVER stop your car in the middle of the motorway and walk or run across the road to help – you will only add to the hazards facing oncoming traffic and secondary collisions will result. Don't allow crash victims to wander around. Leave them in the vehicles if it is safe to do so, or group them together on the embankment with someone looking after them. They will be suffering from shock and should be monitored.

first aid

Where people have been severly injured, time is critical. What happens in the 60 minutes which follow an accident can determine a casualty's fate. There is an 85 per cent survival rate for those who are stabilized at the scene, then transferred to an operating theatre within that time. This is why that first 60 minutes is known as the 'Golden Hour'.

Until the ambulance arrives, it's up to those on the scene to use their first-aid skills to sustain life. Every car should carry a medical kit (see Survival Kits in Essentials), but the equipment inside will only save lives if you know how to make use of it. In a crisis, a proficient first-aider can get by without a medical kit, using whatever is to hand to make improvised dressings and bandages. But you can't get by without basic knowledge of first aid – trying to improvise in that situation can do more harm than good. Did you know, for example, that applying a tourniquet can actually make bleeding worse and result in gangrene setting in?

The techniques given here should enable you to keep a casualty alive until medical help arrives on the scene, but no book can teach first aid as effectively as a qualified instructor. Why not sign up for a course in life-saving techniques which will brief you fully on what you should and should not do, and give you the confidence to act swiftly and effectively in an emergency?

Strategy

A road accident can be chaotic. There may be multiple casualties, people trapped, damaged vehicles leaking fuel, danger from oncoming traffic, hysterical bystanders – it's a daunting task even for professionals to cope in these situations. The way they cope is to work to a plan, and you must do the same.

Your task will be made easier if there are others on the scene who are uninjured and able to help. Where there is a qualified doctor or nurse on hand, follow their instructions, but if no one else is taking charge then it's up to you to put the emergency plan into action. Some onlookers may be distressed or hysterical, but if you remain calm and give clear instructions you should be able to get them doing something useful, like making the area safe or telephoning for help, leaving you free to treat the injured.

RISK OF INFECTION

Don't let the fear of AIDS and other infectious diseases keep you from saving a life. The risk of contracting a disease while giving mouth-to-mouth ventilation is minimal (there are as yet no recorded cases of HIV being transmitted in this way). Infection can be passed through blood, so wear gloves or put your hands into plastic bags when dressing a wound and wash your hands thoroughly afterwards.

Don't try to apply a treatment you are not qualified to give – you could do more harm than good. The techniques described in this book are internationally accepted first-aid practice; stick to the guidelines and you will be doing everything in your power to save a life.

Priorities

Starved of oxygen, the vital organs will fail and death will result. Unconscious casualties take precedence, and your first priority is to check their ABC (remember, don't move them unless their life is in danger):

Once the casualty is breathing and you can feel a pulse, attend to other injuries in the following sequence:

AIRWAY

BREATHING

CIRCULATION

- Stop bleeding
- Dress wounds and burns
- Immobilize fractures
- Treat shock

There are exceptions to the priority rule: for example, if a major artery has been severed, sending a jet of blood several feet into the air, you must stop the bleeding before you do anything else. And if a victim is on fire you must first put out the flames and stop the skin from burning any further by dousing it with water. Only then will you be in a position to check the casualty's vital signs. At all other times, start with the ABC.

EMERGENCY PLAN

- Identify any dangers to the casualty or yourself.
- Where possible, try to remove the danger by making the area safe. Only when this proves impossible should you consider removing the patient.
- Where there is more than one casualty, quickly assess their injuries to determine who should be treated first.
- Call for help. If you are alone, this may have to wait until you have stabilized the casualty. Where you have help, someone can be calling for an ambulance while you administer artificial ventilation or chest compression.

REMEMBER

The casualty may have suffered spinal injury and/or internal bleeding, so do not move them unless it is absolutely necessary, and wherever possible leave it to the emergency services as specialist equipment may be required.

Signs of severe back/neck injuries include a pins-and-needles sensation in the hands and feet, or loss of feeling/movement below the injured area.

Keep the casualty's head steady by supporting it gently with your hands – don't pull the neck or allow them to turn their head to either side. While you continue to support the head, get someone to place folded coats or blankets around the neck and shoulders for added support.

Should fire or toxic fumes make it necessary to move the casualty, four people will be needed: one is responsible for supporting the head and directing the other helpers, the second supports the shoulders and chest, the third takes the weight of the hips and abdomen, and the fourth holds the legs.

The casualty's body should be kept as straight and flat as possible; don't relax your hold so that they sag, or allow the spine to be twisted. All four helpers should place their hands under the body and prepare to lift or lower on the command of the person at the head: 'One, two, three, LIFT.'

emergency!

AIRWAY

Check that the casualty's airway is not obstructed by a foreign body – such as food, dentures, or vomit – or the tongue. Gently sweep a finger around inside the mouth, being careful not to push any matter back into the throat. Well-fitting dentures should be left in place as it's easier to give mouth-to-mouth with dentures in.

If a person regains consciousness while you are fishing around in their mouth they may bite you. To prevent this, pull the mouth to one side while sweeping. If they bite down on your finger, press your knuckle into their cheek.

Having removed any obstructions, open the airway:

Slide your fingers from the Adam's apple to the depression alongside and you should be able to detect the pulse.

With the casualty lying on their back, place one hand on their forehead and two fingers of the other hand under their chin. Now, keeping the head as straight as possible and avoiding any side-to-side movements, tilt the head back and lift the chin. This will prevent the tongue blocking the airway.

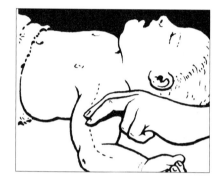

It's not easy to find the carotid pulse on a baby, so use the brachial pulse instead. This is located on the inside of the upper arm midway between shoulder and elbow. Press your index and middle fingertips lightly towards the bone.

BREATHING

To check if a person is breathing, bend over them and place your cheek a couple of centimetres from their mouth. You should feel their breath on your cheek, and see their chest rising and falling as they breathe.

Breathing: If the casualty is breathing, proceed to treat any other injuries they may have, such as bleeding, burns and fractures, then place them in the RECOVERY POSITION.

Not breathing: check for a pulse.

CIRCULATION

To check whether the heart is still pumping blood around the body, check for a pulse. The easiest pulse to find is the carotid pulse in the neck where the main arteries run alongside the windpipe.

Pulse but not breathing: Breathe for the casualty by giving them ARTIFICIAL VENTILATION.

No pulse, not breathing: Start CHEST COMPRESSIONS and CPR. If you are alone with the casualty it is recommended that you send for an ambulance first because your chances of resuscitating the casualty unaided are limited. However, when there is no telephone near at hand, you must start CPR and keep going until you are too exhausted to continue. Try activating the car alarm or sounding the horn as someone living or working nearby may come to investigate.

Artficial Ventilation

When a casualty stops breathing irreversable brain damage can occur after four minutes. You can prevent this by breathing for the casualty, using the 'kiss of life', also known as mouth-to-mouth resuscitation.

Check the airway for obstructions. If the airway is blocked and you cannot dislodge the obstruction with your finger, try back slaps and abdominal thrusts, see AIRWAY OBSTRUCTION.

Loosen any restrictive clothing around the neck and chest. If the casualty is trapped in a damaged car, make sure that there is nothing pressing against the chest – pull away debris and wreckage to leave the chest clear.

Airway Obstruction

If an unconscious casualty's chest will not rise when you give artificial ventilation, try the following:

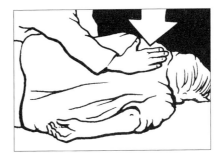

BACK SLAPS
Roll the unconscious casualty on to their side. Kneel alongside so that your thigh supports their chest. Position their head well back to open airway. Slap them up to five times between the shoulderblades with the heel of your hand.

If this fails to dislodge the blockage, try abdominal thrusts. This action is roughly the equivalent of squeezing a plastic bottle with a cork in: the sudden pressure causes the cork to pop out.

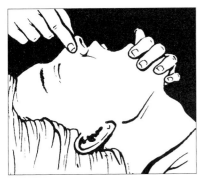

1
Tilt the head back and hold the jaw well open with one hand. Pinch the nostrils closed with a finger and thumb of the other hand. Take a deep breath.

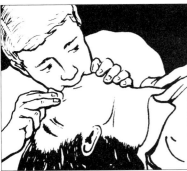

2
Seal your lips over the casualty's mouth and blow until you see their chest rise. (If the chest fails to rise, check that the nostrils are pinched closed and that your lips make a tight seal round the casualty's mouth. If it still won't rise, treat for airway obstruction.) Remove your mouth and take a deep breath while watching casualty's chest fall. Repeat at a rate of 10 inflations per minute until breathing is restored or the ambulance arrives.
After every 10 inflations, check the casualty's pulse to make sure the heart is still beating. If the pulse should stop, you will have to combine artificial ventilation with chest compressions. See CPR.

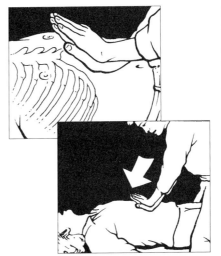

Place the unconscious casualty on their back with their head in the open airway position. Kneel astride them, place your hands one on top of the other just below their ribcage. When you apply pressure, it will be with the heel of the hand. Keep fingers clear.

With both arms straight, press inwards and upwards with quick thrusts. Repeat up to five times to clear the blockage. Once the blockage is clear the patient should start breathing normally. Place them in the RECOVERY POSITION.

emergency!

BABY/CHILD

Gentle back slaps may be used on children and infants. Place the child over your knee (a baby should be laid along your forearm with your hand supporting its chest). Slap between the shoulderblades, but use much less force than you would for an adult.

DON'T attempt abdominal thrusts on a baby. Someone who has not received special training in how to practise this technique on small children could cause internal injuries.

CHOKING

If the casualty is conscious, symptoms of a blocked airway will include difficulty in breathing, inability to speak, distress – they may clasp their throat, and veins in the face and neck may bulge with the effort to breathe. There may also be a tinge of blue around the lips.

Encourage the casualty to cough up the blockage. If they cannot, help them to a chair. They should sit, bending forward until the head is almost between the knees, so that the head is lower than the lungs. Slap them sharply between the shoulder blades. If five slaps later the blockage is not dislodged, try the Heimlich manoeuvre.

HEIMLICH MANOEUVRE
Stand behind the conscious choking person and put your arms around them. Clasp your hands together below their ribcage, and pull sharply inwards and upwards. Repeat up to five times. If the blockage is still not dislodged, try five back slaps followed by five more thrusts.

CPR

When there is no pulse, the heart has stopped pumping blood around the body. Artificial respiration must now be combined with chest compressions in order to keep a supply of oxygenated blood flowing to the brain and other vital organs.

CHEST COMPRESSION
Lay the casualty on their back on a firm surface and kneel by their side. Place the heel of one hand on the lower part of the breastbone – to locate the right point, find the base of the rib cage and run your index finger along the lowest rib until you reach the point where the ribs meet. Place the heel of your hand on the breastbone, about an inch above this meeting point, and then place the heel of the other hand on top, interlinking the fingers and keeping them up off the ribs.

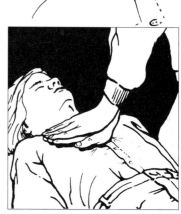

With arms straight, lean over the casualty and press down smoothly and firmly (don't rock and bounce as you could cause further injuries) with all your bodyweight to a depth of approximately 4 cm (1 ½ in) on the breast-bone. Release the pressure, keeping your hands in place. Repeat compressions at a rate of 80 per minute.

Ideally, you need two people for CPR, because it's very tiring to keep going until medical assistance arrives. One person should give artificial ventilation, while the other applies chest compressions. Give five compressions followed by one lung inflation, mouth-to-mouth, on the upstroke of the fifth compression. Allow the chest to rise, then, before it falls, start the next five compressions. The first aider giving mouth-to-mouth should monitor the pulse.

If you are working alone, give fifteen compressions followed by two lung inflations and keep this going until the heart starts again.

As soon as a pulse is detected, stop chest compressions but continue with artificial ventilation. Keep checking the pulse every 10 inflations and restart chest compressions should it disappear. When the casualty is breathing unaided, place them in the RECOVERY POSITION.

BABY/CHILD

For school-age children the techniques are the same as for adults, but they must be done slightly faster and with lighter pressure.

To treat younger children, use one hand only, pressing down 2.5 cm (1 in) at a rate of 100 compressions per minute.

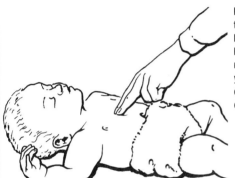

For a baby, use the tips of two fingers placed slightly below the midway point between the baby's nipples. Press lightly with your two fingers to a depth of 1.5 cm (1/2 in) at a rate of 100 per minute.

CPR for babies and children: use the chest compressions described above – five compressions to one lung inflation.

Recovery Position

Once the casualty's airway is clear, and you have checked that they are breathing, their heart is beating, and any wounds and fractures have been attended to, place them in the recovery position. This will allow the casualty to breathe easily and prevent them from swallowing their tongue or choking on vomit. They can then be left unattended for short periods while you deal with other casualties or go to call for help – but keep monitoring their breathing and pulse.

To ensure that the casualty is as comfortable as possible in this position, loosen restrictive clothing, remove glasses, and empty their pockets of keys and other objects which might dig into them.

Assuming the casualty is lying flat on their back with legs straight, turn them as follows:

Arrange the arm nearest to you so that it lies at a right-angle to the body, bent at the elbow, palm upwards. Bend the far arm so that it lies at a 45°-angle across the chest with the back of the hand resting against the casualty's cheek. Place your hand behind the knee of the leg furthest from you and pull it towards you to roll the patient on to their side. Adjust the leg so that it is bent at the knee, preventing the patient from lying flat. Tilt the head and lift the chin so that the airway is open.

Severe Bleeding

The average adult has about 6 litres (10 pints) of blood circulating around the body, transporting oxygen to the vital organs. Blood donors will know that 0.5 litres (1 pint) of blood can be removed with no ill effects other than a mild faintness and slight anaemia. However, if more than this amount is allowed to leak from the system through an open wound (or as a result of internal bleeding), the supply of

emergency!

oxygen to the brain, heart and lungs is reduced to the point where the casualty will collapse. If more than 2.24 litres (4 pints) is lost, they could die.

When you see someone bleeding profusely, it's easy to lose sight of your first-aid priorities. Some wounds look far worse than they really are: a cut to the scalp, for example, will bleed alarmingly, but it is not immediately life-threatening. You should attend first to checking the ABC (Airway, Breathing, Circulation), and only worry about the bleeding once you have confirmed that the person is breathing and has a pulse. The exception to this rule is arterial bleeding. When an artery is severed, the heart will pump bright red blood out through the wound in powerful, rapid spurts. Arterial bleeding must be staunched immediately. If the patient has also stopped breathing, you must try to deal with both emergencies at the same time.

PRIORITIES
- Check airway, act to restore breathing and pulse if necessary
- Staunch the flow of blood by applying direct or indirect pressure
- Dress the wound
- Minimize the risk of infection, both to the casualty and yourself. Wear gloves or cover your hands with clean plastic bags. Always use clean dressings.

STAUNCHING THE FLOW
With the casualty laying down or seated, carefully remove any clothing covering the wound and check that there is nothing embedded in it, such as glass or sharp pieces of metal.

NEVER try to remove embedded objects – they may be plugging the wound and restricting bleeding. If it is a small wound, squeeze the edges together, pressing down with your fingers or thumbs on either side of the object. For a large wound, see INDIRECT PRESSURE.

When bandaging a wound with something stuck in it, prevent the dressing forcing the object deeper into the wound by placing padding on either side to the same height as the protruding object.

Where there are no foreign objects in the wound, place a sterile dressing over it and apply firm pressure with your fingers or palm. If you have no dressings, use any clean, non-fluffy cloth. Elevate an injured limb (carefully, because there may be a fracture) and support it. Conscious casualties will be able to do this for themselves while you attend to others. Where possible, they should lie down as this will help prevent SHOCK.

A continuous firm pressure MUST be kept up for at least 10 minutes. In the meantime the body will be trying to heal itself by releasing clotting agents into the bloodstream and reducing blood pressure. Blood vessels are elastic; when severed, they should spring back into the muscles, reducing blood loss. DON'T lift the dressing to check the wound as you will start the bleeding again.

Once the bleeding has stopped, place a clean dressing over the top of the original dressing and bind firmly in place with a bandage. Make sure the bandage is not twisted or so tight that it cuts off the blood supply. Immobilize the limb as you would for a FRACTURE.

VARICOSE VEINS
The veins in the legs have valves which stop blood from draining downwards. When these valves fail, blood collects in pools, causing the veins to swell. Injury to a varicose vein can cause severe bleeding. This can be stopped by lying the casualty on their back and elevating the injured leg as high as possible. Cover the wound with a clean dressing and apply direct pressure. Make sure the casualty is not wearing tight undergarments (such as a girdle or elastic topped stockings) which might restrict the blood as it flows back towards the heart.

Indirect pressure
If large amounts of blood are being lost from a number of wounds on one limb, or if for some reason you cannot apply direct pressure, find the point where the relevant artery crosses a bone and apply pressure with your fingers to slow down or cut off the blood supply. Elevating the limb will make it easier to reduce the flow.

NEVER apply pressure to cut off blood supply to a limb for more than 10 minutes. And NEVER apply a tourniquet.

BLEEDING ARM/HAND
Press the artery inwards and upwards against the bone which can be found between the muscles on the inner side of the upper arm. Watch the wound(s). If the blood flow is not reduced, adjust the position of your fingers until it is.

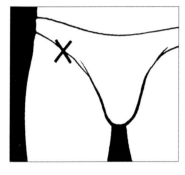

BLEEDING LEG/FOOT
With the casualty lying on their back, raise the knee of the bleeding limb and apply pressure to the centre of the fold where the thigh joins the groin. Press down with your thumbs or the heel of your hand. Watch the wound(s). If the blood flow is not reduced, adjust the position of your fingers until it is.

CHEST WOUNDS

In vehicles which are not fitted with an airbag, there is a danger of the driver being thrown against the steering wheel in a collision. This can break the ribs and force them inwards so that they penetrate the chest cavity. If the wound allows air can to enter the space occupied by the lungs, it will put pressure on the lung on the damaged side, possibly even causing it to collapse.

The casualty will have difficulty breathing, and you may hear a sucking noise when air enters the lung cavity. As their condition deteriorates the mouth and extremities will turn blue from lack of oxygen, they might cough up frothy, bright red blood, and shock will set in. When a casualty shows signs of panic due to breathing difficulties, always check, front and back, for a penetrating chest wound.

Seal a sucking wound immediately to prevent air entering – if nothing else is available, use the palm of your hand. Where possible, apply a sterile dressing, then cover it with kitchen film or aluminium foil and bandage firmly or secure with adhesive tape so that the dressing is airtight. Either prop up the casualty in a half-sitting position, or lay them in the recovery position, with the unaffected lung uppermost.

IMPALED!

If a casualty is impaled on a steering column or other debris, DO NOT attempt to free them. Send for help – the fire brigade and ambulance service will both be needed – and while waiting for the emergency services to arrive, reassure the casualty. If you hear sucking noises from the wound, try to seal it as best you can without moving them. Support the casualty's weight and make them comfortable, but do not give them anything to eat or drink.

ABDOMINAL WOUNDS

If the gut is sticking out through the wound, DO NOT attempt to push it back into place. Without touching it with your hands (because of the high risk of infection) cover it with a plastic bag or kitchen film to keep the moisture in.

If no organs extrude, place a large sterile dressing over the wound. Where there is a danger of the airway becoming blocked, put them in the recovery position and keep applying pressure to the dressing – a bandage may not be sufficient to hold the contents of the abdomen in if they start coughing.

AMPUTATION

If a limb is torn off as a result of an accident the muscle in the wall of the artery will probably go into spasm, shutting down the flow of blood. What blood loss there is can be controlled by applying direct pressure or elevating the limb.

Surgeons may be able to re-attach the severed limb if it is properly preserved. Without handling it or trying to clean it up in any way, put the limb in a plastic bag or wrap it in kitchen film, then wrap a thin piece of cloth round the bag and place it in a container filled with crushed ice (or frozen peas – anything you can lay hands on that will keep it cool). Make sure there is a protective layer between the limb and the ice. See that it is given to the paramedics so they can take it to the operating theatre with the casualty.

INTERNAL BLEEDING

Always look for signs of internal bleeding after a violent collision:

emergency!

- Casualty feels light-headed and thirsty
- Skin pale, cold and clammy
- Pulse weak but very fast
- Signs of shock developing
- Slight bruising under the skin that takes the pattern of clothes or other objects touching the body
- Pain and tenderness around the affected area
- Coughing up or vomiting blood
- Blood in faeces or urine
- Watery blood trickling from the ear – see HEAD INJURIES.

Lay the casualty down with their legs elevated and head low – this makes it easier for the heart to pump blood to the brain. Loosen tight clothing, and keep the patient warm – but watch that they don't get overheated as blood will be diverted away from the internal organs to the skin.

CRUSHED!

Try to free a casualty who is trapped under a vehicle within 10 minutes of the accident occurring. If you cannot lift or move the vehicle within that time, it must be left to the emergency services to free them. Someone who has been crushed for more than 10 minutes can suffer kidney failure when the weight is removed, so it is vital that trained paramedics are on hand to treat them the moment they are freed. All you can do in the meantime is to calm and reassure the victim.

LESSER BLEEDING

Scalp wounds will bleed profusely, making them look worse than they really are. Provided there is nothing embedded in the wound, and no fragments of broken bone, control the bleeding by applying direct pressure. Where there is something stuck in the wound, DON'T try to pick it out; simply cover the area lightly with a dressing to prevent the blood from running down into the casualty's face.

The head should be elevated, so treat the patient while they are sitting or reclining with head and shoulders propped up. If the casualty loses conciousness, place them in the recovery position and monitor their pulse and breathing constantly.

Nosebleeds can occur after a blow. Thin watery blood from the nose (or ear) is a symptom of serious injury to the brain (see HEAD INJURIES), but most nosebleeds are unpleasant rather than life-threatening. To control blood loss, sit the casualty down with their head forward and ask them to remain in this position, pinching the soft part of the nostrils for 10 minutes while breathing through their mouth. They must not sniff, and should try to keep as still and relaxed as possible to allow the blood to clot.

Bleeding in the mouth must be controlled to prevent blood getting into the airway. If the casualty has bitten their tongue or lip, or lost a tooth in the accident, get them to sit down with their head forward and inclined to the injured side so that blood can dribble out of the corner of their mouth. Severe bleeding should be controlled by holding a dressing over the cut and applying direct pressure, or plugging a tooth socket and biting down on the dressing.

Most small cuts and grazes will stop bleeding on their own. Ask the casualty to apply direct pressure and elevate the injured part. Leave them while you attend to any serious injuries. To minimize the risk of infection, lightly wash the cut with clean water or a sterile wipe and cover it with a dressing or plaster.

EYE WOUNDS

NEVER attempt to remove a foreign body embedded in the eye – this must be left to the experts. Keep the casualty calm and still, preferably lying on their back, until help arrives. Head and eye movements must be avoided, and it may help if you gently cover the injured eye with a dressing then lightly bandage both eyes (otherwise using the good eye will cause the injured one to move).

Shock

The medical condition known as shock is caused by poor circulation due to heart failure or loss of blood, or a reduction in body fluids brought about by severe burns or prolonged vomiting or diarrhoea.

If untreated, shock can kill, so watch for the symptoms:

- Skin cold and clammy, pale and grey colour
- Loss of colour in lips

emergency!

- Casualty feels nauseous, faint and weak
- Pulse and breathing are shallow and rapid
- Restless, anxious or even aggressive behaviour
- Vomiting
- Thirst

As the brain is starved of oxygen the casualty may gasp for air or yawn frequently. Eventually they will lose consciousness and the heart will stop beating.

Apply first aid to BURNS or SEVERE BLEEDING. If you can see no obvious injuries there may be internal bleeding. To encourage the supply of blood to the heart, brain and lungs:

1 If the casualty is conscious, have them lie on their back with head low and legs elevated about 30 cm (12 in). Support the legs using folded blankets or coats – bear in mind that there may be fractures to the limbs.
2 Loosen tight clothing and cover them with a blanket, but DO NOT use direct heat (like a hot-water bottle) as warming the surface of the body will draw blood away from the vital organs.
3 Keep the casualty calm and still. Reassure them – your attitude is vital because any sign of distress or agitation from you will alarm the patient.
4 DO NOT give anything to eat or drink. To alleviate thirst, moisten the lips with a damp cloth.
5 Stay by their side monitoring their pulse and breathing. If they lose consciousness, vomit or have difficulty breathing, place them in the RECOVERY POSITION.

NEVER leave a shock victim on their own if you can avoid it.

Burns/Scalds

Burns can be very painful, and if they cover a large area there is a risk of shock developing due to fluid loss. In addition to treating the burn, monitor the casualty for signs of SHOCK.

A variety of burns can occur in a road accident: dry burns are caused by flames, or contact with hot metal; chemical

HEART ATTACK

Symptoms of a heart attack are in many ways similar to those for shock:

- Severe gripping pain in the chest which may spread to the shoulders, throat and down one or both arms.
- Casualty may feel faint or dizzy. They may seem withdrawn.
- As with shock, the skin may lose colour, with a faint blueness at the lips and extremities.
- Breathing may be rapid and shallow.
- Pulse rapid, weak, and erratic.
- Casualty may lose consciousness.

Calm and reassure the casualty. Avoid exciting or worry them, and don't move them any unnecessarily. If possible, help them to a comfortable half-sitting position, propped up against a solid object such as a wall. Bend the knees slightly. Loosen any restrictive clothing. Monitor breathing and pulse until help arrives. Be prepared to give artificial ventilation or CPR if necessary.

burns result from contact with corrosive agents such as battery acid; scalds from hot liquids or steam; electrical burns from electrical currents or lightning. In addition to these accident-related burns, you might encounter cold burns (when skin comes in contact with freezing metal) and radiation burns (sunburn).

Regardless of the cause, treat as follows:

1 Eliminate the cause. Extinguish the fire without fanning the flames. Turn off electrical current. Wash away caustic chemicals, taking care that they do not splash and cause further injuries. Remove clothing which has been soaked in a corrosive substance or scalding liquid.
2 Reduce the temperature by drenching the burned area with clean cold water to cool it down. Keep irrigating the area until it produces no further relief and withdrawal from water can be achieved with no increase in pain. If no water is available, milk can be substituted – but beware of liquids such as antiseptics, alcohol or acidic soft drinks which will inflict further pain and tissue damage.
3 Check the casualty's airway, breathing, and circulation and treat if necessary.

emergency!

4 Remove jewellery and clothing which will constrict if swelling should start. But DO NOT try to remove any material which is sticking to the burn.

5 DO NOT burst blisters/remove loose skin or interfere with the burned tissue in any way. Resist the impulse to apply lotions, ointments, butter/fat, antiseptic or anything else to the injured area – this will make matters worse.

6 Cover the burn with a sterile non-fluffy dressing to prevent infection. Burn sheets make the best dressing because they have a non-adherent surface and trap moisture. If you don't have anything suitable in your first-aid kit, use kitchen film or a clean plastic bag.

7 Constantly reassure the casualty, monitoring them all the while for signs of SHOCK. They may be given sips of water unless in shock, in which case moisten the lips with a damp cloth.

ON FIRE!

Avoid anything that will fan the flames. The instinctive reaction of most victims will be to panic and run – this must be prevented because the draught will feed the fire.

• Lay the casualty on the ground, head upwind, with the side which is burning uppermost. Rolling over and over along the ground will spread the burning rather than put it out. Get them to lie still.

• EITHER smother the flames with a heavy coat or blanket (this MUST be non-flammable and preferably made of natural fibres; some man-made fabrics catch light easily, others melt in extreme heat) OR douse the flames with water.

Head Injuries

Head injuries may involve damage to the skull or brain, so even where the patient does not lose consciousness and there are no obvious wounds to the head, immediate medical attention is required.

CONCUSSION

A severe blow to the head can jolt the brain within the skull. Unconsciousness may or may not occur as a result, but even if the patient complains of nothing more than a slight headache their condition must be carefully monitored. Symptoms include:

- shallow breathing and rapid weak pulse
- cold, clammy, skin and pale complexion
- possible nausea and/or vomiting
- disorientation/loss of memory

In addition, there may be a trickle of watery blood or fluid from the nose, ears or eyes. This is cerebrospinal fluid leaking from the brain. Notify the emergency services when you telephone for help that the casualty has a suspected skull fracture.

If the casualty loses consciousness, place them in the RECOVERY POSITION (exercising great caution if spinal injuries are suspected). When fluid is leaking from one ear only, turn the casualty so that side is facing downwards, allowing the fluid to drain. Be very gentle. Monitor their breathing and pulse, and be prepared to give artificial ventilation or CPR.

FRACTURES

Although any broken bone is very painful, fractures are seldom life-threatening. The main danger is that the broken bone could rupture an artery or cause internal damage. Your main aim must be to keep the casualty still until the injured limb is immobilized and supported.

Where there is an open wound, control the bleeding by applying pressure over a sterile dressing. DO NOT press down directly on the broken bone – use INDIRECT PRESSURE instead.

If they must be moved, try to immobilize the fracture first by securing the injured limb to an adjacent uninjured part. For example, a broken arm can be bound in a sling against the chest. To secure a broken leg, straighten both legs and place a folded blanket or coat between them for padding, then bandage the injured leg to the good one.

DROWNING

When an accident results in a vehicle being submerged there is a danger that the occupants will swallow water in their panic as they try to escape. This can send the airway into spasms, causing asphyxiation. If the water is cold, there is also a risk of hypothermia.

Act quickly. Remove any debris in the casualty's mouth and give ARTIFICIAL VENTILATION and CPR if necessary. Once their condition is stable, place them in the RECOVERY POSITION and cover with a blanket to keep them warm until help arrives. The foil blanket in your survival kit is ideal for this purpose.

A drowning victim who has been successfully revived must still seek urgent medical attention. Water remaining in the lungs can cause delayed drowning up to 72 hours later.

HYSTERIA

The fright of being in a collision, or even just witnessing one, can bring on hyperventilation or hysteria. Be calm and gentle but firm. Don't allow someone who is hysterical distract you from attending to more serious casualties. If possible, ask a bystander to help by taking the distressed person to a quiet place. So long as they remain on the scene they will hinder you and upset other casualties.

If they are hyperventilating (breathing abnormally in rapid, deep gasps), get them to breathe into a paper bag. Slapping someone's face or throwing water at them will NOT cure hysteria. Calm them down by talking quietly and positively to them.

insurance claims

In most countries it is a legal requirement that you notify your insurance company within 24 hours of an accident. Even where you are not legally obliged to do so, it's a good idea to deal with the paperwork while everything is still fresh in your mind. In fact, you can get things underway at the scene of the accident by noting down the following details:

- Name and address of the other driver (and vehicle owner, if different), the name of their insurance company and, if possible, the number on their certificate of insurance.
- Registration number, make and model of the other vehicle.
- Names and addresses (and registration numbers) of any independent witnesses. Ask other motorists and any passing pedestrians if they saw what happened and where they were at the time. Persuade them to give a brief statement (see below).
- The number of the police officer attending the scene (where applicable).
- A description of the accident location including the road name or route number. List all road markings and signs, conditions (potholes, roadworks, debris on road, etc), posi-

tion of parked cars or other hazards (including pedestrians or animals) which may have contributed.
- Weather conditions and time of day. If it was dark at the time, note whether streetlights were working and whether the vehicles involved had lights switched on.
- The speed at which both vehicles were travelling and their position on the road.
- Describe in full any damage to vehicles or property. While checking out the other vehicle, make a note of its general condition – are the tyres badly worn or the lights defective? Does it look roadworthy? If you have a camera, take photographs of the damage.
- If someone has been injured, record this. Was everyone involved wearing a seat belt?
- Take photographs or make a rough sketch of the scene, showing the positions of the vehicles before and after the accident. Measure the width of the road by pacing it out. Draw in road markings, signs, streetlights, bollards and cones, hazards, skid marks, position of witnesses. If you can do this quickly on the scene, you may be able to get an impartial witness (someone other than a passenger) to verify the accuracy of your sketch map.

emergency!

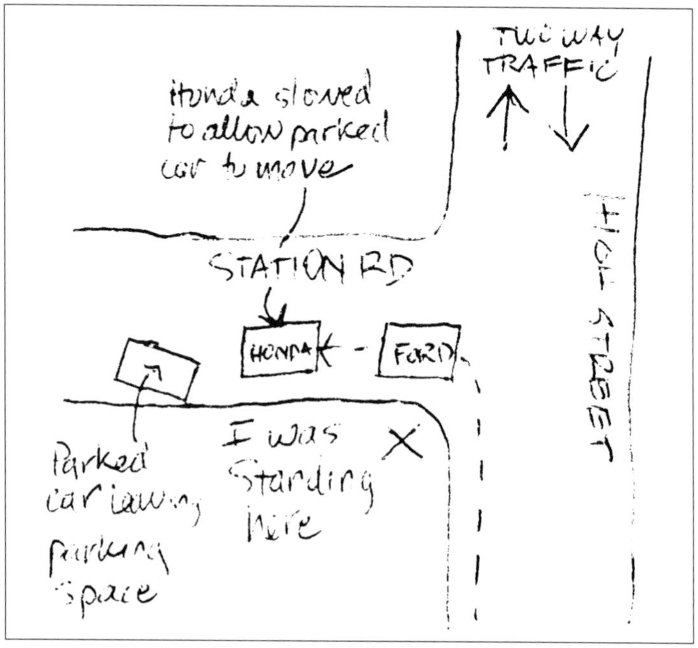

Honda slowed to allow parked car to move

TWO WAY TRAFFIC

STATION RD

HIGH STREET

HONDA — FORD

Parked car leaving parking space

I was standing here X

WITNESS STATEMENT

I, John Wiseman of 3 Survival Close, Hereford, was standing on the corner of High Street and Station Road at 1305hrs. I saw a red Ford reg, no. P123 ABC turn left on to Station Road and run into the green Honda N456 CVB. The Ford's driver was doing up his seat belt and talking to his passenger, a blonde lady.

Signed: J. WISEMAN tel: 0123 56789
1st August 97

If your car needs to be repaired, check your insurance policy before telling a garage to go ahead with the work. Some insurers now offer a repair service and will collect the car, fix it and deliver it back to your door. Some insurers will not allow the car to be repaired until an assessor has examined it and given the go-ahead. Others will insist that you get at least two estimates for the cost of repairs. The garage cannot start work on the car until they receive written authorization from the insurance company.

7

As anyone who watches television or reads a newspaper will know, attacks on motorists are on the increase. Minimize the risk of becoming a victim by taking precautions to deter would-be attackers. And learn how to defend yourself, in case the worst should happen.

personal security

REDUCING THE RISKS Basic precautions • Security on the move

UNDER ATTACK Road rage • Hitch hikers • Being followed • Forced to stop • Joy riders • Caught in a crowd

BREAKDOWNS AND ACCIDENTS Being a good Samaritan

BE STREETWISE Using reasonable force • Offensive weapons

reducing the risks

In general, you are much less vulnerable to attack when driving in your car than you would be on foot. Nevertheless, many motorists, particularly women, are afraid to drive alone at night. Some are nervous of driving alone even in daylight, for fear of what will happen to them if they break down or if they should come across a driver in the grip of road rage.

Although the last few years have seen an increase in violence and aggression on the roads, there are steps you can take to protect yourself. Start by being alert to the potential dangers. Too often drivers are lulled into a false sense of security because they follow the same route every day without event. Instead of focusing on potential hazards, they allow their minds to wander. Such complacency not only leads to accidents, it prevents you noticing threats to your security until it is too late to do anything to protect yourself. The bag-snatcher loitering by the traffic lights will have reached in through the open window, grabbed the laptop or handbag from the passenger seat, and made their escape before you know what's happened.

A driver who is scanning the road ahead and checking the rear-view mirrors to see what vehicles behind are doing will soon notice irregularities. Having observed something suspicious, quickly evaluate the potential risks and decide what course of action you will take if the threat turns out to be genuine. An attacker's greatest weapon is often the element of surprise. A victim who is totally unprepared may be so startled that they take several seconds to respond; one who is prepared can react positively and prevent or repel the attack.

BASIC PRECAUTIONS

Women should take care to leave nothing in the car that might advertise the fact it is driven by a woman. A rapist in search of a target might decide to lie in wait for the return of a driver who has left her make-up bag on the dashboard, her spare shoes in the driver's footwell, and the driver's seat set forward so that her legs will reach the pedals.

Car stickers which give away your gender, advertise what an expensive audio system you've got, or just generally attract attention to your car should also be avoided.

> A well-maintained car with a full tank is less likely to break down, so the first step to guarantee your personal security is to carry out regular maintenance and service checks to make sure that the car won't let you down.

There are a range of devices on the market aimed at deterring potential attackers, including the inflatable passenger – a lifesize rubber figure intended to create the illusion that the lone female driver has a man aboard. This seems as likely to attract unwelcome attention as to deter it, so you would do better to spend your money on a screeching personal alarm which should be kept somewhere close to hand, like the driver's door pocket. Test the alarm periodically to be sure that it works, especially if it's battery-operated. Some car alarm systems can be activated by the driver hitting a panic button, so that sirens sound and lights flash. Don't count on passers-by coming to your aid – use the few seconds while the attacker is confused by the alarm to make your escape.

A mobile phone can be both a lifeline and a deterrent. The sight of a driver summoning help on their mobile will often be enough to send would-be assailants on their way. Make sure that you keep the battery fully charged, though. And choose a system which is designed for hands-free in-car use and covers the maximum possible area; some networks are very limited in range and will be useless if you intend to leave the big cities behind. Many companies offer low connection rates and low rental charges for infrequent users – the cost per minute for calls may seem astronomical, but remember, you will only be using the phone in an emergency.

Membership of a motoring organization will place a nationwide rescue service at your disposal. Vulnerable drivers such as lone women or disabled drivers will be given priority treatment in the event of a breakdown. As well as being cheaper than calling out a local garage to recover your vehicle, many motoring organizations offer a relay service to get you to your destination even if the car cannot be repaired on the spot.

Long journeys through unfamiliar territory should be planned carefully. Plot the route you will follow, the junctions or landmarks where you need to turn off, and the points where you will stop for a break. When travelling after dark, aim to use well-lit main roads where possible and fill the tank at the start of your journey in case there is nowhere to refuel later on. Carry an up-to-date road atlas so that if you do get lost there will be no need to stop and ask for direction. Let someone know your route and estimated time of arrival so they can raise the alarm should you fail to reach your destination.

SECURITY ON THE MOVE

Make it a habit, whenever you get into or out of the car, to lock the doors behind you. In some cities car-jackers prey on cars waiting at traffic lights or junctions, gaining entry through an unlocked door and then using force to eject the driver. This requires less effort than overcoming a sophisticated immobilizer or alarm system on a parked vehicle. Traffic can grind to a halt even on the motorway, so rather than waiting until you find yourself in slow-moving traffic to lock the doors – and running the risk of forgetting – train yourself to do it as a matter of course. The risk of rescuers being prevented from gaining access to you in the event of an accident is minimal compared to that of being mugged at traffic lights. Many cars are now fitted with locks designed to spring open on impact.

Keep valuables out of sight. Don't leave handbags or laptop computers sitting on the passenger's seat, don't stick your arm through an open window if you're wearing an expensive watch or jewellery, and don't sit using a mobile phone with the window open.

under attack

To prevent thieves reaching in, the windows should not be open more than a couple of centimetres. If someone does try to stick their hand through the gap, hit them hard using any improvised weapon you can: fire extinguisher, torch, high-heeled shoe, de-icer aerosol, hairbrush, etc.

When a thief sees a very valuable object within reach, he may decide it's worth smashing a window to get to it. If you fear this is going to happen, sound your horn continuously or, if you have one, use your panic button to activate the car alarm system. Should the thief succeed in gaining entry it's better to give up your valuables rather than risk injury, but if you come under attack defend yourself by going for vulnerable parts such as the eyes, nose and neck (see Self-Defence, below).

Not all attackers are motivated by a desire to steal your property. Sex attackers and other violent criminals may target lone motorists, particularly women.

Avoid making eye contact with pedestrians, cyclists, motorcyclists, or occupants of other vehicles. If someone tries to attract your attention, pretend you haven't seen them. Don't do anything to acknowledge their presence as this will only encourage them.

In the event that an attacker forces his way into the car and threatens you with violence, stay calm and act as though you are going to co-operate. Do as he says, while at the same time trying to attract the attention of the police or passers-by. For example, exceed the speed limit in a restricted zone, cross double white lines or drive into a box junction before your exit is clear. In a car with manual choke, try pulling out the choke unnoticed – this may fool the aggressor into thinking that the car is malfunctioning and it's time to find alternate transport.

When your life is threatened, desperate measures may be called for to prevent your attacker from carrying you off to some location where there will be no hope of rescue. One risky tactic is to use the car as a weapon against the intruder. If road conditions allow – the road surface is good and there are no vehicles following closely behind you – build up speed and then, bracing yourself and gripping the wheel firmly, execute an emergency stop. Make sure your seat belt is secure first, and if your attacker is sitting in the front passenger seat wearing a seat belt, reach out at the last moment and release it so there is nothing to prevent him being thrown against the windscreen. Either shove them out of the car and drive away, or, if that's not possible, grab the ignition keys and run from the car. In a remote area, wait until you are near an inhabited building before doing the emergency stop so that you don't have to run too far to get help.

On a city road, try overtaking a bus or a vehicle carrying a number of people, then brake sharply (but not so abruptly that the bus runs into the back of you), sounding the horn continuously. Take the key out of the ignition, open the door and throw it away. This will certainly attract attention and prevent the vehicle from proceeding.

IF YOU ARE BEING FOLLOWED
Be suspicious when a vehicle or motorcycle keeps pace with you but declines the opportunity to overtake when you slow down to allow it to pass.

If you think you are being followed:

- Don't lead them to your home (especially if you live alone and the house will be in darkness when you arrive)
- Don't stop where there's no one else in sight
- Don't allow yourself to get isolated on a remote road by trying to outrun the other vehicle
- Don't engage in vehicular combat. If your car gets

HITCH HIKERS
Hitch hiking is risky for both the driver and the person hitching a ride. Even though it's tempting to offer some poor bedraggled hitcher a ride in heavy rain or on a remote road, a lone driver should NEVER give a lift to a stranger. Even when you are travelling with someone else, it's still risky to stop for a stranger who may be armed with a knife or other weapon. People have been robbed, assaulted, and even killed after picking up hitchers.

Male drivers may think there's no risk in offering a ride to a young woman standing alone by the roadside, but it's possible that the damsel in distress is a decoy. When you pull up to let her in, a gang of male accomplices will pop out from their hiding place and force you from the car. And even if she is travelling alone, what are your chances if she pulls a knife? Don't take the risk. When driving alone, whatever your gender, DON'T pick up strangers.

damaged you will be at the mercy of your attacker.
- Stick to busy roads and drive to a police station or a well-lit public place such as a bus terminus or service station.
- Don't get out of the vehicle. Stay in the car and, if you have a mobile phone, call the police. If the other vehicle parks close by, sound your horn continuously and switch on your hazard lights to draw attention to yourself.
- Don't be embarrassed to flag down a passer-by and get them to phone the police.

Make sure you can give the police an accurate description of the vehicle and its occupants. Note the make and model, colour, licence number, distinguishing features (roof rack, stickers, fog lamps, aerial, scratches or dents). Write down a few details which will help you describe the occupants: number, sex, age, height and build, hair colour and length, skin colour, facial hair, clothes, tattoos, etc.

IF YOU ARE FORCED TO STOP
If someone steps out into the road or pulls up in front of you, forcing you to stop, stay in the car with the engine running. DON'T switch off the ignition because you may not be able to start the car quickly enough to make your escape should the need arise. Make sure your doors and windows are

securely fastened.

If the other driver gets out of the vehicle to approach you, switch on your hazard lights and sound the horn continuously even if it's the middle of the night. Stay calm. To escape a threatening encounter, engage reverse gear and back up until you have room to turn your car around and make a getaway. But don't try and do it too fast because you could lose control or damage the car.

Be wary if the driver claims to be a police officer – don't take them at their word, ask for proof. A genuine unmarked police car driven by a plainclothes policeman should have a detachable blue flashing light or a siren of some description, and the officer will be able to produce official identification. Do not open the door or window until you have seen proof of identity to convince you that the driver is what he says. Examine the ID carefully to be sure it's genuine. If you have a mobile phone, call the police and ask for verification.

> The law states that you must obey signals by uniformed police officers. Failure to stop is an offence and you will be prosecuted. But where the police officer or vehicle is not clearly identified as such, so that you have no way of knowing that the occupant is indeed a bona fide police officer, in most countries there is no legal requirement compelling you to stop.

Road Rage

Road rage makes the headlines all too frequently these days, as drivers fail to keep a rein on their frustration or lose all self-control in the face of what they interpret as provocation. The chapter on Safe Driving gives tips on controlling your own aggression and making sure that your driving does not give rise to road rage in others. But no matter how careful a driver you are, there may come a time when your path crosses that of a motorist in the grip of road rage.

The first rule when dealing with an enraged driver is stay calm. If you lose your temper it can lead to an escalating spiral of aggression. Seek instead to defuse the situation. It's most likely that the other driver is simply tense from over-work, domestic problems, or sitting in a traffic jam getting later and later for an important engagement. They may be yelling at you purely because they need someone, anyone, to vent that pent-up frustration on. On the other hand, it may be that you are dealing with a drug-crazed psychopath. Either way, it doesn't pay to get into a confrontation with them.

Backing down, even when you know that you are in the right, is a sign of sense, not cowardice. Women, being physically smaller and more vulnerable, generally seek to disengage as quickly as possible, having thought through the possible consequences of taking on a madman. Men are more likely to rise to the bait and exchange heated words with an aggressor – especially if there's a frightened wife, girlfriend or child in their vehicle who has been upset by the other motorist's dangerous driving. The best way to defend your family from a lunatic is to withdraw to a place of safety. The aggressor may well be armed, and in that state of mind they will probably use any weapon that comes to hand.

If your vehicle is rammed or damaged in any way and you suspect that it has been done deliberately, think twice about getting out to remonstrate with the other driver or even to exchange details. It may be safer to remain inside the car while you note the other driver's registration, then drive on to the nearest police station to report the incident.

To de-escalate an intense situation:

- Avoid establishing eye contact. Return a hard stare and you could end up locked in combat. Look away to indicate that you are peaceful and not a threat.
- If you do make a mistake, apologize by mouthing 'Sorry'. Most reasonable people will accept this.
- After making a mistake the worst thing you can do is to speed away, change lanes, or make a turn. This often leads to further mistakes and you will end up annoying even more drivers.
- If you judge that a little humour might help (and bear in mind that in some situations it can make things worse), acknowledge that you have made a mistake by slapping yourself on the back of the hand in an exaggerated manner.
- Don't do anything that could be interpreted as a challenge to the other driver.

- If you proceed calmly and at a steady, safe speed in the inside lane the chances are they will lose interest.
- Don't retaliate when another driver shows poor judgement. Don't sound the horn or flash your lights or take it upon yourself to teach them a lesson. They will get their comeuppance with no help from you – just make sure you're well clear when it happens.
- A bully who gets his kicks frightening people will enjoy seeing you terrified. Stay calm.
- Don't be panicked into taking risks to escape pursuit.
- Pull over – preferably in a well-lit public place – and remain in the car with your doors and windows locked. Take a note of the aggressor's registration number and, if you have a mobile phone, call the police.
- If the other driver gets out of their car ranting and raving so that there is no hope of quietly exchanging details, try to drive away from the scene. Drive to a police station or a busy public place such as a motorway service station.
- Report the incident to the police as soon as possible.

JOY RIDERS

Young thieves who steal cars for kicks show a complete disregard for safety. They're not picking up the bill, so they don't care what damage they do. Get well clear if you suspect a car is being driven by joy riders. Inform the police and leave the pursuit to them.

CAUGHT IN A CROWD

An angry mob of demonstrators or football supporters can be extremely dangerous. Riots can arise when an unruly element decide to engage one another or the police in battle.

Unless you are actually attending an event, try to stay away from venues where crowds are likely to gather. On match days, steer clear of football grounds if at all possible – and make sure you don't display the colours of either team in your car, or you could make yourself a target for marauding groups of troublemakers.

If you see a large crowd approaching, turn the vehicle round and find a different route to your destination. There is a danger that the mob will engulf the car, climbing on top of it and breaking windows. If you have a chance, abandon the car and head for a place of safety. Failing that, remain in the car, with all doors and windows locked and the engine switched off.

Avoid eye contact as this may be interpreted as provocation, but don't sit looking timidly at the ground. Keep your head up and appear alert.

Breakdowns and Accidents

Detailed advice on what to do in the event of a breakdown or accident is given in **Emergency!** The main security points to remember are:

- Try to park the car as safely as possible before coming to a grinding halt. Keep an eye on the instrument panel so that you don't miss any warning signs.
- Try to park in a well-lit, public place. On a motorway, park alongside a phone. In most countries these are located at mile/kilometre intervals along the hard shoulder.
- If you cannot park near a telephone, walk to call for assistance – never hitch or accept a lift.
- It's a good idea for a woman travelling alone to carry some baggy masculine clothing – a baseball cap, overalls, or a large reflective jacket of the kind road maintenance engineers wear. This will make it less obvious that you are female and may help to prevent unwelcome attention.
- Women travelling alone should mention this when phoning for help, as they will be given priority to ensure that they are not left stranded by the roadside for very long.
- Give the operator a description of any vehicles or persons who approach while you are using the emergency telephone.
- The safest place to wait after breaking down on a motorway is on the embankment. Leave the nearside door of the car ajar, so that if another vehicle pulls up you can hop in and lock the door behind you.
- If you prefer to wait inside the car, wear your seat belt, lock the doors and windows, and sit in the passenger seat to create

the impression that you're waiting for the driver to return.

- In case you break down miles from a telephone, buy or make an emergency sign with 'do not approach – please call police' in big letters.
- Should anyone approach the car, communicate through a small gap in the window.
- If you are suspicious of any good Samaritans who come to your aid, tell them that the emergency services are on their way – even if no call has been made. If they look trustworthy, ask them to call the emergency services for you, but don't accept a lift or any other offers of help.
- Ask the driver to show you some identification when the recovery vehicle arrives.

BOGUS BREAKDOWNS

Exercise caution if another vehicle flashes its lights and the occupants point down to a wheel or try to tell you that your car has developed a fault. This ruse has been used to stop motorists in order to rob them.

Don't stop. Ignore suggestions from the other driver that you pull off at a deserted lay-by or other remote spot. Even if the car is behaving strangely, proceed slowly until you reach a well-lit area where there are other people about before investigating the cause of the problem. It's better to risk damaging a tyre or the engine than to expose yourself to attack.

BEING A GOOD SAMARITAN

When you see a broken-down vehicle or someone flags you down, especially at night, be cautious. With your doors locked and a window only partially open, slow down – changing to a low gear so that you can accelerate away if need be – using your main-beam headlights to check out the area. If something strikes you as suspicious, do not stop. Signal to the driver as you pass that you will telephone the police. Give the police a description of the occupant and the car – registration, make and model, etc.

If it looks genuine, keep the engine running with the clutch engaged while you communicate through a small gap in the window. Offer to summon help as soon as you reach a telephone (if you have a mobile telephone, stop a little way down the road and call the breakdown services or police).

Be Streetwise

When you leave your car parked on a dark, secluded street or in a poorly lit multi-storey car park, it isn't only the vehicle that's at risk. Follow the tips on parking listed in Vehicle Security, and bear in mind the following:

- Think before you park what that area will be like after dark, bearing in mind that you may have to return to the car alone.
- Always try to park in a busy, well-lit place. Stay clear of bushes, walls, trees, hedges, where attackers might wait in ambush.
- Before leaving the car, scan the area for any suspicious types loitering nearby. Some multi-storey car parks provide a hunting ground for muggers, who pounce on unsuspecting drivers as they enter or leave their cars.
- When you get out of the car, check that all doors and windows are secured and the alarm/immobilizer activated, then quickly make your way out of the car park.
- Conceal expensive jewellery and clothes underneath a plain-looking outer garment.
- If you know you are faced with a late-night walk, dress suitably. Wear flat, comfortable shoes that you can run and walk in, and clothes that allow you to move freely.
- Don't carry all your cash, cheque books, and credit cards in the same place. Keep your wallet in an inside pocket. For women, a small shoulder bag worn under a coat or jacket is ideal because it allows you to keep both hands free. Always carry a handbag or briefcase on the side away from the road – some opportunist bag snatchers use motorbikes.
- Try to look confident and alert, but avoid eye contact with strangers. Walk purposefully, even if you're lost. Don't let your body language signal uncertainty or fear.
- Don't take short cuts through dangerous areas, no matter how late you are.
- Be aware of dark alleys, doorways, groups of people loitering, people sitting in parked cars with the engines running. It's not paranoia but risk awareness. Most people and situations turn out to be harmless, but prepare yourself to act

if a threat should materialize. Cross the road to avoid potential dangers. Memorize the locations of public telephones, restaurants, pubs, service stations, and other places where you might find help if pursued by an aggressor.

- Walk facing oncoming traffic to avoid cars pulling up behind you. If a car should draw up alongside you, quickly turn in the opposite direction. A pedestrian can change course faster than a car.

- When you return to the car, especially by night, have your keys in your hand ready to open the door.

- If the car is in a shady spot, it's a good idea to carry a torch. Don't use it to light your way to the car as this will only make you a clear target. Use it to quickly check that the locks have not been tampered with and that no one is hiding in the back seat. It will also come in handy as an improvised weapon if anyone should attack you.

- Don't get into the car if it has been vandalized or broken into. Walk briskly to a telephone, preferably in a well-lit busy place, and call the police. Tell them if you are alone and afraid to return to the car.

- Provided the car has not been tampered with, open the door and get in without delay. Never lean into the car arranging your belongings in the boot or back seat – someone could easily approach from behind and rob you.

- If you live or work within a dangerous neighbourhood, try arranging a lift-share scheme with colleagues or neighbours so you won't have to travel alone.

- Never give lifts to strangers, and refuse all offers of lifts – even from those claiming to be minicab drivers.

- Many rapists target their victims, watching their movements and planning the attack. Try to avoid following the same routines and routes day after day.

Using Reasonable Force

The law permits the victim of an attack to ward off their assailant using as much force as is 'reasonable'. In most countries there are strict regulations to prevent unauthorized persons from carrying offensive weapons, even

---

TAXIS

You may have to take a taxi home if the car should break down. Unless you are in a city where taxi drivers licensed by the police authority ply their trade on the streets, it is best to telephone for a taxi. Anyone can eavesdrop on cab firms' radio broadcasts and turn up pretending to be a minicab, so ask the controller to describe the car and driver who will collect you.

There are a growing number of taxi companies employing female drivers, and women travelling alone at night may feel more comfortable booking a taxi through one of these.

---

though their intention may be only to use them in self-defence. But if you come under attack it is unlikely that you would be prosecuted for making use of a tool or piece of equipment as a weapon in self-defence, provided it was carried for some other legitimate purpose.

OFFENSIVE WEAPONS

The definition of what constitutes an offensive weapon varies from country to country. Guns and certain types of knife are subject to strict controls in most countries, but in the USA and parts of Europe it is legal for members of the public to carry disabling chemical sprays and even 'stun guns'. In Britain, however, such devices are illegal.

In certain circumstances, tools such as spanners and screwdrivers may be considered offensive weapons, unless you have a legitimate reason for carrying them in a public place. It's against the law to carry an object which has been adapted to cause injury, such as a sharpened comb or chisel. But there's nothing to stop you making use of an umbrella or walking stick, a torch, a high-heeled shoe, or a can of hairspray to beat off an attacker.

Any action you take to defend yourself must not be excessive. Your aim should be to disable your attacker sufficiently to allow you to escape. However, in cases of extreme violence escape may prove impossible, and there may be no alternative but to kill an aggressor in order to protect yourself. This must be considered strictly as a last resort.

Defensive driving doesn't mean using your car as a weapon by engaging in vehicular combat. It's all about following a strategy which will keep you safe when faced with hazardous road conditions and the careless actions of others.

defensive driving

MOTORING DRILL The driver • The drill

HAZARD RECOGNITION Visual skills • Mirrors • Signalling

RISK EVALUATION Anticipation • A driving plan

COURSE

SPEED

STEERING

GEAR CHANGING

DEALING WITH HAZARDS Cornering • Overtaking

COMMON ACCIDENT SCENARIOS Reversing • Parked cars • Cyclists • Pedestrians • Junctions • Roundabouts • Avoiding a head-on collision

motoring drill

Motorists who attain a high, consistent standard in their driving do so by following a simple formula, sometimes referred to by professional drivers as the system of car control. This is a drill whereby the process of driving is divided into a series of mental and physical actions which must be performed in order to negotiate a hazard safely.

By learning and practising this drill until you have succeeded in mastering it, you will achieve maximum control and safety behind the wheel.

It takes time and dedication to become a skilled driver rather than a competent one. Too many drivers stop learning the day they pass the driving test. For the rest of their lives they drive on autopilot – and it shows. Resolve to make your self a better driver, starting today.

The Driver

Statistics show that most road accidents occur as the result of driver error. In the majority of cases the accident could have been avoided if only the driver had spotted danger in time.

Part of the problem is that, having passed the driving test and gained a few years' – maybe many years – experience behind the wheel, drivers tend to over-estimate their own ability. Comfortable at the controls, and confident that they can handle a vehicle at speed, that their reflexes are sharp and their reaction times better than average, they get themselves into lethal situations by taking what they think are calculated risks. So the first step to becoming a better driver is a little honest self-analysis. You're not going to put in the time and effort it takes to eradicate bad habits if you won't own up to having any.

To drive like an expert you need to observe what is happening, anticipate what might happen next, and devise a strategy which will allow you to cope with whatever situation should arise. When confronted with a number of hazards at once, you need to be able to determine which pose the greatest threat to your safety – and having decided, you need to act without delay.

Using the drill will help you to evaluate risks quickly and respond in a calm, confident manner. A driver who appears to be under pressure, making a fuss about other motorists or using exaggerated movements when manoeuvring, leaves passengers feeling uneasy. But even those nagging back-seat drivers will be able to relax and turn their minds to other things when it becomes obvious that you are fully in control, proceeding smoothly at the right speed, in the right gear, with the car positioned in the correct part of the road.

By weighing up situations and options the whole time, you will be in a position to react speedily, reducing your speed well in advance of a hazard and averting the need for sudden braking or violent swerving.

defensive driving

Panic is not conducive to clear thinking. A good driver starts looking for 'escape routes' which will get them out of danger the moment a potential hazard is sighted – and because their eyes are trained to scan the whole of the road for clues to dangers ahead, they are likely to recognize a hazard while it is still a long way off.

Skilled drivers wait and evaluate rather than committing themselves to a course of action and then rushing in, hoping for the best. This cautious approach should not be confused with hesitation, which is born of uncertainty. 'He who hesitates is lost,' as the saying goes. Only by waiting until you have fully assessed a situation can you make well-judged decisions on your next course of action.

Your aim should be to drive with deliberation, assessing risks and taking into account changing circumstances, forming a plan as to how you will deal with those risks, and then having the flexibility to adapt your driving plan to suit.

The Drill

When you set off in your car you are entering an unpredictable environment. The law does what it can to make driving more predictable by stipulating that vehicles must be well maintained and roadworthy, and that drivers must pass a proficiency test and follow the Highway Code. This reduces the risks somewhat, but a basic level of competence (which is all that is required to pass the driving test) is no guarantee of safety.

To improve safety margins still further, the driver needs to be able to compensate for adverse conditions and the sometimes irrational behaviour of other road users – not to mention their own occasional lapses in concentration. Military and police drivers – who have to deal with the most hazardous conditions on a daily basis – have found that the best way to do this is to follow a drill which instils a methodical yet flexible approach to driving.

The purpose of the drill is to provide a framework which can be adapted to any situation. By putting it into operation you will become a safer driver, able to negotiate hazards with the minimum risk to yourself and others.

The hazard recognition phase goes on continuously, because new hazards can arise at any time and you may need to change your of plan of action as a result. Practise co-ordinating your mental skills (looking for clues, weighing up information, anticipating what might happen next, deciding whether a signal would be helpful in the circumstances, formulating a plan based on your observations) with the physical skills (braking, steering, changing gears, accelerating, signalling) required to maintain control of the vehicle at all times. Be realistic about your capabilities and adjust your speed accordingly.

Each phase of the drill should be considered in sequence at the approach to a hazard. But be flexible: only implement those phases applicable to the particular circumstances.

The drill consists of five phases:

HAZARD RECOGNITION:
look, evaluate, decide, signal if necessary

COURSE:
adopt a position which will allow you to see and negotiate hazards

SPEED AND STEERING:
adjust your speed and time steering so that the maximum tyre grip can be attained

GEAR:
engage the correct gear to match your speed

ACCELERATION:
where appropriate, accelerate smoothly away from the hazard

Hazard Recognition

 In order to react to danger, you must first be aware of it. It's vital therefore to develop the habit of using your eyes, ears, and even your nose to register potential hazards in good time to act upon them and avert disaster.

VISUAL SKILLS

There's more to effective observation than 20/20 vision. On a busy road the motorist is surrounded by visual information – movement, bright colours, things happening in every direction – much of which catches the eye but has no relevance whatsoever to your driving. What sets skilled drivers apart is their ability to look selectively, to read the road. They do this by filtering out all the irrelevant details and concentrating on the ones that matter.

This is a skill which is not acquired overnight. Inexperienced drivers will often look straight at something without recognizing the element of risk involved. They see a sharp corner; it doesn't occur to them that beyond the bend children might have strayed into the road, too young to understand the risk they're taking.

Or, having seen a potential hazard and recognized it as such, the novice driver will focus on that to the exclusion of all else. For example, seeing an emergency vehicle racing through the traffic with flashing lights and sirens, the novice might be so eager to pull over that they fail to notice the cyclist on their nearside.

To improve your visual skills:

- Keep your eyes moving. Continuously. scan the road ahead, from immediately in front of your vehicle to the furthest point on the horizon. And use your mirrors to scan the view to the sides and rear.
- Be on the look out for hazards in general rather than in particular. If you're thinking, 'Windy day, must watch for high-sided vehicles,' you might overlook smaller road users such as cyclists and pedestrians who are likely to be swept into your path by the wind.
- Avoid focusing on any one object or in any one direction. While your eyes are fixed on one hazard, a dozen others could materialize without your being aware of it. Having identified a potential hazard, monitor it by glancing back that way at regular intervals. Don't stop scanning the road as a whole.
- Use your peripheral vision to register movements to the side. Don't forget the hazards that pedestrians and animals can pose when they cross your path unexpectedly.
- Children sometimes run out from behind or between

parked vehicles. Check for signs of movement as you approach and where possible look underneath – you may be able to see the feet of hidden pedestrians. Be especially wary of ice-cream vans and buses.

- If there is someone inside a parked vehicle there's a possibility that they will open a door without warning. At night, the interior light coming on may signal that someone is about to get out. If the engine is running the car could pull out suddenly, so watch for brake lights and emissions coming from the exhaust.
- On fast, open roads such as motorways, look as far ahead as possible. The majority of drivers do not look far enough ahead and fail to see warning signs such as the brake lights of cars forced to slow down because of a hazard.
- Where the layout of the road or an obstruction restricts your view, use whatever aids exist. Reflections in shop windows or polished metal surfaces may help you to see round corners on blind bends. Look through vehicle windows or gaps in hedges to see what lies beyond. By night, use the angle of approaching headlights to judge the curvature of a bend.
- On winding country roads, use any high, open stretches to assess the road ahead. It may be possible to see oncoming vehicles – or obstructions, such as herds of cattle – far in the distance.
- Observe road signs and markings. These exist to give prior warning of hazards ahead – make use of the information they provide.
- Check your mirrors every five seconds to keep abreast of what's going on behind you.

MIRRORS

Effective use of the mirrors is essential if you are to avoid accidents. If there's something behind you – whether it's a four-wheeled vehicle or a cyclist – you need to know how far away it is and how fast it's travelling in order to determine whether you can safely change speed, change lanes, or change direction. This is why driving instructors drum the maxim 'mirror signal manoeuvre' into their pupils until they can repeat it in their sleep.

Correct adjustment of mirrors can significantly reduce blind spots, but even with mirror inserts fitted there will be some areas to the rear and side where your vision is obscured by the car's framework. Make sure that you know where these blind spots occur on your vehicle, and take a quick glance over your shoulder to check for hazards when pulling out at junctions or joining a motorway.

SIGNALLING

Signals between road users provide an invaluable guide to intentions, provided they are given clearly and in good time. You should give a signal whenever you think it would be helpful to other road users, but make sure there is no room for ambiguity.

Certain signals, such as flashing headlights, are subject to a variety of interpretations. In Britain, drivers often flash their lights to indicate to another road user that they may proceed. French motorists, on the other hand, use this signal when they are claiming the right of way. To avoid confusion, flash your headlights only to alert another driver to your presence, then wait to assess their next move before proceeding.

In situations where flashing headlights are unlikely to be seen, use a quick toot of the horn to alert other road users to your presence. A long, deafening blast might do more harm than good, causing a cyclist or pedestrian to start suddenly and fall into your path. Bear in mind that background noise or deafness may prevent their hearing your signal, so never assume that it is safe to proceed until you are certain that the other person has seen you and conceded the right of way.

In many countries it is illegal to sound the horn in built-up areas outside daylight hours, or while your vehicle is stationary (unless a moving vehicle has not seen you and is on a collision course with your parked car).

The only time you should give a long blast is when approaching a hazard such as a blind bend or hump-back bridge where the view is very restricted.

In addition to using direction indicators, flashing headlights, the horn, and arm signals, road users can communicate in a variety of ways:

- When it's necessary to lose speed, warn following traffic by giving several short pumps on the brake pedal. This will attract attention to your brake lights.
- The position of a vehicle on the road will indicate when it is about to overtake a parked vehicle (this may be preferable to using the direction indicator in some situations, as it might be thought that you were going to turn off to the side rather than merely overtake).
- Eye contact is often the surest guide to whether it is safe to proceed or wait.

IMPROVING YOUR AWARENESS

A simple exercise which will improve your powers of observation and concentration is to deliver a running commentary as you drive. Once you get over feeling self-conscious about talking to yourself, this technique will help to make you a more aware driver.

Report everything you see:

- weather conditions
- road signs and markings
- road surface
- junctions, bends, hills and other areas where visibility is restricted
- position of pedestrians and animals by the side of the road
- actions of other road users (note the speed and position of vehicles in front, behind and to the side)

Describe in each case the risks you anticipate as a result, and how you intend dealing with them. Because it makes you more conscious of hazards and your response to them, this technique can quickly effect a marked improvement in the way you drive.

HAZARDS

Anything that presents an element of risk and requires an adjustment in the vehicle's speed or course can be classified as a hazard. These fall into three main categories:

'**physical features**' – sharp bends, road junctions, roadworks, hill crests

'**other vehicles and road users**' – pedestrians, cyclists, animals

'**adverse conditions**' – wear and tear on road surfaces, bad weather, poor visibility

Hazards can take many forms:

- Parked vehicles, especially those which have been illegally or carelessly parked, or where the occupants put others at risk by opening doors or driving off without checking their mirrors.
- Some drivers allow themselves to get distracted by road-works instead of concentrating on the road ahead. Keep your wits about you and maintain a safe gap between your vehicle and the one in front.
- Be prepared for sudden changes in road surfaces, especially if driving at night on country roads.
- Faulty traffic lights. Some drivers see out-of-order traffic lights as an invitation to speed across a junction. Treat with caution, especially if the lights control a crossroads. Follow the procedure you would for an unmarked junction or crossroads.
- Motorists who ignore the Highway Code. Impatience with traffic delays can lead to vehicles speeding through lights after they have turned red, overtaking on the inside, or barging in to a queue of traffic. Be patient and always allow extra time for hold-ups.
- Motorists driving without due care and attention. Drivers who miss their turning and stop suddenly or perform illegal manoeuvres to get back on track cause chaos. If you see the occupants of the car in front pointing or gesticulating, they may be looking for a parking space or street number. Keep back in case they make a sudden stop or turn in the road.
- Learner drivers are unpredictable and should be given plenty of room in case they make mistakes – like rolling backwards on a hill start or stalling at a junction.
- Children walking to and from school or disembarking from school buses can behave unpredictably. Too busy playing to realize the risks they're taking, they can without warning run into the road.
- Be careful when driving past pubs at closing time. Drunken pedestrians (and, worse still, drunken drivers exiting pub car parks) need to be watched and avoided.
- Try to avoid driving in rush-hour traffic if possible. The roads are gridlocked in many areas and tempers rise as a result.

- In bad weather, make allowances for pedestrians whose view of the road is restricted by an umbrella or rain hood. People are less likely to wait patiently for the lights to change when they're getting soaked, so be prepared for pedestrians running across the road.
- Ice-cream vans attract small children. They race across roads to get to them and stroll away licking their cones oblivious to all thoughts of safety. When you see an ice-cream van, slow down and give it a wide berth.
- An animal by the side of the road may dart out at any time. Slow down, and prepare to brake if one should run in front of you, but never swerve violently to avoid it as you could endanger human life.
- When you encounter a herd of sheep or cattle on a country road, it's best to pull up and wait for them to pass.
- Never accelerate, rev your engine, sound your horn, or do anything else to startle animals – they may behave unpredictably as a result.
- Be careful when passing young, inexperienced riders who may have difficulty controlling their horses.
- Exercise caution when following a bus. People running for buses, or disembarking from them, sometimes take insane risks. Give way to buses whenever you can do so.
- Taxis will turn on a sixpence if they see a prospective fare waving them down. Watch out for people hailing one from the kerb and be prepared for sudden, often illegal, manoeuvres.
- Give cyclists a wide berth – the same space (a door's width) as you would a parked car. In bad weather, anticipate them getting blown off course or swerving to avoid a puddle.
- If a cyclist looks over their shoulder, be prepared for them to make a turn.
- Because of the helmet and engine noise, motorcyclists might not hear you coming. If you overtake a motorcycle, try to make sure that they have seen you in their mirrors.
- If you see two motorcyclists together, there's every likelihood that they will try to remain together by overtaking at the same time and negotiating lights and junctions together. Bear this in mind, because if one pulls out, cutting it fine, the other may well follow.
- When scanning for hazards, think BIKE. Cyclists and

motorcyclists are difficult to see – especially if they're not wearing fluorescent strips or bright colours – and even when you have seen them there's a tendency to lose track of them when you are concentrating on finding a gap. Bear in mind that the stopping distances for motorbikes are greater than those for cars.

- Slow-moving vehicles such as tractors and JCBs will cause a tailback. Be patient and wait for a clear road before overtaking. Stay well back to obtain a clear view and avoid stones and clods of earth thrown up by the wheels.
- Articulated trucks and other long vehicles often need two lanes when manoeuvring round a corner or roundabout. Leave them plenty of room. Never overtake a truck which is signalling to turn, even if the indicator has been flashing for some time and it seems that the driver may have forgotten to turn it off. Give a polite toot on the horn to let them know you are there.
- DON'T drive in a truck driver's blind spots for any longer than you have to on straight roads.
- When you see a vehicle is carrying a load, always ask yourself whether it looks safe and well secured. A flapping tarpaulin indicates a sloppy driver – stay back, especially on bends. If you see a load that is obviously not secure, flash your lights and use the horn to draw the driver's attention to this.
- If you do see a load slip, pump the brakes to activate your brake lights and give warning to those behind.

Risk Evaluation

Once you have identified a potential danger, the next step is to assess how great a risk it poses and determine what action must be taken.

This sounds straightforward enough, in theory. But in real life things have a way of getting complicated. On congested roads and in adverse conditions it's more than likely that you will find yourself faced with a variety of hazards and potential dangers in quick succession or even simultaneously. You then have a matter of seconds to decide which hazard presents the greatest risk and therefore takes priority, and to

formulate a plan which will allow you to cope with each hazard in turn, without jeopardizing your safety or that of any other road user.

The risk potential of a hazard fluctuates according to the nature of the danger, how far away it is, how fast the gap between you is closing, whether it is stationary or moving, and what escape routes are at your disposal. As the level of risk changes, your priorities will change too.

For example, a slip road joining the motorway ahead of you presents a hazard. While it remains clear of traffic the risk is negligible. The only action you need take is to watch for vehicles approaching the motorway.

The risk increases when you see a vehicle proceeding along the slip road, because if the driver fails to check his mirrors and blindspot he might not see you. At this point you check the progress and speed of the other vehicle and start thinking about adjusting your speed or changing lanes.

Should it become apparent that the other car is being driven recklessly, the risk potential rises dramatically. Joy riders in a stolen vehicle or a macho driver out to show he's the fastest thing on the road present a very real danger. You don't want to engage in a motorway duel, so you need to get out of their way quickly without putting drivers behind you at risk. If they've entered the slip road at breakneck speed you will have little time to register their presence before they hit the motorway. It may be necessary to brake hard or change course.

ANTICIPATION

Anticipation plays a crucial part in formulating a driving plan. Rather than acting purely on what can be seen, you must take into account what is obscured from view and try to predict what might happen next. This means using your experience to deduce what circumstances may arise on the basis of the few visual clues you have.

It doesn't pay to be complacent where the abilities and behaviour of other drivers are concerned. Never assume that they will check their mirrors before pulling out, or that, having signalled, they will turn as indicated. Even a driver who seems to be driving carefully can have a sudden lapse in concentration and do something irrational.

A skilled driver does not simply observe the road, they try

to interpret what they see. When a vehicle in the distance does something out of the ordinary – a sudden change of course or speed – they ask themselves what obstacle in the road has caused this action.

Driving Plan

By looking and planning well ahead you will make life much easier for yourself. If you don't spot a hazard until the last moment – or if you see it in good time but fail to act – you will be left with two options: brake hard or swerve violently. With planning, on the other hand, you will be able to negotiate a succession of hazards by making minor adjustments to your speed and position; corrections so smooth that they will go unnoticed by your passengers.

For a plan to work, it needs to be based on accurate and continuous assessment. There's no sense making a rash decision on the basis of a few clues and then committing yourself to it regardless. As more information becomes available, your original assessment should be revised. Make contingency plans to deal with those 'what if' scenarios.

While this information-gathering process is going on, apply the five phases of the drill:

- identify and evaluate hazards
- adopt a course which will improve your view
- adjust your speed
- engage the correct gear
- when safe to do so, accelerate away from the hazard

So long as there is any element of doubt as to the correct course of action, keep your options open and your speed low to maintain safety margins.

Course

The position of your vehicle on the road has a critical bearing on safety. The safest course will vary according to the circumstances, because the layout of the road, volume of traffic, position of parked cars, location of hazards such as roadworks, presence of pedestrians, and road markings will all have a bearing on your position.

If you drive too close to the nearside your view of the road will be restricted and you risk clipping the kerb, a cyclist, or a pedestrian straying off the pavement – or being clipped by the door of a parked vehicle opening without warning. Your position may be seen as an invitation to following vehicles to overtake, and could render you virtually invisible to drivers joining the road from a junction or driveway on the nearside, especially if they are reversing out. There's also a greater risk of puncturing a tyre, because broken glass and other debris is often allowed to accumulate in the gutter.

On the other hand, if you drive too close to the middle of the road your vehicle may obstruct oncoming vehicles attempting to overtake or negotiate hazards.

In normal driving conditions on a two-way, single carriageway you should position the nearside wheels about one metre from the kerb. This will be sufficient to dominate your side of the road and avoid conflict with most of the nearside hazards mentioned above. Be prepared, however, to adapt your course to fit the circumstances. Keep an eye out for road markings indicating bus or cycle lanes, and allow adequate clearance when passing cyclists and stationary vehicles.

On wider roads you can drive nearer to the middle of the road. This position will improve your view of the road ahead and to the sides, permitting you to drive at higher speeds. Again, be prepared to adjust your course and reduce your speed should changing conditions make it necessary.

PARKED VEHICLES AND OTHER HAZARDS

When passing stationary vehicles, cyclists, pedestrians, or road-works, allow as much clearance as you can. Don't weave in and out of a line of parked vehicles. Move out towards the crown of the road, leaving at least a door's width between your vehicle and the obstacle.

Where oncoming traffic prevents your adopting this course, you may have to stop and allow the oncoming vehicle to pass. Try to stop some way ahead of the obstruction so that you will have plenty of room to pull away without having to steer your way out of a tight corner.

FOLLOWING POSITION

While driving along it's important to keep up with the flow of traffic – driving too slowly will irritate those motorists who have the misfortune to be stuck in line behind you – but at the same time you must always leave a safe gap between your vehicle and the one in front.

Following too closely is dangerous because it reduces the time available to you to anticipate, let alone react to, the actions of the driver in front. Some drivers will argue that their speed of reaction is such that they can get away with travelling faster and closing the gap. But what if the driver in front has exceptionally slow reflexes or is prone to lapses in concentration? What if their vehicle has faulty brakes, defective brake lights, or worn tyres? It is impossible to gauge what another driver will do next. It may be the very opposite of what they ought to be doing or what you would expect them to do.

To accommodate the unexpected, on the open road maintain a gap which allows one metre/yard for every mile per hour. Check the distance by watching the vehicle in front as it draws level with a marker of some kind, then reciting: 'Only a fool breaks the two-second rule.' If you pass the marker before completing the phrase, the gap needs to be increased. When travelling at high speeds or in adverse conditions, an even greater gap should be maintained.

At speeds below 10 mph – when travelling in a slow-moving queue of traffic, for example – allow a minimum of one foot for each mph.

Even when you come to a complete halt, held up behind a line of vehicles at traffic lights or road works, you should make sure that you can see both tarmac and the rear tyres of the vehicle in front of you. That way you can move forward if a vehicle coming up behind should brake too late. Remember that rear-end shunts are one of the commonest forms of accident, and if you're too close to the vehicle in

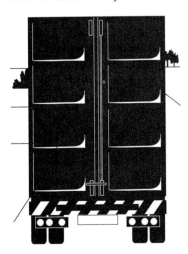

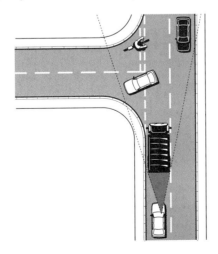

The closer you are to the vehicle in front, the less you will be able to see, especially if it is a van or lorry. Keep well back to obtain the best possible view of the road ahead.

front you'll suffer damage to the front and rear.

By maintaining a safe distance you will gain the following advantages:

- Your view of the road will be improved.
- Only a very slight adjustment in course will be required to obtain an even better view to the near or offside.
- In heavy traffic it is safer to look through the windows of the vehicle in front than to pull out for a better view of the road ahead.
- You are less likely to have to slam on the brakes should the vehicle in front stop suddenly. This in turn gives the driver behind more time to react and reduces the likelihood of their rear-ending you.
- An impatient driver following along behind will be able to use the gap to overtake.
- Should you wish to overtake you will be well placed to see when it is safe to do so.

Speed

'Slow into trouble, fast out,' as the saying goes. Speed should be used intelligently, as a means of getting you away from danger rather than into it. Use of the accelerator must be combined with observation, anticipation, accurate assessment of traffic conditions, and an awareness of the capabilities and limitations both of the vehicle and yourself as a driver.

Thrilling as it may be to feel the power surge as you floor the accelerator, safety considerations must come first. Remember, at speed:

- tyres will have less grip on the road
- steering control will be reduced
- skids are more likely to occur
- stopping distances will be increased
- in the event of a crash the impact will be more severe.

Let the prevailing conditions dictate your speed. Observe whatever speed limits apply, and drive well within those limits if visibility is poor or the road surface is slippery. Above all, make sure you can safely stop on your side of the road within the distance you can see to be clear.

There can be a drastic variation in the acceleration capabilities of different vehicles, so no matter how experienced a driver you are, when you get behind the wheel of a car you're not familiar with, take the time to learn which is the best gear for overtaking, how the brakes respond, get the feel for the controls and determine whether the vehicle has a tendency to oversteer or understeer on bends. Acquaint yourself with what it can do before attempting any potentially dangerous manoeuvres such as overtaking or trying to merge with motorway traffic.

A SMOOTH RIDE

Try to progress at a steady speed. Don't be one of those macho drivers who accelerates at full throttle every time he sees a gap, only to brake hard when traffic builds up again a little further down the road. This style of driving increases fuel consumption, engine wear, tyre wear and pollution. A jerky ride is also uncomfortable for passengers, and if they get car sick you'll have only yourself to blame.

The mark of a skilled driver is a smooth ride. Practise controlled, precise use of the pedals. Advanced observation and planning should make it possible for you to anticipate the need to reduce speed and do it progressively. Gradual variations in speed can be achieved without touching the brakes; all you need do is gently release the accelerator. In slippery conditions it is far better to lose speed in this way and rely on engine braking (see Bad-Weather Driving).

Harsh braking should be avoided, even if you have the luxury of ABS. For maximum control – and to reduce wear and tear on the vehicle – apply these braking principles:

- Start to apply the brakes in good time.
- The pressure should be gentle to start with, increasing in force until the car slows down to the correct speed.
- To bring the car to a standstill, brake progressively and then reduce the pressure to prevent the car stopping with a sudden jolt.
- Brake firmly only when travelling in a straight line.

- Vary brake pressure according to condition of the road surface. Use cadence or pulse braking if you feel the wheels begin to lock (see Skidding in Bad-Weather Driving).
- When faced with a steep downhill run on a winding road, engage a low gear before you start the descent. Stay off the brakes as far as possible. If you must apply the brakes, do it on the straight stretches and not the bends.

BRAKE TESTS

To check the efficiency of your vehicle's brakes:

1 Find a straight section of road which is free of traffic. The weather conditions and road surface need to be good for this exercise; don't jeopardize your safety or that of other road users by trying this in poor visibility or on a slippery road.
2 Drive the vehicle in a straight line at 60 mph and apply the brakes firmly and progressively. The vehicle should remain on a straight course with no pulling to one side.
3 Reduce speed until you reach 15 mph, then ease off the brakes and reapply firmly to test the operation of the inertia seat belts.

If the vehicle pulls to one side or swerves violently under braking in a straight line, have it checked by a professional mechanic.

Now let's try an emergency stop:

- Drive in a straight line in third gear at around 30 mph.
- Press the foot brake down hard to stop the car in the shortest possible time and distance.
- At the last moment, press the clutch to prevent the car stalling.

Steering

The pull–push method of steering taught by driving instructors is a safe, efficient technique which enables the driver to turn the wheel smoothly and accurately under full control. The disadvantage is that it's difficult to master and too cumbersome for situations when the car is skidding out of control and the driver needs to apply a speedy correction. At such times it's better to forget the textbook style and do whatever it takes to control the vehicle's course – even if it means crossing hands in the process.

There are, however, certain steering rules which should never be ignored:

- Adjust the driver's seat so that you can reach the controls comfortably.
- Hold the wheel lightly but firmly with your hands in the ten-to-two or quarter-to-three position on the rim. Don't try using a spoke to turn the wheel.
- Be ready to tighten your grip should the need arise. For example, to prevent the wheel being wrenched from your grasp when there are strong crosswinds, or when steering round a corner.
- While the engine is running, never take BOTH hands off the wheel.
- When you have to take one hand off the wheel to change gear, operate a control, or give a hand signal, always replace it the moment you finish the task.
- Don't drive with an elbow resting on the window frame or arm rest.
- Time your gear changes so that you can keep both hands on the wheel when cornering or braking hard. Don't change down while on a bend.
- Turn the wheel smoothly. Avoid short, jerky movements.
- After turning, the self-centring action of the wheel helps to return it to the original position, but don't allow the wheel to spin back on its own. Feed it back using both hands to control and guide its movement.
- On slippery roads all steering movements should be delicate and gradual. Harsh steering is a common cause of skids (see *Skidding* in **Bad-Weather Driving**).
- When travelling on badly maintained roads or driving off-road, make sure your thumbs are not hooked round the rim. When you run over a bump there's a danger of kick-back wrenching the steering wheel violently to one side – with sufficient force to dislocate a carelessly placed thumb.
- If you're accustomed to standard steering, be careful when driving a car with power-assisted steering. The vehicle will

respond more than you expect to the amount of turn you give the wheel. Go gently!

- Don't turn the steering wheel while the car is stationary. This puts unnecessary strain on the steering linkage.

Gear Changing

The ability to select the correct gear for the road speed and conditions is one of the most important skills a driver needs to master – unless, of course, the vehicle has an automatic gearbox.

The art of gear changing involves:

- an understanding of your vehicle's gear ratios and acceleration capabilities – the maximum road speed for each gear can vary considerably between vehicles, so check the manufacturer's handbook
- listening to the engine: when it start's labouring, it's time to change gear
- taking into account traffic conditions (can you maintain a steady speed or will you have to slow down or go faster?); road surface (on icy, slippery roads, tyre grip will be reduced); hills and bends (on steep ascents and descents you may need all the power you can get)
- the precise operation of clutch, brakes or accelerator, and gear lever to achieve smooth, flowing gear changes
- the ability to change gear selectively rather than sequentially
- getting your timing right, so that the correct gear is engaged on the approach to a hazard, and not while you're negotiating it

There's every incentive to perfect your technique: abusing the gearbox – as many drivers do, either by driving in too high a gear or changing down rather than braking to reduce speed – increases wear and tear on engine components and wastes fuel.

First or bottom gear is the most powerful, but because it drives the wheels more slowly it gives little road speed.

Top gear is the least powerful but produces the most

speed. On some cars the highest gear (fifth) is designed for cruising at motorway speeds. For sudden bursts of speed – needed when overtaking, for example – you would engage a lower gear.

DOUBLE DE-CLUTCH TECHNIQUE

Modern cars have synchromesh gears, which gives the driver some leeway when it comes to matching road speed and engine speed because the speeds of the gears are synchronized before they engage. If, however, you drive a vehicle which does not have synchromesh gears, you will have to master the art of double de-clutching:

- Place your hand on the gear lever
- Depress the clutch pedal fully and take your foot off the accelerator
- Move the gear lever to neutral
- Release the clutch pedal
- Quickly depress and then release the accelerator pedal
- Clutch down quickly
- Change into lower/higher gear
- Let the clutch pedal come up fully and, at the same time, press the accelerator (or brake pedal, as appropriate)

CHANGING UP

Remaining in a low gear beyond its optimum performance will damage the engine. Check the manufacturer's handbook for your vehicle's peak engine performance recommendations.

Accelerate smoothly away from a standing start, working your way up through the gears as you gather speed. When the engine's optimum performance for a particular gear is reached, change up to the next.

If you're cruising at 50 mph in top gear and find you need extra power – to overtake, or climb a steep hill, for example – change down to a lower gear. This can be done without losing road speed, using the following technique:

1 Place your hand on the gear lever
2 Press the clutch pedal down quickly
3 At the same time, depress the accelerator and then release it immediately

4 Select the next gear down

5 Bring up the clutch and accelerate away

SELECTIVE GEAR CHANGING

There is no need to change down sequentially through the gears in order to lose speed – no matter what your driving instructor may have taught you all those years ago. For maximum control and stability you need both hands on the wheel when approaching a hazard, and the best way to achieve this is to skip all those intermediate gears and go straight for the one you want – having reduced speed first, of course.

A snatched, last-minute gear change will destabilize the vehicle and could prove dangerous, so it is vital that you plan ahead. If you are following the drill properly, you should be using your powers of observation and anticipation to spot a hazard in good time. Your next step will be to lose speed either by braking or deceleration, depending on the traffic conditions and how far away the hazard is. Once the correct road speed has been achieved, and only then, you can ease off or release the brake, depress the clutch and change directly from, say, fourth gear to second. Both hands can then be back on the wheel in time to steer round the hazard.

> Gear-assisted braking (changing down through the gears to reduce speed) should only be used in icy conditions, when the tyres' grip on slippery roads would be reduced by applying the brakes. Or when travelling down a steep downhill gradient. At such times, your speed should be kept low to begin with – this technique is intended to help you maintain control of the vehicle's speed; it cannot suddenly reduce excessive speeds to a safe level. See Bad-Weather Driving for more information.

TIMING

Like braking, gear changing is best done when travelling in a straight line. You don't want to have only one hand on the wheel while steering a corner or negotiating a hazard, and you definitely don't want to run the risk of bungling a gear change mid-way through overtaking another vehicle.

The gear change should be effected on the approach to a hazard, so that the power to accelerate out of trouble is at your command by the time you reach the hazard. This can sometimes mean that you have to change up a little early. For example, when planning to overtake, you must change down in readiness to pull out – and you should remain in that gear until you are past the vehicle being overtaken.

> ### REMEMBER
> DON'T leave anything to chance. Plan your gear changes and time them so that they are over and done with by the time you come to negotiate any hazard or changes in direction.

AUTOMATIC TRANSMISSION

Automatics take a lot of the effort out of driving, especially for those who spend much of their time behind the wheel in urban traffic jams. The transmission automatically picks the optimum gear, reducing stress on both the engine and the driver.

The gear selector offers a range of options:

'park' locks the transmission and should be selected only when the vehicle is stationary

'reverse' and 'neutral' have the same function as in a manual car, as do the gears: 1st, 2nd, etc.

'drive' automatically selects the most appropriate gear for driving forwards.

You will find yourself having to use the brakes more often than in a manual car, because automatics have a tendency to creep forward unless held stationary by the handbrake or foot brake. Make sure you apply the brakes while starting the engine and selecting drive or reverse while stationary. Don't select neutral for temporary stops when held up in traffic.

It's advisable to use one foot to control both the brake and accelerator, as this encourages good driving practices such as early release of the accelerator and progressive braking.

Every driver of an automatic car should make sure that they know how to use the gearbox in manual mode. Although 'drive' may see you through most situations, there is no substitute for manual control when overtaking, cornering, or negotiating a steep downhill gradient – especially in icy conditions.

defensive driving

dealing with hazards

Though bad weather, traffic conditions, road layout, road surface, and other variables play their part in making sure that each hazard poses a different set of problems, the motoring drill provides you with a strategy that can be adapted to suit any situation.

By applying the various phases of the drill – identifying and evaluating hazards, adopting the correct course; maintaining vehicle control through carefully judged use of acceleration, braking and steering – you will be able to negotiate hazards smoothly and safely.

Start getting into the habit now.

Cornering

Driving round a corner or bend is a kind of balancing act. The stability of the vehicle will be affected by a number of forces:

- vehicle characteristics: rear-wheel, front-wheel, or four-wheel drive? Tendency to understeer or oversteer?
- distribution of load
- condition of tyres
- sharpness of the bend
- camber of the road
- condition of the road surface
- centrifugal forces
- speed
- use of brakes
- how much steering you use
- use of accelerator

APPROACHING BENDS

Now it's simply a question of applying the drill, starting with hazard recognition. Road signs and markings will warn of an approaching bend, and may even indicate its severity, but look for other clues as well. Hedgerows, trees and streetlights may help you to judge how sharp the bend is. At night, observe the angle of approaching cars' headlights as they negotiate the bend. Turn off the radio and listen for oncoming traffic.

When the weather is bad, road surfaces can be treacherous. You could turn the corner to find a vast puddle or a sheet of black ice. Watch the behaviour of vehicles ahead – what seems to be erratic steering may be due to a slippery road.

If the bend is too sharp for you to see into it, look through gaps in buildings, fences or hedges for a view of the road on the other side. Try to gauge the speed of oncoming traffic, and keep an eye out for HGVs and other large vehicles which will have difficulty steering a tight corner.

Don't forget that danger can come from behind, as well. Use your mirrors to check what's going on to your rear. And don't forget to use signals where necessary, so that your intentions are made clear to other road users.

> ### VEHICLE CHARACTERISTICS
> Safe cornering starts with getting to know how your vehicle handles on a bend. You need to be able to judge how much steering to apply, and that will depend on whether the vehicle has power-assisted steering, traction control, front- or rear-wheel drive, and the condition of the tyres and suspension. Your driving will have to be adapted to suit the vehicle's characteristics.
>
> Bear in mind that the vehicle will behave differently when carrying a full load or a roof rack. If you're used to driving alone, don't assume that the car will feel the same when it's full of passengers or heavy luggage. You may need to adjust the tyre pressures (see the manufacturer's recommendations in the handbook). Drive extra cautiously until you get used to it.

POSITIONING ON BENDS

As you approach the bend, you need to set a course which will give you the best possible view, while at the same time keeping out of the path of other road users. There's always the possibility that a vehicle approaching from the opposite direction might have crossed over to your side of the road in order to improve their view of the road – or because they've veered off course as a result of misjudging the bend or taking it too fast. There may also be parked cars or other obstructions just around the corner.

SPEED

Your speed should be determined by:

- your view into the bend
- the severity of the bend
- the camber of the bend
- the width of the road
- the condition of the road
- prevailing weather conditions
- other traffic
- the handling and road-holding capabilities of your vehicle

Cornering places heavy demands on the tyres. Remember, there's only a limited amount of grip available – harsh braking or acceleration while steering round a bend will destablize the vehicle, resulting in a skid. To minimize the risk of skidding, adjust your speed and select the appropriate gear before you get to the bend.

If you get all your braking and gear changing over with while travelling in a straight line on the approach to the corner, both hands can be back on the wheel for maximum steering control as you turn into the bend. (For more information on the various types of skid and how to control them, see Skidding in Bad-Weather Driving.)

If the worst happens and you feel the wheels start to skid, come off the accelerator and follow the procedure for cadence braking – unless you have ABS, in which case all you need do is depress the brake pedal and hold it there while the ABS does the rest.

Right-hand bends

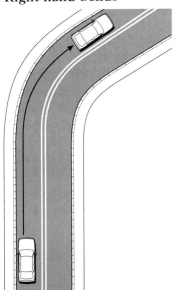

When approaching a right-hand bend, stay close to the nearside kerb for the best view into the bend. Watch out for pedestrians and cyclists – especially on country roads where there is no pavement. Don't be tempted to increase your speed even if the road ahead looks clear.

Left-hand bends

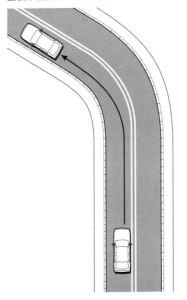

On a left-hand bend, provided traffic conditions allow, position yourself towards the centre of the road but stay in your lane. If you stray too far over you could find yourself on a collision course with oncoming traffic.

defensive driving

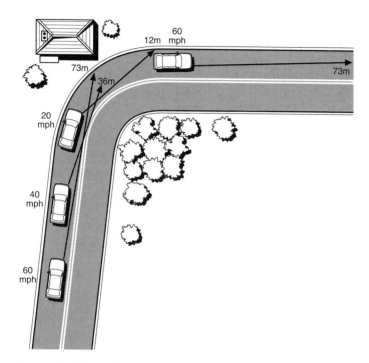

You cannot safely negotiate a blind corner at 60 mph, even if that is the legal maximum speed limit for the road your are on. Remember, the minimum stopping distance at that speed is 73 metres. So, the moment you find yourself 73 metres or 18 car lengths from a tight bend it's time to apply the brakes. At 40 mph your stopping distance is 36m or 9 car lengths, but you still can't see into the bend so your speed needs to come down further still. At 20 mph the vehicle can be brought to a halt in 12m or 3 car lengths, and the view is starting to open out again. This is the correct speed for the bend. Change down to second gear and maintain a steady 20 mph as you turn the corner. Once you are on the straight again and can see far into the distance, it's time to start gaining speed again.

WARNING

The stopping distances shown above apply to a roadworthy car on a good road surface. If the road is wet, double the stopping distance. In icy conditions, you could easily cover three or four times that distance before the car comes to a halt.

Be careful, too, when following another vehicle. Remember to maintain a safe distance. Don't blindly follow the leader into danger.

Overtaking

Overtaking can be a dangerous manoeuvre. Always weigh up the risks before committing yourself, and continue to review the situation throughout. Prepare contingency plans in case you need to reconsider at any stage – sometimes hazards materialize with no warning, so you must have an escape route in mind.

Don't make a move until you are certain that it is:

NECESSARY

LEGAL

SAFE

There's no point trying to overtake a vehicle which is signalling its intention to turn off at the next junction, or if it is only travelling a couple of miles slower than you are.

Check road signs and markings to make sure that you won't be breaking the law. If you plan to take the car abroad, familiarize yourself with the road signs and regulations before you go. In most countries, for example, it's illegal to overtake on the approach to a pedestrian or level crossing, even though there may not be anything you'd recognize as a 'No Overtaking' sign. In some countries drivers must signal their intention to overtake by flashing their headlights at the car in front as they pull out.

Hazards to bear in mind:
- road layout: especially where there are bends in the road, hills, and other features which will obstruct your view
- road surface
- poor visibility – driving at night or in bad weather
- traffic on the road ahead
- vehicles behind
- side roads
- dangers posed by oncoming traffic on a two-lane road

OVERTAKING SEQUENCE

1 Read the road: identify and evaluate risks. Scan as far as you can see in every direction. Use your mirrors to check

OVERTAKING DOs AND DON'Ts

- Don't pull out without first checking your mirrors for vehicles coming up fast from behind.

- Always make sure there's room to move back to the nearside in good time.

- Don't cause other vehicles to take evasive action. No one should be forced to alter their speed or course to avoid you.

- Do bear in mind that on two-lane roads you will have to drive on the 'wrong' side of the road when passing. This means that oncoming traffic will be meeting you head on – and the gap between you will be closing at approximately twice the speed you are doing.

- Check both sides of a single-carriageway for side roads and entrances. A vehicle approaching the main road might pull out suddenly, not expecting to find you there.

- Avoid getting sandwiched between the vehicle you're overtaking and a vehicle travelling in the opposite direction.

- Don't overtake where visibility is poor because of a bend in the road, a hump bridge, or where the road dips out of sight. Road signs and markings will warn of approaching junctions, bends, and other hazards.

- Do make sure the road is wide enough.

- Don't get too close to the vehicle you are overtaking – you won't be able to see the road ahead properly.

- A large vehicle may be following closely behind a car, hiding it from view. Look for shadows, and look underneath an HGV in case you can spot the car's wheels.

- Do be extra careful when overtaking at night or in bad weather. It is more difficult to judge the speed and distance of traffic in poor visibility.

- Do make sure that the vehicle you are about to overtake is not about to change lanes.

- When you see a slow-moving vehicle approaching in the distance, anticipate that faster vehicles coming up from behind will be trying to overtake it.

- NEVER follow another vehicle as it overtakes. They may pull quickly into a space on the nearside, leaving you exposed.

---

what is happening behind you. Gauge the speed of other vehicles and try to judge how far away they are.

Think how that type of vehicle may be expected to behave. For example, heavy goods vehicles will slow down considerably on an uphill gradient and gain speed going downhill; sports cars appeal to drivers who like to travel at the maximum speed limit and beyond.

Assess how quickly the gap will close by combining your speed with theirs: if you are both travelling at 70 mph, the gap is shrinking at a rate of 140 mph – which translates as 64 metres (210 feet or 16 car lengths) per second.

2 Course: maintain a proper following distance. Don't close in on the vehicle in front, because your view of the road will be restricted. The larger the vehicle you are following, the further back you need to be.

3 Speed: while in the following position, match your speed to that of the vehicle in front.

4 Gear: select a gear which will give you sufficient power to overtake when the road ahead is clear. Change down from fifth gear to fourth, or even third.

5 Assuming that the way is clear for you to pull out, and that you have identified a safe gap, recheck your mirrors to make sure it's safe to pull out and signal your intention to overtake. This gives the driver in front the opportunity to warn you if they themselves are about to turn off or overtake another vehicle. If you are in any doubt as to whether the driver has noticed you, use your headlights or horn to alert him to your presence. Check your blind spot. Remember to look out for motorcyclists.

6 Move out smoothly and decisively. Check that it is safe to proceed by scanning for hazards which may not have been visible to you before. Accelerate to pass the other vehicle, leaving plenty of room between you. Make sure that you can see the vehicle in your interior mirror before you pull back in to the nearside.

> If in doubt, at any stage, about the safety of overtaking
> **DON'T DO IT.**

defensive driving

common accident scenarios

Most accidents are avoidable, the result of bad judgement or carelessness. Statistics show that more accidents occur in summer – when driving conditions are far less hazardous than in winter – and that late evenings (especially around closing time for public houses and night-clubs) and Sunday afternoons are the 'peak period' for crashes and collisions.

Among the most common causes of accidents are:
- Speeding and/or ignoring road signs and signals (often these accidents occur on straight sections of road)
- Overtaking dangerously
- Tailgating
- Reversing without due care and attention
- Not allowing adequate clearance when passing parked cars
- Not giving cyclists enough room
- Ignoring pedestrian crossings or trying to zip through on amber
- Turning at junctions
- Pulling out without stopping to check that it is safe to do so
- Failing to look or signal on roundabouts

Reversing

In most countries it is illegal to reverse for any great distance because of the danger this presents to pedestrians and other road users. Even if they register the presence of a vehicle with someone at the wheel, people tend to assume that it's going to move forwards, not backwards. Never assume that another driver or pedestrian knows that you are about to reverse; they may not have seen your reversing lights – and a child probably won't know what those white lights mean even if they do see them. The onus is on you to exercise caution when reversing and avoid endangering others.

Continuous observation is essential when driving backwards. It's not enough to rely on your mirrors to tell you what is going on behind, as these offer only a restricted view. Turn in your seat and look all around to check your blind spots before moving. A child crouching behind the car would be below your line of vision – if there is any possibility that a child might be playing in the area, get out and check that it's all-clear behind before reversing, or ask a passenger to get out and direct you.

You cannot reverse safely if the rear parcel shelf is full of clutter or the windows are filthy. Make sure you have an unobstructed view – or have someone standing on the roadside guide you.

At night or in poor visibility, use your hazard lights to illuminate the road behind you – but take care not to mislead other road users.

Remember that the front of the vehicle will swing out as you reverse round a corner. Keep checking what's going on at the front of the car throughout the manoeuvre.

Brakes are less effective when reversing, so always reverse at a slow speed with delicate use of the clutch, accelerator and brake pedals.

NEVER reverse on to a main road, either from a side road or a driveway. It's best to reverse into your driveway and drive out; otherwise your view of the road will be severely restricted and you will present a dangerous obstruction to others as you negotiate your way out.

If you miss your turning or enter a one-way street by mistake, NEVER reverse to where you want to go. Drive on and turn when it is safe and legal to do so.

Saftey At Work
Each year many accidents occur in the workplace as a result

of goods vehicles with restricted rear-vision reversing into people or property. The loss of life, injury and damage to property could be avoided if:

- All company vehicles were fitted with a reversing alarm
- Traffic systems were designed in such a way as to minimize the need for drivers to reverse (using one-way systems and drive-through delivery bays)
- A properly trained banksman or guide was on hand to guide any reversing vehicles

Parked Cars

Keep well clear of parked cars in case a door is thrown open or a child steps out from between two cars. Look for clues such as feet underneath vehicles, people inside cars, lights coming on, or other signs of movement.

Never assume that an oncoming vehicle will give way, even if the obstruction is on their side of the road. Slow down and be prepared to hold back if you see that there is not room for both of you to proceed through the gap.

Cyclists

A vehicle travelling at speed creates a considerable slipstream, enough to cause any cyclist it overtakes to wobble or swerve. They may also weave erratically in order to avoid potholes or debris in the road, or as a result of strong winds and heavy rain.

Always allow cyclists plenty of room. If you cannot move out to allow them the same clearance you would a car, slow down and hold back until you can get by safely.

Remember that at night or in bad weather cyclists can be difficult to see, especially if they've not taken the precaution of wearing fluorescent strips or bright colours.

Child cyclists can be especially unpredictable, practising stunts to impress their friends, or simply not looking where

they are going. Be patient and leave even more room than you would for an adult cyclist.

Pedestrians

It's dangerous to assume that pedestrians will look and assess the hazards before stepping into the road. Be alert and make allowances for pedestrians, especially vulnerable groups such as children and the elderly. Slow down and be prepared to brake if they should step out without having seen you. Drive extra cautiously near schools, buses, and ice-cream vans.

In winter, and on country roads where there is no pavement, look out for pedestrians walking in the road. In poor light it can be very difficult to see them, but you should anticipate coming across pedestrians and drive accordingly: slow down and prepare to pull up if necessary.

As you approach a pedestrian crossing, check for people waiting to cross. The law gives pedestrians precedence once they set foot on the crossing, so you must give way to them. Be patient with elderly and disabled people who take a long time to cross – don't rev the engine or try to rush them.

Be careful when turning right at a crossroads where there are pedestrian crossings. By the time you've waited for

---

ARM SIGNALS

Should your indicators ever fail, use arm signals to advise other road users of your intentions.

TURNING RIGHT: Extend your right arm out of the window with the palm forward and fingers extended and together.

TURNING LEFT: Extend your right arm out of the window and rotate it slowly in a circular motion, with the palm of the hand facing forward.

STOPPING: Extend your right arm, palm downwards, fingers together, and gently raise and lower the arm a few times.

GOING STRAIGHT ON: Raise your left arm, palm facing forwards. Point ahead, if need be.

oncoming vehicles to leave a way clear for you, pedestrians may have received the signal that it's safe to cross. They now have the right of way and you must wait until they're safely across before proceeding.

Junctions

At a junction, you generally have three choices: keep going straight ahead, turn left or turn right. Whichever option you intend to take, remember to apply the drill. Scan in all directions to identify, anticipate and evaluate hazards; signal your intentions and steer a course that will put you in the correct lane and give you the best possible view; reduce your speed to negotiate any hazards; change gear on the approach so that you will be prepared to change direction or accelerate away.

If you are planning to drive straight on, beware of traffic entering from either side and oncoming traffic turning across your path. There's no guarantee that other drivers will give way to you, even though you have priority in the eyes of the law. When visibility is poor, in thick fog or heavy rain, there's a very real danger that they won't even see you – and vice versa. Be on your guard; reduce your speed to match your vision of the road and consider making them aware of your presence by tooting your horn. Try to establish eye contact so you can be certain the other driver is aware of your presence.

If the vehicle in front of you is signalling its intention to turn, decide whether it's necessary for you to alter your position or reduce your speed. Where the road is too narrow for you to pass safely, be prepared to stop and wait until the other vehicle has made its turn.

TURNING LEFT

When approaching a junction where you intend to make a left-hand turn, steer a course towards the left of the road about a metre from the kerb. Keep checking your mirrors and the road ahead, noting all road signs and markings, and the position and speed of other vehicles – particularly motor-

bikes and cyclists. Remember, too, that pedestrians will often cross the road at a junction.

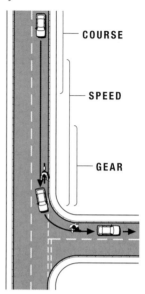

Reduce your speed and change gear while travelling in a straight line. If you take the corner too fast, there's a danger that you could go wide – try to remain a metre from the kerb throughout. Where parked vehicles, trees, or other obstructions restrict your view, slow down even more than usual.

TURNING RIGHT

A right-hand turn involves turning across the flow of approaching traffic, which makes it that much more difficult and risky.

Scan the road ahead, as much as you can see of the road you will be turning into, and the road behind. As always, be on the lookout for cyclists and motorcyclists, weaving in and out of traffic.

Steer a course as close to the centre of the road as is safe, signalling your attentions to other road users. Adjust your speed to match your vision of the road, traffic conditions, road surface and layout, etc. Change gear before you arrive at the point where you will turn.

You may have to hold your position until there is a gap in the traffic. Stop level with the middle of the road you will be turning into, and make sure your wheels are pointing straight ahead. In the event of a rear-end shunt, you'll be pushed forward rather than into the path of oncoming traffic.

Don't rush the turn because you're worried about traffic behind being held up, but do check your mirrors before turning in case an impatient driver or motorcyclist tries to overtake on the offside.

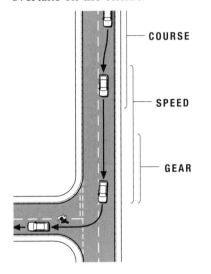

— COURSE

— SPEED

— GEAR

Always look into the road you are about to turn into in case there are obstructions, pedestrians crossing, or vehicles emerging.

PULLING OUT

When emerging from a side road on to a major road, always pause at the stop or give-way line. Scan the road in all direc-

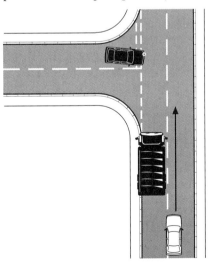

> When queuing behind another vehicle waiting to emerge on to a main road, concentrate on watching the vehicle in front rather than looking for gaps in traffic which would allow you to make your turn. Most rear-end shunts occur when drivers fail to see that the car in front of them has stopped for some reason – perhaps because the other driver hasn't seen the gap, or has stalled.

tions – a vehicle could be travelling on the wrong side of the road to overtake or pass an obstruction.

ROUNDABOUTS

One of the problems with roundabouts is that not everyone follows the rules. Drivers do all sorts of unexpected things – some signal their intention to do one thing and then proceed to do something else entirely, others fail to signal at all, and some seem to have no idea as to who has priority and who should give way.

In some countries traffic approaching from the right has priority, in others it's traffic approaching from the left. There are even roundabouts where traffic on the roundabout must give way to traffic entering. When driving abroad, make sure to familiarize yourself with the regulations which apply. When driving at home, stay well back from cars with foreign number plates!

Never rely entirely on another driver's signals. Try to judge their intentions from the vehicle's position and speed, and keep assessing and re-assessing the situation.

As soon as you see a road sign indicating that there is a roundabout ahead, position yourself in the correct lane for the exit you intend to take. Reduce speed on the approach to match the traffic conditions and your view of the roundabout and its approach roads. Select a gear to match your speed and give you the power to accelerate on to the roundabout.

> You must be prepared to stop and give way – but keep monitoring the situation so that you're ready to seize the opportunity and go the moment it's safe to do so.

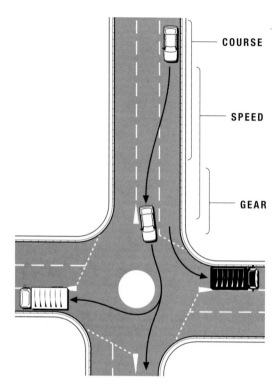

COURSE

SPEED

GEAR

Negotiating a roundabout

Turning left: approach in the left-hand lane, signal left, and keep to the left until you reach your exit.

Going straight ahead: approach in the left-hand lane or, if that lane is blocked, the one next to it. Do not signal. Remain in the same lane through the roundabout. Signal left as you pass the exit before the one you intend to take.

Turning right: signal right and get into the right-hand lane as you approach. Keep to the right-hand lane and signal right until you pass the exit before the one you want. Check your mirrors and the nearside blindspot. Signal left and leave by the left-hand lane if possible.

Avoiding A Head-On Collision

If another vehicle is heading straight for you – perhaps because the driver is drunk or has suffered a seizure, or because a mechanical failure has caused them to lose control of the car – and it seems that a head-on collision is inevitable:

- Look for an escape route. It is better to leave the road rather than risk a collision. Steer towards a piece of open ground such as a field or garden, or a hedgerow that will slow your vehicle down and soften the impact.
- If there is nowhere else to go, it is better to run into a parked car than a moving vehicle. Aim to use the parked car as a shield from the oncoming vehicle.
- For every mile of speed that you can lose, the impact will be reduced considerably – but beware of causing a skid by braking too hard and locking the wheels.
- Where there is no escape, angle your vehicle so that you will be side-swiped rather than hit head-on. If your front corner is the point of impact, the car may be spun away in the collision instead of bearing the full brunt of it.
- Warn your passengers to assume the impact position (see below).
- Everyone in the vehicle must be wearing a seatbelt. Passengers who are not securely strapped in will be slung forward and could injure others or prevent the driver dealing effectively with the emergency.

IMPACT POSITION

- Drop your chin to your chest.
- Place your hands at the back of your head to pull it down and keep it firm against your chest.
- Tuck your elbows in.
- Keep your knees tight together and pull your feet underneath you.

Terrorists and hostage-takers know that VIPs are at their most vulnerable when they leave their secure homes and offices and take to the road. Evasive driving techniques are designed to protect those who are targeted and allow them to escape unharmed.

evasive driving

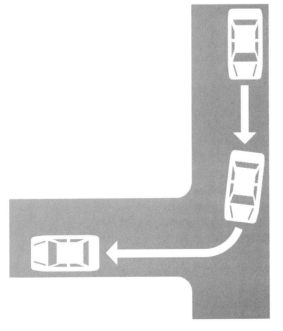

TARGET SELECTION

COUNTERING THE THREAT High security • A top security vehicle • Searching the vehicle

SURVEILLANCE & COUNTER-SURVEILLANCE

RISK LIMITATION Securing the route

UNDER FIRE Attack recognition • Countering surprise • Vehicle escort drills • Breakdowns

AMBUSHED! Evasive manoeuvres: Two-point turn • J-turn • U-turn • Handbrake turn

ESCAPE ROUTES

TAKEN HOSTAGE

target selection

A planned attack is the culmination of a multi-stage process which starts with target selection. An individual or family may be targeted for political or financial reasons, or out of revenge or jealousy.

Terrorist attacks on members of the general public tend to be random, indiscriminate affairs – a matter of the victims being in the wrong place at the wrong time. When travelling to a region where there is political instability, consider how this might affect you and consider altering your plans. Extremist groups sometimes attack tourists in an attempt to destabilize the economy by driving away foreign visitors.

Planned attacks are usually directed at prime targets and their families. VIPs, government officials, leading industrialists, military leaders, and celebrities are all at high risk. But civil servants, members of the armed forces, embassy officials, and employees of companies whose activities attract terrorist attention should also toughen up their security.

Countering the Threat

Stage two in the terrorist's strategy, having singled out a target, is to keep them under surveillance, gathering information which will help them to plan an attack. If the attack sequence is allowed to proceed to its final stage there is every likelihood that it will succeed, but if detected in the early stages it can be thwarted by instigating extra security measures.

HIGH SECURITY
If you fall into a high-risk category, take the following precautions:

- Be a grey person. Don't advertise your presence – avoid personalized number plates or other distinguishing marks which will make your vehicle too easily identifiable.
- Don't use a parking space with your name or company status painted on it.
- Don't follow a predictable routine. Vary the routes you use to travel to and from work. Try to avoid roadworks and areas where you know there will be heavy traffic jams.
- Leave at different times so that no one can establish a set pattern.
- If possible, change vehicles frequently.
- When booking into a hotel, use an assumed name.
- Before leaving your home, office, or car, check for people loitering suspiciously or sitting in parked vehicles.
- Check your rear-view mirrors for vehicles which might be tailing you. When on foot, use reflective surfaces such as glass windows to check whether anyone is following you – this is less obvious than looking over your shoulder the whole time.
- To build up a profile on you, someone carrying out surveillance might make enquiries at your place of work, or any clubs or organizations you belong to, or by contacting your

neighbours, friends or family. Make sure that people know to inform you if anyone starts asking questions or taking an interest in your movements.

- Always telephone ahead when setting out on a journey, and call base to let them know when you've arrived.
- In case something does go wrong, work out a coded phrase to warn your associates that you are in danger. Choose something innocuous that you can drop into normal conversation without arousing suspicion. Make sure that it's not a phrase you might let slip by accident.

SEARCHING THE VEHICLE

Although the vehicle should be attended at all times and garaged in a secure facility when not in use, it should nevertheless be searched daily in case there has been a breach of security.

To help you spot any changes or signs of tampering:

- Fill keyholes with soft wax or a smear of Vaseline so you

will be able to tell if someone has inserted a key.
- Hubcaps make a good hiding place for a bomb, so mark all hubcaps with a discreet dot, scratch, or other identifying mark and line up the marks carefully. Check that the marks are correctly aligned when you return to the car.
- Fix thin, near-invisible strips of clear adhesive tape across the door, bonnet, sunroof, boot. Look to see that the tape hasn't been broken by someone gaining entry to the car.
- Overnight, the garage floor surrounding the car should be covered with a bed of sand so any intruder will leave footprints.

A TOP SECURITY VEHICLE

Any large four-door saloon can be modified to improve security for its occupants. To accommodate the extra equipment and armour which must be carried, it's best to opt for a large multi-cylinder car.

Tinted glass will hide the occupants and still be discreet enough not to attract too much attention. The glass should also be armoured, as should the body panels. Layers of kevlar, a virtually unbreakable man-made fibre used in bulletproof jackets and other protective clothing, can be sandwiched between steel or plastic shielding. This will prevent an explosion damaging the interior of the vehicle. The extra weight this involves will necessitate upgrading the suspension and fitting chassis stiffeners.

A larger than usual tank will be needed to deal with the high fuel consumption of a heavier than average car. The tank should be modified with an explo-safe filling to render it self-sealing and puncture-proof in case the car comes under gunfire.

Run-flat tyres are essential. These have special inserts which prevent the rubber tyre from coming away from the rim, so that the car can be driven even if the tyres have been punctured.

Heavy bumpers offer good protection and will allow the driver to ram a hostile car or burst through a road block set up by ambushers. Keeping the same profile, extra brackets can be fitted with metal inserts to beef up the bumpers.

High-powered lights will be needed for night driving. These can be turned on in addition to the standard dipped and main-beam headlights to dazzle attackers or illuminate a threatening environment.

Air conditioning is a must. For security reasons, the windows should never be opened in case someone throws a missile into the car.

To save the driver and passengers being thrown about the car while executing evasive manoeuvres, standard seat belts should be replaced with racing-style harnesses.

Finally, if you are serious about security, the car should be fully equipped with radios to allow continuous communication with any escort vehicles and the control room at base. This should, if possible, be compatible with the police net.

NEVER leave the vehicle unattended. It should always be kept secure and garaged when not in use. Servicing and maintenance must be carried out in-house or by carefully vetted personnel.

evasive driving

SEARCH PROCEDURE

- Approach the vehicle at an angle of 45 degrees. Without touching it, look around the vehicle and underneath it. At this angle all four wheels can be seen and anything hanging down underneath will be spotted.
- Crouch down and look for objects under the vehicle. Examine each wheel arch and follow the exhaust system from manifold to tailpipe. Look behind bumpers and inside spoilers.
- Check that the hubcaps have not been replaced or adjusted.
- Look for pieces of wire, insulating or adhesive tape used to fix explosives to the car.
- Check the outside of the car for any signs that it has been tampered with or a forced entry effected. Make sure the tape seals on the doors, windows, bonnet and boot are intact.
- Keep the car spotless and well polished so that fingerprints or smudges on the bodywork will show when someone has been to the car in your absence.
- Look in the engine compartment. Carry out the first parade routine, checking fluid levels, lights, wipers, brakes, etc.
- Check the boot to ensure that all equipment – tools, spares, etc – is in place.
- Examine the interior of the car. Make sure the medical pack and extinguisher are stowed correctly.

Even if you are not a member of a high-risk category, it's a good idea to search your vehicle if it has been parked near a potential target at a time when terrorists are waging a campaign of violence.

It's possible to obtain, from a security equipment supplier, a tool consisting of a flashlight and mirror attached to a pole. This device will allow you to get a clear view of the underside of the car, one of the most common bomb concealment areas.

If ever a high-risk target vehicle has been left unattended for some reason, it should not be used until passed clear by a

WARNING

If you should find a suspicious-looking object in the course of your search, DON'T tamper with it or touch the vehicle. Evacuate the area and send for the police. Tell the operator that you suspect a vehicle bomb.

trained specialist after undergoing a detailed search. The vehicle may have been rigged to explode when the key is turned in the ignition or when the engine heats up to a certain temperature. Don't take any chances.

Surveillance

A successful plan of attack depends to a large degree on good surveillance. In order launch a successful ambush, the bad guys need to determine the place and time when the target will be at their most vulnerable. By making it standard practice to vary timings, routes, vehicles and personnel, you will make it difficult for them to get a fix on the target. The longer they have to maintain their surveillance in the hope of establishing a pattern, the more chance you have of detecting

Poor surveillance can be easily detected by a trained security operator. Look for the following indicators:
- Vehicles parked in prohibited zones.
- Parked vehicles with occupants sitting in the front seats. Be suspicious if the vehicle remains in place for any length of time for no apparent reason.
- Motorcycles and vehicles that appear to be following the target.
- Vehicles that overtake the target as it pulls in, only to park a little further along the road.
- Vehicles travelling too fast or too slow, weaving erratically or making sudden stops.
- Any vehicle, two or four-wheeled, that pokes its nose round a corner and withdraws.
- Vehicles that signal a turn but carry on.
- Vehicles that turn a corner slowly.
- Any vehicle that follows the principal through a red light.
- Vehicles that slow down or try to hide behind other vehicles as the principal slows.
- Vehicles that close on the target in heavy traffic and fall behind in lighter traffic.
- Vehicles that park when the target does – especially if no one gets out.

their operations. Your tight security, based on good observation and awareness, will force them to make mistakes and to take more chances.

A poorly planned attack based on sketchy information is doomed to failure.

Much of the time vehicles which appear to be following the target will be perfectly innocent, but if tell-tale signs keep occurring it is unlikely to be mere coincidence. When you are responsible for the safety of a VIP you cannot afford to be complacent. Take heed of any indicators which suggest that the target is under surveillance and be prepared to act.

Be on the look out too for bogus maintenance workers. It's worth surreptitiously checking out road maintenance gangs. Their footwear is usually a giveaway – polished leather shoes worn with an overall should arouse your suspicions. Phone the depot to verify that workmen are genuinely in the employ of the water/gas board or telephone company. If the vehicle bears no signs to indicate which company they are from, try checking with the local government offices to find out whether anyone has been authorized to carry out road-works at that location.

Counter-Surveillance

Once signs of surveillance have been detected, collect as much information as possible about those responsible.

While the principal remains safely under guard – either at home or at a secure location – send out a decoy in the target's car and note the make and licence number of any vehicles tailing it, together with descriptions of all persons involved.

Pass this information to the authorities without delay. The police and security forces can then keep those individuals responsible under surveillance in an effort to discover who is behind the plan. Always leave it to the experts to apprehend the culprits, who may be armed and dangerous.

> **ALWAYS** co-operate with the authorities. Notify the police of any suspicious activity and seek their advice on how best to combat the threat. The anti-terrorist forces are trained in combating dangerous extremists and criminals, and their intelligence network is far superior to anything you may have access to. **NEVER** try to go it alone.

risk limitation

You can minimize the risks of attack by taking a positive approach to anti-terrorist measures, assessing the risks and devising strategies to cope in advance of undertaking any journey:

> **1 Vary timings and routes**
> **2 Select routes with care**
> **3 Secure the route and test communications**

Journeys

Journeys fall into various categories:

'Private visits' to friends and family, usually during the evening or at weekends. Distances tend to be short and the route familiar.

'Official visits' such as public functions where many people are present. If the principal is well known, crowds can pose a problem. Uniformed police may provide an escort.

'Short notice trips' Business people and politicians may be called away unexpectedly. As a result you will have to do some hasty route planning and negotiate unfamiliar roads.

evasive driving

'**Long journeys**' Because of the distances involved, refuelling and accommodation will have to be planned carefully.

Whatever the nature of the journey, the principal must be dissuaded from following a fixed routine. If they start and finish work early one day and late the next, this will have the added benefit of dodging the rush hour when traffic is at its heaviest. When there is any suspicion that the principal is under surveillance, or if intelligence reports suggest that an attack is imminent, visits which unavoidably follow a fixed routine (such as church attendance for a Sunday-morning service) should be abandoned.

All journeys must be planned in advance. It's not enough just to plot a route on the map. The safest route will not necessarily be the shortest one, and you will need to take into account roadworks or special events such as fairs, demonstrations, sports fixtures, or street markets, which might create temporary bottlenecks and lead to congestion.

A trial run should be carried out. If the journey is to take place on a Monday, the route should be checked out the Monday beforehand to get an accurate appreciation of conditions – it may be that one stretch of the road is calm every day but Monday, when it's total bedlam.

> Test communications all along the route to ensure that there are no radio black spots which will prevent your making contact with base.

Check out possible escape routes. Note the location of dead-end streets and roads with speed bumps and other hazards.

Always note the location of hospitals with a casualty department en route in case of an emergency. You won't want to remain on the scene of an accident until the emergency services come to you.

SECURING THE ROUTE

Where there are bottlenecks (choke points) en route to the destination which cannot be avoided because of the location of the residence or office, these are the points where the enemy will set up surveillance. Around 80 per cent of ambushes occur at these choke points.

When you see someone loitering in the vicinity of a choke point, make a note of it. Should the choke point be 'manned' a couple of times in succession, don't take chances – alert the authorities.

under fire

Early recognition of an attack is vital if the occupants of the car are to survive. An unwary driver whose mind is in neutral will have handed the advantage to the terrorists: the element of surprise is their greatest tactical advantage.

Attack Recognition

A good driver must have a feel for the ground and the ability to recognize potential danger areas. Alert at all times, the driver must concentrating even harder when passing through choke points and other hazardous places, watching for situations and incidents which could be the prelude to danger. The vast majority of these situations are innocent, but the driver must still be ready to act each and every time.

A well-planned attack will come when you least expect it. The terrorists hope is that the security detail will be too surprised to react positively. By the time they recover their wits the target will have been abducted or murdered.

The best way to combat surprise is to be alert for anything out of the ordinary. When something causes you to slow down or stop, prepare to react. Potential dangers to look out for include:

- People in the road
- Broken-down vehicles
- An accident
- Road works
- Cars overtaking.
- People using mobile phones or waving – possibly signalling to someone in the distance to announce your arrival.

Don't be complacent. Until proven otherwise, assume that danger looms.

COUNTERING SURPRISE

Everyone reacts differently to surprise. How a person reacts will depend on their temperament, experience, and the degree of surprise.

Expert training in VIP protection improves reactions, putting drivers through a variety of different types of ambush to give them realistic experience of every possible scenario and test their ability to respond instinctively. It soon becomes clear whether a driver has what it takes.

An untrained driver may go into shock and fail to respond at all. For an experienced VIP driver the level of surprise will be minimal and the response will be swift and well judged.

Vehicle Escort Drills

The driver needs to be familiar with the vehicle – there is no time in an emergency to wonder where on the dashboard a certain switch is located.

The doors and windows should be secured as soon as the passengers have climbed inside. Everyone must wear their seat belts at all times to protect them in the event that the vehicle is rammed or forced to make an emergency stop.

Normal traffic regulations apply, regardless of who you are driving. If in convoy, proceed in tight formation and don't allow any other vehicles to slip between the detail. When travelling alone, maintain a gap between your car and the vehicle in front which will leave you plenty of room for manoeuvre. A common ambush scenario is for the attackers

to suddenly pull up in front of the target car, forcing it to slam on the brakes. Another enemy car will then block the road to the rear, preventing escape. Unless you have left yourself with room to move, you will be sandwiched between hostile forces with no way out.

Keep checking your rear-view mirrors. Assassins on a motorcycle or driving a rugged 4WD vehicle will sometimes drive alongside and either shoot through a window or attach a magnetic explosive device to the bodywork.

You are particularly vulnerable to attack when passing under bridges (including footbridges over motorways) and flyovers. Attack from above is lethal. Roundabouts are another danger area: it's difficult to keep the convoy together, so other vehicles can get in close to attack and then choose from a variety of escape routes.

Be especially alert where there is close cover to the roadside on a sharp bend or hill. An enemy sniper might be concealed at the point where the vehicle must slow down.

Concentrate on reading the road and driving defensively. Don't let yourself be distracted by chatter or the local beauties. Don't have the tape or radio on, and don't smoke.

Drive smoothly and travel at the maximum legal speed. Accelerate smoothly and brake lightly. The principal wants to relax or read, and they can't do either while being bounced around in the back.

A vehicle is at its most vulnerable when stationary, so as soon as the principal is aboard the cavalcade must be moving. When parking the vehicle it is better to reverse into a space so that you can get away as fast as possible, should the need arise.

Have the doors open, ready for the security crew to get in quickly. Remind everyone of the dangers of getting a hand shut in a door. Don't set off with someone still trying to get in half in the car, hopping down the road on one leg like something out of the Keystone Kops.

VEHICLE BREAKDOWNS

When the vehicle has to stop for any length of time, the security crew must get out and surround it. If the principal's car breaks down, he or she should be transferred to an escort vehicle and conveyed to their destination. Leave a few members of the security detail to guard the limousine until it can be recovered.

---

evasive driving

ambushed!

Should the vehicle come under attack, the golden rule is KEEP MOVING.

Try if possible to drive through the ambush. The way may well be blocked, in which case you will have to ram the car or obstacle in your path. Try to hit it at an angle rather than head-on, as this will reduce the force of the impact. Brace your arms, gripping the wheel tightly, and warn all occupants to brace themselves. This is where the seat harness and strengthened bumpers earn their keep.

Alternatively it may be possible to get round a barrier by mounting a kerb and driving along the pavement. Hit the kerb at an angle of about 20 degrees. Use a drop kerb or driveway, if present, and try to avoid deep drain holes.

> Do not practise the following manoeuvres on the public highway – they are intended strictly for emergency situations and you could be prosecuted for performing them on normal roads. To learn how to execute these manoeuvres, find an instructor who specializes in teaching evasive driving skills and practise on private land.

Evasive Manoeuvres

THE TWO-POINT TURN

If you are travelling slowly (say, 30 mph) and you see something suspicious ahead, or if the way forward is blocked and it is impossible to clear the obstacle by mounting the pavement, perform a two-point turn to go back the way you came.

Bear in mind the camber or slope of the road. Some roads peak in the middle (the crown) and slope down steeply on either side to allow drainage. As you reverse, you may have to go uphill to cross the crown, downhill to reach the far kerb, then uphill again to go forward and turn around. This takes careful and sensitive accelerator control to make sure that you don't lose control and shoot backwards into a hedge, or stall the vehicle by being too tentative on the ascent.

- Brake hard when you see the road block ahead – you don't want to collide with it or allow the enemy an opportunity to swarm your vehicle.
- Engage reverse gear and bring the clutch pedal fully up.
- Check quickly to make sure your way is clear to the rear – try to find a point where you can turn without hindrance from parked cars or roadside obstacles such as bollards and trees. If the road is narrow you may need to run on to the pavement.
- Accelerate backwards, turning the steering wheel towards the offside and applying full lock.
- As the car's rear approaches the kerb, brake and depress the clutch.
- Turn the steering wheel hard in the opposite direction so that the wheels will be pointing the way you want to go next.
- If the camber is steep, you may need to apply the hand brake to stop the vehicle rolling back any further.
- Engage first gear and release the hand brake.
- Complete the turn as you accelerate away. Get back into the correct lane as soon as possible in case you meet oncoming traffic.

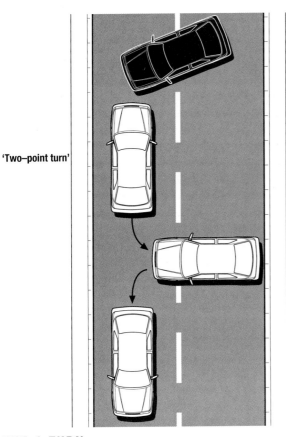

'Two–point turn'

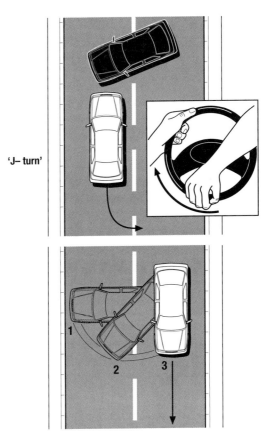

'J– turn'

THE J-TURN

If the road block has been sited at a bottleneck where there is insufficient room to execute a two-point turn, a J-turn will allow you to escape – provided the road to your rear is still clear.

- Check your mirrors to make sure that the road behind you is clear.
- Execute an emergency stop so that you pull up well before reaching the road block. Remember to keep both hands on the steering wheel to maintain full control.
- Glancing in your rear-view mirror to make sure the road behind is still clear, engage reverse.
- Accelerate back down the road using your mirrors to keep you straight.
- Go back far enough to get you clear of anyone pursuing on

foot, or until the car has gained enough momentum to allow you to take your foot off the accelerator for a moment.
- Now spin the steering wheel to the right. The usual, pull–push method of steering is too cumbersome for the turn you are about to execute, so while holding the wheel with your left hand at the ten o'clock position, reach across with your right hand and grip the rim just to the left of the bottom, at seven o'clock. Don't hook your thumb inside the rim. Now use both hands to turn the wheel to the right, quickly repositioning the left hand near the bottom of the wheel to help push the wheel to the right.
- Do this as quickly as possible and the car will do a 180-degree turn, anticlockwise, so that you will be facing in the direction you've just come from.
- Engage first gear and accelerate away to safety.

THE U-TURN

If the road is wide enough, you can turn the vehicle completely around without having to stop to reverse. Obviously, you need to be certain that both lanes are free of traffic. The obstruction blocking the road ahead of you will prevent anything coming from that direction, so glance in your rear-view mirror quickly to make sure that there's nothing behind.

- Brake to reduce your speed as you approach the obstacle – aim to get down to 20 mph if possible.
- Engage second gear as you approach the point where you will turn. Let the clutch out quickly. The clutch pedal should be released before you turn the wheels or the vehicle may skid.
- Keep well over to the nearside.
- Turn the steering wheel towards the offside, applying full lock.
- Once the car is facing in the opposite direction, straighten up and accelerate away to safety.

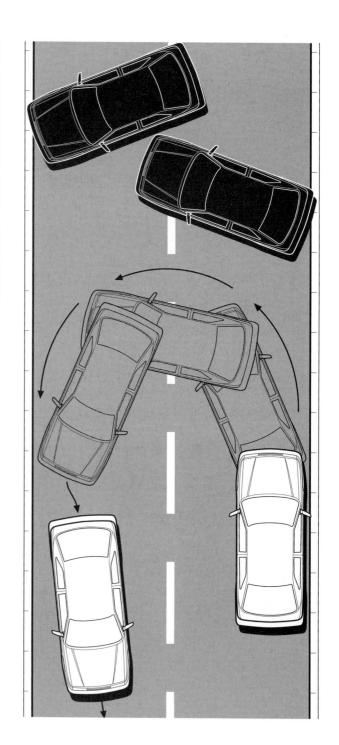

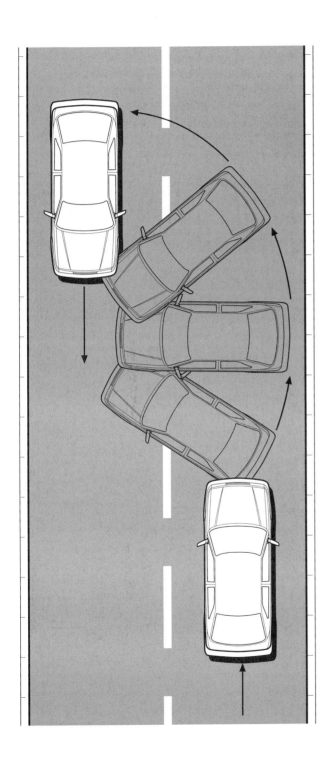

HANDBRAKE TURN

Probably the most difficult evasive manoeuvre to control, a handbrake turn may be used in an emergency to spin the car in the road and drive away before the ambush can be sprung. The disadvantage is that because it is difficult to control it is less precise than the manoeuvres described above, making it sometimes hard to predict where the car will end up and which direction it will be pointing in.

- Change down to a lower gear but keep up the revs
- Spin the wheel to the right or left, depending which side of the road you're driving on.
- Pull up hard on the handbrake as you turn.
- This will cause the rear wheels to lock and pivot the front of the car round the rear axle.
- When 180 degrees has been reached, release the handbrake and accelerate away.

It takes a lot of practice to master this technique, but NEVER attempt it on public roads.

Escape Routes

Use any route you can to get out of immediate danger, whether it means driving across gardens or through advertising hoardings.

Your priority is to keep the principal safe, so take the option that will shield the VIP and offer the most protection. Execute whatever turns will place him furthest from the enemy. Order passengers to get down so that they will present less of a target.

> While you drive, someone in the security detail should make radio contact with control to let them know that you are under attack. The police should be informed immediately and given a precise location, the number of assailants, weapons used, description of vehicles, etc.

Don't hesitate to drive straight at the attackers if they are strung out across the road to block your escape. This will cause confusion and has been used successfully in the past to defeat an ambush.

TAKEN HOSTAGE

If the worst happens and you are taken hostage, do not struggle or attempt to escape unless you are certain of success.

• Behave as though you are going to co-operate. Being aggressive could get you hurt.

• If you are tied up or gagged, fill your lungs with air to expand your chest while being tied. There may be some useful slack in your bonds when you exhale.

• If being tied to a chair, sit in a slouched position, keeping your spine away from the back of the chair.

• Try to catch a gag between your teeth. If it's forced back into your mouth you may have difficulty breathing or making a sound.

• To remove a blindfold, try rubbing against any handy object to push it upwards rather than down.

• When tied up with rope or other fibres which may fray, find a sharp object to rub your bonds against.

• Listen to your captors' conversations. You may find clues as to where you are that will help you if an opportunity to escape should arise.

REMEMBER

A hostage is more valuable alive than dead. It is not in your kidnappers' interest to kill you – if they wanted you dead they would have killed you at the scene of the ambush. Co-operate and keep your head down, and you should come out of this situation alive.

Driving a car gives you the freedom to travel from one end of the country – or continent – to the other. There's no need to plan your trip like a military campaign, but a little research and preparation will smooth the way and lead to hassle-free travels.

long journeys

MOTORWAY DRIVING Joining the motorway • Lane discipline • Leaving the motorway

HOLIDAY TRAVEL Sunburn and heat exhaustion • Motion sickness

LOADING THE CAR The luggage compartment • Roof racks • Loading a roof rack • Roof boxes

CARAVANS AND TRAILERS The towing vehicle • Weight limits • Loading the caravan • Caravan safety tips • Hitching up • Unhitching

TOWING TECHNIQUES Changing direction • Overtaking • Reversing • Snaking

TRAVELLING ABROAD Red tape • Planning your trip • Essential accessories • Hire cars • Ferries

DRIVING ON THE WRONG SIDE

long journeys

Here's a recipe for disaster that thousands of holidaymakers follow every year: take one average family which has poured out of bed at the last minute; fill a car in double-quick time with anything that comes to mind, loading the heaviest items on one side (the same side where the heaviest passenger will sit); join the motorway at the same time as all the other holidaymakers and crawl along at snail's pace; open road atlas and discover that the last exit was the one you should have taken; have heated argument about whose fault it was as you retrace your steps; discover that fuel tank is almost empty; stop to refuel at service station where prices are 20 per cent higher than what you'd normally pay; break speed limit in order to catch ferry; realize on arrival at port that ferry tickets are still on mantelpiece at home.

Sound familiar? Or did I leave out the part where the engine overheats under the strain and you end up parked on the hard shoulder, praying that the recovery vehicle will get there soon?

Before You Go

Many of the pitfalls of long trips can be avoided with a little forward planning and research. This is true no matter what the purpose of your journey may be.

Some people will argue that travel should be spontaneous and fun. But where's the enjoyment in getting held up at border control because you haven't got the right documentation, or being stuck in some dull industrial town just off the motorway for days on end because a fuse has blown and the local garage doesn't carry spares for foreign vehicles?

The more carefully you prepare for a trip, the more carefree you can be when you reach your destination.

PREPARE YOURSELF

Consult your doctor before travelling abroad for up-to-date advice on which vaccinations are mandatory or advisable for the destinations you intend to visit. It's always a good idea to check that your vaccinations are up to date and that you're not due for a booster shot.

If you are on prescribed medication or suffer from a medical condition for which special drugs are required, the doctor will be able to issue you with a prescription for sufficient medicine to last the trip.

> NEVER assume that you will be able to obtain the medication you need abroad. It may be unavailable or prohibitively expensive.

Invest in a phrase book and a reliable guidebook for each country you plan to visit. Read up on the climate (so you will know when is the best time of year to go, and what to pack), red tape (visa requirements, insurance, customs allowances), currency (how much currency are you allowed to import? Is it better to carry sterling or dollar traveller's cheques?) and the local customs (Western styles of casual dress are considered offensive in some countries, and women may attract unwanted attention if they wear shorts or mini-skirts; alcohol may be frowned upon for religious reasons; even eating in public may be taboo).

THE VEHICLE

To reduce the risk of breakdowns, make sure your car is given a thorough check-up before setting off on a long journey. If you don't feel competent to carry out the service checks described in **Maintenance**, take your vehicle to a reputable garage.

It's particularly important to seek professional advice if you're going to be towing a trailer or carrying a very heavy load, as it may be necessary to have extension mirrors or a tow-bar stabilizer fitted, and the car's cooling system may need to be modified to prevent the engine overheating.

When travelling to a country where they drive on the 'wrong' side of the road, you will need to fit headlamp beam deflectors. These alter the direction of the light beam so you won't dazzle other road users.

Don't set off on a long trip unless you are confident that the battery is in good condition; that all fluids (fuel, oil, coolant, screenwash) have been topped up to the correct level; that your tyres (including the spare) are roadworthy and the pressures are suited to the load you will be carrying; that windscreen wipers and all lights are working; and that your survival kit, complete with all tools and spares you are likely to need, is in place.

Regulations making it compulsory to carry certain spares (and illegal to carry others) vary from country to country. In much of Europe it is a legal requirement that you carry a warning triangle; some countries also insist that all cars be equipped with a fire extinguisher and first-aid kit. While in Austria, Greece, Italy and Luxembourg it is illegal to carry a spare can of fuel.

Check with one of the major motoring organizations for an up-to-date list of the rules which apply in the countries you will be visiting.

THE ROUTE

Even if you think you know the route, carry an up-to-date road map in case traffic jams or diversions throw you off course. When your journey involves travelling unfamiliar roads, spend some time devising a route and jotting it down on a route card (see *Planning Your Journey* in **Reading the Signs**). This simple precaution should help you to avoid taking wrong turns and wasting fuel on unnecessary detours.

> **REMEMBER**
>
> Remember, if you are to remain alert you will need to take regular breaks , so check the map for places where you will be able to rest, eat, and fill up with fuel.

Away from the motorways, fuel stations may be few and far between, and in some countries garages on rural roads are closed on Sundays and late at night. Many garages won't accept credit cards, so make sure you have enough cash to meet your needs. Depending where you are travelling, it may be difficult to obtain your usual brands of fuel. Investigate before you go what the most acceptable local substitute is (one of the major motoring organizations should be able to tell you).

On motorways and bridges there may be tolls to be paid – and the further you travel, the more it will cost you. On French motorways, for example, expect to pay 0.34 francs per kilometre travelled on a toll road – so if you plan on travelling the length and breadth of the country by motorway you will certainly pay for the privilege. In Switzerland all drivers wishing to use the motorway must buy a permit or vignette, which is valid for one year and costs around 40 Swiss francs. Those who feel that there are better ways to spend their holiday money should stay off the motorways and take the scenic route instead.

If your journey involves a ferry crossing, check with the ferry companies whether it is necessary to book in advance. Some routes need to be booked months ahead if you plan to travel during the school holidays. Turn up without a ticket and you could find yourself stranded.

long journeys

Motorway Driving

Drivers who rarely use motorways are often nervous about travelling on them because of the high speeds and the number of heavy goods vehicles. Although it's true that when accidents do happen they tend to be more serious, motorways are, on the whole, safer than dual carriageways.

There are no roundabouts, sharp bends, hump-backed bridges, to restrict your view. Most motorways follow the straightest possible route from A to B, so you can see far into the distance. You don't have to worry about cyclists, pedestrians, learner drivers, buses pulling in at stops, or traffic turning across your path to reach a side entrance on the right. Provided everyone observes the rules and maintains lane discipline, everything should go smoothly.

Problems which do arise usually occur because of driver error. Motorway driving can be very monotonous. Mile upon mile, everything looks the same, and with so little visual stimulation it's difficult to maintain your concentration. What's worse, you may not even realize that fatigue is taking its toll: your ability to identify and evaluate risks may be undermined long before you start to feel sleepy.

Even the most experienced driver should start the journey feeling fresh and rested, and schedule a rest break every two hours to make sure they stay that way. No matter how late you are running, and regardless of whether or not you feel tired, it's important to pull over at a lay-by or service station and take a while to unwind. Have something to drink, maybe a light snack. Take the opportunity to use the lavatory. Go for a short walk or do a few exercises to stretch your aching limbs. If you are travelling with young children, find a safe place where they can run around and wear themselves out so that they'll sleep when you get back on the road.

While you are on the move, have a window ajar so you get a supply of fresh air. Play tapes and sing along, talk to a passenger, or follow any of the other tips listed under **Fatigue** in the chapter on Safe Driving. Make a conscious effort to stay alert and keep your eyes scanning left to right, near and far the whole time. Don't let fatigue get a grip on you!

JOINING THE MOTORWAY

Some motorways begin as a regular main road which widens from two lanes to three or four, but usually you will join at a junction where a slip road leads into an acceleration lane, which in turn feeds into the left-hand lane of the motorway.

The traffic already on the motorway has priority, so your aim should be to find a safe gap and adjust your speed on the acceleration lane so that you can slot into that gap without causing any disruption to the traffic flow. In order to achieve this, you must:

- Keep well back from the vehicle in front of you on the slip road.
- Begin looking for a safe gap as soon as the left-hand lane of the motorway comes in sight. Do this by taking lots of quick glances rather than by staring hard.
- Don't forget to keep an eye on vehicles sharing the slip road with you. If your attention is fixed on finding a gap, you could run into the back of a vehicle which has slowed down or stopped in front of you.
- Don't enter the acceleration lane too quickly. Increase your speed to match that of vehicles in the left-hand lane only when you have identified a safe gap.
- Use your mirrors and signal your intentions. Check quickly over your shoulder in case a vehicle is hidden in your blind spot.
- If there isn't a suitable gap, slow down – checking your mirrors to make sure drivers behind have seen – and stop well before you come to the end of the acceleration lane. That way, when a gap does occur, you will have room to accelerate up to speed.
- Steer gently – avoid harsh, aggressive movements of the wheel.
- Remain in the left-hand lane until your senses have adjusted to the speed.

LANE DISCIPLINE

At high speeds it becomes even more important to maintain a safe distance between your vehicle and the one in front. If you are the victim of tailgating (a vehicle behind driving too close), increase the gap in front to preserve your margin of safety.

Scan the whole picture rather than focusing on the car in front of you or the one in your rear-view mirror. Everything happens very fast on a motorway, so you need to continuously update your 'picture' of the road. Don't let your mind wander; snap back to attention by giving a running commentary on signs, hazards, traffic, etc. Apply the motoring drill to help you identify hazards in good time and react to them. Try to anticipate and plan ahead rather than reacting at the last minute.

To avoid inciting road rage in others, observe correct lane discipline:

- Drive in the left-hand lane unless you need to overtake vehicles which are moving more slowly than you.
- When overtaking, make sure the driver of the vehicle you are about to overtake is aware of your intention before moving out. When it is safe to move, accelerate to complete the manoeuvre quickly – don't remain in another driver's blindspot any longer than necessary. Once the vehicle you are overtaking can be seen in your interior mirror, it's safe to move back in.
- Always move back to the left-hand lane once you have finished overtaking. Heavy goods vehicles get very frustrated with drivers who hold them up by hogging the middle lane. (HGVs are not permitted to use the outside lane of a three-lane motorway, and it's illegal for anyone to overtake on the inside lane, so you leave them with nowhere to go but nose-to-tail with your rear bumper.)
- If others want to break the speed limit, it's not your job to try and stop them. Move back into the inside lane and let them through.
- Don't leave it until the last moment to change lanes. Harsh steering at high speeds can lead to a skid. Any alterations to your course should be planned well in advance, so watch for anything that might give rise to a lane change: exit signs, roadworks, traffic joining from slip roads, and slow-moving vehicles up ahead. Don't wait until you've arrived at the hazard, choose your moment so you have the maximum room for manoeuvre.

Check your mirrors, signal, check your blind spot, then steer gently into the next lane.

LEAVING THE MOTORWAY

When planning your route, always note the number of the exit you intend using. Look well ahead for signs warning of junctions, and when you know your exit is imminent look for an early and safe opportunity to move into the left-hand lane.

- Signal your intention to turn off between the 300 and 200 yard/metre countdown markers.
- Be on the alert for drivers who suddenly realize that they need to turn off and cut across lanes of traffic to reach the exit in time.
- It's a good idea to check your nearside blindspot in case someone is trying to overtake on the hard shoulder (although it's illegal, some drivers will take the risk to beat others to the exit).
- When you reach the deceleration lane leading into the slip road, reduce your speed to the limit displayed. There may be sharp bends and/or queues of traffic waiting for lights to change at the junction, so take care.

It can take a while to adjust to driving at 30 mph after you've been acclimatized to motorway speeds. Keep checking your speedometer to make sure you're not going faster than you think. If your schedule allows, take a short break to give yourself a chance to unwind.

 A three-mile shopping trip or school run will consume fuel at roughly twice the rate of a hundred-mile motorway journey. Try to avoid short trips by combining several errands into one long journey.

And to make your journey even more economical, let friends and relations know you are planning a long-distance trip – someone may just want to share the ride and your fuel costs.

holiday travel

One of the great things about taking the car on holiday is that you don't have to limit yourself to a couple of suitcases light enough to carry around airport and station concourses. You can load the family car with the kids' favourite toys, your sports equipment – even the family pets – so you'll have everything you need to enjoy your time away from home. But remember that the vehicle, and the driver, can only take so much strain!

Getting Started

Get your holiday off to a good start by setting off when the roads are at their most peaceful: early in the morning or late at night. In summer it's a pleasure to drive early in the day – although you do need to be careful when driving eastwards into the dazzling sun. Watch out too for wildlife on the roads.

If you have small children, a late-night drive avoids all the bother of entertaining youngsters throughout a long ride. Provided they've had plenty of exercise the day before, they should sleep right through the journey – which makes for a less stressful drive for you, too. (But see the section on night-time hazards in Bad-Weather Driving for details of potential pitfalls and how to deal with them).

Everyone will be a lot more comfortable if they dress in loose-fitting garments. Opt for elasticated waistbands rather than belts, and natural fibres that allow the skin to 'breathe' rather than man-made fabrics that get hot and sticky. In winter, wear layers of warm thermals and fleeces. In summer, white cotton garments are best. Cotton absorbs sweat, unlike nylon and other man-made fabrics which trap the moisture, causing skin rashes and prickly heat. White clothing reflects the light, reducing the solar heat absorbed by up to 50 per cent.

If you are starting out very early in the day it may be cool to start with, but you are going to get hotter as the day progresses. Wear layers that can be removed as the temperature rises – and that goes for feet, too! Trapped inside socks and shoes, overheated feet can swell up, making it painful to get out and walk. You will be much more comfortable wearing sandals which allow the air to get to your feet.

Motion Sickness

Around 50 per cent of travellers experience some degree of motion sickness when travelling by road, sea, air, or rail. For a lucky few, the symptoms are limited to a slight feeling of discomfort or a headache, but others will suffer excessive sweating and salivation, nausea, and vomiting.

The problem originates in the organ of balance within the inner ear. This responds to movement by sending signals through the nervous system to trigger reflexes which will enable the body to right itself when thrown off balance. Unfortunately, some of the nerves connect with the part of the brain which controls vomiting.

The condition will be aggravated by psychological factors: a person who has been sick in the past – and feels anxious about travelling because of this – is more likely to be sick than someone who's had no previous experience of the condition. Focusing on nearby objects or trying to read can also bring on an attack.

There are various drugs on the market which will prevent or help control motion sickness, but some cause drowsiness and are therefore unsuitable for drivers.

Other measures to prevent motion sickness include:

- Looking at a point on the far horizon.
- Keeping your mind occupied – but not by reading. Children can listen to story tapes rather than looking at

SUNBURN AND HEAT EXHAUSTION

It can get very hot in the car when the sun is beating down, especially if the vehicle is stuck in heavy traffic and there's very little breeze.

Heat exhaustion causes dizziness, fatigue, blurred vision, nausea and fainting. If anyone inside the car starts showing symptoms, break your journey as soon as it is safe to do so. The casualty will need to be moved to a cool place and given sips of cold water to drink. If he or she loses consciousness place them in the Recovery Position (see First Aid in Emergency!) and seek medical attention.

To prevent this situation arising:

• Try to avoid travelling during the hottest part of the day (between 11 a.m. and 2 p.m.)

• Always have a cold drink available and sip it frequently to avoid dehydration.

• Don't drive with an arm resting on the window ledge. The slip-stream hides the heat and you won't realize you're being burned till the damage has been done. It's also a security and safety risk. Keep both hands on the wheel and bear in mind the risks of snatch thieves making off with your expensive watch or jewellery.

• The sun can burn even through glass, clothing and in shade. Apply a high SPF (sun protection factor) cream or lotion on all exposed parts – especially if you are fair-skinned and burn easily. Reapply the cream every time you stop for a break; one application will not last an entire day.

• Protect children from sunstroke by sitting them in a shaded part of the car. Put up a screen to create shade if necessary – these can be bought from most car accessory shops.

• Babies must be monitored continuously to ensure that they do not become overheated.

• If you drive a convertible or a car with a sunroof, wear a hat to protect the back of your neck.

• Sunglasses are a must when driving in bright sunshine. Cheap glasses can do more harm than good. Invest in a pair that meet internationally agreed safety standards.

---

books, or encourage them to play I-Spy.

• A stuffy or fume-filled atmosphere will make matters worse. Open a window to let in fresh air. (On a boat it may help to go out on deck.)

• Try sitting with your head tilted back.

• Suck a peppermint.

• Don't eat too much – and don't go without food altogether. Small, plain snacks may help settle your stomach.

• Some people swear by acupressure bands. Available from all good pharmacies, these bands are worn on the wrist, with the ball positioned so that it applies light pressure on the radial pulse.

REMEMBER
If someone feels sick while travelling along the motorway, you cannot just pull over – the hard shoulder is a dangerous place and you must not park there unless it's an emergency.

Carry a sick-bag or two in case you have a passenger who can't make it to the next service station. If you haven't laid by a stock of bags collected from car ferries and airlines, line a heavy-duty brown-paper bag with a plastic bag.

• Others claim that an earth strap is the answer. This strip hangs down from the car to the ground, getting rid of static electricity.

Loading the Car

Before you start filling the luggage compartment and piling the roof-rack high with excess baggage, check the manufacturer's recommendations on maximum permitted loads in the handbook – and don't forget that the total weight must take into account your human cargo, too.

A light car will consume 33 per cent less fuel than one which is carrying a heavy load, especially if the journey involves a lot of stop–start driving in heavy traffic. So it pays to think of ways you might reduce the load.

Start by clearing the luggage compartment of all those bits and pieces left over from the last family holiday. Then sit down and make a list of essential items. Be firm about what gets included in the list, because if one person is allowed a non-essential item, everyone else will want to pack something extra as well. Check each item off as you load the car and then, if there's room, consider squeezing a few extras in – but remember that could mean less room for souvenirs and keepsakes on the homeward journey.

> **Don't leave home without the really essential items: ferry tickets, passports, travellers' cheques, credit cards, cash, etc. Carry them in a zip-fastened pocket or moneybelt at all times – don't leave your valuables unguarded in the car.**
>
> **Make sure that you leave a number where you can be contacted with a trusted friend in case of emergencies.**
>
> **Keep a loaded camera in the car. In the unlikely event that you have an accident, photographs will expedite an insurance claim.**

The Luggage Compartment

To prevent the vehicle's stability and road-handling being impaired, it's essential that heavy luggage is evenly distributed.

Wedge the heaviest suitcase at the back of the luggage compartment, so it's level with the middle of the rear seat, and fill in the spaces on either side with smaller items to stop it moving around. If you have two big, heavy suitcases, lay them down one on top of the other. Coats and spare items of clothing can be used to plug gaps and prevent things rattling around, but don't overfill the boot. In an emergency you will have to empty everything out by the roadside to get at the spare wheel.

Items which may be needed en route, like pushchairs, should be packed last so they can be unloaded first.

Roofracks

If there isn't enough room in the luggage compartment for all your luggage and sports equipment, you might want to consider extending your car's storage capacity with a roof rack.

Borrowing a roof rack from a friend may be the cheapest solution but, unless they drive the same make and model of car as you, it's not a good idea. If the rack is to fit securely, it must comply with the recommended specifications for your vehicle (check the handbook or consult an authorized dealer to find out what these specifications are).

 Studies have shown that roof racks, cycle- and ski-holders increase drag or air resistance, even when empty, and this makes for significantly higher fuel consumption. You will save yourself a lot of money if you take off the rack whenever it is not in use.

Always allow yourself plenty of time to fit the roof rack. It's a fiddly business and all the instructions must be followed carefully if the rack is to sit securely in place at motorway speeds and when turning corners or driving into high winds

Care must be taken, too, when loading. Uneven weight distribution will affect the vehicle's stability, and a poorly secured load could fly off into the road causing damage to your property and endangering the lives of other road users.

WARNING

If anything should fall from your vehicle on a single or dual carriageway, you should stop and attempt to retrieve it – provided this can be done safely. Where it is unsafe, or the item poses a danger to other road users, contact the police and, if possible, try to warn oncoming traffic.

On a motorway you must not attempt to pick up any fallen articles. Stop at the next emergency telephone and notify the police.

LOADING A ROOF RACK

All too often you will see a roof rack where the largest suitcases have been stacked upright at the front, creating a very effective wind barrier. This wrecks the aerodynamic performance of the vehicle, reducing speed by around 15 mph and increasing fuel consumption.

The correct way to load a roof rack is as follows:

1 Check that the roof rack is fixed securely to the anchor points or roof rails, and that all nuts and bolts are tightened properly. Ensure that the rack does not interfere with the opening and closing of doors.

2 Lay a heavy plastic sheet one third of the way down the rack with the excess over the front. (DON'T use thin polythene as it will tear, exposing your luggage to the elements and flapping about distractingly in the wind.)

3 Arrange the load evenly across the rack, holding the cover in position. The bulk of the weight should be situated at the bottom of the pile in the middle of the rack. Lie suitcases flat to keep the overall height as low as possible; place smaller items to the front and larger ones to the rear for an aerodynamic wedge shape which will keep wind resistance to a minimum.

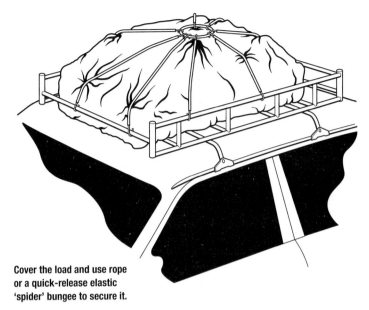

Cover the load and use rope or a quick-release elastic 'spider' bungee to secure it.

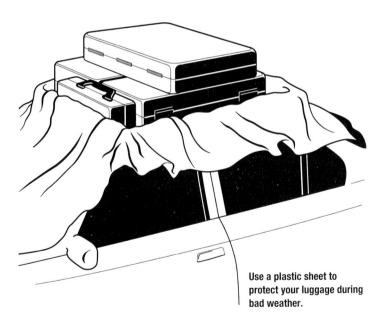

Use a plastic sheet to protect your luggage during bad weather.

4 DON'T overload the rack.

5 Working from the front to the rear, cover the load with the waterproof sheet.

6 Use a strong, eight-stranded elastic bungee or plenty of rope to secure the sheet. Tuck excess material and loose ends in so that they can't flap around or billow out like a sail in the wind.

WARNING

Any load will be vulnerable to theft, so never leave the vehicle unattended. It will take a thief only a couple of minutes' work with a sharp knife to relieve you of your possessions.

DANGER! STRONG WINDS

A roof rack will have a significant effect on the vehicle's road-holding capabilities. Load the really heavy items in the luggage compartment and save the roof rack for bulky lightweight objects.

It's also advisable to have a trial run with the roof rack before you go on a long journey. Load it up and take the car out for a short run to feel the difference it makes to your steering. Notice how susceptible you are to strong winds and how much care needs to be taken when overtaking or being overtaken by high-sided vehicles.

REMEMBER

When you stop for a break, always check that your roof rack and its load have not worked loose. Tighten any loose fittings and secure any flapping bits of sheeting.

long journeys

ROOF BOXES

If you regularly carry valuable sports equipment it may be worth purchasing a purpose-built roof box. These are constructed of durable weatherproof materials, and the streamlined shape gives a better aerodynamic performance than a roof rack. But the greatest advantage of all is that they can be locked to protect your belongings from thieves. So instead of having to stand guard over the car, you can leave it unattended while you take a break.

MAKING ADJUSTMENTS FOR HEAVY LOADS

A heavy load, whether carried in the boot or on a roof rack, can affect the angle of your headlight beams. With some new cars you can adjust the angle of the beam using a switch on the dashboard. Remember to change the setting back from 'full load and all seats occupied' to 'driver only' or whichever position applies for your next trip.

And don't forget to increase your tyre pressures to cope with a heavy load, as per the instructions in your handbook.

caravans and trailers

There's a lot more to towing a caravan or trailer than just hitching up and driving away. If you've never towed anything before it can come as a surprise to discover how much heavier the car's controls feel, not to mention the strangeness of trying to manoeuvre something that's higher, longer, and wider than your vehicle, with a tendency to move as though it had a mind of its own.

In some countries there is no legal requirement for drivers to seek professional training before towing a caravan on the public highway – but I would strongly recommend that you sign up for a course regardless. The large caravanning associations run excellent courses for beginners. Expert instructors will teach you all there is to know about manoeuvring, reversing, and loading a caravan, and give you the confidence to enjoy caravanning anywhere. And you can also pick up tips about accessories, safety devices, and which makes and models of car are best for towing.

Laws governing the towing of caravans and trailers vary from country to country. As a result of a European Community directive, member countries are imposing restrictions on what can be towed without a special licence.

In Britain, anyone who passed their driving test after 1 January 1997 cannot tow a trailer (or a boat or horsebox) weighing more than 750 kg (0.75 tonne) unless they apply for a special licence. This involves taking an additional driving test where you will be asked to execute a number of manoeuvres with a trailer in tow.

To find out what restrictions apply to you (either at home or in any countries you will be visiting) consult one of the major motoring organizations.

The Towing Vehicle

Towing a caravan takes a lot of power and places considerable strain on a vehicle. If you are thinking about buying a caravan and making regular use of it, consult an authorized dealer for your make of car.

As well as being able to tell you the maximum trailer and towbar weights for your car (and the correct tyre pressures for towing a loaded trailer), the dealer can advise on modifications to the cooling system, rear suspension, indicator circuits, and other components.

They can also fit the correct type of tow bar and stabilizer for your car, and any additional mirrors you might need. The most useful mirror for this purpose is an oversized wing mirror that sits at the end of an extended arm. These give a clear view of the road to your rear and, if hit, they fold back rather than breaking off.

WEIGHT LIMITS

The handbook will tell you the maximum caravan and trailer loads permissible for your vehicle. Do not exceed those limits.

As a general rule, what you are towing should not weigh more, even when it is fully loaded, than your car does when it is empty. Ideally, your loaded caravan or trailer should weigh 15 per cent less than the empty towing vehicle.

LOADING THE CARAVAN
Be careful how you load your caravan, its stability depends on getting the weight distribution right. Even a light load, if positioned in the wrong place, can put undue strain on the towing hitch.

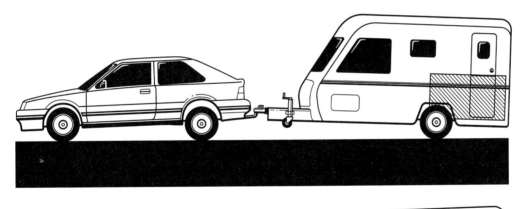

Don't overload the tail as this will cause the caravan to snake when being towed.

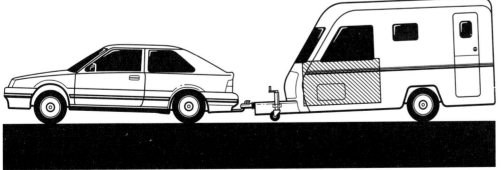

Too much weight at the front will make the towing vehicle's steering feel light and cause the headlights to shine upwards even on dipped beam.

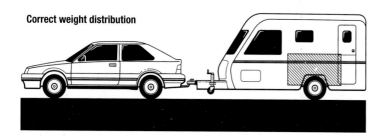

Correct weight distribution

To check that the noseweight (the load exerted on the towing coupling) is correct, buy a special gauge from a caravan accessory shop or dealer.

Pack heavy items like containers of food and water in the centre of the caravan, over the axles, at floor level or just above.

Medium items such as bedding materials can be spread about at front and rear to achieve an even balance.

Only very light items should be placed in high cabinets and shelves, otherwise the caravan will be top heavy and unstable.

HITCHING UP

It's best to hitch up on level ground, as this makes things much easier. But before you start the process of hitching the caravan and towing vehicle, run through the following safety checks:

- Inspect the tyre walls for signs of cracks, cuts, bulges and blisters. Make sure they comply with the minimum tread depth.
- Check that the tyres are inflated to the correct pressure for the load carried. This applies equally to car and caravan.
- The caravan must have a roadworthy spare wheel, together with the correct wheel brace. A jack will also be required if the towing vehicle's is unsuitable.
- If the caravan has been laid up for a long period, it's a good idea to check the wheel bearings and brakes. Using the leg braces, jack up one side of the caravan until the wheel is clear of the ground. Take a firm grip of the wheel and try moving it back and forth. Any side movement indicates worn or badly adjusted wheel bearings. Remove the wheel and adjust or replace as necessary. Grease the bearings, thoroughly packing grease into the protective covers before replacing them.

CARAVAN SAFETY TIPS

- Disconnect the caravan's battery when towing.
- Ensure that the gas cylinders are turned off.
- It's a good idea to turn the fridge on for 24 hours before departure to cool it down. Fill it with any perishable items and they will stay cool for the duration of the journey even though the power has been disconnected.
- Keep all the food in boxes on the floor and load the shelves only when you reach your destination.
- Secure all loose items, either by wedging them into tight spaces or securing them with bungees.
- Corrosive items like disinfectants and lavatory cleaners must be kept away from clothes and food. Screw the tops on tightly and stow the containers so that they will remain upright.

NEVER allow passengers to travel inside the caravan. It is both illegal and extremely dangerous.

Although there's no law against carrying animals to travel in a moving caravan, it is best if you don't. They might get hurt – and they will probably have a field day breaking into your holiday rations!

- Tighten wheel nuts and bolts to the correct torque setting.
- Inspect the brakes. Take off the wheel hub and check the thickness of the brake linings. If they seem very thin, get them replaced.
- Make sure brake cables are properly connected and that there is no sign of damage or leaks.
- Test the handbrake. It should be capable of holding the caravan on all gradients. Release it and pull it up several times.
- Check the tow hitch for full movement, and inspect all bolts to make sure they're tight enough.
- Check that the breakaway cable is connected properly. When towing a trailer or caravan you should always use a supplementary restraining chain or breakaway cable to prevent the trailer breaking free in the event that the tow hitch fails. If your caravan is not fitted with such a device, have one installed.

- Hook up the caravan and plug in the electrics. Check all road lights: indicators, brake lights, and number-plate lights.
- Make sure that the number plate matches the towing vehicle.

Once you have completed the safety checks, call in a helper to assist you in hitching up. Ask them to stand to the side of the caravan and give directions as you reverse the car into place.

- The caravan's legs and corner steadies should be wound up, the handbrake on, and the tow hitch release catch open.
- Reverse slowly, using your mirrors and your helper's guidance to locate the hitch. As soon as they give the signal to tell you the towbar and hitch are aligned, switch off the engine and engage the hand brake.

Under no circumstances should the helper get between the car and caravan while you are reversing – or they could get crushed.

- Lower the jockey wheel until the connection is made.
- The jockey wheel and assembly can then be fully retracted and stowed away. Double check that it is secure before you set off.
- Inspect the connecting cable to make sure that it is looped securely around the towing bracket and not running along the ground or fouled on anything.
- Use your gauge to check that the noseweight load does not exceed the car manufacturer's limit.
- Disengage the caravan's handbrake.
- Check that all gas cylinders and other fuel supplies have been shut off.
- Close all windows, doors and the skylight.

You are now ready to go!

UNHITCHING THE CARAVAN

When you reach your destination:

- Apply the hand brake.

- Unplug the electrics.
- Disconnect the safety cable/chain.
- Lower the jockey wheel.
- Pull up the hitch release and wind the jockey wheel down until the hitch disengages.
- Use a spirit level to make sure that the caravan does not slope to one side. Always carry a few flat blocks of wood that you can prop under the corner steadies or legs to compensate for any slight unevenness in the ground.
- Put the socket cover on, or use a plastic bag to protect it from the weather.

TIPS FOR CARAVAN HOLIDAYS

Carry one full water container and leave the rest empty. These can be filled once you have settled at your destination.

Take a few essential food items only. Buy the rest from a market, grocery, or supermarket near the site – there's bound to be one.

Don't try transporting fragile foods like eggs – they damage too easily.

Remember to pack the tin opener and corkscrew!

It's always advisable to pull over to a lay-by after 15 minutes or so and inspect the caravan, inside and out, for anything you may have missed or that may need readjusting.

Check that the tyres are cool and properly inflated, that nothing has shaken loose inside, and that no windows or skylights have blown open.

Towing Techniques

When towing a caravan or trailer you have to get used to making allowances. Because of the extra weight, you need to allow three times your normal stopping distance and to exercise caution on steep gradients. Because of the extra length and width, you need to allow more room for manoeuvre when cornering or overtaking. Because of the extra height, you have to allow for the effects of crosswinds and the slipstream of high-sided vehicles. You will also need to watch out for low bridges, overhanging trees, and arched gateways.

As always, you should apply the motoring drill to help you spot hazards well in advance and formulate a plan which will allow you to deal with them. With a trailer or caravan in tow, last-minute decisions and hurried manoeuvres are out of the question. Reduce your speed to give yourself more time to react to hazards. Use your mirrors frequently, and signal your intentions clearly and in good time.

If you're not careful, things can get out of control going down steep hills. Don't ride the brakes all the way down. To avoid overheating the engine, change down to a lower gear at the crest of the hill.

CHANGING DIRECTION

When you steer round a corner with a caravan in tow, the wheels of the caravan will follow those of the car. This means that you are effectively driving a vehicle that's twice as long as the average car. If you take the corner too tight, the caravan/trailer will cut across at a dangerous angle. So you must swing wide in order to corner safely.

OVERTAKING

Plan carefully before overtaking. Your judgement of speeds and distances needs to be even more accurate than when driving a car, because

- you will have less power to accelerate
- you will need a larger gap to pull into
- to avoid harsh steering, you must alter course gradually over a greater distance.

This means that you need to look well ahead for hazards and junctions where other traffic might conflict with you.

REVERSING

To reverse around a corner, you have to steer the car in the opposite direction to where you want the caravan to go. Until you get used to turning the wheel while watching the caravan in the mirrors – and at the same time keeping an eye

out for pedestrians and other road users whom you may need to give way to – reversing can be tricky, to say the least!

Even at low speeds the smallest steering input can result in a drastic change in the caravan's angle. If you over-correct your steering, reverse too fast, or stare too long at an obstacle you want to avoid rather than checking the position of the caravan, you will jack-knife the vehicles.

Use the mirrors, and always have a helper at the nearside to direct you. They should stand on the nearside – well clear of the reversing caravan – so that they can see into your blind spots. Proceed very, very slowly.

SNAKING

Avoid exposed bridges and roads when it's windy, and always adjust your speed to suit the conditions. Caravans become unstable in high winds and at high speeds.

Even when you are not speeding, a high-sided vehicle overtaking you can create sufficient air turbulence to cause snaking. This swaying, side-to-side motion can get out of control – especially if you make the mistake of trying to cure it by harsh braking, steering or accelerating.

The correct way to correct snaking is to:

- Slowly ease off the accelerator to reduce your speed.
- Try to stay off the brake pedal. If you have no alternative but to brake, do it very gently to lose speed progressively rather than suddenly.
- DON'T try to correct the steering by pulling hard to one side or the other. Keep a firm hold on the wheel and try to keep the car pointing straight ahead. Avoid hooking your thumb round the rim as the wheel may twitch suddenly with sufficient force to dislocate the joint.
- Keep losing speed until the snaking stops.
- Consider fitting a stabilizer to improve stability in gusty conditions.

TOWING ETIQUETTE

When towing a caravan or trailer, try not to cause a nuisance to other road users. Allow a large gap between your vehicle and the one in front so that faster vehicles can overtake. Make your intentions clear by signalling well in advance of a turn or lane change. And if a queue of other vehicles builds up behind you, look for a lay-by where you can pull in and allow traffic to pass.

Trailers

If you are a keen gardener with an allotment, a DIY enthusiast who makes regular trips to the builder's yard, or if you enjoy camping holidays, a trailer may be the solution to your problems.

Easier to load than a roof rack, and easier to clean out than the luggage compartment of your car, it can be used to transport household or garden refuse to the tip, sand and cement from the DIY centre to the site of your latest project, and all the bulky equipment you'll ever need on a camping holiday.

The techniques and safety measures for towing a trailer are the same as those for towing a caravan, but here are a few additional tips to bear in mind:

- Always follow the manufacturer's recommendations when loading. Place the heaviest items as near to the trailer axle as possible, and make sure that the load does not exceed the maximum nose weight.
- Be careful when carrying loads of sand or soil. If the trailer is left uncovered in rainy weather, the weight of the load can double as it absorbs water.
- Make sure the load is well secured and covered with a heavy-duty plastic sheet to prevent loose or lightweight items from blowing away. Objects falling off trailers can endanger other road users – and you would be held liable for the consequences, which could prove costly.
- Because trailers are not in everyday use they tend to get neglected and problems develop, like wheel-bearing failures, punctures, and faults in the electrics. Always check your trailer's roadworthiness before hitching it up.
- Examine the tyres for signs of damage. If they are worn, replace them. Carry a spare tyre attached to the trailer.
- Make sure the trailer lights are functioning.

travelling abroad

Package holidays are not to everyone's taste. Being herded into a tourist hotel in a tourist resort, eating the same food you would find at home, not having to worry about language barriers because the only locals you meet are the ones who serve you food and drinks... It may be a comfort to those who are nervous about venturing abroad, but some prefer the freedom of an independent holiday. They want to get off the beaten track, experience different customs and cultures – to feel like a traveller rather than a tourist.

A driving holiday abroad allows you to indulge that spirit of adventure. And provided you take a few sensible precautions and remember to observe the local rules and customs, your journey should be enjoyable and trouble-free.

Red Tape

Depending on your destination, there are a number of documents and certificates which you may need on your travels. The major motoring organizations will be able to advise you which of the following are required for the countries you will be visiting:

- Passport
- Visa
- Driving licence
- International Driving Permit
- Vehicle registration document
- Vehicle Excise licence (road tax disc)
- Certificate of roadworthiness (MOT)

- Bail bond
- Motor insurance certificate
- Personal/medical insurance

All persons travelling abroad must hold a valid passport (children under 16 may be included in a parent's passport). Some countries also require a visa or special vaccination certificates before you will be allowed to enter: check with the relevant tourist office, embassy or consulate before you go. Before travelling to any trouble spots like the former Yugoslavia, parts of Africa, or the Middle East, contact the Foreign Office for advice.

You must also carry a valid driving licence. Your national driving licence may be sufficient, but it's a good idea to obtain an International Driving Permit as well, even for countries where there is no legal requirement that you carry one. An IDP shows your photograph and lists your details in a number of different languages, so if you're stopped by the local police and asked to produce your documents there won't be a lot of head-scratching and phoning around while they try to decipher the piece of paper you're waving at them. To obtain an IDP, apply to one of the major motoring organizations (you don't have to be a member).

You will also need to carry the original vehicle registration document. If you've lost the original, or have just bought the car and the paperwork hasn't come through yet, apply for a temporary certificate of registration. If you are hiring a vehicle, the car-hire company must issue you with a certificate authorizing you to take their car abroad.

Make sure that your road tax won't expire while you are abroad. You could be fined if your tax disk is out of date when you return. The same goes for your MOT certificate.

To drive in Spain, you will need a bail bond. It's not compulsory, but without one you could be imprisoned and your vehicle impounded after even a minor traffic accident. The bond simply guarantees that your insurer will pay your bail so that you don't have to wait in prison until the case gets to court. Get one from your insurance company.

You will be denied entry at most borders if you cannot produce an internationally recognized certificate of motor insurance. Third-party insurance is the minimum cover permitted for most countries, but with personal injury awards, recovery and breakdown costs tending to be much higher abroad than at home, you should arrange fully comprehensive cover with your insurers before you go.

Read the small print carefully: some policies will meet the full cost of bringing the car back home if it requires major repair, others will only pay a small proportion of the costs – yet the two policies could cost pretty much the same. Shop around for the best deal before you commit yourself.

Don't leave home without adequate health insurance for the whole family. Not all countries offer free emergency medical care, and some will even demand money up front. There are reciprocal health arrangements between EC member states (consult the Department of Health for details and the necessary forms), but the cover is fairly basic so it's a good idea to arrange additional insurance before you travel. Get the best you can afford: in some countries the cost of medical care can be frighteningly expensive.

Planning Your Trip

As with any long journey, you should plan your approximate route before travelling. A wide range of maps and guides are available, but make sure that any you buy are up to date.

When looking at a map of an entire continent like Europe or the United States, it's easy to lose sight of the vast distances involved. Don't set yourself over-ambitious targets; even on motorways it's no fun trying to cover several hundred miles a day for days on end. Split the journey up into manageable portions and allow plenty of time for sightseeing and resting.

Any of the motoring organizations will be happy to offer advice and help in planning your trip. They can provide estimates on how long a journey will take, what it will cost in tolls and fuel, where to break your journey, etc. If you wish, for a small fee they will even provide you with a full itinerary for the entire holiday, and book your accommodation.

To prevent yourself going way over budget, find out as much as you can about the costs you are likely to incur. Some things, like ferry tickets and hotel accommodation, can be paid for in advance. A good tourist guide or literature from the relevant tourist offices will help you to estimate the cost of bed and breakfast accommodation, campsites, food (whether you plan on self-catering or eating out), motorway tolls, and fuel.

Don't just assume that you can put everything on your credit cards. In some countries the majority of garages will only accept cash. And in parts of Eastern Europe fuel is obtained using vouchers, which you must purchase before entering the country.

Visit a bank or bureau de change before you depart and obtain a small cash float in the relevant currency for each country you will visit. There will probably be currency exchange facilities at each border crossing, but the rates will be far less favourable.

The bulk of your holiday money can be carried in the form of travellers' cheques. You have to pay a commission charge to the bank or travel agent, but in return you get a guarantee that the cheques will be replaced if lost or stolen. Make sure you make a note of the cheque numbers, and don't lose the leaflet telling you how what to do and who to contact in an emergency.

> Draw up a detailed route card, and make a list on the back of emergency numbers and garages or dealerships which carry spares for your particular car (ask your local authorized dealer or the car manufacturer for a list of overseas stockists).
>
> Your route card should look something like this:

From	To	Route	Distance	Direction	Time
Calais	Orly	A476	55 km	south	1 hr 20 min
Orly	Luppen	B316	18 km	east	50 min
Luppen	Greerly	M2	100 km	south	2 hr
REST SERVICES JCT 6					
Greerly	Pasith	A119	54 km	south/west	1hr 30min

ACCESSORIES

Headlights are adjusted by vehicle manufacturers so that, when the dipped beam setting is selected, oncoming drivers will not be dazzled by the light. But when you take a left-hand drive vehicle to a country where they drive on the right, or vice versa, your factory-adjusted dipped beams will

REMEMBER
Always carry enough cash to pay motorway tolls, feed parking meters, and to cover emergencies like on-the-spot speeding fines.

be shining straight into the eyes of approaching motorists. The solution is to fit specially designed lenses which alter the direction of your dipped beams. No technical know-how is required to fit the lenses, and you can still use your headlamp washer/wipers, if fitted. Make sure that you buy lenses which redirect the light rather than blocking it. Yellow is the preferred colour for headlamp lenses in much of Europe, although there is no legal requirement forcing you to comply.

Although it makes a lot of sense to carry a full emergency kit wherever you go, if your own government hasn't made it compulsory to carry warning triangles, fire extinguishers or first-aid kits, you may feel that you don't want to go to the expense of buying these things for a fortnight's holiday. The solution is to hire an emergency kit from one of the motoring organizations. They can also loan roof racks and boxes, bike and ski racks, snow chains, and other useful equipment.

In addition to making sure you have all those accessories required by law in the countries you are visiting, take a few spare parts for the car – especially if it's an old model. Left-hand drive parts are not always interchangeable with those for a right-hand drive car of the same make and model, so don't count on foreign garages having the item you need available in stock.

Even in countries where it is not a legal requirement, carry a set of spare bulbs for your car in case replacements are difficult to find.

> Take some spare parts for the driver, too! If you wear contact lenses or glasses, carry a spare pair in case of emergencies. In some countries this is a legal requirement.

ESSENTIAL ACCESSORIES

Whereas most visitors to North America and Australasia will hire a car which is equipped to comply with local regulations, Europeans face a new set of rules with each national boundary. When you take your car across borders, it must have a plate showing the country of origin (for example GB for Great Britain) fixed to the rear. Other items which you should carry when visiting European countries are shown below.

COUNTRY	SEAT BELTS	HEADLAMP DEFLECTORS	WARNING TRIANGLE	FIRE EXTIN-GUISHER	FIRST AID KIT	SPARE BULBS	ILLEGAL TO CARRY FUEL CAN
Austria	C	C	C	R	C	R	–
Belgium	C	C	C	R	R	R	–
Bulgaria	C	C	C	C	C	R	–
Cyprus	C	C	C*	R	R	R	C
Czech Republic	C	C	C	R	C	C	
Denmark	C	C**	C	R	R	R	–
Eire	C	C§	R	R	R	R	–
Finland	C	C**	C	R	C	R	–
France	C	C	C	R	R	C	–
Germany	C	C	C	R	C	C	–
Gibraltar	C	C	R	R	R	R	–
Greece	C	R	C	C	C	R	C
Hungary	C	C	C	R	R	R	–
Italy	C	C	C	R	R	R	C
Luxembourg C	C	C	R	R	C		
Netherlands	C	C†	C	R	R	R	–
Norway	C	C**	R	R	R	R	–
Poland	C	C††	C	R	R	R	–
Portugal	C	C	C	R	R	R	–
Romania	C	C	C	R	C	R	–
Russia (CIS)	C	C	C	C	C	R	–
Slovakia	C	C	C	R	C	C	–
Spain	C	C	C	R	R	C	–
Sweden	C	C**	C	R	R	R	–
Switzerland	C	C	C	R	C	R	–
UK	C	C§	R	R	R	R	–

C compulsory   **R** recommended
§ traffic drives on the left; right-hand drive cars need headlamp converters
* two warning triangles must be carried

** Dipped-beam headlights must be used at all times
† Dipped-beam headlights compulsory in bad weather
†† Dipped-beam headlights compulsory in winter

Hire Cars

By the time you add up the cost of the ferry, fuel, motorway tolls, overnight accommodation, etc – not to mention how tiring it can be to drive the length and breadth of a country to reach the resort of your dreams, and the wear and tear (and depreciation) to your car – it may just be cheaper and quicker to take a charter flight to your destination and hire a car when you get there.

If you are used to driving on the other side of the road, it will feel strange at first to find the gear lever and hand brake on the wrong side, but take your time and you will soon get used to it.

Choose a reliable car-hire firm rather than some shady local outfit, and make the booking in advance to guarantee that the car of your choice will be waiting for you.

All the major car-hire firms have outlets at international airports and ferry terminals, so it may seem like the most convenient option to pick up your hire car as you step off the plane or boat. If, however, you have just flown for several hours or endured a rough crossing, getting into a car and driving on the wrong side of the road is the last thing you should do.

Statistics show that most accidents occur within a few kilometres of the ferry terminal or airport. Drivers who are unfamiliar with the handling of a hire car and confused by unfamiliar traffic signs, road markings, and traffic behaviour are prone to make mistakes.

Jetlag disturbs your pulse rate, body temperature, reaction time and decision-making abilities. And the effects are twice as bad flying West–East as they are going East–West (North–South journeys should not cause jetlag). On arrival, you should try to take it easy for the first twenty-four hours, or at least take a taxi to your hotel and get seven or eight hours' sleep before you think about driving.

And if you have taken tablets to control motion sickness, remember that the medication will remain in your system for several hours. So long as the effects last you could suffer fatigue and your judgement will be impaired, making you unfit to drive.

HIRE CAR CHECK LIST

Never sign for a hire car until you have looked it over. No reputable firm will mind you running through the following checks:

- Inspect tyre treads and pressures.
- Take a look at the spare tyre, too. Is there a jack and tools for changing the wheel?
- Make sure the tank is full.
- Check the oil level, the water level in the coolant system and screenwash reservoir, and the general condition of the engine compartment.
- All seat belts should fasten, unfasten and retract properly.
- Make sure all the doors open and close, and that the locks operate.
- Any dents, scratches and chips in the bodywork should be recorded before you leave, otherwise you could be charged for existing damage.
- Check the documentation you have been given. Query anything you are not certain about.
- Make sure you are given the handbook. It will help you to locate unfamiliar auxiliary controls and put right any problems that may occur.
- Satisfy yourself that the insurance meets your requirements and includes a damage waiver so that you don't end up paying for any damage to the hire car.

Take a final test drive round the block to make certain that the engine starts first time, that the clutch is smooth, the gears easy to find and operate, the brakes are even and don't screech, and all the instruments work.

Try not to look too much like a tourist. Muggers and thieves have been known to lay in wait on airport roads or in tourist areas, targeting hire cars filled with people who look like they're strangers in town.

If someone appears to be tailing you, or if they try to flag you down by indicating that something is wrong with the car, keep your doors locked and your windows up. Follow all the precautions listed in Personal Security.

long journeys

Ferries and Terminals

 Safety standards on all European ferry lines are strictly enforced, with the result that you should have little to worry about other than high seas and the occasional industrial dispute. The crew will direct you to the part of the car deck where you should park. Follow all guidelines displayed on the car deck and any instructions you are given by crew members:

- Leave the car in first gear rather than neutral, with the handbrake applied
- No smoking is permitted on the car decks.
- You will not be allowed to return to the car deck until the end of the voyage, so take everything you need with you. DON'T leave money or valuables in the car.
- If you have a caravan, make sure all forms of power supply such as gas cylinders are shut off.

- Before leaving the car, make a note of the location indicators so that you can find your way back.

On the passenger decks you will find rest areas, children's playgrounds, bureaux de change, duty-free shops, toilets, restaurants and bars.

> If the ferry ride will last only a couple of hours and you intend to drive on arrival, DON'T drink alcohol and DON'T take travel sickness pills which cause drowsiness.
> Even on an overnight crossing you should limit the amount you drink. Remember, the alcohol will stay in your system for up to twelve hours.

As the vessel approaches port, there will be an announcement telling all drivers to return to their cars. Be careful as you make your way through the lines of parked cars in case someone opens a door without looking first. Once in the car, ask everyone to fasten their seat belts and lock their doors, so you will be ready to go when the crew give the signal.

driving on the wrong side

! It takes time to adjust to driving on the 'wrong' side of the road, so take it easy and concentrate. Be especially careful after a short break, or when emerging from a service station or garage: unless you think about where you are and which side of the road you should be driving on, your instinctive reaction will be to drive on the side you're used to. Try sticking a piece of tape to the top of the steering wheel and writing on it 'DRIVE RIGHT'.

Getting Adjusted

If you are at the wheel of a hire car you will need to get used to the handbrake and gear lever being in an unfamiliar position – and you have to get used to the fact that first gear is now the one nearest to you and fifth is the furthest. But at least the pedals are in the right place and you have a clear view of the road to the offside.

If you are driving your own vehicle, the controls will feel familiar but you will have to contend with sitting on the side nearest the kerb and having a restricted view of the road. From this position, it is very difficult to see around the vehicle in front of you in order to judge whether it is safe to overtake or turn left.

A front-seat passenger who understands how to read the road and can judge speeds and distances accurately will be able to tell you when it is safe to pull out – but someone who doesn't drive shouldn't be asked to assume that sort of responsibility. Remember how long it took you as a learner to master the art of judging when it was safe to overtake.

The mirror on the passenger's side must be correctly adjusted so that you can see traffic approaching from behind. If you drive an old banger that doesn't have a mirror on that side, buy one that clips on, or the kind that sticks to the windscreen.

The Summit Europa mirror is an ingenious device which makes it possible to see around the vehicle in front without having to edge out of your lane.

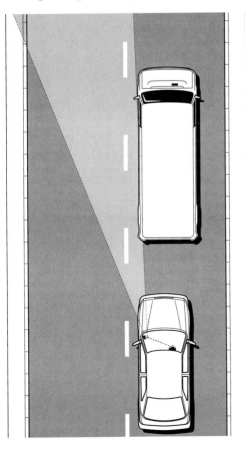

The dual mirror fits to the windscreen so that mirror A reflects the view of the road ahead into mirror B, which is positioned where the driver can easily glance at it.

Motoring Laws

Road signs and markings follow an internationally agreed standard (see Reading the Signs), so you should have little difficulty recognizing hazard warnings even if you don't speak the language. Most of the traffic regulations will be the same too, but BEWARE: there are bound to be some laws which you are not familiar with.

Penalties for infringing against the law can be severe – and the fact that you are a foreigner will not count in your defence. In many European countries the police are authorized to impose on-the-spot cash fines, and if you can't pay the fine (in cash or by credit cards) your car will be impounded.

> Don't run the risk of being stopped by the police and fined – familiarize yourself with the motoring regulations which apply in the countries you will be visiting before you leave home. Contact one of the motoring organizations for a list of guidelines.

SPEEDING

Speed limits vary from country to country and on different classes of road. In France, they change with the weather, too: when it's wet the speed limit will drop 10–20 kph, as signs by the roadside will warn you.

It's tempting to speed on motorways and main roads, especially when everybody else seems to be doing it, but speed traps are common and chances are you will get caught.

Keep your speed down whatever the maximum limit as this will give you more time to react to unfamiliar traffic customs and hazards. Also, you will find that road surfaces on some secondary roads leave a lot to be desired, with deep potholes and manhole covers standing proud of the tarmac.

> **REMEMBER**
> In Europe speed limits are given in kilometres per hour, not miles.

DRINKING AND DRIVING

Even though you're on holiday and it's tempting to enjoy a few glasses of wine or beer with your lunch, DON'T indulge if you are driving.

Permitted blood levels of alcohol vary from country to country (and in the USA, from state to state). In some countries the ban is absolute. You will fail the test in Sweden if you have more than 0.02 per cent of alcohol in your bloodstream. In Norway they're more lenient: you can get away with 0.05 per cent!

The penalties are severe too. Driving with 0.15 per cent alcohol in your system in Finland will land you in prison. Carrying an opened bottle of alcohol in the car in France and certain American states is an offence, even if you're not drinking from it. Elsewhere, the police will impose heavy fines for failing the blood test, with prison sentences for those whose drunken driving leads to accidents.

> Citizens of EC member states should know that if they are found guilty of a motoring offence in an EC country, the authorities back home will be made aware of it.

LIGHTS

For commonsense reasons, most countries insist that you switch on dipped headlights when driving at night. Sidelights and main-beam headlights are not acceptable. And if you are driving a left-hand drive car on the right (or a right-hand drive car on the left) headlamp beam deflectors must be fitted to avoid dazzling other road users.

In Denmark, Norway, Sweden, Finland and Iceland it is compulsory to have your dipped headlights on at all times – even in broad daylight.

On the approach to tunnels in Switzerland and Italy you will see signs advising you to switch on your dipped headlights. You should comply even if the tunnels appear well lit – the police will fine anyone they catch disobeying the law.

MINIMUM DRIVING AGE

You may have passed your test to become the proud owner of a valid driving licence, but that will not entitle you to drive worldwide if you fall below the minimum age limit.

In the following countries no one under the age of 18 is permitted to drive: Austria, Belgium, Bulgaria, Czech Republic, Finland, France, Hungary, Italy, Luxembourg, the Netherlands, Poland, Romania, Spain, Switzerland and Turkey.

> Throughout the EC there are restrictions prohibiting small children from travelling in the front passenger seat (unless they are carried in special baby or child seats). As a rule, children under 12 are safest travelling in the rear seats.

Tourist Traps

Some foreign rules and customs can take the unsuspecting visitor by surprise. Here are a few examples:

- In some Islamic countries there are laws against women driving.
- Trams always have priority in Belgium.
- It's customary to sound your horn (except in built-up areas) when overtaking in Belgium.
- Accidents involving elk and reindeer on Finnish roads must be reported to the police.
- When a French driver flashes his headlights at you, it's a warning that he's claiming the right of way, not an invitation for you to proceed.
- Running out of petrol on a German autobahn will earn you an on-the-spot fine.
- Rein in your road rage in Germany: the police will fine anyone they hear using foul language or making rude gestures.
- On Gibraltar the maximum speed limit is 30 kph (20 mph).
- Athens police have a novel way of letting drivers know they've parked illegally: they remove their registration plates.
- If you dent your car in Hungary or the Czech Republic, tell the police. You can't take a damaged car out of the country without a police report.
- It's against the law to sound your horn in Budapest.
- Illegal parking in Rome can land you in prison.

- Drivers in Milan never leave the handbrake on when parking on the city's crowded streets. Space is so tight that others wanting to park will roll cars back and forth to make a space.
- Nepalese drivers use the horn to tell people to overtake.
- Visit a car wash before driving in Romania, Russia or the Ukraine: it's illegal to drive a dirty car in these places.
- When parking on one-way streets in Spain and parts of Italy, check your calendar: on even dates, park on the side with even house numbers, on odd dates use the other side.

WARNING

Foreign or hired cars packed with luggage are favourite targets for local thieves. Try not to make life too easy for them by leaving the car unlocked.

Ensure your own security by trying not to look and act like a tourist who's lost in a strange land. Carry your valuables in an inside zipped pocket or a shoulder bag with a secure fastening. See Personal Security for more detailed advice on staying safe.

Breakdowns and Accidents

Breakdown procedures are pretty much the same wherever you go in the world:

- Try to get the car out of the way of traffic if possible.
- Get your passengers clear of the vehicle and away from the road.
- Warn other traffic. Use your hazard lights and sidelights.
- Place a red triangle 50 metres behind the car on a main road, 150 metres back on a motorway.
- Make sure no one stands behind the vehicle, obscuring the warning lights.

If you break down on the motorway, try to stop near an emergency telephone. A local recovery service will be sent to retrieve your vehicle.

Wait in a safe place, off the hard shoulder, just as you

Check your breakdown insurance policy. Some companies operate 24-hour phone lines which will organize assistance for you. This is especially helpful if you don't speak the language and would have difficulty explaining what you need.

would if you broke down on a motorway at home. Don't accept lifts from strangers, and don't hitch hike.

In the event of an accident, try to stay calm. Again, follow the same procedure as you would had the accident happened in your own country. Administer first aid and send for the emergency services if anyone is hurt.

In many countries it is a legal requirement that all accidents are reported to the police. Make sure you know the emergency phone numbers for each country you will visit.

- Exchange names, addresses, and insurance details with any other parties involved in the accident.
- Get statements from witnesses if the language barrier permits, otherwise settle for taking their names and addresses.
- Make a sketch map of the accident scene, and note the time, date, location, weather conditions, and any hazards which may have had a bearing on the accident.
- Use your camera or camcorder to photograph the scene, the position of the vehicles – showing any damage – and try to film any hazards that may have contributed to the incident.
- Co-operate with the police. They may seem biased towards their fellow countrymen, but don't challenge them on this. Hostility will get you nowhere.
- If the vehicle has to be towed away, make a note of the garage.
- Report the accident to your insurers as soon as possible. You should always carry their address with you.

Recovery and repair costs can be very high. Make sure your insurance cover includes recovery, repair charges, medical expenses, alternative transport, and accommodation.

COUNTRY	BUILT-UP AREAS KPH	NON-URBAN ROADS KPH	MOTORWAYS KPH	EMERGENCY PHONE NUMBERS		
				POLICE	FIRE	AMBULANCE
Australia	60	100	110	000	000	000
Austria	50	100	130	133	122	144
Belgium	60	90	120	101	100	100
Czech Republic	60	90	110	158	150	155
Denmark	50	80	100	112	112	112
Eire	30 mph	55 mph	55 mph	999	999	999
Finland	50	80	120	112	112	112
France	50	90 (80)*	130 (110)*	17	18	15
Germany	50	80	130†	110	112	110
Greece	50	80	100	100	199	166
Italy	50	90	130	113	113	113
Luxembourg	60	90	120	012	012	012
Netherlands	50	80	120	0611	0611	0611
Norway	50	80	90	‡	‡	‡
Portugal	60	90	120	115	115	115
Spain	50	90	120	091	091	091
Sweden	50	70	110	90000	90000	90000
Switzerland	50	80	120	117	118	144
United Kingdom	30 mph	60 mph	70 mph	999	999	999

*Figures shown in brackets are wet weather speed limits
† On some sections of the autobahn there is no upper speed limit
‡ See front cover of local telephone directory under SOS

For excitement and adventure, and the opportunity to really get away from it all, off-road driving is hard to beat. It can, however, be dangerous, so to make sure the fun doesn't get spoilt, you need to master techniques which will allow you to negotiate rough terrain safely.

off-road driving

BECOMING AN OFF-ROADER

KNOW YOUR VEHICLE Transmission systems • Locking hubs • Ground clearance

DRIVING A 4WD

ROUGH TERRAIN Mud • Driving in wheel tracks • Fording deep water • Dust and sand • Subkah • Steep hills • Pinnacles • Tobogganing • Rocky ground

RECOVERY Towing • Winching

EXPEDITIONS Supplies and equipment

becoming an off-roader

 Off-road driving requires certain skills that must be mastered before attempting a cross-country route. Though your vehicle may have been designed to cope with all kinds of terrain, it will take many hours of practice before the same can be said of the driver. If you are new to four-wheel drive, you must first take the time to familiarize yourself with the capabilities and performance of your vehicle. Start on flat ground, and wait until you've got the feel of the gears, braking, suspension, etc before moving on to even the gentlest of slopes.

Rather than learning by your mistakes, which can prove costly and dangerous, prepare yourself and your vehicle for the sorts of conditions you are likely to encounter. This chapter outlines some techniques for nursing a vehicle through rugged terrain, but the best way for a novice to learn is by watching an expert put the theory into practice. There are a number of off-road clubs and specialized training schools – check out the various magazines dedicated to off-road driving for details.

> Some areas are off-limits to 4WD vehicles. Always observe local bye-laws and regulations, and be a responsible driver. You have an obligation to avoid causing damage to the environment and property.

Know Your Vehicle

A four-wheel drive vehicle (4WD) has more gear levers and gadgets than a conventional car, making them seem complicated to the uninitiated. But once behind the wheel you'll soon get the hang of it.

In addition to constant four-wheel drive vehicles, it's possible to get models which can switch from rear-wheel drive to four-wheel. It's important, though, to revert to rear-wheel drive on Tarmac roads as leaving 4WD engaged could result in transmission problems.

TRANSMISSION SYSTEMS

Four-wheel drive vehicles have two gear ranges: high range for moderate terrain (or for Tarmac in icy or slippery conditions), and low range to give extra power and traction performance for cross-country driving and towing over difficult ground. To allow the driver to switch between gear ranges, 4WDs are fitted with a transfer box to maximize engine torque and ensure that there is always a suitable gear within the engine power band. On a constant 4WD the transfer box also houses a central differential lock which links the two differentials, one on each axle.

For maximum traction, the vehicle should be fitted with cross-axle differential locks. With open differentials, if one wheel loses traction then progress will depend entirely on the other axle. A limited slip (or self-locking) differential senses the amount of traction and automatically feeds power through to any wheel which stops, giving it traction. A fully-locking differential does the same thing, but is operated by the driver rather than kicking in automatically.

LOCKING HUBS

If you drive a 'part-time' 4WD rather than a constant, it's a good idea to fit freewheel hubs to the front wheels. When driving on normal roads you can then disengage the hubs (or,

TRANSMISSION WIND-UP

When travelling on uneven ground the front and rear axles will turn at different distances and speeds. This variation in tail-shaft rotation can result in transmission wind-up. On constant 4WD vehicles wind-up can be observed when the centre diff lock has been engaged.

Symptoms include wheel slippage on soft or loose surfaces, and tyres squealing on firm surfaces. The transfer lever becomes difficult to move, leading eventually to complete seizure, and a major component such as a differential or axle could fail.

On loose surfaces the transmission should gradually unwind of its own accord. If not, the situation can be remedied by reversing the vehicle until the transfer lever moves easily again.

if they are automatic, this will happen as soon as you switch from four-wheel drive to two-wheel) to reduce wear, and improve performance and fuel economy.

REMEMBER

Where manual freewheel hubs are fitted, you must engage them before setting off cross-country. If you forget, and the vehicle gets stuck in mud, you'll have a very messy job on your hands.

GROUND CLEARANCE

To prevent your rearranging the underside of your vehicle on boulders or other obstacles, you need to have an accurate idea of the distance from the chassis to the ground, and the angles of approach and departure.

The handbook will give the dimensions of your vehicle, or you can measure it yourself. To check ground clearance, look under the vehicle for the lowest point – usually the axle differentials – and measure the distance to the ground. Remove accessories such as foglights and tow bars which might snag on objects protruding from the ground.

To measure the approach and departure angles, with the car parked on flat ground, take a piece of cord and hold one end against the bumper (front for approach angle, rear bumper for departure angle) and the other against the point

PREPARING THE VEHICLE

• Fit a full-length sump guard made from a strong metal such as titanium to protect both the engine and gear box. It will also help the underbelly of the vehicle to slide through mud and sand.

• Wrap-around bull bars will protect the radiator and sidelights from collision damage, but don't fit bars which are much wider than the vehicle.

• To prevent damage caused by flying stones, fit covers over all lights. These can be removed for cleaning. Cling film will protect glass from the abrasive effects of sand.

• Insert canvas thorn gaiters between the tyre and inner tube to prevent thorns penetrating.

• If you're heading for a quagmire, invest in mud clogs. These are strong plastic devices with deep treads which can be fitted to a wheel in minutes, giving a greater surface area. In effect, they help the vehicle to float over the mud.

• Sand channels will get you out of trouble if you're planning on crossing sandy spaces. These are metal or plastic strips, usually 2 m long by 50 cm wide. Laid under the wheels, they will provide a firm surface to drive on.

• Armour the brake hoses.

• You may have to reroute the exhaust system to protect it and give better ground clearance. To ford deep water it may need to be raised so the tail pipe is above the cab.

• A full roll cage should be installed and padded.

• Check that everything under the bonnet – particularly the battery – is securely clamped in place.

where the nearest tyre touches the ground; the angle between the cord and the ground gives you the approach/departure angle.

NEVER tackle a slope which has a gradient higher than your vehicle's approach/departure angle.

off-road driving

WARNING

Keep a firm hold on the steering wheel, positioning your thumbs on the outside of the wheel rim. If you hook them inside the steering wheel and the vehicle hits a rock or pothole, the wheel will jerk with sufficient force to break your thumbs or dislocate them.

Driving a 4WD

A slight adjustment to your driving position is required for graded and off-road driving. The driver's seat should be raised and set closer to the steering wheel, and less inclined than for road use. Make sure that you are well supported.

On long cross-country journeys, it's advisable to wear a neck brace to support your head and reduce discomfort. A brace to support the back can also be worn. Elbows should be kept near to your sides.

Make sure that each of your passengers has a seat and seatbelt, securely anchored to the vehicle. Everything inside the passenger compartment should be tied down so that if the vehicle should roll over or collide with an obstruction you won't be hit by flying objects.

The secret to driving on difficult terrain is to keep the vehicle moving without losing traction. Inexperienced drivers tend to apply too much pressure on the controls, leading to excessive wheelspin. As with a conventional car, the wheels may lock when you try braking hard on a loose surface, so go gently on the brakes. Generally engine braking alone will be sufficient. Use rapid gear changes to keep the engine within the power band. Practise the technique on a flat track or field (but remember to get the owner's permission first) to build up your confidence before putting it to the test on rough terrain.

Go easy on the accelerator, too. If you drive slowly you will allow yourself time to assess any obstacles. When in doubt, stop the vehicle and carry out reconnaissance on foot (or, better still, get your passengers to climb out and check that you have sufficient clearance – the vehicle will be that much lighter and the clearance greater as a result).

Maintain a safe distance between vehicles and only allow one vehicle at a time to negotiate an obstacle. This way, only one vehicle will get stuck and it can be recovered by the others.

Don't try showing off – your passengers won't be impressed if you misjudge a hazard and the vehicle overturns. And don't let the speed creep up even when the going is good; dust and mud may conceal rocks or potholes which will bring you to an abrupt and uncomfortable halt. Second or third gear will see you through most off-road situations, switching to first for steep downhill runs.

The height of 4WD vehicles makes them prone to roll over when they corner badly, so exercise caution and don't try cornering on a hill unless you are experienced enough to judge accurately whether it's possible or not.

rough terrain

 Once you leave the Tarmac behind the nearest thing you will find to a conventional road surface is 'Black Top'. These metal roads are occasionally found in remote areas, but for the most part you will be driving on tracks made by animals or humans, and graded roads.

Graded roads are made by scraping the surface with a bulldozer blade; they have no prepared surface, drainage, or road markings – which can make driving hazardous. In dry weather you may have to contend with dust clouds which limit visibility; in wet conditions the road may be washed away by heavy storms, or, undermined by rain, it could collapse under the weight of a vehicle; at best there will be slippery sticky mud and, if the road is much-travelled, deep ruts; in places the road may be hard to define, especially where it crosses streams and river beds; and even where you can see the road, the way may be blocked by fallen trees and other obstacles.

On gravel roads, stones will be thrown up from the loose surface, making it vital that you leave a safe distance between yourself and the vehicle in front. Braking on gravel is not unlike driving on ball bearings; apply too much pressure on the pedal and the wheels will spin like crazy.

Tall grass and brush may conceal dangerous hazards such as barbed wire, rusting farm machinery, rocks, holes, and ant hills. If in doubt, get out and walk the route to check that it's passable. In arid areas, vegetation is protected by tough thorns which can penetrate tyre sidewalls.

Wildlife can also pose problems. A high-speed collision with a large animal such as a deer, kangaroo, or buffalo can write off a vehicle. Smaller animals can also wreck your 4WD by undermining the road with their burrows or digging holes that will cause you to overturn. Keep your speed down and your eyes peeled to avoid these hazards.

Mud

Mud is one of the trickiest surfaces to deal with. It's slippery, causing loss of traction, it creates a sucking effect which retards the vehicle's progress, and it can be very difficult to gauge the depth of the mud – or what hazards lie concealed beneath it.

Soft ground can be identified by lush vegetation, particularly rushes and tall grasses. Low-lying areas and water courses must always be treated with suspicion. Before committing your vehicle, always check the depth of the mud using a stick and a brave volunteer – after all, your passengers must have known they were in for a dirty weekend! The consistency of the mud should also be taken into account as it will affect your progress. Heavy clay is easier to cross than wet soft soil stirred to a liquid.

The secret to driving on mud is to prevent wheelspin and keep the vehicle moving. Chains or ropes fixed to the tyres will give more traction. Low range second gear will provide all the power and control you need. Don't over rev, and keep the wheels straight. Select a route that will take you directly across the mud rather than having to deviate around a tree or large rock, and proceed one vehicle at a time. Don't enter the mud until the vehicle in front has successfully cleared it.

If you do lose traction or the vehicle sinks in deep mud and grounds the chassis, STOP. No amount of power will free the wheels, and the more they spin the deeper you will go. Provided you're not in too deep, it may be possible to get

When the trail is blocked by a fallen tree, cross it at an angle rather than head on. Make sure you have sufficient ground clearance. If the tree is exceptionally large, you will have to build approach and departure ramps on either side.

off-road driving

CROSSING DEEP RUTS

Always aim to cross ruts or a deep ditch at a diagonal angle (30° should do it) rather than head on. If you try crossing at right-angles the front wheels will probably end up stuck in the rut while the rear wheels spin helplessly, unable to gain sufficient traction to pull the vehicle out.

To keep all four wheels on the ground throughout, approach the ruts diagonally and as slowly as possible. If one wheel should lift and spin, your lockable differential will ensure that the wheels in contact with the ground will still drive.

out by selecting reverse and backing out slowly. Failing that, you will have to put your recovery equipment to use: see **Recovery** below.

After a muddy trip, always wash the vehicle down thoroughly and inspect the hubs and wheel bearings for signs of damage.

DRIVING IN WHEEL TRACKS

Although it may seem to be the simplest solution, driving in ruts left by other vehicles is not always a good idea. For a start, you need to be certain that the ground clearance on your 4WD is equal to that of the vehicle which left the track, otherwise you could be grounded.

Rather than driving in a deep rut or channel, straddle the sides. Keep one wheel on the central ridge and the other on the verge, proceeding slowly and making sure the vehicle remains on the level. If it is allowed to tilt to one side, the lower wheels will probably sink into the ground.

When there's no alternative but to drive in the rut, imagine that you're driving a train along a railway line. Resist the temptation to oversteer; all it takes is a light touch on the steering wheel to keep the vehicle following the tracks. If traction is minimal, rock the steering wheel from side to side to allow the tread to clear and bite on the edge of the ruts.

Keep watching the way ahead to make sure the ruts don't get deeper than your ground clearance will tolerate. When the time comes for you to turn off, stop the vehicle and dig an exit point. Use logs or stones to form a ramp which will get you clear of the ruts.

Fording Deep Water

Before attempting to cross any stretch of water make sure the vehicle is well prepared – especially if you drive a petrol-engine 4WD. Protect all parts that will be affected by the water – electronics, air intakes, breather tubes, engine compartment – by coating with a de-watering spray/WD40. The exhaust may need to be extended and raised so that the tail pipe is clear of the water level. Slackening the fan belt will prevent the fan from splashing water over the engine, but remember to tighten it again once clear of the water.

Look out for hazards such as sunken branches, large rocks, and deep holes. Ripples or waves that appear to stay in one position usually indicate an obstacle on the bottom deflecting water upwards. A calm area of surface water may be a sign that the water is exceptionally deep at this point.

Avoid weed beds as these can be hazardous. Shingle is the easiest surface to negotiate.

Stop the vehicle and assess the entry and exit points. The vehicle must be able to enter the water and climb out safely without getting stuck or hung up. These points will not necessarily be in line. Choose the best sites available.

Next, take a good look at the current. Strong currents can easily sweep a vehicle away. Beware of flash floods: a low-lying river or stream can be turned into a raging torrent in minutes by water flowing down from nearby hills after heavy rain.

Throw in a small stick and watch its progress. Water runs faster where the banks converge and on the outside of bends. Shallows tend to be rocky and wide, offering the best fording place.

Clear water can be deceptive – there may be hidden depths or underwater obstacles. The only way to check the depth is to test it physically. Adult passengers should wade across to select the best route. All unnecessary clothing should be removed to keep it dry, but leave boots on as these will give better grip than bare feet. Each person in the group must be linked by a safety rope as they line up behind the strongest, who should carry a pole to aid balance and test for depth. Turning at a slight angle, back towards the opposite bank, the group should follow the leader slowly and carefully across, taking cautious sideways steps rather than great strides, and testing each foothold before using it.

The driver should unfasten his or her seatbelt and wear a flotation device when fording deep water. Everything inside the vehicle should be lashed down securely. Delicate water-sensitive items such as radios and perishable rations should be removed or wrapped in waterproof material.

Select low-range gear and drive slowly across, making sure that the bow wave at the front of the vehicle doesn't rise high enough to flood the engine. Proceed at a steady crawl until you reach the other side. Don't change gear and don't stop – the water will wash away the silt under your tyres making pulling away again difficult.

Resist the temptation to speed up as you get closer to the far bank. Climb clear of the water and if possible leave the vehicle on the slope so water will drain, but don't park on a steep slope as you may have trouble getting started again. Stop for a while so that the heat from the engine can dry the electricals. Before moving off, check all equipment and test the brakes. Drive with a light pressure on the brake pedal to heat the pads and dry them.

Dust and Sand

Dust is a killer. It accounts for many accidents and must be treated with the greatest respect. Never drive blindly into a dust cloud. Try to keep upwind, and allow sufficient space between vehicles for the dust to settle. The lower the speed the less the dust, so ease off the accelerator.

Extra filters and more frequent servicing will be required for vehicles operating in dusty conditions. All grease and oil will attract dust, causing components to seize up.

The best time to drive on sand is early in the morning, after a heavy dew. As the day progresses and the sun heats the sand, it becomes more 'fluid' and difficult to drive on. Always proceed one vehicle at a time, keeping the windows closed and following the tracks of the vehicle in front.

Smooth-treaded sand tyres allow the vehicle to float over the loose surface. Alternatively, you can deflate the tyres to around 12 psi (0.83 bars), but remember that ground clearance will be reduced as a result, so special care must be taken to avoid small rocks and scrub that would normally be straddled without difficulty. Don't forget to reinflate the tyres as soon as you reach firm ground. If the tyres are deflated too much and wheelspin occurs, the valves could be ripped out. Short valves are better than long ones and dust caps must be fitted. Use a gauge to check the pressure when reinflating, preferably when the tyres are cold.

The basic principle for crossing soft sand is keep moving in high range 4WD and don't change gear. If you suddenly come upon an area of soft sand engage 4WD and change down quickly – don't keep revving up because wheelspin will just dig the vehicle in deeper. On flat stretches take the sand at speed. As the vehicle slows down, rapid gear-changing will be required to maintain momentum. Keep the front wheels straight to reduce resistance. As momentum is lost, swing the wheel from side to side to carry on going forward. Getting crew members to bounce up and down over the driving wheels will improve traction.

If you start to sink, select reverse gear and drive out backwards over your own tracks. When this doesn't work, you may need to rock the vehicle: select reverse and accelerate, then quickly engage second gear and accelerate to create a rocking motion which should free the vehicle.

Should the vehicle get completely stuck:

- Don't switch off the engine as this will cause overheating. Leave the engine running and lift the bonnet if the delay looks set to be a long one.
- Reduce the tyre pressures.
- Place anything available under the wheels to aid traction. Canvas sheets are ideal. Attach them to the vehicle with strings so they can be pulled aboard without your having to stop and retrieve them. Seats, sacking, brushwood, stones, and vegetation, can also be used, but be careful when placing them to stay clear of the hot exhaust pipe or you could get burnt. And stand well clear when the vehicle starts moving as items can come flying out as the wheels spin.
- Dig channels for the wheels and clear sand away from the chassis and any components.
- Drive slowly to avoid wheelspin. Once moving don't stop

until firm ground is reached. If you have no alternative but to stop on sand, wait until you come to a downhill section.

SAND DUNES

Sand dunes are unstable, particularly the smaller, less well-established ones, and inexperienced drivers would do best to avoid them.

Stop and assess the route before driving up the side of a dune, and make sure you know what's on the far side of a ridge before committing yourself to a descent. You may have to knock the top off a sharp ridge to reduce the chance of grounding your vehicle.

Red sand is normally harder than white, which tends to be freshly blown. Dunes always follow a distinctive pattern determined by the prevailing wind. Slip faces occur on the side away from the wind direction, and are always softer than the upslope.

SUBKAH

Wet subkah or quicksand is found on the fringes of lakes and rivers. It can be well above the water level and appears dry. Be suspicious of patches of sand darker than the surrounding area. Dry subkah is the residue left after a lake or river has dried up. Sometimes it has a hard crust on top like white powder.

Look for entry and exit points made by other vehicles and stick to these tracks. Treat subkah as you would loose sand. Maintain a constant speed and try to avoid stopping or making sharp turns.

After crossing dry subkah, clean the vehicle using an air line to blow away the fine dust. Engine filters should be cleaned too.

Steep Hills

The best way over steep hills is straight up and down. The steeper the climb, the less deviation across the slope can be made – driving diagonally is the quickest way to roll over. Select the correct low-range gear for the climb and remain in that gear throughout the ascent. Keep the revs up and if you feel vehicle struggling to maintain momentum, accelerate the vehicle gently.

Using the clutch or brakes can cause the wheels to lock, making the vehicle slide out of control. If the vehicle stalls on the ascent, resume the climb by restarting the engine without touching the clutch. To do this, select the correct gear and use the starter motor. The vehicle will creep forward; when the engine fires, drive on up the slope.

If the vehicle cannot make the climb and you need to retreat, apply the handbrake (or, if the handbrake won't hold the vehicle, use the brake pedal), depress the clutch quickly and select reverse gear in the lowest range, making sure that the front wheels are straight. Come off the clutch and press the brake pedal to hold the vehicle, then release the handbrake and allow the vehicle to back down the slope under control. Don't touch the clutch until you're on level ground or the vehicle will freewheel.

If the engine has stalled, keep your foot on the brake while turning the ignition. As soon as the engine fires, lift your foot but don't remove it from the pedal until you are certain that reverse gear has been engaged. It is now safe to remove your foot from the brake as engine compression will control the vehicle.

PINNACLES

Avoid high points where the vehicle chassis grounds on the summit leaving all four wheels in the air. To recover a vehicle perched on an obstacle, get crew members to bounce up and down on a bumper – taking great care that no one falls under a wheel as the vehicle comes off.

DESCENDING A SLOPE

Stop on the crest just as the vehicle is balanced to descend and select the best route down. Keep in the same low gear and let the vehicle descend using engine braking power to control your speed. Stay off the clutch and brake pedals. If an emergency arises and you need to stop mid-descent, switch off the ignition to halt the vehicle.

TOBOGGANING

Descending a steep slope in too low a gear can lead to stones and mud building up under the wheels so that the vehicle toboggans. If this happens, accelerate a little to leave the build-up behind.

Rocky Ground

Rocky ground is hard on a vehicle's suspension and tyres. Proceed slowly, memorizing what lies in front, and crawl over the obstacles. Use low-range 4WD to give maximum control. Always ensure that you have sufficient ground clearance. Straddling large rocks can cause damage to the sump, mountings, differentials, and exhaust. Have a passenger direct you by standing to the front and giving hand signals – if you have to lean out of the window you could bang your head when the vehicle hits a bump.

Rocky tracks that carry a high volume of traffic tend to get corrugated, like the surface of a washboard. If you drive too slowly the vehicle shakes itself to bits. Adjust your speed so this effect is reduced.

BLOW HOLES

Where possible, take a detour round these deep holes. Where this is impossible, the best way out of a blow hole is to drive in a straight line using forward and reverse gears. Select the best route and reverse back in a straight line as far as possible, then drive forward to get as high as you can. Reverse back and repeat. Each time it should be possible to get a little further.

recovery

When you've dug yourself into a hole, bearing down on the accelerator is not going to get you out – it will only make the wheels spin and dig you in even deeper. You may just be able to dislodge yourself by rocking the vehicle, switching quickly from reverse to forward gear and moving a little further each time. Failing that, get out of the car and assess the situation from ground level. Will it help to place sacking or brushwood under the wheels to improve traction? Will digging a trench do the trick? Or would it be possible to jack up each wheel so that stones can be packed beneath each wheel for extra traction? Whichever of these options you choose, you will need plenty of bin liners handy to put the soiled kit in.

Towing

Inertia or snatch ropes are among the most popular for recovery use. These store kinetic energy as they stretch, so when the towing vehicle accelerates forward stretching the rope to its limit, the inertia built up in the rope is suddenly released, contracting the rope to its normal size and snatching the stuck vehicle free.

To tow a vehicle free, first select the best exit route. Make use of downhill slopes where possible, but it's more important to go where the firm ground is.

WARNING

Inertia ropes exert tremendous force – if there is any rust or structural weakness in the anchor point on either vehicle, that piece of metal work will be torn loose and sent flying through the air, endangering bystanders and vehicles nearby. Snatch ropes should therefore only be anchored to structurally sound vehicles.

off-road driving

Dig around the wheels and any other parts that are grounding. Fill in holes that might hinder the tow and place sacking or other materials under the wheels to aid traction. Prepare the vehicle by straightening the wheels and disengaging the handbrake; put the gear in neutral.

Attach the rope to a secure tow hook (these should be fitted front and rear on a 4WD). Tow ropes should be fitted with a shackle and pin at either end. Never tie a knot in a tow line as this reduces the breaking strain by half.

Once the line is fitted, start both engines. One helper will be needed to supervise the operation and signal to both drivers; he should stand at a distance double the distance of the towing line in case it snaps. All other bystanders should retreat well beyond this point and leave the talking to the supervisor.

With a conventional tow rope, take up the slack and, when the line is taut, the supervisor should signal both vehicles to proceed in low gear. When using a snatch rope there is no need to take up the slack first; the towing vehicle does this by accelerating forward. Once both vehicles are on firm ground, stop and retrieve the gear.

Winching

Winching can be dangerous. To ensure that no one gets hurt, follow these rules:

- Always wear protective gloves when winching as the cable develops burrs which can cause deep cuts. Wear strong boots with a good grip to reduce the risk of slipping.
- Never straddle or jump a winch cable when in use.
- Don't jerk the winch line or use it like a tow strap.
- Place the hand control on the dashboard or bonnet while people are handling the cable. If you hold it in your hand, one slip of the thumb could cause injury.
- Don't pull your hook into the roller fairlead. Release power at least a metre (3 ft) from the winch and secure hook around bumper.
- Don't overrun your winch line. Always make sure there are at least five turns left around the drum before winching.

- Place a piece of canvas over the middle of the cable. This will prevent the line recoiling completely if it breaks.
- Don't try to rewind the spool evenly while winching. Finish the job, then pull out the line and rewind it neatly.
- Keep everyone well clear during winching.
- Always use the tow hooks on the vehicle being recovered, or the chassis or a spring shackle. If you have to operate your vehicle while it is being recovered, raise the bonnet to give protection in case the cable snaps.

An 8000 lb winch will provide sufficient power to recover a 4WD vehicle. In addition, you will need a strap or tree sling, snatch blocks, and shackles.

Using a snatch block will double the winch rating and make recovery safer. Where there is no good anchorage directly ahead of the winch, you can use the pulley to link two anchorage points and effectively pull round a corner. If no natural anchorage points are available, attach the cable to the spare wheel then bury it.

To prevent damage to trees, always use a sling placed low round the trunk. If there are only small trees to hand, place the strap low around several of them.

A vehicle that isn't tightly stuck may be freed by a direct pull from a second vehicle. The winching vehicle should be in low-range reverse gear, apply power slowly while winching. The stuck vehicle should be in low range first gear, gently applying power to assist with the recovery.

If this proves ineffective, use the double blocking method. Attach the snatch block to the stuck vehicle and run the winch cable through this back to the towing hook on the winching vehicle. As before, reverse while winching with the stuck vehicle assisting by applying power.

To remove a fallen tree blocking the path, select a strong point such as a rock or mature tree and attach the strap and snatch block to it. Place a second strap round the tree and attach the cable. Run the cable back through the snatch block and use the winch to pull the deadfall clear.

A vehicle which has rolled over can be righted by placing a strap all the way round the vehicle body. Route the cable so that it will cause minimal damage – avoid sharp edges and vital components.

expeditions

Journeys cross-country in remote areas must be thoroughly planned. Study the map to select a route which avoids hazards such as high ground, rivers and streams where possible. Break it down into daily stages, calculating how long it will take you to cover the distance, taking into account the terrain, climate, vehicle loads, quality of tracks. Remember, it's better to over-estimate and end up with time to spare rather than pushing hard all of the time. Determine where you will stop for lunch and other breaks each day, and where you will stop each night. Allow time during daylight hours to inspect and carry out maintenance on the vehicles.

Having plotted your route on the map and marked it to show estimated times of arrival, leave a copy with someone in authority. Call base at regular intervals to confirm your progress. This way, if anything goes wrong they will be able to send rescuers to the correct area.

Good communication is vital. Carry a radio with rechargeable batteries and spare parts. Select frequencies that work in that region and appoint an emergency frequency that will be manned 24 hours a day. Decide on a call sign and set times of day when you will contact base.

Radios are fragile and must be protected. Secure them on a sprung mounting and fix the aerial to the roof – don't forget the additional height when passing under low branches and overhangs.

Supplies and Equipment

Rations should be well packed, easy to prepare, and non perishable. Carry high-energy foods like corned beef, rather than tins of stew which are full of water. Each person will need about 1500 calories per day. In hot countries, allow 5 litres (8 pints) of water per person per day for drinking and cooking only. Large billy cans are ideal for communal cooking and brewing. Each person should have their own plate, mug, and spoon. The cooking stove should run on the same fuel as the vehicle. Pack a large funnel to make filling it with fuel easier.

The contents of the medical kit will depend on the skill of the medic. In remote areas the medic must be prepared to deal with all emergencies from suturing to CPR.

Before setting off, have the vehicle thoroughly overhauled. Get all faults rectified and have any necessary adaptations carried out professionally. Don't exceed the manufacturer's recommended axle loadings for the vehicle.

Large capacity fuel tanks will give greater range. Fit two tanks so if one gets damaged there is a reserve (the same applies to water tanks). All fuel lines should be routed in chassis members for protection. Install extra filters for dusty conditions. Remember to carry oil, brake fluid, de-watering spray, and distilled water. Fit at least two spare wheels to the

Book out

Stick to the planned route where possible

Contact base at regular intervals

Keep the speed down and avoid hazards

Carry out reconnaissance on foot if in doubt

Never risk your life or the lives of your passengers

outside of the vehicle. Position them so they balance and don't affect the vehicle's centre of gravity. You will also need a foot pump or compressor for inflating tyres.

One advantage of carrying extra supplies of water and fuel in cans is that by offloading the cans the vehicle can be lightened to negotiate difficult terrain or a weak bridge. There is an international colour code for containers: water = white, petrol = red, lubricants = green, diesel = yellow. All containers must be strapped down and stowed with the filler caps uppermost.

A front-mounted power winch should be standard equipment. Self-recovery can be achieved with this. If there are several vehicles in the party have at least one vehicle with a rear-mounted winch as well.

A conventional jack will sink into loose surfaces like sand, so you should carry a baseboard to stand the jack on. Or take an air bag of the kind used by the rescue services. These can be inflated by plugging into the exhaust pipe.

Don't skimp on tools, spares and supplies. Out in the wilderness there are no garages, no motoring organizations, no petrol stations, no supermarkets, and no doctors. In an emergency there will be no one to bail you out.

Travelling on unfamiliar roads can be stressful. It's easy to get lost and, because you don't know the lie of the land, hazards can take you by surprise. But it needn't be that way.

reading the signs

PLANNING YOUR JOURNEY Maps • Motorway travel • Route cards • Lost! • Route planners • Navigating

READING THE ROAD Road markings

TRAFFIC SIGNS Junctions • Road layout • Priority signs • Speed restrictions • Hazards • Level crossings

LOOKING FOR CLUES

planning your journey

Stress-free travel begins at home. With a little careful planning you can knock hours off your journey and avoid many of the pitfalls that might otherwise ruin your trip: like getting lost and driving round and round in circles; feeling an increasing sense of panic and frustration because the fuel tank is almost empty or you're going to be late; having to stop and ask the way, even though it means exposing yourself to danger – although it's more likely that the helpful stranger will turn out to be a complete idiot, giving out wrong directions and sending you even further off course.

Maps

There is a huge range of maps available, ranging from large-scale survey maps, which cover a small area in great detail, to road atlases, which cover whole countries – even continents – showing only the motorway networks and main roads.

The scale of a typical survey map is 1:50,000, which translates as 2 cm to 1 km (1.25 in to 1 mile). Every topographical feature is recorded: hills, valleys, rivers, forests, roads, footpaths, field and parish boundaries, buildings, car parks, lay-bys, public toilets, telephone boxes, hospitals, police stations, post offices, public houses, etc.

These maps are ideal where in-depth local knowledge is needed. For example, from looking at the symbol on the map you will be able to see whether a church has a tower or a spire – which can be very helpful when you're looking for a landmark to pinpoint your location.

When travelling on icy roads in winter – or towing a caravan/trailer at any time of year – it's vital to know where the tricky hills are. The contours on a survey map will help you identify steep gradients and devise a route that avoids the worst of them. You can anticipate where the mist will linger on valley bottoms, where ice is likely to form in shaded areas, which areas of high ground will be most exposed in strong winds or blizzards, where rivers may flood in heavy rains, and so on.

For urban driving, you will need detailed street maps. If you drive regularly in a city, it's well worth investing in the largest scale street atlas you can find – preferably one which shows one-way systems operating on main roads. It's much easier to find your place on a map which shows 4 inches to the mile than one where the scale is so small you need a magnifying glass to read the street names. When there's no one alongside to navigate for you, it's possible to sneak a glance at a large map while held up at traffic lights; with a small street atlas the lights will have changed several times before you figure out where you are on the map.

BOTTLENECKS

Given the choice, it's always better to take a detour around a town or city rather than getting caught up in heavy town-centre traffic. The ring road may look to be the longer route, but you can bet it will be faster than crawling through congested streets with traffic lights at every junction.

If, however, you find yourself with no alternative but travel into town, study a street map beforehand and try to identify potential bottlenecks where rush-hour traffic will be at its most congested. For example, where a city is divided in two by a river, crossing points may be few and far between, leading to jams on the approach roads to bridges, tunnels and ferry services. And if one crossing point is closed to traffic for any reason, those on either side will be twice as congested as usual. Monitor traffic bulletins on the radio or television before you set off, or call one of the telephone information lines run by the major motoring organizations to check that the route is clear.

MOTORWAY TRAVEL

It's impracticable to use survey maps for motorway driving. Because each map covers only a few miles only a tiny fraction of the journey would appear on any one sheet. You would need to fill the car with maps, changing from one to another every five minutes. And none of the minute detail would be of use to you in any case.

Motorway route-planning is a matter of noting road numbers and the junctions where you will enter and exit the motorway, as well as the location of service stations where you will stop to rest and refuel. Use a road atlas to get you to the general vicinity of your destination, and save the survey maps for finding your way around once you're there.

ROUTE CARDS

If you are travelling alone, it won't be possible to keep your eyes on the road and study the map at the same time. Before setting off on an unfamiliar route, use a road atlas to draw up a route card. Keep it simple and use large, clear handwriting so that all you need do is glance quickly at the card to remind yourself of the route.

List a series of checkpoints that will keep you on course:

- The number of each motorway or major road you will be using.
- The junctions where you need to turn off.
- Names of major towns or cities along the road – it may be easier to spot a sign for OXFORD than one for the A420, for example.
- Jot down the approximate mileage for each stage of your journey, then you'll know if you overshoot the mark.
- Plan your rest breaks. For safety reasons, you should stop every two hours (less, in hazardous conditions or when driving by night), so identify the places where you will pause for a rest along the way and write them on your route card.

Fatigue is a killer, and it can creep up on you so subtly that you will hardly be aware of the symptoms. Stop, regardless of whether you're running late, and even if you don't feel that you need a break. It's better to be safe than sorry.

A seatbelt that has been worn in an accident should be checked by an expert. The whole assembly may need to be replaced even if there is no visible sign of damage.

Country Road Checkpoints

Country roads are more difficult to navigate than motorways because it's not simply a question of counting the junctions until you reach your turn-off point. There may be tracks leading off which are not marked on the map, and it can be difficult to tell whether a narrow lane is the entrance to a private property or the road to the next village.

Use a survey map to locate landmarks which will provide clearly visible checkpoints. Bear in mind that unforeseen delays or bad weather could mean that you reach the area after dark, in thick fog, or when the whole area is covered by a blanket of snow. Look for features that will be obvious even in poor visibility, such as hills, bridges, level crossings, or large buildings set close to the road.

In daylight you should be able to see signposts for attractions such as theme parks, places of interest, airfields and golf courses. Use these to verify your position.

Make a mental note of place names that you pass. If you have to stop and check your position on the map, knowing where you've been will help you to determine where you have arrived!

LOST!

If you do get lost, provided you're alert it should soon become apparent that all is not well. As soon as you realize that, according to your calculations, you should have reached a certain landmark or place by now but it's nowhere in sight, find a safe place to park – preferably within sight of a signpost or landmark.

Check the map and try to identify place names or landmarks you have passed. If you are still totally confused, retrace your steps until you can identify with certainty where you are on the map.

Obviously, a sense of direction is a valuable instinct in these situations. Provided you have a rough idea of where your destination lies in relation to your current location, you can improvise a route. But always build in a safety factor – 'If I don't reach landmark x in 3 miles, I've guessed wrong about my location – rather than driving on for miles in hope.

Route Planners

If studying maps and plotting a route from A to B doesn't thrill you, help is at hand.

Most motoring organizations offer a route-planning service which is free to members (non-members may have to pay a small charge). Simply let them know your starting point and destination, and they will provide a full computer printout giving directions. The route will be tailor-made to suit your specifications, whether you are looking for the quickest route; the cheapest (avoiding toll roads); the most scenic; or one which avoids low bridges and steep hills (if you're driving a high-sided vehicle or towing a caravan).

If you have a personal computer at home or in the office, there a number of software packages which will generate maps and/or detailed itineraries. Some will even estimate the costs involved.

Even more convenient are handheld or dashboard-mounted computerized route planners. Simply type in your starting point and destination, together with any special requirements (for example, routes which avoid motorways or low bridges), and you will be given step-by-step directions, plus estimated time of arrival and fuel costs. And if you run into heavy traffic along the way, the routefinder will offer you an alternative at the press of a button. The database is held on a memory card, so you can update the system, or insert data on foreign countries, simply by buying a new card.

At the top end of the price range, you can subscribe to a service which provides not only route guidance and traffic information but also breakdown assistance. Run by the larger motoring organizations, systems such as OnStar connect you with an operator who, having pinpointed your vehicle's location using the satellite global positioning system, will talk you through the route to your destination and warn of traffic delays in the area. With this system installed, you don't have to worry about giving your location in the event of a breakdown – the recovery vehicle will be issued with a precise map reference for your position the moment you contact the operator.

Navigating

Whatever method you use to plan your route, carry an up-to-date road map in the car so you can verify your location. Make sure you know how to read a map properly – it's amazing how many people get it wrong.

Start by making sure that the map is facing the way you are travelling. This makes it much easier to follow directions on the page: a left-hand junction on the map will appear on your left. Turn the map every time you adjust your course.

TRAINING TO NAVIGATE

Rally drivers can negotiate difficult courses by day or night and at very high speeds because there is always a navigator sitting alongside them, reading out pace notes. These notes record accurately every bend, elevation, turning and obsta-

MAP-READING AIDS

Many people experience motion sickness when reading a map while travelling. The secret is to hold the map as high as possible (obviously, you can't do this while you're driving!).

To avoid eye strain, fix a flexible light on the navigator-passenger's side, and carry a magnifying glass to help you read maps with small type and lots of detail.

A car compass mounted on the dashboard will keep you on course and help you make the correct decision when faced with an unmarked junction. It's also invaluable in large towns when a one-way system carries you off in the wrong direction. Provided you know the general direction you should be heading in, the compass will set you back on target.

cle. The driver will be told the distance between points, and warned of the severity of each adverse camber, bend or gradient. Thanks to the navigator, he knows exactly when to turn and what to expect.

In everyday driving, pace notes are replaced by a route card, but the principles should be the same. To test your navigational skills, try this simple exercise.

NAVIGATION EXERCISE

With the aid of a survey map, select a route in a remote area where there are lots of tracks and minor roads. The 'course' should include lots of changes of direction and different gradients.

Now compile pace notes which record each bend and gradient, and any distinctive features that will help to verify your position. For example:

'Short climb, 100 metres to crest; sharp right over crest; 200 metres down to bridge; slight right-hand curve; house on left; straight on for 500 metres to crossroads; turn left...'

Have a friend drive while you navigate the course.

Remember, this is a navigation exercise, NOT a race. Drive slowly and carefully.

You will soon come to appreciate the value of pace notes and see how helpful it can be to a driver to have advance warning of each hazard.

Now try preparing a route card for a drive in the country using the same techniques. Take a survey map and plan a route from A to B. Section off each stage of the journey using significant landmarks along the way – bridges, crossroads, churches, etc – as checkpoints.

For example, imagine that stage one begins at a hump-back bridge. Continue until you reach the crossroads and turn left – at which point stage two begins. Count the junctions – the turning you want is the fourth (stage three). A short way along the road, to the left hand side, lies a wooded area. The inn you are heading for is situated on the edge of the woods.

Your imaginary route card would read:

HUMP-BACK BRIDGE
LEFT AT CROSSROADS
TAKE 4TH TURNING
WOODS ON LEFT
INN

reading the road

The ability to anticipate what lies around the next bend or over the brow of a hill is something every driver should cultivate. There's no mystery or magic involved, and you don't have to be a clairvoyant. It's simply a matter of knowing how to read the signs and act upon the information they provide.

Road markings and signs serve two purposes. They remind drivers of the rules and regulations which must be obeyed. And they give warning of potential dangers up ahead. Those who ignore the warnings often find out about hazards the hard way. Instead of applying gentle, progressive corrections to the car's course and speed, they have no option but to slam on the brakes and swerve clear – if they're lucky – at the last minute.

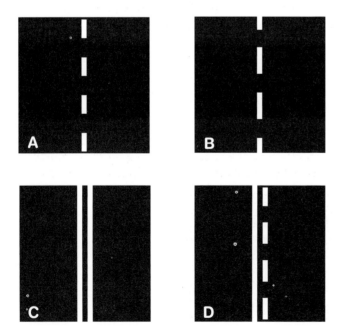

Road Markings

Don't take road markings for granted: those lines along the centre or edges of the road give useful information about the traffic conditions you can expect and whether it is safe to overtake.

Short broken lines with long gaps (A) are used where there are no permanent hazards to mark the centre or divide the road into lanes. You should keep to your own lane where possible, but you can cross the line if you need to overtake, provided it is safe (remember to check your mirrors and signal your intentions).

A single broken line with long markings and short gaps is a hazard warning line (B). It is telling you to be especially careful and only cross if the road is clear well ahead. The occur on the approach to hazards such as bends and junctions. DON'T cross the line unless you can be certain that the road ahead is clear.

As a rule, the amount of paint on the road increases in proportion to the danger.

By night, cat's eyes – reflective studs in the road – indicate where the white lines are. The more cat's eyes you see, the greater the hazard: double white lines will be marked with twice as many cat's eyes as hazard warning lines. Red studs mark the left-hand edge of the road, white studs mark centre-of-road lines. You may also see amber studs on the right-hand edge of a dual carriageway or motorway, and green studs across slip roads.

Where there are unbroken double white lines (C) along the centre of the road, it means that your vision will be restricted. Overtaking is not permitted, and you should reduce your speed until you have a clear view of the road once more.

If the line is continuous on one side but broken on the other (D), drivers on the side where the line is solid must not cross the line unless they need to pass a stationary obstruction or turn into an entrance on the far side (and then only if it is safe and won't inconvenience anybody). Vehicles on the side nearest the broken line, however, are permitted to overtake – so long as they can get back in lane before reaching an unbroken line on their side. Arrows on the road warn when the broken line is about to turn into a solid one: get back into lane when you see them.

Some roads have areas where the central double line open out and the space between is filled with white diagonal stripes. This is done to separate traffic streams. Where the outer lines are solid, you must not enter the painted area. But if the outer lines are broken, you may enter provided it is safe to do so.

On country roads where the side of the road would be difficult to make out in poor light, white lines are painted at the very edge of the road. Where the line is broken the road will be fairly straight; solid lines at the edge of the road indicate a curve.

Solid or broken white lines a metre from the edge designate a cycle lane. You must not cross a solid white line, and should avoid crossing a broken white line unless it is unavoidable.

A solid white line painted across the road (A) is often seen at the point where a side turning feeds into the main road. There will also be a stop sign on a pole nearby to reinforce the message. You should always stop, even if the road appears to be clear. Often visibility is restricted in some way, either from the side road or the main road, so the driver must take the time to check it is safe to emerge.

Where the end of the road is marked with double broken white lines and a painted triangle, you must give way to traffic on the major road (B). Enter only when you can do so without causing anyone to change speed or direction.

In the Netherlands, triangular markings indicate that you should give way to traffic on the main road.

Road markings follow an internationally agreed form, with slight variations from country to country. In Austria and Switzerland, for example, road markings are yellow rather than white. If you are hiring a car, you should be given a copy of the Highway Code for the country you are visiting. Drivers taking their own car abroad should be able to purchase a copy from any tourist information centre on arrival.

Yellow lines running parallel to the kerb warn of waiting and parking restrictions. Nearby there will be a sign mounted on a post telling you when the restrictions are in force. Yellow zigzag lines warn against parking outside schools.

A junction where the road is painted in a yellow crisscross pattern is known as a box junction. You may not cross the stop line and enter the box unless your exit is clear. Traffic turning right can sit in the box and wait for a gap in the oncoming traffic, but the exit must be clear so that they are in a position to seize the opportunity when it arises.

Red lines alongside the kerb indicate that you are on an urban clearway. There is no stopping on these routes at any time – not even a short stop to pick up or put down passengers.

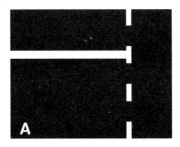

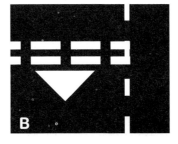

traffic signs

Every learner prepares for the driving test by memorizing as many traffic signs as possible. By the time they take the test, they can identify well over a hundred different road signs and markings. But often when they throw away the L-plates, the Highway Code gets discarded too. When was the last time you tested your recall? You may be surprised to find how much you've forgotten.

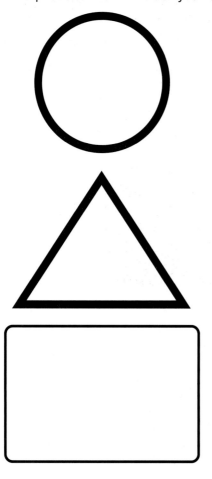

Once you know the basic code, it's easy to work out the meaning of a traffic sign:

CIRCULAR signs give orders that must be obeyed: red ones are prohibitive, telling you what you MUST NOT do, blue ones give positive instructions like 'turn left ahead'.

TRIANGULAR signs give advance warning of how the road ahead is laid out and hazards that you should prepare to encounter.

RECTANGLES give information. A blue background indicates that the sign gives general information; green signs give route directions on primary roads; white signs with black borders give directions on non-primary roads.

JUNCTIONS

Warning signs are posted at the approach to a junction to tell you what to expect and what to do. Stop and give way signs reinforce the message of those white lines on the road surface. There may be other signs posted 50 to 100 metres ahead of the junction warning you of the presence of a stop or give way sign. When you see one of these, it's time to start losing speed.

There are five types of junction: side roads, T-junctions, staggered junctions, crossroads, and roundabouts. All junctions can be dangerous, because there is no guarantee that drivers will look before emerging. The line which is thickest represents the priority road, but even if you have priority you should still apply the motoring drill: be on the lookout for danger, and prepare to adjust your course and speed if necessary.

At a staggered junction, for example, you should anticipate vehicles joining the road you are on from both sides. Expect the unexpected. Impatience can lead drivers waiting to emerge to take risks, muscling their way on to the main road and forcing other road users to brake or swerve to avoid a collision. If you flash your lights at the driver waiting to emerge, the signal may be misinterpreted as an invitation to proceed. Your safest course of action is to reduce speed, move towards the crown of the road, and give a toot of your horn to let him know you're there. The position of your car and the flashing of your brake lights should warn drivers behind that it is not safe to overtake.

On the approach to a roundabout, always observe the direction of the arrows on the sign (a blue circle for mini-roundabouts, a red-bordered triangle for roundabouts): these tell you who has priority on the roundabout. The general rule is to give way to traffic on the roundabout. In Great Britain and Eire, this means that traffic approaching from the right has priority; in countries where vehicles drive on the right, however, you would give way to vehicles approaching from the left. Always read the signs on the approach in case a different set of rules apply to that particular roundabout.

In France it was once the custom that traffic entering the roundabout had priority. This has now changed, and signs have been posted on approach roads to remind drivers that they do not have priority and must give way to traffic approaching from the left.

ROAD LAYOUT

Signs also give information the layout of the road ahead, such as bottlenecks where the road narrows from one or both directions; where a dual carriageway ends; or where traffic merges from either side.

Bends in the road are indicated by a triangular sign with a line bending to the right or left. Bends often occur on slopes as the road hugs the contours of a hill or mountain. Reduce speed and change gear while you are still travelling in a straight line. Apply the motoring drill to negotiate the bend safely.

> ### REMEMBER
> On sunny days turning the corner can take you from shade into dazzling sunlight. Don't let the sun blind you on a dangerous corner: prepare for its effects by lowering your sun visor and reducing speed.

Signs on the approach to a double bend will tell you whether the road bends first to the left and then right or vice versa. Reduce your speed and alter your course to give you the best possible view of the road ahead without putting you in conflict with oncoming traffic. Anticipate oncoming vehicles straying over to your side of the road after misjudging a turn.

A sharp deviation will be marked with black and white chevrons.

Signs warning of gradients will tell you whether the slope goes up or down, and how steep it is. A 20 per cent downhill gradient drops one foot for every five feet you travel. Riding the foot brake the whole way down is not the best way to negotiate a steep gradient as it could lead to brake failure. Select a lower gear instead and let the engine control your speed.

Where the road is not strong enough to carry heavy vehicles, or where low bridges and narrow tunnels entail height and width restrictions, you will see red circles prohibiting certain classes of vehicle.

reading the signs

PRIORITY SIGNS

These, mostly circular signs, give orders which must be obeyed. Arrows indicate which direction you may or may not proceed in, whether the road is one-way or no entry, whether oncoming traffic has priority.

No overtaking signs some-times apply to specific categories of vehicle only. For example, this Danish sign prohibits overtaking by lorries, coaches and vehicles towing trailers.

SPEED RESTRICTIONS

Red circular signs indicate maximum permitted speeds, blue circles tell you the minimum speed allowed.

Remember, when travelling in Europe, speeds are shown in kilometres, not miles! The maximum limits vary from country to country, and on-the-spot fines may be imposed if you are caught speeding.

In many countries it is left to the driver's discretion to reduce speed when it rains, but in some parts of the Continent mandatory reduc-tions are imposed. This French motorway sign warns that the 130 kph speed limit is reduced to 110 kph in rain.

Road authorities try, in a variety of ways, to remind drivers that they must maintain an adequate safety margin between vehi-cles. In France, chevrons are painted at intervals on the road's surface, while signs alongside stress the importance of remain-ing two chevrons or 'marques' – the equivalent of the 'two-second' gap – behind the car in front for safety's sake.

HAZARDS

Hazard warning signs tend to rely on internationally recog-nized symbols, so even if you don't know the language, you should still get the message.

A slippery road sign may be accompanied by foreign words you don't understand. It may be that because the road is exposed black ice develops in winter, or that autumn leaves turn the road into a skid pan. Whatever the cause, your action on seeing this symbol should always be to reduce speed.

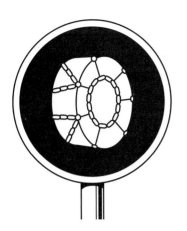

In areas where winter conditions make the roads too treacherous for standard tyres, you may see signs like these indicating that snow chains or tyres should be fitted.

It may be time to look for a detour when you see signs warning of long queues ahead.

Children pose a hazard the world over! Always be on the alert and kill your speed when you see signs warning of small children crossing or schools in the vicinity. This sign warns drivers that a crossing patrol operates at this point to see school children safely across the road.

LEVEL CROSSINGS

The points where roads cross railway lines are controlled in a variety of ways, so there are several types of level crossing sign to reflect these differences.

Always approach level crossings with caution. Never drive nose-to-tail over a crossing; wait until the vehicle in front has cleared the crossing before entering it. Never enter the crossing after the alarm has been activated, but if you are already crossing when it starts, keep going. There will be flashing lights and an audible warning to let you know when a train is coming.

A blue circle showing a dipped-beam headlight tells you that it is compulsory to switch your lights on. These signs are often seen at the entrance to long tunnels.

This sign warns motorists to expect:
• a bumpy ride where the tracks run across the road
• a gate or barrier which will close shortly after the alarm sounds, to prevent motorists crossing the path of an oncoming train
• an automatic crossing – in other words, there will be no attendant on hand. There will, however, be an emergency telephone link to the signal operator, so you can raise the alarm if your car breaks down on the crossing.

reading the signs

In remote rural areas you may come across level crossings with no traffic signals to warn you when a train is coming. It should be possible to judge whether it's safe to cross by stopping the car and looking and listening for a train in the distance. Close any gates behind you once you are clear.

If your car breaks down on a crossing, your first priority must be to get everyone out of the vehicle. Even though the train driver may see the obstruction on the line ahead and apply the brakes, the train will take a long time to come to a halt. If you can see a train approaching, stand well clear as wreckage can be thrown a long way by the force of the impact.

Tramways

There are no level crossings at points where tramlines cross traffic lanes, but there will often be separate traffic lights signals for tram drivers and ordinary drivers.

When you see a hazard sign showing a tram, it means that there is a crossing point ahead. You must ALWAYS give way to trams. Don't try to race them or cut in front of them, and stay out of tram lanes marked on the road surface.

Remember that trams can be extremely long. Wait until the last carriage has passed you before pulling out across a tram line – on a tight corner it can be difficult to see other carriages towed behind the first.

LOW-FLYING AIRCRAFT

When a road passes close to an airfield, you will see a sign warning of low-flying aircraft. If there are traffic lights, stop when the signals flash and wait until the plane has landed and the alarm has stopped before proceeding.

In fact, the planes are probably the least of your worries. Most accidents near airfields occur because drivers allow themselves to be distracted by the sight of aircraft landing and taking off, so pay attention to your driving and keep your eyes on the road.

In the vicinity of international airports you will also find foreign drivers, tired after a long journey and possibly not accustomed to driving on the 'wrong' side of the road. Unfamiliar with the route, the language, the priorities and traffic regulations, they are liable to make errors of judgement. Be patient and don't add to the pressure on them by driving too close.

As with buses, you should keep an eye out for pedestrians running across the road to catch a tram, or disembarking passengers stepping into your path.

Metal tram rails can be extremely slippery in wet weather, causing problems for cyclists and motorcyclists who have to cross the lines. Leave extra room in case they skid or fall over into your path.

INTERPRETING TRAFFIC SIGNS

Don't just take traffic signs at face value. The simplest sign can provide a wealth of information. Take the hazard sign which warns of wild animals for example. When you see this leaping deer symbol beside a country road, it means that you should slow down in case a wild animal runs across your path. But there are a number of other, less obvious, meanings:

• This stretch of road might be fairly uninhabited. If you are running low on fuel, perhaps you should turn round and find a petrol station rather than running the risk of breaking down miles from anywhere.

• On the other hand, in summer it might be far from deserted. Many motorists will stop here to let the kids stretch their legs, or to exercise the dog. Look out for children playing near the road and cars pulling out without warning.

• During the evening, when animals are at their most active, you may see wildlife crossing the road. They may behave unpredictably: motorists coming the other way might spook the animals and cause them to panic, running blindly in your direction. When you see an animal in the road, check your mirrors, and if possible slow right down to a crawl, or stop and switch on your hazard lights. The animals should soon disappear back into cover.

• These signs are often placed where roads run through woodland. In addition to wild animals you should expect falling branches in windy weather, and a slippery carpet of leaves in autumn.

It is safer to read too much into a sign than to ignore its significance.